Friends and enemies

Manchester University Press

Friends and enemies

The Allies and neutral Ireland in the Second World War

Karen Garner

Copyright © Karen Garner 2021

The right of Karen Garner to be identified as the author of this work has been asserted by them in accordance with the Copyright, Designs and Patents Act 1988.

Published by Manchester University Press
Oxford Road, Manchester M13 9PL

www.manchesteruniversitypress.co.uk

British Library Cataloguing-in-Publication Data
A catalogue record for this book is available from the British Library

ISBN 978 1 5261 5729 4 hardback
ISBN 978 1 5261 7203 7 paperback

First published 2021
Paperback published 2023

The publisher has no responsibility for the persistence or accuracy of URLs for any external or third-party internet websites referred to in this book, and does not guarantee that any content on such websites is, or will remain, accurate or appropriate.

Typeset by
Servis Filmsetting Ltd, Stockport, Cheshire

For my mom and dad, and in memory of their wartime generation

Contents

List of figures	viii
Acknowledgments	x
Map of Eire during the Emergency	xi
Introduction	1
1 Agreements made, pledges broken: Europe in the 1930s	21
2 Neutral states in a world at war, September 1939 to May 1940	43
3 "Unstoppable" Germany, "unbeatable" Britain, June to December 1940	81
4 In pursuit of America's friendship, January to June 1941	109
5 British friend, Irish foe, July to December 1941	140
6 Efforts to "break the backbone" of Irish neutrality, January 1942 to December 1943	168
7 Eire, neutral to the bitter end, January 1944 to June 1945	198
Conclusion	222
Bibliography	237
Index	246

Figures

0.1 Map of Eire during the Emergency. Artist Bonnie Faith Bolton, October 2020. — xi
1.1 Helen Paull Kirkpatrick, *c.* 1941. Carroll Binder Papers, The Newberry Library, Chicago. — 25
1.2 Eamon de Valera, *c.* 1939. P104/3268. Courtesy of University College Dublin Archives. Reproduced by kind permission of UCD-OFM Partnership. — 31
2.1 Winston Churchill leaving 10 Downing Street after a War Council Meeting, *c.* 1939. Photographer Unknown, Imperial War Museum. © Imperial War Museum. — 45
2.2 Eamon de Valera and members of the Irish Diplomatic Service, *c.* 1939. P150/3818. Seated, front row, left to right: John Dulanty, Joseph Walshe, Eamon de Valera, Robert Brennan, Thomas Kiernan. Standing, back row, left to right: John Hearne, Frank Gallagher, Frederick (F. H.) Boland, Michael McWhite, Seán Murphy, Leo Kearney, Michael Rynne. Courtesy of University College Dublin Archives. Reproduced by kind permission of UCD-OFM Partnership. — 55
2.3 Sir John Loader Maffey, Lord Rugby, January 1931. Bassano Ltd., Public Domain. — 57
2.4 David and Maude Gray in Dublin, *c.* 1940. Coll. 03082, David Gray Papers, American Heritage Center, University of Wyoming. — 65
4.1 Eamon de Valera and Frank Aiken at Dublin Airport, as Aiken begins journey to the United States, March 1941. P104/3819. Courtesy of University College Dublin Archives. Reproduced by kind permission of UCD-OFM Partnership. — 121
5.1 Prime Minister Winston Churchill and President Franklin Roosevelt seated on the quarterdeck of the HMS *Prince of Wales* following the Sunday religious service, Atlantic Conference, August 1941. Photographer Major W. G. Horton,

List of figures

	War Office Official Photographer, Imperial War Museum. © Imperial War Museum.	144
5.2	Prime Minister Winston Churchill looks out from deck of HMS *Prince of Wales* as the USS *Augusta* sails away following the Atlantic Conference with U.S. President Franklin Roosevelt on board the vessel, August 1941. Photographer Major W. G. Horton, War Office Official Photographer, Imperial War Museum. © Imperial War Museum.	146
5.3	Helen Kirkpatrick [far left] with David and Maude Gray on United States Legation grounds, Phoenix Park, *c.* 1941. Coll. 03082, David Gray Papers, American Heritage Center, University of Wyoming.	150
6.1	Winston Churchill and Franklin Roosevelt relax in the grounds of the White House in Washington, DC, prior to the daily meeting with the Joint Chiefs of Staff from the United Kingdom and the United States to discuss war strategy, *c.* June 1942. Photographer Unknown, Imperial War Museum. © Imperial War Museum.	178

Acknowledgments

During the last several years spent researching and writing this book, the following individuals and institutions gave me their generous assistance. Thank you to Professors Tom Zeiler at the University of Colorado and Tim Borstelmann at the University of Nebraska, who read multiple outlines of this book project and sent their recommendations as I applied for research grants. I am also grateful to the many professional archivists who shared their vast knowledge of collections with me at the American Heritage Center at the University of Wyoming, the Boston College Burns Library, the British National Archives, the Franklin D. Roosevelt Presidential Library, the Newberry Library, the Public Records Office of Northern Ireland, the Sophia Smith Collection at Smith College, and the University College Dublin Archives. Thanks are also owed to SUNY Empire State College which provided institutional support in the form of Faculty Development Awards and sabbatical release for this extended research project. Special thanks to Emma Brennan, Editorial Director at Manchester University Press, who shepherded the book through the review and publication process, and to the anonymous reviewers who provided astute comments and suggestions that most certainly improved this work. To my friends and my family who listened to me talk about this project and provided their moral support for years, I also thank you. I am especially grateful to my niece Bonnie Bolton who drew the map of Ireland included here. And to my husband, Chuck Vosganian, thank you for the daily love, laughter, and support you have always shared with me, especially through the long months of 2020 when we were each other's constant companions.

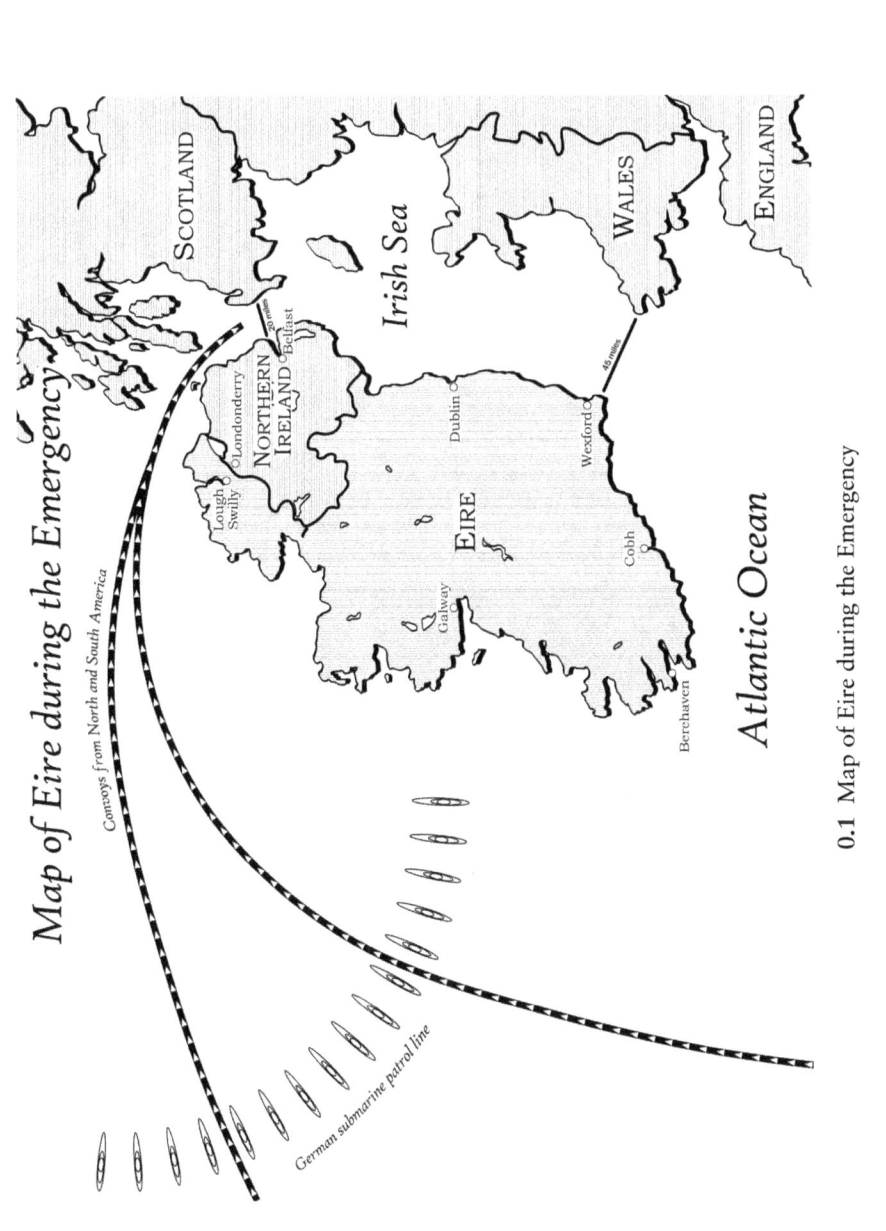

0.1 Map of Eire during the Emergency

Introduction

What happens when sentiments of friendship and enmity are politicized and when distinctions between individual self-identities and national identities and allegiances dissolve during times of war? This history explores those questions through the words and actions of a few key male leaders who determined national policies for Great Britain and America in relation to neutral Ireland during the Second World War. It examines the personal friendships and embittered conflicts among British, American, and Irish national leaders and their Dublin-based advisers, as those relationships warmed and cooled, shifting in response to their nations' fortunes during the six years' war. The dominant personalities of Winston Churchill, Franklin D. Roosevelt, and Eamon de Valera, marked by their distinctive individual prejudices and predilections, in combination with the culturally and historically specific British, American, and Irish masculine ideologies that prescribed their privileged and powerful roles, determined the ways that they each constructed politically useful national identities and war stories. Their constructions of those identities and narratives helped to shape the collective emotional, patriotic, and gendered experiences of the Second World War among their nations' people, as well as their nations' foreign policies. Succeeding generations of national leaders drew upon the stories and gendered national identities that these wartime leaders defined and symbolized as they reconfigured and reaffirmed state-to-state "special relationships" – Anglo-Irish relationships, Anglo-American relationships, Irish-American relationships – long into the postwar era. To be sure, some scholars reject the notion that a distinctive national identity exists in any empirical or "factual" sense, or that it is in any way a "stable or monolithic" concept.[1] Moreover, gender scholars may theorize a "hegemonic" or "normative" masculinity with a "national" character that delineates the boundaries of "ideal" male behavior, as they also recognize that individuals rarely lived up to the ideal.[2] Nonetheless, the leaders under study here deliberately, through their public addresses and in their private correspondence and recollections, constructed unitary, masculine national identities, as they equated their own values and personalities with the nations they each led. They associated specific character traits, behaviors, allegiances, and affinities with themselves, their nations' male citizens, and with their personal "friends" and national allies, as they distinguished themselves from their "enemies" in order to rally their compatriots to either support – or reject – the most consequential of all political projects: to go to war.

The Anglo-American leaders and their close advisers who are examined here created the dominant gendered, racialized, and moral narratives of the Second World War as it was being fought in order to make sense of the catastrophic devastation that engulfed Europe, North Africa, Soviet Russia, East and South Asia, and the Pacific Islands for their nations' peoples when the fascist Axis Powers launched their empire-building crusades. Through these narratives, Churchill, Roosevelt, and their Anglo-American policy advisers also aimed to legitimize the often-merciless retaliations that the Western Allies perpetrated against their enemies. They told stories of heroism and collective courage and resistance displayed by their nations' soldiers and citizens on and off the battlefields. They emphasized the "manly" virtues of the Western Powers as a brotherhood of "civilized," "democratic," yet "muscular" Christian nations that fought to defend the highest moral values and protect weak and vulnerable peoples of all races, religions, and cultures from enslavement and from the blood-lust and genocidal atrocities committed by the German Third Reich army, directed by its demonic Nazi Party leaders, whose crimes against humanity were mirrored in the brutal war-making of the Axis Powers alliance. By forging and cultivating their personal fraternal friendship and together defining and redefining who was a "friend" and who was an "enemy" of their noble cause and just fight, Churchill and Roosevelt tried to persuade the pre-eminent leader of neutral Ireland, Eamon de Valera, to join the Western Powers alliance. Their efforts to demarcate and circumscribe the dominant narratives of "war and manhood" for de Valera and his wartime policy advisers, and through them for the Irish people, were pursued with a vigorous tenacity throughout the war because, at crucial moments in the anti-fascist campaign, a formal alliance with Southern Ireland was deemed critically necessary to Britain's survival, if not the Western Allies' eventual triumph over the fascist powers. Churchill and Roosevelt and their Dublin-based advisers understood that "triumph" must come in the form of a strategic and absolute military victory; it would also depend on winning a deeply symbolic, moralistic, propaganda victory in the hearts and minds of their friends and their vanquished enemies.

Introduction 3

Anglo-Irish, Anglo-American, and Irish-American special relationships

Both formal diplomatic enticements and pressures that Churchill and Roosevelt and their emissaries exerted on de Valera, as well as friendly and not-so-friendly covert operations that took place in Ireland to undermine Irish neutrality policy, failed to move de Valera and his cabinet advisers away from their firm refusal to ally with the Western Powers.

Irish leaders rejected Britain's overtures during the Second World War, wary of Winston Churchill's and his emissaries' representations of Britain as "friend" to the Irish people or its nationalist aspirations, when the recent history of Anglo-Irish relations had been so fraught with interstate violence and political ill will. The dominant counternarratives that de Valera and his fellow Irish nationalists related to explain Ireland's contentious late nineteenth- and early twentieth-century history with Great Britain, and the Irish national identity that de Valera and his advisers actively created during the 1930s and 1940s, were based on their own experiences as revolutionaries and statesmen and on their strong sense of their own destinies being intertwined with their homeland's historic fight for independence from Britain's colonial empire and full restoration of Irish sovereignty throughout the Irish isle. In the early twentieth century, Irishmen fighting for independence from the British Empire had formed their own "oppositional" male identity: the "muscular Gael (with undertones of Catholicism) in opposition to that of muscular Christianity (rooted in Anglo Protestantism)," who must fight to protect the colonized, feminized, and disempowered Irish nation.[3] Eamon de Valera and his advisers were of the generation that lived through the nationalist Easter Rising of 1916 and fought to dislodge British colonial rule during the First World War and in its immediate aftermath. As Irish historian Brian Girvin has explained the Irish nationalist identity of the close circle surrounding de Valera who served in his cabinet during the Second World War, they were, like de Valera, "radicalized during the First World War. ... driven by memories and experience of that other great conflict ... literally bloodied by that experience which had a profound influence on them. They held a parochial view of Irish national identity, one that was suspicious [of] if not openly hostile to Britain."[4]

During the First World War, a small band of radical nationalists known as the Irish Republican Brotherhood, de Valera among them, guided Ireland in an ill-fated attempt to gain full independence in the 1916 Easter Rising. The rebellion was launched at a moment when British power was supposed to be most vulnerable,[5] but British Army troops quickly rallied to restore colonial control; they established martial law and executed many of the captured rebel leaders. In de Valera's case, he was captured and imprisoned and narrowly escaped execution for treason. As the First World War ended in 1918, Irish radicals renewed attacks on colonial institutions and on British loyalists throughout the country, while the Royal Irish Constabulary (RIC) and the notorious "Black and Tans" recruited by the British government met nationalist violence with their own harsh counterforce.[6] To end the bloodshed, the British Parliament passed the Government of Ireland Act in 1920 and partitioned Ireland into two separately governed entities: the six counties of Northern Ireland occupied by a "foreign" British power, in the Irish nationalists' view, and governed locally by "Ulster Unionist" Northern Irish Protestants who remained loyal to the Crown; and the twenty-six counties that comprised the Southern Ireland Dominion of the British Empire, populated by an Irish Catholic nationalist majority. Ongoing anti-British violence in the South led to a diplomatic compromise embedded in the December 1921 Anglo-Irish Treaty that established the "Irish Free State" in the twenty-six counties governed by the Dáil Éireann (Irish Assembly) in Dublin. Following the contested settlement, civil war erupted between the Sinn Féin (Ourselves Alone) revolutionary movement and its military wing, the Irish Republican Army (IRA), who rejected the 1921 Treaty (as did Eamon de Valera until the mid-1920s), and the Southern Catholic and Protestant political factions who led the Free State government and favored political solutions over continued violence. By 1925, the tide of public opinion had turned against violence and a proximate peace ensued.[7]

After a period of political exile in the 1920s, de Valera and his supporters recaptured governing power through popular support at the ballot box. De Valera established a political party, Fianna Fáil (Soldiers of Destiny), in 1926, and formed a coalition to win the majority seats in the Dáil Éireann in 1932. At that time Fianna Fáil became the Irish Free State's governing party, de Valera became President of the Executive Council, and, after 1937, he became Taoiseach (head of government), a position he held until 1947 (and would hold again in the 1950s). During the decades of the 1930s and 1940s, de Valera and his governing Cabinet ministers delegitimized and overcame political challenges from staunch Anglo-Irish Unionists on the far right, conciliatory advocates of "Home Rule" who accepted British Dominion status for the Free State on the center right, and Sinn Féin revolutionaries and its IRA who continued a violent campaign for complete Irish independence on the far political left and who went as far as declaring open war on Britain in January 1939. Through these critical decades, de Valera and his cohorts seemingly recognized few distinctions between their own political, ideological, and Catholic religious affiliations, the unified Irish national identity and Irish manhood that they were promoting, and the feminized Irish Gaelic nation they were protecting.

Introduction 5

De Valera's demands for complete independence from the British Empire and assertion of Ireland's sovereign rights, during the 1920s and 1930s, were the foundation of his government's neutrality policy throughout the Second World War, 1939–1945. Even with the close geographic proximity, interdependent trade relations, and fairly unrestricted travel and labor exchanges between Britain and Ireland that continued throughout the war, Eire's official and unchanging neutrality policy was claimed by de Valera as a right of the Irish nation's self-declared sovereign status, a status that the international community was only beginning to recognize in the 1930s. In the name of neutrality, de Valera's government preserved Eire's formal diplomatic relations with Nazi Germany, Fascist Italy, and imperial Japan and the Axis Powers retained legations in Dublin throughout the Second World War. Eire's diplomats continued to serve in Irish legations in Berlin, and in Rome at the Holy See, and in German-occupied Vichy France, as well as in London and Washington, DC.[8]

De Valera's stubborn refusal to abandon the official neutrality policy throughout the "Emergency" period, as the war years were referred to in Ireland, frustrated and at times infuriated Churchill and Roosevelt and the British and American wartime governments they led. However, as Irish politician and historian Conor Cruise O'Brien once explained Ireland's foreign policy from the 1920s onward, the overarching goal was to gain international recognition for Ireland's sovereignty by focusing on "identity, legitimacy, symbolism, [and] status."[9] In other words, the relationship between Ireland's national identity and its foreign policy should be understood as "mutually constitutive,"[10] as de Valera linked Ireland's national sovereignty, Irish manhood, and his government's neutrality policy during the crucial decades of the 1930s and 1940s.

A history of conflict marked Britain's relations with its former North American colonies as well, beginning with the colonists who sought religious, economic, and social freedoms they couldn't achieve in their mother country. Their aspirations led to brutal battles to break away from the British Empire waged during the American colonists' successful fight for independence and establishment of the sovereign United States in the eighteenth century. Throughout the nineteenth century, Britain's imperial government challenged the United States' territorial, political, and economic sovereignty as well as American claims to their own colonial holdings and dominant sphere of influence in the Western hemisphere – all told, "an impressive catalogue of sources of enmity."[11] But as the United States' national wealth grew and its world power status was established by the turn of the twentieth century, a "special relationship" developed as the two Great Powers "reappraised" their interests. At that time, "the things they shared began to take on new importance, and the problems that would arise if they came to blows with each other were seen to outweigh any possible advantages."[12]

White male leaders dominated both Britain and the United States and asserted their hegemonic power to rule over all others. They also developed related conceptions of their nations' "exceptionalism." For British leaders, national exceptionalism led to assertions of their "White Man's Burden" and global "civilizing" (and colonizing) mission; for American leaders, exceptionalism led to the articulation of their "divinely inspired" "Manifest Destiny," to be a model for democratic societies to follow worldwide. According to historian Alan Dobson, who has written extensively about the Anglo-American special relationship, "Towards the end of the nineteenth century these ideas came together in the minds of those who advocated a form of Anglo-Saxonism" that encompassed a cultural, racial, and gendered sense of superiority over all other peoples.[13] In 1898, future U.S. president and then-Assistant Secretary of the Navy Theodore Roosevelt, the "embodiment" of the "marriage" of muscular Christian manhood and U.S. imperialism in turn-of-the-century America,[14] lauded the strong ties that already existed between the two nations' "English-speaking peoples" (that is, more accurately, between the white male elite that comprised the British and American Anglo-Saxon ruling classes): "for their interests are really fundamentally the same, they are more closely akin, not merely in blood, but in feeling and principle, than either is akin to any other people in the world."[15]

During the First World War, European imperial rivals led by Britain and Germany fought for continental dominance and for the preservation of their own colonial empires in Africa and Asia. The United States government maintained a policy of neutrality for nearly three years, from August 1914 to April 1917, protecting its own national interests. This was, to be sure, a neutrality that gave heavy preference to Britain in terms of wartime financing, sales of weapons, and wartime trade. Moreover, British propagandists won the war for moral superiority, at least in the view of U.S. President Woodrow Wilson and his pro-British advisers, by portraying Germany's use of newly developed and increasingly more destructive weapons that targeted civilian populations as the barbarous actions of a tyrannical power that must be halted by united democratic powers.[16] In April 1917, President Wilson appealed to Congress for a declaration of war and the United States joined the British-led Western European alliance in its righteous crusade against the German-led Central Powers, with nothing less than Christian "civilization itself seeming to be in the balance."[17] With the declaration of war, and a renewed influx of supplies, munitions, and soldiers, the Western Allies prevailed and Germany conceded defeat in November 1918.

A "twenty-year truce" followed the German defeat before the economic inequalities, national resentments, and social dislocations caused by the ill-conceived and mismanaged peace settlements of the First World War led to the outbreak of a second world war in Europe in September 1939.[18] The Anglo-American alliance forged during the First World War was strained during these two interwar decades, as the global capitalist economy faltered, and shortsighted economic nationalism led to a severe global economic depression. The rise of the Communist Party-led Soviet Union challenged the Western-dominated international order in the 1920s, and the rise of fascist states led by aggressive and militaristic dictators in Germany, Italy, and Japan rejected Western-defined global security agreements in the 1930s. In the United States, "Anglophobia," that is, long-standing antipathy for British imperial power and cynicism expressed by many Americans who never shared faith in Britain's moral leadership, along with the dashing of idealistic hopes for a cooperative and rational liberal world order as promised in wartime rhetoric, led to the prevalent national isolationist mood of the 1930s. Reflecting isolationist sentiment and disillusionment, the U.S. Congress passed a series of laws enshrining "neutrality" as the nation's foreign policy, prohibiting economic entanglements through sales of war materiel or munitions to belligerent powers, should war break out in Europe, or in other parts of the world, again.

U.S. President Franklin Roosevelt, elected in 1932 at the nadir of the Great Depression on a promise to restore the national economy and protect the national welfare, was bound by political imperatives to serve his electoral base. Yet his recognition of the growing threats to U.S. national security and to global peace and human security emanating from the rise of the militaristic fascist powers converged with a sense of his own destiny to lead the United States back into prominence as a world power. From September 1939 until December 1941 when the United States became an active belligerent, the United States was nominally a neutral power. Yet during this period of neutrality, President Roosevelt took significant steps to aid the British war effort, making public addresses expressing moral support for the Western democracies and persuading Congress to amend the Neutrality Laws to shore up British resistance, stopping just short of direct military engagement with the Axis Powers. The American government provided this aid in large part because Franklin Roosevelt and Winston Churchill shared a fundamental understanding of the existential fascist threat to democratic nations.[19] After Churchill replaced Neville Chamberlain as Britain's Prime Minister and took over the direction of Britain's war policy in May 1940, Roosevelt and Churchill worked together to devise creative aid strategies and to use the combined power of their rhetorical skills to persuade Americans that the British were fighting to create a world where human freedoms were protected, a world that most Americans hoped for in the future.[20]

These collaborations were possible, and they were effective, because the two national leaders developed an extraordinarily close political and fraternal friendship, which is documented in their voluminous wartime correspondence, as well as in other official documents and in the private papers of their advisers. Historian Warren Kimball, who edited the "steady stream of telegrams, letters, and memoranda" that recorded Churchill–Roosevelt wartime communications, noted, "no two national leaders ever corresponded on such intimate and personal terms."[21] Churchill and Roosevelt shared a strikingly similar patrician upbringing during their formative years that shaped their masculine political identities. In his study focusing on U.S. foreign policy makers, historian Robert Dean describes the common experiences of the Anglo-American male elite who emerged in the late nineteenth and early twentieth centuries. They were each educated in "exclusive male-only institutions," the "boarding schools, ... elite military service, metropolitan men's clubs – where imperial traditions of 'service' and 'sacrifice' were invented and bequeathed to those that followed," producing "the ritual creation of a fictive brotherhood of privilege and power."[22] With social class, race, and gender in common, Churchill and Roosevelt understood each other instinctively and intimately from their earliest associations.

While the two leaders did not always agree on wartime strategies regarding Allied military operations, and Churchill envisioned the continuation of a postwar British Empire that Roosevelt did not share, their "Anglo-American partnership" constituted a special relationship that strengthened their individual positions as national leaders as well as their nations' militaries' abilities to fight together to defeat a common foe.[23] Jon Meacham, who published a well-researched account of Roosevelt and Churchill's "epic friendship," offered a similar analysis:

> Though they had differences – Churchill wanted the British empire to survive and thrive; Roosevelt largely favored self-determination for colonial peoples around the world – they cared passionately about the same over-arching truth: breaking the Axis. They also shared a conviction that they were destined to play these roles. ... Victory was the common goal, and only Roosevelt and Churchill knew the uncertainties that came with ultimate power.[24]

As this history will document, they also shared the foreign policy goal to bring de Valera's Ireland into the wartime Western Alliance. Their foreign offices and their Dublin-based advisers worked together to bring this about, and Churchill and Roosevelt shared frustrations when their governments' pressure campaigns failed them.

Ireland's historic relations with America can also be described as a special relationship, one that was established by the large Irish immigrant population that settled in the United States from the nineteenth century onward and that maintained close familial, religious, and cultural ties with the Irish homeland. In the nineteenth century, poor Irish Catholic immigrants experienced formal and informal discrimination, which solidified their ethnic community bonds. The relatively large immigrant populations were concentrated in primarily Irish-American neighborhoods in several U.S. cities where they dominated the workforce in a few industries and selected professions. These demographic patterns encouraged a cultural cohesiveness that led to a unified political voting bloc that could sway election outcomes. Dominant white Anglo-Saxon Protestants, so-called "native" American politicians, whose governing power was tied to success at the ballot box, such as Franklin Roosevelt, were sensitive to Irish American voting behaviors, especially during the first half of the twentieth century. Irish politicians, including de Valera and his Fianna Fáil cohorts, claimed to play an influential role in determining the political attitudes of the Irish diaspora, especially those who had settled in the United States. During the Second World War, de Valera and his Cabinet advisers often used threats of their ability to mobilize Irish American political opinion and votes in warnings to Anglo-American leaders to respect Ireland's sovereign rights as a neutral power.[25]

Eamon de Valera's personal history also linked Ireland and America in a special relationship. De Valera was born in New York, son of a poor Irish mother and Spanish father, both immigrants. When he was still an infant his mother sent him back to Ireland where he was raised by his uncle.[26] His dual citizenship may have saved his life after he was arrested by the British following the 1916 Easter Rising. Historian T. Ryle Dwyer has asserted that "The British planned to execute [de Valera] then, but commuted the sentence because they were afraid that executing an American citizen would antagonize people in the United States at a crucial stage of the First World War. The following year the British even granted amnesty to de Valera and others involved in the Rising in order to win public favor in the United States."[27] De Valera traveled to the United States in 1919–1921, on a very successful fundraising and public relations tour promoting the Irish nationalist cause, vowing when he left the States that "Ireland will not forget" American support for Irish independence.[28] Even though neither Republican nor Democratic U.S. political parties officially recognized an independent Irish republic at that time, historian Diarmaid Ferriter has written that:

> The American trip was also significant in terms of the evolution of the cult of personality. ... The connection with the United States remained significant,

and was one of the main factors contributing to what Owen Dudley Edwards termed de Valera's "remarkable international sense". His American origins and connections provided him with a source of friendship, sympathy and funds and increased his sense of the effectiveness of public opinion and the marshalling of international sentiment. The American trip and dimension also added to his fame.[29]

IRA leaders, including Sean Russell who collaborated with Nazi Germany's *Abwehr* (Intelligence Organization), also traveled to the United States to raise funds and rally Irish American support for the IRA's anti-British violence during the 1930s, and cultivated their own special relationships with Irish Americans who supported the Irish republican cause.[30]

In addition to exploring the special relationships that existed between British, American, and Irish governments and wartime leaders, this history exposes emotional foundations of the political relationships that animated and motivated Churchill's, Roosevelt's, and de Valera's foreign policy advisers on the ground in Dublin: British Representative Sir John Loader Maffey, American Minister David Gray, and Irish Cabinet Secretaries Joseph Walshe and Frank Aiken. In the cases of these policy advisers in Dublin, and of their counterparts in London and Washington, DC, pragmatic calculations of state power were always combined with intense emotional and highly personal interactions that colored their political relationships. Except for the reserved and experienced British diplomat John Maffey, emotions frequently surfaced in both public and private communications as these diplomatic advisers expressed their love or hate for one another in very personal terms, which they often related to the state of their nations' friendly or hostile relationships and used to justify their own individual actions as well as their nations' wartime actions.

This study also highlights the informal interventions of another key individual, American journalist and London-based war correspondent Helen Paull Kirkpatrick, who took a personal interest in Anglo-American efforts to overturn Irish neutrality policy. Because of her energetic anti-fascist and pro-Allied reporting on diplomatic intrigues in neutral Ireland, U.S. Minister David Gray befriended her and at times made her his co-conspirator, feeding her information about German spy activities and sensitive Anglo-Irish trade relations that she used in her reports printed in the *Chicago Daily News* and in her wartime speeches and radio addresses to criticize Irish neutrality policy. Churchill's government appreciated her dramatic firsthand reporting of the Battle of Britain 1940–1941, and her pro-Allied reporting throughout the war years, but they were wary of the political damage she might cause when she reported on classified war policies gleaned through her insider connections with Anglo-American government and military officials. Kirkpatrick wasn't the only American correspondent reporting critically on Irish neutrality during the war,[31] but her friendship with David Gray and bold reporting from London and continental war zones brought her some notoriety among Allied and Irish, military and government, leaders.

Male political friendships, enmities, and nationalist identities

Other studies that have examined links between expressions of friendship and enmity in the interpersonal and political spheres have informed this analysis of Anglo-American diplomacy toward neutral Eire during the Second World War.[32] Simon Koschut and Andrea Oelsner have argued that the term "friendship" can be applied to international relationships that can include state-to-state relationships as well as other people-to-people relationships that diplomats, policy makers, interest groups, and social movements establish. All these international relationships can "resemble" interpersonal friendships.[33] With regard to state-to-state friendships, they cite the work of international relations scholar Alexander Wendt who has asserted that "friendly" states don't go to war with one another to settle disputes and will fight together if one state's security is threatened. Therefore, state-to-state friendships that form to address national security issues are akin to "open-ended alliance(s)."[34] If interpersonal friendship is defined by its qualities of "camaraderie, comradeship, fellowship, closeness, affinity, understanding, harmony and unity," or shared feelings of "sympathy and empathy" for one another, nation-states can also conclude "strategic" friendships with similar descriptive attributes and with expectations of mutual benefits through treaties, and so forth. But nation-states may also form "normative" friendships when they share "ideational and emotional" bonds, and establish friendships for "normative and moral reasons as opposed to strategic friendships." These normative friendships may be rare among nation-states and more common regarding people-to-people international relationships, but they can occur. They just take more time to develop and nurture, such as the mid-twentieth-century Anglo-American "special relationship" described above.[35] For example, Koschut and Oelsner quote political scientist Michael G. Fry: "the US–British special relationship that existed during the Second World War, … 'was something above and beyond a mere alliance, founded on more than interest.' It showed a 'potential to transcend individuals and governments, to continue even as the external threat changed.'"[36] The emotional elements of these special relationships "can intensify with a so-called 'defining moment'." State-to-state special relationships, and the personal international friendships that can develop as a consequence of state relations, "ensure and maintain exclusivity vis-à-vis outsiders, ... engage in 'secret' discourse, develop a language, symbols, and code of their own, and perform joint rituals and practices that highlight the wall between insiders and outsiders."[37] All these elements were present in the Anglo-American and Irish-American wartime diplomatic relationships scrutinized in this history.

Sociologist Danny Kaplan has argued that the emotional components of affection and loyalty one finds in interpersonal friendships are at the core of public expressions of nationalism.[38] Beginning with traditional conceptions of the nation a "as a great family, invoking associations of common ancestry, of the warmth and support of kin relation,"[39] Kaplan analyzed the imagery of friendships that bind two or more individuals to each other, focusing on "fraternal friendships" that exist between male citizens in the civic realm. In his 2006 study, Kaplan defined the characteristics of fraternal friendships:

> Fraternal friendship holds a hegemonic space in the philosophical canon, a phallocentric domination excluding both feminine friendships and heterosexual friendships. The figure of "the brother" is eventually the core structure of the civil regime. It plays an organizing role in the definition of justice, morality, and democracy. Political issues of sovereignty, power, and representation are marked by the privilege granted to brotherhood.[40]

Democratic societies, Kaplan notes, tend to be "characterized by egalitarian and relatively open networks of friends" that "would encourage the formation of productive alliances and coalitions and enable citizens to take responsibility and be accountable for their actions."[41] Among the elements of these civic and fraternal friendships there are bonds of affection and loyalty that also define nationalism, or love of one's country, and one's "feelings toward fellow nationals"; "Nationalism is therefore, at first, a union of sentiment. ... As a process of collective identification, national solidarity may be as emotional as interpersonal bonds."[42]

In contrast to the bonds of affection described above, fraternal friendships can also be forged on shared hatred of the "enemy." For example, the sentiments that bonded Irish Catholic nationalists to one another in the twentieth century, according to political historian Timothy White, were like sentiments in other postcolonial states that struggled:

> to establish a national identity, to achieve self-determination, and reinvigorate the indigenous cultural and practices that have been threatened by imperial power. Nationalism derives its strength in these circumstances from the vigor of the anticolonial movement, its reaction to oppression, and its hostility toward others. Typically, discontented intellectuals lead the nationalist movement for a collective political purpose. It is through this process that the "imagined community" of a nation is created.[43]

In other words, rather than brotherly love and affection acting as the prime emotions underlying nationalism, enmity toward their former colonizers may have been the primary emotion driving nationalists in de Valera's Ireland, fused with an emotional attachment to a "holy Catholic" Irish nationalist identity that opposed the Anglo Protestant "other."[44]

The gendered nature of fraternal friendships in wartime

The friendships in all cases described in this study, whether between individuals or between nations, whether they involved only the male principals named here or whether they also included Helen Kirkpatrick, were fraternal, masculine-gendered friendships. "Citizens" are often defined in both classical and modern Western political theory as "male." Traditionally, men took up arms to defend the *polis*, or the modern nation, in the public sphere (and therefore men had a "right" to govern), while women were protected by men within the private sphere (and therefore were excluded from political power).[45] Male-gendered friendships privileged affectionate male bonds such as those that exist between the "brotherhood" of self-sacrificing male citizen-soldiers or among male national leaders and diplomats who dominated policy making in wartime and peacetime, in most world cultures and for most of human history.[46] Kaplan references Benedict Anderson's seminal study of modern nationalism in which Anderson noted that modern nations were "imagined communities," of relative strangers that exhibited "a deep, horizontal comradeship" among nations of peers.[47] Kaplan also amends Anderson's gender-blind thesis, noting the contributions of feminist international relations scholars to give greater emphasis to the male-gendered affectional relationship of "fraternity" that "shapes the nation-state ... as a political community of [male] friends."[48] Jean Bethke Elshtain, for example, describes the history of wartime demonstrations of brotherhood and gendered love of nation as one that has long roots in Western Christian traditions.[49] Certainly, the male elite – the national leaders and their advisers who are examined here and who devised their nation's war policies – touted the virtues of hegemonic masculine behaviors, asserting "virile, strong, brave" power through physical strength and (violent) aggression toward their "degenerate, weak, cowardly" and intrinsically evil enemies, as they also displayed zealous protection of the weak, feminized nations and members of the national community.[50]

Men were the consequential actors in this wartime Dublin drama. Many international relations scholars have also exposed the gendered nature of political concepts, noting that "the nation" and nationalism are "man-made" masculine institutions.[51] In the case of the Anglo-American leaders and diplomats who aimed to bring the leaders of neutral Ireland into the wartime brotherhood of Allied Power "friends," masculine-gendered maneuvering and posturing prevailed. Helen Kirkpatrick, too, knew how to maneuver and posture within the male world of war and power and diplomacy. As a political journalist and war correspondent, she was a woman in a "man's profession." She had to fight for the respect of her male professional colleagues and the male leaders that she reported on, but she earned that respect. She was trusted for her political acumen and admired for her physical courage. After the war, she was awarded the French Legion of Honor, the French Médaille de la Reconnaissance, and the U.S. Medal of Freedom.[52] If Helen Kirkpatrick's name is not recognized and if the role she played in shaping international relationships in Dublin during the Second World War is less well known, it speaks to our continued gendered assumptions that war stories are men's stories; these assumptions shape our individual biases and our collective memories of war.

Plan of the book

This history of Anglo-American efforts to overturn Ireland's neutrality policy adds complexity to the grand narrative of the wartime Western Alliance against the Axis Powers. Although the British and American governments' foreign policies regarding Irish neutrality policy have been explored in previous studies and their foundation is fully acknowledged here,[53] this analysis takes a new approach: it explores relatively unexamined emotional, personalized, and gendered politics that underlay policy making and alliance relations. It combines the methodologies of diplomatic history through its close reliance on archival documentation with attention to new theoretical understandings regarding the roles played by personal friendships and enmities and competing masculine ideologies in shaping international relationships and in understanding the construction of national identities, especially in times of war. This book also includes elements of a collective biography or prosopography[54] in its focus on a select, small multinational group of individuals: the national leaders, their close Dublin-based foreign policy advisers, and the journalist who knew and reported on them all. It teases out the connecting threads of their associations, exposing their interactions, intrigues, biases, and agendas, and highlighting the emotional language they used to describe each other as "friends" or "enemies," as they constructed war stories to influence each other's national war policies and to shape the collective memories of the war for their nations' people. As these personal and political relationships evolved over the course of the Second World War, chapters proceed chronologically.

Chapter 1, "Agreements made, pledges broken: Europe in the 1930s," focuses on European relations up to August 1939, as Britain's government led by Prime Minister Neville Chamberlain took the lead among the Western democracies in appeasing the increasingly aggressive European fascist dictators, and attempted to settle some long-running disputes with Ireland's Taoiseach Eamon de Valera. Chapter 2, "Neutral states in a world at war, September 1939 to May 1940," examines the first months of war, as Chamberlain and Winston Churchill (called back into government service in the War Cabinet after a decade of political exile in the 1930s), struggled to establish Britain's war footing in response to the German *blitzkrieg* attacks on Poland and Western European allies. During these months, Eamon de Valera and Franklin Roosevelt also established their nations' strikingly dissimilar neutrality policies. Chapter 3, "'Unstoppable' Germany, 'unbeatable' Britain, June to December 1940," covers the period when Winston Churchill became Britain's wartime prime minister and led his nation's singular struggle against German military advances. During these months, Churchill's government focused its most intense diplomatic pressure on de Valera's government to overturn Irish neutrality policy, and received some much-needed moral support, if not the critical material support it lobbied for, from Franklin Roosevelt's government. Chapter 4, "In pursuit of America's friendship, January to June 1941," focuses on the months when the British and Irish governments each campaigned fiercely for America's friendship and for the Roosevelt administration's aid and sympathetic understanding of their nations' competing wartime imperatives, as Winston Churchill and Eamon de Valera each defined them. Chapter 5, "British friend, Irish foe, July to December 1941," examines the period when Britain and America cemented the Anglo-American "special relationship," personified in Churchill and Roosevelt's deepening fraternal friendship. In December, when Japan, Germany's Axis ally, attacked the United States' Hawaiian territory and Germany declared war on the United States, America formally entered the anti-fascist war. Churchill and Roosevelt again tried to persuade de Valera that the time to join the united nations' alliance was "now or never." Chapter 6, "Efforts to 'break the backbone' of Irish neutrality, January 1942 to December 1943," covers the steady deterioration of Ireland's relationships with the Anglo-American Allies, following the heightened pressures exerted by Anglo-American diplomats on de Valera's government to curtail the activities of German diplomats and operatives in Ireland. Chapter 7, "Eire, neutral to the bitter end, January 1944 to June 1945," covers the final eighteen months of the war in Europe. Ireland regained some strategic importance in the spring of 1944, as military preparations for Operation Overlord, the invasion of Normandy, went forward. Liberation of the

Axis concentration camps in spring 1945 revealed the depths of depravity of Nazi Germany's Holocaust policy, and Anglo-American propaganda campaigns condemned amoral Irish neutrality as Irish counter-propaganda waged a vigorous campaign of self-defense. The conclusion evaluates the legacies of the highly personalized fraternal friendships and intensely felt animosities of the Irish, British, and American national leaders and their close foreign policy advisers who either shaped or responded to Ireland's neutrality policy during the Second World War.

To be sure, the importance of Ireland's alliance with the Anglo-American powers with regard to safeguarding British national security and to supporting an Allied military victory against the fascist aggressors was greatest during the first two years of the war, and then regained some urgency in 1944, as the Allies planned Operation Overlord to reopen the Western Front. Moreover, Winston Churchill's and Franklin Roosevelt's attention to Irish relations took place within the context of their global war policy considerations as they strategized with the Soviet Union and a host of British Dominions and Western Allies to win a world war against the fascist powers. Helen Kirkpatrick's attention was also diverted from Ireland's neutrality policy as her reporting assignments took her to North Africa and Italy in 1943 and into France in 1944. Nevertheless, as these individuals all believed – the national leaders as well as their on-the-ground diplomats in Dublin – the importance of an Irish alliance to the winning of the propaganda war did not fade. When the wartime alliance did not occur, it affected the national identities and collective memories of the war that these individuals did so much to define and had a negative effect on Ireland's postwar international status and its global relationships.

Notes

1 Siniša Malešević, "The Chimera of National Identity," *Nations and Nationalism* 17: 2 (2011), 272–290.
2 Joane Nagel, "Masculinity and Nationalism: Gender and Sexuality in the Making of Nation," *Ethnic and Racial Studies* 21: 2 (1998), 242–269. See also Charlotte Hooper, *Manly States: Masculinities, International Relations, and Gender Politics* (New York: Columbia University Press, 2001), and R. W. Connell and James W. Messerschmidt, "Hegemonic Masculinity: Rethinking the Concept," *Gender & Society* 19: 6 (December 2005), 829–859.
3 Sikata Banerjee, *Muscular Nationalism: Gender, Violence and Empire in India and Ireland, 1914–2004* (New York: New York University Press, 2012), 16, 45.
4 Brian Girvin, *The Emergency: Neutral Ireland 1939–45* (London: Pan Macmillan, 2007), 30.

5 Richard English, *Irish Freedom: The History of Nationalism in Ireland* (London: Pan Macmillan, 2007), 271.
6 Thomas E. Hatchley and Lawrence J. McCaffrey, *The Irish Experience Since 1800: A Concise History* (New York: Routledge, 2010), 135.
7 English, *Irish Freedom*, 317–318.
8 Joseph Walshe, Minister for External Affairs, to Eamon de Valera, Notes for a Conversation with the Representative of Germany Concerning Ireland's Neutrality, 25 August 1939, P150/2571, Eamon de Valera Papers (on microfilm), University College Dublin Archives (hereafter: EdV Papers, UCD).
9 Conor Cruise O'Brien quoted in Francis M. Carroll, "Ireland Among the Nations of the Earth: Ireland's Foreign Relations from 1923 to 1949," *Irish Studies* (2016), 41.
10 David Campbell, in *Writing Security: United States Foreign Policy and the Policies of Identity* (Manchester: Manchester University Press, 1992), has explained that foreign policy is both the "external representation of a state," as well as a producer and reproducer of the state's identity. Campbell quoted in Ben Tonra, *Global Citizen and European Republic: Irish Foreign Policy in Transition*, e-book ed. (Manchester: Manchester University Press, 2007), 6.
11 Alan P. Dobson, *Anglo-American Relations in the Twentieth Century: Of Friendship, Conflict and the Rise and Decline of Superpowers* (New York: Routledge, 1995), 14.
12 Dobson, *Anglo-American Relations*, 15.
13 *Ibid.*, 8.
14 Nagel, "Masculinity and Nationalism," 249–250.
15 Theodore Roosevelt quoted in Walter LaFeber, *The American Age: United States Foreign Policy at Home and Abroad since 1750* (New York: W. W. Norton, 1989), 174.
16 Pearl James, ed., *Picture This: World War I Visual Culture* (Lincoln, NB: University of Nebraska Press, 2009), 16–19, 316–320.
17 Woodrow Wilson, War Messages, 65th Cong., 1st Sess. Senate Doc. No. 5, Serial No. 7264, Washington, DC, 1917, 3–8; https://wwi.lib.byu.edu/index.php/Wilson%27s_War_Message_to_Congress (accessed 30 November 2020).
18 William R. Keylor, *The Twentieth Century World and Beyond: An International History Since 1900*, 6th ed. (New York: Oxford University Press, 2011), 44.
19 Carlo D'Este, *Warlord: A Life of Winston Churchill at War, 1874–1945* (New York: HarperCollins, 2008), 498.
20 Dobson, *Anglo-American Relations*, 73.
21 Warren F. Kimball, ed., *Churchill and Roosevelt, The Complete Correspondence*, vol. 1, *Alliance Emerging, October 1933–November 1942* (Princeton, NJ: Princeton University Press, 1984), 3.
22 Robert D. Dean, *Imperial Brotherhood: Gender and the Making of Cold War Foreign Policy* (Amherst, MA: University of Massachusetts Press, 2001), 4–5.
23 Dobson, *Anglo-American Relations*, 78.
24 Jon Meacham, *Franklin and Winston: An Intimate Portrait of an Epic Friendship* (New York: Random House, 2004), xvii.

25 For an early expression of this strategy, see Joseph Walshe, Minister for External Affairs, Report on Visit to London 6–10 September 1939, P150/2571, EdV Papers, UCD.
26 Tim Pat Coogan, *Eamon de Valera: The Man Who Made Ireland* (New York: HarperCollins, 1993), 5–9. (Published in London by Hutchinson as *De Valera: Long Fellow, Long Shadow* in 1993.)
27 T. Ryle Dwyer, *Irish Neutrality and the USA, 1939–47* (Dublin: Gill & Macmillan, 1977), 3.
28 This, according to David Gray's memoir *Behind the Emerald Curtain*, in Paul Bew, ed., *A Yankee in De Valera's Ireland: The Memoir of David Gray* (Dublin: Royal Irish Academy, 2012), xxxvi. See also: English, *Irish Freedom*, 325.
29 Diarmaid Ferriter, *Judging Dev: A Reassessment of the Life and Legacy of Eamon de Valera* (Dublin: Royal Irish Academy, 2007), 36.
30 John P. Duggan, *Herr Hempel and the German Legation in Dublin, 1937–1945* (Dublin: Irish Academic Press, 2003), 61–62; Eunan O'Halpin, *Defending Ireland: The Irish State and Its Enemies Since 1922* (New York: Oxford University Press, 2000), 194.
31 See Leah Susan Egofske, "A Contested Policy: Irish and American Perspectives on Eire's Neutrality," MA thesis, Graduate School of Clemson University (May 2013), 55; https://tigerprints.clemson.edu/cgi/viewcontent.cgi?article=2621&context=all_theses (accessed 30 November 2020). Egofske names Ben Robertson and Roi Ottley of New York's *PM* newspaper, Quentin Reynolds representing *Collier's* magazine, Vincent Sheehan writing for the *Nation*, among Kirkpatrick's colleagues reporting on neutral Ireland.
32 For an overview of scholarly approaches to the study of friendship and politics, including a literature review, see Heather Devere and Graham M. Smith, "Friendship and Politics," *Political Studies Review* 8 (2010), 341–356. See also Frank Costigliola, *Roosevelt's Lost Alliances: How Personal Politics Helped Start the Cold War* (Princeton, NJ: Princeton University Press, 2012).
33 Simon Koschut and Andrea Oelsner, eds, *Friendship and International Relations* (New York: Palgrave Macmillan, 2014), 7.
34 Koschut and Oelsner, *Friendship and International Relations*, 9.
35 Ibid., 12, 14–15.
36 Ibid., 16, citing Michael G. Fry, *The Suez Crisis of 1956* (Pittsburgh, PA: Pew Charitable Trust, 1988).
37 Ibid., 18–19.
38 Danny Kaplan, "What Can the Concept of Friendship Contribute to the Study of Nationalism?" *Nations and Nationalism* 13: 2 (2007), 225–244.
39 Kaplan, "What Can the Concept of Friendship Contribute?" 227.
40 Danny Kaplan, *The Men We Loved: Male Friendship and Nationalism in Israeli Culture* (New York: Berghahn Books, 2006), 8.
41 Kaplan, "What Can the Concept of Friendship Contribute?" 232.
42 Ibid., 233.

43 Timothy J. White, "Nationalism vs Liberalism in the Irish Context: From a Postcolonial Past to a Postmodern Future," *Eire-Ireland* 37: 3&4 (Fall/Winter 2002), 27–28.
44 White, "Nationalism vs Liberalism in the Irish Context," 28.
45 Joyce P. Kaufman and Kristen P. Williams, "Nationalism, Citizenship, and Gender," in *Oxford Research Encyclopedia of International Studies*, online ed. (Oxford University Press, November 2017), 10, 16; https://oxfordre.com/internationalstudies/view/10.1093/acrefore/9780190846626.001.0001/acrefore-9780190846626-e-58 (accessed 30 November 2020).
46 Joshua S. Goldstein, *War and Gender: How Gender Shapes the War System and Vice Versa* (New York: Cambridge University Press, 2001), 252.
47 Benedict Anderson, *Imagined Communities: Reflections on the Origin and Spread of Nationalism* (London: Verso, 1983).
48 Kaplan, "What Can the Concept of Friendship Contribute?" 226, 242.
49 Jean Bethke Elshtain, "Sovereignty, Identity and Sacrifice," in *Gendered States: Feminist (Re)Visions of International Relations Theory*, ed. V. Spike Peterson (Boulder, CO: Lynne Rienner, 1992), 145: "The death of the warrior *pro patria* was interpreted as self-sacrifice for others", a "work of *caritas*." (Greater love hath no man than this …) The theme of brotherly love was struck again and again. Men who have killed in a campaign (the example is the Crusades) died "for the love of God and his brothers" and received "eternal beatitude according to the mercy of God." In the thirteenth century, "the Christian virtue of *caritas* became unmistakably political" and was "activated to sanctify and justify, ethically and morally, the death for the 'political fatherland.'"
50 Kaufman and Williams, "Nationalism, Citizenship, and Gender," 19.
51 See for example, Cynthia Enloe, *Bananas, Beaches, and Bases: Making Sense of Feminist International Relations* (Berkeley, CA: University of California Press, 1989); Nagel, "Masculinity and Nationalism," 242–269; Anne Sisson Runyan and V. Spike Peterson, *Global Gender Issues in the New Millennium*, 3rd ed. (Boulder, CO: Westview Press, 2009); Laura J. Shepherd, *Gender Matters in Global Politics: A Feminist Introduction to International Relations*, 2nd ed. (New York: Routledge, 2015); Nira Yuval-Davis, *Gender & Nation* (London: Sage, 1997).
52 Interview with Helen Kirkpatrick Milbank by Anne Kasper, Women in Journalism oral history project of the Washington Press Club Foundation, 3–5 April 1990, Oral History Collection of Columbia University and other repositories; Kerrie Logan Hollihan, *Women of Action, Reporting Under Fire: 16 War Correspondents and Photojournalists* (Chicago, IL: Chicago Review Press, 2014), 69, 103; Obituary: Helen Kirkpatrick Milbank, *Independent* (8 January 1998), www.independent.co.uk/news/obituaries/obituary-helen-kirkpatrick-milbank-1137424.html (accessed 30 November 2020).
53 See for example, Paul Bew, *Churchill and Ireland* (Oxford University Press, 2016); T. Ryle Dwyer, *Behind the Green Curtain: Ireland's Phoney Neutrality During World War II* (Dublin: Gill & Macmillan, 2009) and *Irish Neutrality and the USA*; Robert Fisk, *In Time of War: Ireland, Ulster and the Price of Neutrality*,

1939–1945 (London: Andre Deutsch, 1983); Girvin, *The Emergency*; Dermot Keogh and Mervyn O'Driscoll, eds, *Ireland in World War Two: Neutrality and Sustainability* (Cork: Mercier Press, 2004); John Day Tully, *Ireland and Irish-Americans, 1932–1945: The Search for Identity* (Dublin: Irish Academic Press, 2010); Ian S. Wood, *Britain, Ireland, and the Second World War* (Edinburgh: Edinburgh University Press, 2010).

54 Lawrence Stone, "Prosopography," *Daedalus* 100: 1, in *Historical Studies Today* (Winter 1971), 46–79.

1

Agreements made, pledges broken: Europe in the 1930s

When Helen Kirkpatrick began her graduate studies in history and politics at the Institute des Hautes Études Internationales in Geneva, Switzerland in September 1931, her goal, at the young age of twenty-two, was to travel throughout Europe and to learn at first hand about the conduct of world affairs. Kirkpatrick (1909–1997) was a hardworking and ambitious young woman, raised in a middle-class family in upstate New York. She enrolled at Smith College in 1928 and graduated in June 1931 near the top of her class. At the time she had no clear vision of the path her life would follow. The future that many bright young Americans faced at the depths of the Great Depression was uncertain, yet Kirkpatrick sensed that new opportunities could open for her in the city where the League of Nations, the decade-old forum for member state delegations and global activists, gathered to debate the most pressing issues of the day. In fall 1931, planning for the World Disarmament Conference that the Great War's victor nations had promised to convene in postwar peace settlements was finally underway. Preparations, however, were marred by a new global security crisis that erupted in September when the rising Japanese imperial power invaded and occupied Chinese Manchuria. In Geneva, the proposed disarmament conference and Japan's not-yet-officially-acknowledged act of war dominated the conversations in her classes, in League of Nations public sessions, and at the flurry of social events hosted by foreign delegations and global lobbyists that Kirkpatrick attended.

The opening of the annual League General Assembly in mid-September launched both the social and political seasons in Geneva. Advocacy groups hoping to influence their nation's leaders, whose policies and governing decisions shaped their constituents' fates, mingled with businessmen hoping to gain inside information regarding the direction of the world economy that affected their financial futures, and with journalists gathering news they could report to readers across the globe. In 1931, the world's leading statesmen, along with their nations' often jaded diplomatic envoys and global civil servants, joined earnest advocates of "peace" through disarmament. The women's international organizations, veteran soldiers, socialists and labor unionists, and university students who represented a postwar generation that hoped for a different fate than those who lost their lives in the last war all converged on the international capital with plans and schemes, intent on shaping their national leaders' disarmament pledges and global governance treaties.

Helen Kirkpatrick set out to learn from them all. In classes taught by a host of elite male scholars and government dignitaries whose international reputations were well established – including Swedish economist Gunnar Myrdal, former Italian foreign minister Count Carlo Sforza, Spanish diplomat Salvatore Madariaga, and historian of the Great War Bernadotte Schmidt – Kirkpatrick's studies focused on debating world events and the relative merits of democratic, socialist, and fascist governments to lead their peoples through dangerous global transformations. She also attended League of Nations sessions presided over by General Secretary Sir Eric Drummond, where the foreign ministers of the world's "Great Powers," including Aristide Briand, Sir John Simon, Dino Grandi, and Heinrich Brüning, addressed the global Assembly. An awestruck Kirkpatrick "sat not ten feet away from ... all the men I have read about and studied so long."[1]

Years later, Kirkpatrick wrote about the actions taken by the League member states during her days as a graduate student in Geneva from 1931 to 1933, and marked these years, as many of her contemporaries would, too, as the inception of the fascist powers' aggressive imperial projects that culminated in a second world war. Yet even at the time, in her youthful naivety, she noted the moral and political failures of world leaders who refused to recognize Japan's war in China for what it was and continued the charade that they were honestly debating the terms of an international disarmament treaty that would preserve an already shattered world peace.[2] Following two years spent back in the United States, from 1933 to 1935, when Kirkpatrick tried without success to land a job as a newspaper reporter and was married briefly to a New York businessman, she returned to Geneva in September 1935 to establish herself as a journalist and commentator on international affairs. She was immediately drawn back into the self-serving and backroom-deal-making world of League of Nations politics. In 1935, Fascist Italy led by Benito Mussolini launched a territorial land grab to establish their colonial power over defenseless League member state Ethiopia, and throughout the fall session the League's leading Western European powers deliberated inconclusively regarding collective sanctions that were never imposed on the Italian aggressors. Kirkpatrick also jumped back into Geneva's swirling social life that accompanied League Assemblies, and cultivated networks of diplomats, League civil servants, and foreign reporters, parlaying these contacts into journalistic assignments that paid her rent and served her professional ambitions.[3]

Over the next two years, Kirkpatrick witnessed intergovernmental relations in both public and private arenas that shaped her distinctive reporter's blend of cynicism and idealism as she searched for the "real" story behind increasingly violent global conflicts. One shocking episode that took place in July 1936 helped to define her anti-fascist reportorial perspective throughout the cataclysmic next decade. She was standing next to a Jewish journalist, Stefan Lux, in the League general meeting hall as Italy's annexation of Ethiopia was announced to the member states. Following Italy's attack on Ethiopia in October 1935, Britain and France negotiated a "peace" in January 1936 that ceded 220,000 square miles of Ethiopian territory to Italy.[4] When Ethiopia rejected the settlement and fought back, Italy dropped poison gas bombs on both military and civilian targets until Ethiopia surrendered in May.[5] The terms of Ethiopia's capitulation were announced at the July League session; Lux leapt to his feet, shouted "This is the last blow," and shot himself. He died from his wounds as the assembled government delegations looked on helplessly. Kirkpatrick became a part of the media reports, as she had overheard his last words calling out to the Secretary General, Joseph Avenol, to take charge of his briefcase. The case contained letters explaining his suicide to Britain's Foreign Minister Anthony Eden, King George VI, and to several journalists.[6] Lux's letters expressed his despair at the failure of the League to stand up to the fascist powers and to call attention to the plight of the Jewish peoples in Nazi Germany, and he urged the British government to form a European alliance to halt the dangerous dictators directing Germany's and Italy's violent assaults on undefended populations.[7]

In 1936, Kirkpatrick's reports from Europe focused on Germany's and Italy's provocative empire-building policies that threatened the continental peace, including German-Italian interventions in the Spanish Civil War, and German occupation of the Rhineland.[8] She also joined critics of Britain's Conservative Party government then led by Prime Minister Stanley Baldwin, denouncing the government's failures to check the fascist powers' aggressive rearmament programs or to establish a vigorous British rearmament program in response.[9] In 1937, Kirkpatrick relocated to London to work with *Daily Telegraph* reporter Victor Gordon Lennox and *Economist* deputy editor Graham Hutton on a new publication, the *Whitehall Letter*, an international affairs newsletter that circulated through private subscriptions and was able to avoid some of the press censorship that stifled reporting in other mainstream newspapers.[10] Articles published in the *Whitehall Letter* were based on inside information Kirkpatrick, Gordon Lennox, and Hutton gleaned from their closely guarded diplomatic contacts and on their own investigative reporting.[11] While Gordon Lennox continued his post as the *Daily Telegraph*'s diplomatic correspondent and he and Hutton remained anonymous,[12] Kirkpatrick wrote and edited copy for the *Whitehall Letter*. Together they built up a "small but influential" readership that included Winston Churchill and Anthony Eden, among other government-affiliated European and American subscribers.[13]

The *Whitehall Letter* was, in Kirkpatrick's words, "objective in its approach and designed to inform its readers of the realities of world politics."[14] In fact, the *Whitehall Letter* was anything but objective; it actively opposed the appeasement policy that Neville Chamberlain (1869–1940) adopted when he succeeded Stanley Baldwin in May 1937 as Prime Minister and leader of the Conservative Party government. Kirkpatrick, Gordon Lennox, and Hutton set out to cultivate American anti-fascist, anti-isolationist public opinion in league with an "Old Guard of Tory dissenters," who also opposed appeasement.[15] In 1938–1939, British anti-appeasers joined forces with American expatriate reporters, including Kirkpatrick, Edgar Mowrer, Dorothy Thompson, John Gunther, Vincent Sheehan, and Bill Stoneman, whose firsthand experiences covering European politics had already convinced them of the existential fascist threat. The Brits introduced American reporters to Britain's ruling elite, and shared insights regarding the inner workings of British government.[16] At the suggestion of Victor Gordon Lennox and other British friends, Kirkpatrick wrote two books that focused on the follies of the British appeasement policy and the dangers that the Nazi German Reich's imperial expansion and attacks on European Jewish people posed to world peace, both books intended to explain American responses to European affairs to British readers and to undermine American isolationist opinion in the United States. *This Terrible Peace*[17] was written after Neville Chamberlain orchestrated the Munich Agreement in September 1938, forcing the Czechoslovakian government to cede the Sudetenland to Germany. *Under the British Umbrella* was published several months after Britain went to war with Germany following the German invasion of Poland in September 1939.

Kirkpatrick's harsh critiques of Neville Chamberlain and his government's "weak" and "foolish" and "ignorant" foreign policies made her a target of British government surveillance.[18] Kirkpatrick recalled her impressions of Chamberlain years later in an oral history interview:

> At that time, in late 1936–37, it was clear to the three of us [Kirkpatrick, Gordon Lennox and Hutton] that we were headed – or Britain was headed – for war with Germany. ... but there were those who didn't want to believe it to be inevitable. Many thought that they could avoid it – as did Mr. Chamberlain, who perhaps was very naïve. He was naïve in many ways – though not in

1.1 Helen Paull Kirkpatrick, *c.* 1941

street politics. His election in Birmingham and to Parliament, [and] subsequently to the leadership of the Conservative Party attested to that. But he was naïve in sensing what the situation was with Hitler and Mussolini.[19]

Some of Chamberlain's contemporaries, most notably Winston Churchill (1874–1965), who was advocating for a united front against Nazism at the time,[20] as well as succeeding generations of scholars, were even more critical of Chamberlain's appeasement policy and of his character flaws. Diplomatic historian Greg Kennedy, for one, pronounced him "guilty" for promoting appeasement in the 1930s:

> Chamberlain was a guilty man. ... There is little doubt that Chamberlain was an arrogant man in a hurry, prone to making judgements with insufficient evidence. He believed in his own personal ability to persuade others of the rightness of his position no matter what, and immediately discounted anyone that was not swayed by the brilliance of his analysis. His narrow views on Britain's defense position; his interference with the working of the Foreign Office; the bypassing and manipulation of policy making bodies; his desire for the premiership; and his limited knowledge of how other nations were involved in Britain's defense planning requirements, all made him guilty of an arrogance and conceit in his own abilities.[21]

Neville Chamberlain's ascent to the leadership of Britain's ruling Conservative Party and to the post of Prime Minister was preceded by his tenure as Chancellor of the Exchequer in PM Stanley Baldwin's Cabinet. From those leading government positions, Chamberlain consistently gave way to the attacks of European dictators Benito Mussolini and Adolf Hitler on weaker states and vulnerable populations and acquiesced to their aggressive rearmament programs that violated postwar international treaties. At the same time, the British government launched its own rearmament program and Chamberlain pursued strategic bilateral alliances to preserve the veneer of "peace" among Europe's four Great Powers: Britain, Germany, Italy, and France.[22] Unwilling to tolerate criticism of his conduct of foreign relations, Chamberlain instituted a strict policy of government censorship of foreign news reporting that was followed without much pushback by the editors and proprietors of the mainstream British press. In his study of the British government's manipulation of the media and its efforts to control political messaging before and after the Second World War began, historian Nicholas Cull recounted that the Chamberlain government routinely stonewalled reporters regarding its response to fascist aggression, operating behind a veil of polite but firm deflections.[23]

Press censorship had moral consequences. It kept the British people uninformed about the dangerous implications for British national and global security when the fascist powers attacked the human rights of targeted populations and the sovereign rights of weak states with impunity.[24] At the time, Kirkpatrick wrote that the Chamberlain government's attitude seemed to be that "the truth is not good for the public,"[25] and she wasn't far off the mark. Chamberlain's censorship policy controlled the major British news outlets, and he also exerted strict control over Britain's official relationships with the fascist powers, conducting delicate diplomatic negotiations between Britain, Italy, and Germany privately:

> The result was a conspiracy of silence that obscured deep divisions over Chamberlain's policy in Whitehall, Westminster, and the country at large – a silence that effectively precluded both the articulation of any alternative policy and the presentation of the facts and figures to the British public that might have prompted alternative policies. Thus, the later defense of appeasement as the only policy possible because the country was not sufficiently educated to support a stand against dictators is specious in the extreme, considering that Chamberlain did his utmost to ensure that there was no "education" of the country.[26]

Chamberlain bypassed the British Foreign Office and his Foreign Secretary, Anthony Eden, at several key junctures, prompting Eden to resign his Cabinet post on 21 February 1938, when Chamberlain forged a peace pact with Benito Mussolini, in spite of Mussolini's continued violation of a League of Nations agreement not to intervene with arms or aid in the Spanish Civil War. Reacting to the news, Winston Churchill wrote that "my heart sank, and for a while the dark waters of despair overwhelmed me." Anthony Eden, whom Churchill then considered to be the "one strong figure standing up against long, dismal, drawling tides of drift and surrender, or wrong measurements and feeble impulses," now joined the anti-appeasement Conservative Party critics on the ineffectual sidelines of government power.[27]

Neville Chamberlain also rejected several overtures, between 1937 and 1939, from U.S. President Franklin Roosevelt (FDR) (1882–1945) to present a united front of the Western democracies and to conduct multilateral diplomacy to curb Italian and German aggression. Greg Kennedy lays the blame for this consequential foreign policy decision on Chamberlain's personal antipathy toward the United States, revealing the ongoing influence of the historic rivalry among the masculine Anglo-American elite national leaders documented by Alan Dobson. Franklin Roosevelt may have shared his cousin Theodore's faith in the affinity of Anglo-American patrician cultural and political values, but Chamberlain dismissed the American powerholders:

> Chamberlain's view of the United States as untrustworthy, unimportant and marginal in the British strategic foreign policy process, as well as his jealous,

petty and uninformed view of the nation as a whole, continued to plague attempts by the Foreign Office, Admiralty and other government bodies at manufacturing closer Anglo-American strategic relations throughout his career. This was particularly true after 1937, once he had attained the long sought after position of Prime Minister. ... As a result of his style of governing and politics, Chamberlain helped prevent any prewar formal Anglo-American security arrangement. Without such a pact there was little hope of impressing aggressor nations, and certainly no ability to use a formal alignment to good use as a deterrent in the Far East.[28]

As Chamberlain set the direction of British appeasement policy, Roosevelt grew increasingly alarmed at the rise of the "leading gangsters"[29] directing policy in Fascist Italy and Nazi Germany who flouted international law, especially after Germany's annexation of Austrian territory in March 1938 and Czechoslovakia in 1938–1939,[30] and dismayed at Neville Chamberlain's reluctance to challenge the dictators. In early 1938, prior to Joseph Kennedy's appointment as U.S. Ambassador to Britain, U.S. Minister to Ireland John Cudahy sent FDR frequent reports on British foreign policy. Cudahy provided his analysis of Eden's resignation and its political repercussions, confirming FDR's opinion of Chamberlain's dangerous errors of judgment:

> But the outstanding feature of this crisis is that it is a further retreat; a meeting of Mussolini on his own terms. Winston Churchill came closest to making an honest analysis when he said this.[31] All other discussions in Parliament and the press is typical English face-saving. The situation is one of entering into a contract with one who has shown bad faith and repeatedly breached agreements. The Chamberlain Government would have people believe that Mussolini should be treated as one whose good faith can be taken at face value, and Eden held out for some assurance of performance in view of repeated broken promises. ...
>
> The justification of the Prime Minister's policy is that the time has not yet come in the realization of the rearmament program to risk war. But the trouble with this policy is that it marks further retreat, which may be fatal in encouraging the dangerous adventures of both Mussolini and Hitler. When Hitler invaded the Rhineland, it was clear to all that the treaty system had been replaced by force and show of force in diplomacy, and each successive stroke of Rome and Berlin makes this belief more certain.[32]

Cudahy's missives to Roosevelt became even more critical of Chamberlain following Germany's invasion and annexation of Austria in mid-March:

> I think Chamberlain's is the most weak, vacillating, humiliating policy England has ever presented. It is a drifting, not a policy at all and the amazing thing is the unity of the press and the powers behind the Prime Minister. ... Now with Austria gone, and the balance [of power against Germany] with

it, they evade the issue of Czechoslovakia with a face-saving which is incredible. One of the consequences is Mussolini's arrogant speech, thumbing his nose at Chamberlain. If a British-Italian accord is accomplished, it will be on Mussolini's terms. It is an ignominious defeat and yet the criticism of Chamberlain in his own country has no realistic, clean-cut leadership to insist that the issue be met.

That is the tragedy. There is no leadership to oppose the dictators.[33]

In other words, Britain was failing the test of manhood; its leaders were 'too soft' to stand up to the tough and aggressive dictators.

Roosevelt agreed with Cudahy, but he did not take a bold stand against Hitler or Mussolini at the time either, facing political obstacles that also disempowered him:

> Over here there is the same [appeasement] element that exists in London. Unfortunately, it is led by many of your friends and mine. [FDR was referring to de Valera's Irish Government and Irish American voters.] They would really like me to be a Neville Chamberlain – and if I would promise that, the market would go up and they would work positively and actively for the resumption of prosperity. But if that were done, we would only be breeding far more serious trouble four or eight years from now.[34]

The Western democracies faced "far more serious trouble" that arrived the next year when Chamberlain capitulated again to Hitler's demands to expand Germany's control over Czechoslovakia in March 1939. Still not satisfied, Germany invaded Poland in September 1939, in the move that finally provoked British and French declarations of war.

Ireland's Taoiseach, Eamon de Valera (1882–1975), stood out among the leaders of Western democracies in consistently praising Chamberlain's appeasement policy after 1937. Several factors shaped his perspective. After the failures of the League of Nations' major powers to unite against the fascist aggressors in the 1930s and halt their oppression of the "smaller" powers that could not defend themselves, de Valera increasingly leaned toward Irish neutrality with regard to international conflicts since Ireland was too weak militarily to do battle with the well-armed fascist powers. In addition, his government's diplomatic representative in Berlin, Charles Bewley, openly admired the Nazi government, and presented Nazi actions in the most positive terms in his diplomatic reports. Bewley remained in his Berlin post until war broke out in 1939. Moreover, some of Germany's "nationalist" justifications for its reoccupation of the Rhineland, absorption of Austria, and annexation of the Sudetenland, places that were home to German peoples, also seemed necessary in the interests of international "peace" and justifiable to Irish nationalists who rejected the partition of the Irish homeland and "oppression" of Irish Catholics in Northern Ireland who were governed by a "foreign" power.[35] In large part, however, de Valera's support for Chamberlain's European appeasement policy was due to friendly feelings toward Neville Chamberlain based on the concessions he was able to win from Chamberlain, and from Chamberlain's chief negotiating agent, Secretary of State for Dominion Affairs Malcolm MacDonald (1901–1981), during bilateral negotiations with Chamberlain's Foreign Office that opened in January 1938.

The goal of these state-to-state negotiations was to settle several outstanding issues that jeopardized Anglo-Irish friendly relations in anticipation of the outbreak of another European war.[36] These issues were: the reduction of import duties on Irish goods sold in Britain; the settlement of debts that Irish landowners still owed to Britain based on agreements forged decades earlier; the return to Irish government control of several ports at Berehaven, Cobh, and Lough Swilly that were still occupied by British naval forces according to terms of the 1921 Anglo-Irish Treaty; and ending the partition of the Irish Isle, with the return of the Six Counties of Northern Ireland that remained a member of the United Kingdom rather than part of a sovereign Irish state governed from Dublin. Chamberlain and his designated representatives, especially Dominions Secretary Malcolm MacDonald, were anxious to reach a settlement of these issues. Historian Mervyn O'Driscoll has noted that:

> MacDonald in particular was vital. A member of a new British political generation, he had not formed negative preconceptions as a result of the Anglo-Irish conflict during and after Irish independence and he was prepared to discuss Anglo-Irish differences with more even-handedness and sensitivity than most of his more senior cabinet colleagues. ... In his conception of the Commonwealth as "a gentlemanly club of ex-colonial states" he believed Ireland had a role. Between 1936 and 1938 he used his undoubted persuasive powers to overcome the objections of cabinet colleagues and officials to reaching an accommodation with de Valera. MacDonald tended to emphasize the positive elements of de Valera's position.[37]

And, according to historian David Dilks, during the negotiations Chamberlain "made a sincere and sustained effort to understand the Irish claims. He refused to haggle over small matters in the interests of a wider settlement,"[38] even though Chamberlain found de Valera "extremely difficult to negotiate with."[39] In turn, Eamon de Valera and his designated negotiators also sought "satisfactory settlement" of these issues.[40]

De Valera directed the Irish side of the negotiations and demonstrated his fierce determination to assert Ireland's sovereign rights and to press for every advantage throughout the four-months-long back-and-forth between the two powers.[41] According to the terms of the Anglo-Irish Treaty that was

1.2 Eamon de Valera, *c.* 1939

finally concluded in April 1938, Ireland agreed to pay the British treasury £10 million to settle the outstanding land debts, Britain reduced import duties on Irish goods, and the British Navy evacuated the Irish treaty ports, delivering them to the Irish government's complete control with no guarantees that they could be used by British forces during wartime.[42] The major issue from de Valera's perspective – the partition of Ireland and continued compromise of Irish sovereignty – was not settled during the bilateral talks, even though de Valera threatened to scuttle the talks at several points during the negotiations and tried to persuade Franklin Roosevelt to exert the U.S. government's pressure on Chamberlain to withdraw from the Six Counties.[43]

Despite this significant and consequential disagreement over partition that remained unsettled, de Valera and Chamberlain forged a bilateral agreement that represented "an 'act of good faith,' conducive to good relations."[44] De Valera also established political friendships with MacDonald and Chamberlain that led to his public support for Chamberlain's European appeasement policy,[45] and de Valera understood Chamberlain's motivations as Chamberlain hoped the world would understand them:

Chamberlain's best known policy, appeasement, is often derided as a caving into Hitler and Mussolini. But as one of his close colleagues pointed out, "appeasement did not mean surrender, nor was it a policy only to be used towards the dictators. To Chamberlain it meant the methodical removal of the principal causes of friction in the world."[46]

De Valera supported Chamberlain's efforts to eliminate sources of friction between Britain and Ireland and praised the progress toward that goal that the 1938 Treaty formalized:

> In the Dáil I have already paid a tribute to the wisdom of the present British Premier and his Government, a wisdom I had not previously experienced, in recognizing the fact which the National leaders of Ireland for generations have been pressing on them – that a friendly Ireland is a vast international safeguard to Britain herself, and that Irish friendship can be had only by undoing past wrongs and respecting Irish sovereignty. I look forward to the day when there can be real friendship between the two peoples – the day when Partition is undone and Ireland, united, is a sovereign state. The present agreement will, I am certain, hasten that day.[47]

Chamberlain, too, felt his government had made the best settlement that it could at the time. The Anglo-Protestant government in Northern Ireland refused to consider uniting with de Valera's Catholic Nationalist Southern state, and the promise that he believed he received from de Valera, that Ireland would be a "benevolent neutral" state in the event of war in Europe, satisfied him in spring 1938.[48]

Eamon de Valera was elected President of the League of Nations General Assembly in mid-September 1938, as Nazi Germany massed its troops on the Czechoslovakian border intending to "liberate" German peoples living in the Sudetenland region and to "restore" Czech territory to the German Reich. War seemed inevitable, and de Valera noted the "unparalleled anxiety" that gripped the world in his opening League Assembly address. When Chamberlain orchestrated a meeting with Hitler on September 23 that delayed the German advance, de Valera shared his relief at a dinner for delegates from Britain's Commonwealth States: "it is the best thing that England has ever done." And he wrote to Chamberlain, "One person at least is completely satisfied that you are doing the right thing no matter what the result. ... To stop short at any action which held out the slightest hope of success in view of what is involved would be very wrong."[49] One week later Chamberlain negotiated the Munich Pact with Germany, whereby Italy, Britain, and France all agreed on behalf of Czechoslovakia to cede the territory that Hitler desired to Germany. In an effusive address to the League of Nations as it closed the 1938 Assembly session at the September 30 meeting, Eamon de Valera "hailed Chamberlain as a 'knight of peace', who had 'attained the highest peak of human greatness, and a glory greater than that of all the conquerors'" as he had delayed the outbreak of war.[50] To be sure, "de Valera remained convinced that appeasement was both worthwhile and justified" following the Munich settlement,[51] but he also believed that the Munich Pact implied that negotiated transfer of territory from one nation to another was possible. Or, as historian Robert Fisk has explained, "International disputes could illustrate Ireland's difficulties; and suitable examples from the crisis in Europe were selected to emphasize the evils of Irish partition. Thus, the German speakers of the Sudetenland were metamorphosed by de Valera into the Catholics of Northern Ireland."[52] De Valera continued to press Chamberlain to end partition of Ireland in exchange for Irish support for Britain if war broke out. He advocated Ireland's case privately with Chamberlain and the British Foreign Office,[53] and publicly through the British press.[54]

Following the Munich settlement, Chamberlain received a hero's welcome in Britain. Describing the scene in front of Buckingham Palace on September 30, when Chamberlain's car pulled up to the palace gates to report on his mission to King George VI, Helen Kirkpatrick noted that the Mall was packed with cheering crowds:

> Long after the Prime Minister had disappeared behind the high iron gates, the people lingered on, giving cheer after cheer. Then ... the doors on the left balcony of the Palace opened. It was the King and Queen, followed by Mr. and Mrs. Chamberlain. Slightly sheltered from the pouring rain, they bowed and waved to the mass of people. This was Friday, September 30, 1938. Tomorrow the war was to have begun, but Neville Chamberlain has flown to Germany and returned to announce that there would be no war. "I believe it is peace for our time." Did he really believe that? Did all these people who cheered so wildly believe it? How could they?[55]

According to his biographer Robert Dallek, Franklin Roosevelt "deplored the peace-at-any-price attitude" voiced by Chamberlain and French prime minister Édouard Daladier following their meeting with the dictators in Munich. Nonetheless, Roosevelt also supported a peaceful resolution of the Czech crisis because he believed that the Western Powers' militaries were no match for Nazi Germany's forces.[56] In fact, Roosevelt sent a telegram to Chamberlain, pronouncing him a "Good man" when he learned that Chamberlain was invited to Munich to negotiate the peace with the German Führer.[57]

Winston Churchill was one of the few loud voices[58] asserting that Chamberlain "chose dishonor and ... will have war." Churchill pronounced the Munich settlement "a total unmitigated defeat" in a speech to the House of Lords on October 5.[59] It was a defeat that had been a long time in the making, in Churchill's view:

All is over. Silent, mournful, abandoned, broken, Czechoslovakia recedes into the darkness. ... When I think of the fair hopes of a long peace which still lay before Europe at the beginning of 1933 when Herr Hitler first obtained power, and of all the opportunities of arresting the growth of the Nazi power which have been thrown away, when I think of the immense combinations and resources which have been neglected or squandered, I cannot believe that a parallel exists in the whole course of history. So far as this country is concerned the responsibility must rest with those who have had the undisputed control of our political affairs. They neither prevented Germany from rearming, nor did they rearm ourselves in time. They quarreled with Italy without saving Ethiopia. They exploited and discredited the vast institution of the League of Nations and they neglected to make alliances and combinations which might have repaired previous errors, and thus they left us in the hour of trial without adequate national defense or effective international security.[60]

Churchill's blanket rejection of Chamberlain's appeasement policy toward the European dictators was matched by his condemnation of Chamberlain's Irish appeasement policy. Both critiques were grounded in Churchill's belief that Chamberlain's dangerous concessions undermined Britain's national security and weakened Britain's ability to wage a defensive anti-fascist war.[61] Churchill challenged Chamberlain's judgment to act in the best interest of the British Empire, raising objections to the 1938 Anglo-Irish Treaty in a blistering speech to the House of Commons when the Treaty was presented to Parliament on May 5. As a former First Lord of the Admiralty and head of the Royal Navy during the First World War, Churchill focused his attacks on the relinquished Irish naval ports, highlighting their strategic importance in time of war: "These ports are, in fact, the sentinel towers of the western approaches, by which 45,000,000 people in this Island so enormously depend on foreign food for their daily bread, and by which they carry on their trade, which is equally important to their existence." Not only were the ports surrendered, they were handed over to Irish leaders who were Britain's sworn enemies during the Great War, and who had established an Irish government that was committed to rejecting Britain's imperial power: "Now we are to give them up, unconditionally, to an Irish Government led by men – I do not want to use harsh words – whose rise to power has been proportionate to the animosity with which they have acted against this country, no doubt in pursuit of their own patriotic impulses, and whose present position in power is based upon the violation of solemn [1921 Anglo-Irish] Treaty engagements." Churchill asked the House what would Britain do if Ireland declared neutrality during the next war as de Valera had pledged to do, and the British Navy believed it was necessary for Britain's national survival to occupy the ports by force? How would Britain justify its violation of Ireland's neutral rights if it was "fighting in the name of law, of respect for the rights of small countries?"[62] In Churchill's view, the fate of "civilization" was at stake in the coming war with the fascists, and Britain must stand on the side of laws to protect the rights of the people against tyrannical and barbaric powers.[63]

The fascists' march toward war continued in the year following the Munich settlement, with little change in the responses of any of the key persons discussed here. In late October and early November 1938, Nazi Party activists launched vicious pogroms against the German Jewish peoples, "a retreat in a modern state to savagery associated with bygone ages, laid bare to the world the barbarism of the Nazi regime."[64] Roosevelt's response was threefold: to recall the U.S. Ambassador from Berlin;[65] to alert his military chiefs and civilian defense advisers that the United States needed to build up its air force in order to defend against a possible attack on U.S. territory from Nazi Germany;[66] and to issue a moralistic pledge in his annual address to Congress in January 1939 that the United States would do its part to defend democracy and "the tenets of faith and humanity on which their churches, their government, and their very civilization are founded" – in the Western hemisphere.[67] Throughout spring and summer 1939 FDR did little publicly or privately to rescue European Jewish refugees.[68] A contemporary account that laid out the American response to the refugees' "difficulties" noted that over 600,000 Jews facing incarceration in Nazi concentration camps were trying to leave Germany but "no country seems to want the settlers." The United States' quota for German immigrants was 27,000, and politicians were lobbying to reduce that number. The process for those seeking to emigrate from Germany was complicated by a widespread culture of anti-Semitism in the United States that masqueraded as concern that the immigrants would become a "public charge" because they could not prove they had a source of support in America; Germany had prohibited the expelled Jewish people from taking their property with them.[69] In April, Roosevelt had appealed directly to the European dictators for "peace," but issued no ultimatums, no threats of reprisals; Hitler mocked his overtures.[70]

Meanwhile, de Valera's energetic anti-partition campaign, linked to the opening the British government's settlement with Nazi Germany at Munich seemed to provide, inspired rallies in Glasgow, Manchester, and London throughout fall 1938.[71] The failure of de Valera's arguments to sway the British government's position, however, also led to a December 1938 ultimatum from the Irish Republican Army (IRA) to the British imperial forces in Northern Ireland: either withdraw from Irish territory or face IRA bombing of British cities beginning in January 1939.[72] When the IRA carried through with their attacks and declared "war" on Britain, they jeopardized de Valera's absolute control over governing power in Ireland and challenged the legitimacy (and manhood) of the Fianna Fáil government.[73] These challenges, not the IRA's anti-British violence per se, persuaded de Valera to crack down on IRA subversion.[74] In June 1939 de Valera's government passed the Offences Against the State Act that established a military tribunal and allowed for imprisonment and detention without trial in order to prosecute the IRA bombers.[75] De Valera also publicly voiced support once again for Chamberlain's continued efforts to mediate a European peace, while privately pushing Chamberlain to end partition.[76] And, de Valera lodged Ireland's strong objections to the British Cabinet's April 1939 peacetime conscription order that initially included Northern Ireland, still a member of the United Kingdom, in the mandatory military draft. Worried that de Valera would instigate a new wave of anti-British violence in Northern Ireland if Irishmen were drafted into the British armed forces, Chamberlain backed down.[77] De Valera maintained an effective strategy of sending out mixed messages to different constituencies regarding Ireland's loyalties until war broke out in September.[78]

German troops entered Prague in March 1939, completing the occupation of Czech territory, again without any military response from Britain or France. At that point, "most people realized the folly of the Munich Agreement. ... The invasion of Czechoslovakia stunned the world."[79] The exception, of course, was Winston Churchill, who reminded Britons that he had predicted that "The Fruits of Munich" would be further fascist aggression:

> Many people at the time of the September crisis thought they were only giving away the interests of Czechoslovakia, but with every month that passes you will see that they were also giving away the interests of Britain, and the interests of peace and justice. Now I have defended this speech which has been attacked, and I say never did I make a truer statement to Parliament.[80]

After March, Churchill's reputation and the value of his counsel rose in Parliament: "As the certainty of war with Germany grew, so did the campaign that it was essential to have Winston in the Cabinet."[81] Chamberlain's Cabinet, including his Foreign Secretary, Lord Halifax, who previously supported appeasement, asserted that Britain must take a "hard line" against Germany and "Chamberlain reluctantly accepted that limits had to be determined and shown to Germany ... [and] appeasement was abandoned."[82] Chamberlain, however, still rejected calls for Churchill's return to a policy-making post, believing that Churchill's presence in the Cabinet would provoke Hitler to take even more aggressive actions, including an invasion of Poland, a country that, at last, Britain and France pledged to defend from Nazi attack.[83] Yet it was Churchill's words that resonated with the democratic origin stories that animated the British and American peoples and their Western allies and ultimately inspired the world's anti-fascist resistance. In a broadcast to the United States on August 8, 1939, Churchill captured the anxious mood of Europe on the brink of war, managing to warn the Americans of what was to come and to remind them of their shared humanity with European victims of the fascist powers:

> Listen! No listen carefully; I think I hear something – yes, there is was quite clear. Don't you hear it? It is the tramp of armies crunching gravel of the parade-grounds, splashing through the rain-soaked fields, the tramp of two million German soldiers and more than a million Italians. ... No wonder the armies are tramping when there is so much liberation to be done, and no wonder there is a hush among all the neighbors of Germany and Italy while they are wondering which one is going to be "liberated" next ...[84]

Notes

1 Letter to Mother, 10 September 1931, box 9, Helen Paull Kirkpatrick Papers, Sophia Smith Collection, SSC-MS-00103, Smith College Special Collections, Northampton, Massachusetts (hereafter: HPK Papers).
2 "Geneva – Not in Perspective," Helen Kirkpatrick's personal reflections, *c.* 1933, box 7, HPK Papers.
3 Letter to Mother, 19 September 1935, box 9, HPK Papers.
4 Elmer Bendinger, *No Time for Angels: The Tragicomic History of the League of Nations* (New York: Alfred A. Knopf, 1975), 356–360.
5 John H. Spencer, "The Italian-Ethiopian Dispute and the League of Nations," *American Journal of International Law* 31 (October 1937), 614–630.
6 "Suicide Shot Rings at League Session," *New York Times* (3 July 1936), box 12, HPK Papers.
7 David B. Green, "This Day in Jewish History: A Jewish Writer Commits Suicide at the League of Nations," *Haaretz*, 3 July 2013, www.haaretz.com/jewish/.premium-this-day-a-suicide-at-the-league-of-nations-1.5290616 (accessed 30 November 2020).
8 Kirkpatrick, "Impending European War a Theme of Geneva Correspondents Letter," *Montclair Times*, 4 December 1936, box 1, HPK Papers; Kirkpatrick, "General War is Near Unless League Acts, Madrid Holds," *New York Herald Tribune*, 11 December 1936, box 12, HPK Papers.
9 Helen P. Kirkpatrick, *Under the British Umbrella* (New York and London: Charles Scribner's Sons, 1939), 153, 233.
10 Letter to Mother, 21 April 1937, box 9, HPK Papers; Kirkpatrick, *Under the British Umbrella*, 96–98.
11 Interview with Helen Kirkpatrick Milbank by Anne Kasper, Women in Journalism, Oral History Project of the Washington Press Club Foundation, 3–5 April 1990, 25–26; Letter to Family, 24 May 1938, box 9, HPK Papers.
12 Letter to Family, 8 June 1938, box 9, HPK Papers.

13 Letter to Avis Berman, 15 November 1977, box 9, HPK Papers; Leonard Miall, Obituary: Helen Paull Kirkpatrick, *Independent* online, 8 January 1998, www.independent.co.uk/news/obituaries/obituary-helen-kirkpatrick-milbank-1137424.html (accessed 30 November 2020); Victor Gordon Lennox to Winston Churchill, 7 September 1939, CHAR: 2/362, 01, Winston Churchill Archives online, The Chartwell Trust.
14 Kirkpatrick, *Under the British Umbrella*, 98.
15 Nicholas J. Cull, *Selling War: The British Propaganda Campaign Against American 'Neutrality' in World War II* (Oxford: Oxford University Press, 1996), 14.
16 Cull, *Selling War*; Letter to Family, 23 February 1938, box 9, HPK Papers.
17 Helen Paull Kirkpatrick, *This Terrible Peace*, Foreword by Victor Gordon Lennox (London: Rich & Cowan, 1939).
18 Cull, *Selling War*, 15–16; Kirkpatrick, *Under the British Umbrella*.
19 Interview with Helen Kirkpatrick Milbank, Women in Journalism, Oral History Project, 3–5 April 1990, 25.
20 Martin Gilbert, *Churchill: A Life* (New York: Henry Holt, 1991), 584.
21 Greg Kennedy, "Neville Chamberlain and Strategic Relations with the US During His Chancellorship," *Diplomacy & Statecraft* 13: 1 (March 2002), 114.
22 Michael Roi, "Introduction: Appeasement: Rethinking the Policy and Policy-Makers," *Diplomacy & Statecraft* 19: 3 (September 2008), 383; B. J. C. McKercher, "National Security and Imperial Defense: British Grand Strategy and Appeasement, 1930–1939," *Diplomacy & Statecraft* 19: 3 (September 2008), 392.
23 Cull, *Selling War*, 14–15.
24 William R. Rock, "Review of Richard Crockett, *Twilight of Truth: Chamberlain, Appeasement, and the Manipulation of the Press*," *American Historical Review* 95: 5 (December 1990), 1547–1548. Rock wrote: "Those who may wish for a rehabilitation of Neville Chamberlain and British foreign policy from 1937 to 1940 will derive no comfort from this book. Its central themes, consistently elaborated throughout, are that the Chamberlain government shamefully – and sometimes treacherously – manipulated the British press in order to silence the criticism of Adolf Hitler and Benito Mussolini (a seeming prerequisite of any settlement with them) and put the best face on its dealings with the dictators and further that many proprietors and editors, equally shamefully and treacherously, succumbed to manipulation (for various reasons) to the point of losing touch entirely with public opinion and becoming 'not so much the watchdogs of democracy as the harlots of democracy' (p. 187)."
25 Kirkpatrick, *Under the British Umbrella*, 96.
26 Rock, "Review of Richard Crockett, *Twilight of Truth*," 1548.
27 Gilbert, *Churchill*, 587.
28 Kennedy, "Neville Chamberlain and Strategic Relations," 113–114. See also Robert Dallek, *Franklin D. Roosevelt: A Political Life* (New York: Penguin, 2018), 284–284; Kevin Smith, "Reassessing Roosevelt's View of Chamberlain After Munich: Ideological Affinity in the Geoffrey Thompson–Claude Bowers

Correspondence," *Diplomatic History* 33: 5 (November 2009), 840–841, 859–862.
29 Dallek, *Franklin D. Roosevelt: A Political Life*, 300–301.
30 Smith, "Reassessing Roosevelt's View of Chamberlain," 863.
31 Gilbert, *Churchill*, 588. Churchill spoke in Parliament following Eden's resignation and Nazi Germany's interference in Austria's government: "This has been a good week for Dictators. It is the best one they have ever had. The German Dictator has laid his heavy hand upon a small but historic country, and the Italian Dictator has carried his vendetta to a victorious conclusion against my right Hon friend the late Foreign Secretary."
32 John Cudahy to President Franklin Roosevelt, 1 March 1938, box 40, President's Secretary's Files, Ireland 1938–1939, Franklin D. Roosevelt Papers, Franklin D. Roosevelt Presidential Library, Hyde Park, NY (hereafter: FDR Papers).
33 John Cudahy to President Franklin Roosevelt, 6 April 1938, box 40, President's Secretary's Files, Ireland 1938–1939, FDR Papers.
34 Franklin Roosevelt to John Cudahy, 16 April 1938, box 40, President's Secretary's Files, Ireland 1938–1939, FDR Papers.
35 Mervyn O'Driscoll, *Ireland, Germany and the Nazis: Politics and Diplomacy, 1919–1939*, 2nd ed. (Dublin: Four Courts Press, 2017), 187–196, 213–214.
36 De Valera's statement given to *Paramount News* and the *March of Time*, 19 January 1938, P150/2491, Eamon de Valera Papers (on microfilm), University College Dublin (hereafter: EdV Papers, UCD).
37 O'Driscoll, *Ireland, Germany and the Nazis*, 212. See also David McCullagh, *De Valera: Rule*, vol. II, *1932–1972* (Dublin: Gill Books, 2018), 139: "In September 1937 Malcolm MacDonald had two lengthy conversations with de Valera in Geneva, coming away convinced that de Valera was 'really genuine in desiring whole-hearted friendship and cooperation between the Irish Free State and Great Britain', though he 'would rather like to get that friendship on his own terms'."
38 David Dilks, *Churchill and Company: Allies and Rivals in War and Peace* (London: I. B. Tauris, 2012), 252.
39 O'Driscoll, *Ireland, Germany and the Nazis*, 212.
40 Notes on the First Meeting of the Conference between Representatives of the United Kingdom and Eire, 17 January 1938, P150/2480, EdV Papers, UCD. See also Thomas E. Hatchley and Lawrence J. McCaffrey, *The Irish Experience Since 1800: A Concise History* (New York: Routledge, 2010), 175.
41 O'Driscoll, *Ireland, Germany and the Nazis*, 213.
42 McCullagh, *De Valera*, 137: "The return of the Treaty ports is usually described as de Valera's greatest diplomatic triumph. It was certainly a triumph, as it enabled Irish neutrality in the Second World War. How much it owed to de Valera's diplomatic skills, however, is debatable." See also Francis M. Carroll, "Ireland Among the Nations of the Earth: Ireland's Foreign Relations from 1923 to 1949," *Irish Studies* (2016), 48.
43 Notes on the Sixth Meeting of the Conference between Representatives of the United Kingdom and Eire, 23 February 1938, P150.2485, EdV Papers, UCD;

John Cudahy to President Roosevelt, 22 January 1938, Eamon de Valera to Franklin Roosevelt, 25 January 1938, and John Cudahy to Franklin Roosevelt, 1 March 1938, box 40, President's Secretary's Files, Ireland 1938–1939, FDR Papers.
44 Robert Fisk, *In Time of War: Ireland, Ulster and the Price of Neutrality, 1939–1945* (London: Andre Deutsch, 1983), 36; Tim Pat Coogan, *Eamon de Valera: The Man Who Was Ireland* (New York: HarperCollins, 1993), 513–515.
45 Eamon de Valera to Franklin Roosevelt, 22 April 1938, P150/2836; "The Anglo-Irish Agreement; Mr. DeValera on the Ports," *Irish Times* (28 April 1938), P150/2512; Malcolm MacDonald to Eamon de Valera, 17 May 1938 and Eamon de Valera to Malcolm MacDonald, 30 May 1938, P150/2517, EdV Papers, UCD.
46 McCullagh, *De Valera*, 137. See also Alvin Jackson, *Ireland 1798–1998 War, Peace and Beyond*, 2nd ed. (Chichester: John Wiley & Sons, 2010), 295: "The British, unsettled by the development of German and Italian ambitions and fearful of the strategic consequences of having an unfriendly Irish neighbor, were determined to have an agreement, even though the price might be high. The Anglo-Irish Agreement was clearly viewed by Chamberlain not simply within its own terms, but very firmly within the international context as a part of a series of interlocking diplomatic settlements forged between Britain and Italy and Germany."
47 "Points for U.S. Interview," 29 April 1938, P150/2515, EdV Papers, UCD.
48 O'Driscoll, *Ireland, Germany and the Nazis*, 220.
49 McCullagh, *De Valera*, 156–157. See also Fisk, *In Time of War*, 62.
50 Coogan, *Eamon de Valera*, 530.
51 McCullagh, *De Valera*, 159.
52 Robert Fisk, *In Time of War*, 65.
53 Ibid., 56–57.
54 Extract from Taoiseach's interview with London *Evening Standard*, 17 October 1938, P150/2541, EdV Papers, UCD.
55 Kirkpatrick, *Under the British Umbrella*, viii.
56 *Franklin D. Roosevelt: A Political Life*, 318, 320.
57 Smith, "Reassessing Roosevelt's View of Chamberlain," 840.
58 Gilbert, *Churchill*, 598. Churchill's view was shared by First Lord of the Admiralty Duff Cooper, who resigned from Chamberlain's Cabinet, and by Labour Party leader Clement Atlee and Liberal Party leader Archibald Sinclair, but they were in the minority.
59 Dallek, *Franklin D. Roosevelt: A Political Life*, 320. See also Anthony J. Jordan, *Churchill: A Founder of Modern Ireland* (Dublin: Westport Books, 1995), 169.
60 Winston Churchill, "The Munich Agreement, A Speech Delivered in the House of Commons," 5 October 1938, in Winston Churchill, *Into Battle, 1941* (RosettaBooks, 2013), 46–47.
61 "Mr. Churchill & Dictators, 'Volcanic Forces at Work,'" *The [London] Daily Telegraph* (3 June 1938), 11.

62 Fisk, *In Time of War*, 37–38. See also Winston Churchill, Speech to the House of Commons on the "Eire Bill," 5 May 1938, in Churchill, *Into Battle, 1941*, 13. Churchill repeated his prophesies in December 1938: "Mr. Churchill Hits Back at Prime Minister; The Price of Eire's Aid in Time of War," *Irish Times* (10 December 1938), P150/2547, EdV Papers, UCD.
63 Winston Churchill, "Civilization, An Address as Chancellor to the University of Bristol," 2 July 1938, in Churchill, *Into Battle, 1941*, 36.
64 Dallek, *Franklin D. Roosevelt: A Political Life*, 323, quoting Ian Kershaw, *Hitler: A Biography* (New York: W. W. Norton, 2010).
65 *Ibid.*, 324.
66 John A. Thompson, "Conceptions of National Security and American Entry into World War II," *Diplomacy & Statecraft* 16: 4 (December 2005), 673.
67 Franklin Roosevelt's address to U.S. Congress, 4 January 1939, reproduced in Smith, "Reassessing Roosevelt's View of Chamberlain," 859.
68 Blanche Wiesen Cook, *Eleanor Roosevelt: The War Years and After*, vol. 3: *1939–1962* (New York: Viking, 2016), 61–62, 80–81, 90. One egregious incident that exposed Franklin Roosevelt's moral and political failure to rescue fewer than 1,000 Jewish refugees who had managed to escape Europe and set sail for Cuba and the United States on the *St. Louis* ocean liner at the end of May 1939 is recounted on the website of the United States Holocaust Memorial Museum: "Voyage of the St. Louis," *Holocaust Encyclopedia* online (Washington, DC: United States Holocaust Memorial Museum, 16 June 2016). https://encyclopedia.ushmm.org/content/en/article/voyage-of-the-st-louis (accessed 1 December 2020).
69 Clarence E. Pickett, "Difficulties in the Placement of Refugees," *Annals of the American Academy of Political and Social Science* 203 (May 1939), 94–98.
70 Dallek, *Franklin D. Roosevelt: A Political Life*, 341–343. See also Winston Churchill, "Herr Hitler Speaks, An Address Broadcast to the People of the United States of America, 28 April 1939," in Churchill, *Into Battle, 1941*, 94; T. Ryle Dwyer, *Behind the Green Curtain: Ireland's Phoney Neutrality During World War II* (Dublin: Gill & Macmillan, 2009), 11.
71 Robert Cole, *Propaganda, Censorship and Irish Neutrality in the Second World War* (Edinburgh: Edinburgh University Press, 2006), 7.
72 Fisk, *In Time of War*, 73. See also Tony Gray, *The Lost Years: The Emergency in Ireland, 1939–1945* (London: Warner Books, 1998), 8: "In December 1938, the IRA suddenly took it into its head to serve an ultimatum on the British Home Secretary, demanding the instant withdrawal of British troops from Northern Ireland and threatening reprisals if Britain failed to comply. This action was a direct result of de Valera's failure to secure any concrete concessions on the partition issue in his 1938 negotiations with the British"; and T. Ryle Dwyer, *Irish Neutrality and the USA, 1939–47* (Dublin: Gill & Macmillan, 1977), 13: "In January 1939 the IRA issued an ultimatum to the British government to leave Northern Ireland within four days. And when London failed to comply, the organization – encouraged by Germany and financed mainly by money from the United States – initiated a bombing campaign in a number of British cities,

placing explosives in mailboxes, railroad stations, bridges and other public places."
73 John Duggan, *Herr Hempel and the German Legation in Dublin* (Dublin: Irish Academic Press, 2003), 48; Coogan, *Eamon de Valera*, 523.
74 McCullagh, *De Valera*, 162. De Valera made a speech to the Irish Seanad in February 1939 during which he stated: "I am not a pacifist by any means. I would, if I could see a way of doing it effectively, rescue the people of Tyrone and Fermanagh, South Down, South Armagh, and Derry city from the coercion which they are suffering at the present time ... If we had behind us the strength of some of the continental powers ... I would feel perfectly justified in using force ..." He then qualified what he just said: "I do not want, and I am not advocating, force – I hope that is clear – because I do not think it would succeed ... I think it would embitter relations which were improving."
75 Gray, *The Lost Years*, 10.
76 Eamon de Valera to Malcolm MacDonald, 13 April 1939, P150/2553, and Eamon de Valera to Neville Chamberlain, 4 May 1939, P150/2548, EdV Papers, UCD. See also John Cudahy to Franklin Roosevelt, 6 April 1939, box 40, President's Secretary's File, Ireland 1938–1939, FDR Library.
77 Telegram from State Department to Franklin Roosevelt, 27 April 1939, box 40, President's Secretary's File, Ireland 1938–1939, FDR Library. See also Fisk, *In Time of War*, 80–83. Northern Ireland's Unionist government prime minister, Lord James Craigavon, was anxious to prove Northern Ireland's loyalty to the British government. But due to the Catholic/IRA resistance and civil violence in Northern Ireland that de Valera "predicted" (or "threatened," according to Craigavon), Chamberlain refused to extend conscription to Northern Ireland in 1939. The contentious conscription issue resurfaced in 1941. Brian Barton, *Northern Ireland in the Second World War* (Belfast: Ulster Historical Foundation, 1995), 16–18.
78 Fisk, *In Time of War*, 74, 76.
79 Jordan, *Churchill*, 169.
80 Winston Churchill, "The Fruits of Munich, A Speech Delivered at Altham Abbey, 14 March 1939," in Churchill, *Into Battle, 1941*, 73.
81 Jordan, *Churchill*, 170. See also Carlos D'Este, *Warlord: A Life of Winston Churchill at War, 1874–1945* (New York: HarperCollins, 2008), 325.
82 McKercher, "National Security and Imperial Defense," 424.
83 Dilks, *Churchill and Company*, 35.
84 D'Este, *Warlord*, 322.

2

Neutral states in a world at war, September 1939 to May 1940

In summer 1939 the anxious mood across Europe and the United States intensified. Following the German occupation of Czechoslovakia in March, Britain and France had finally drawn the line to halt German Führer Adolf Hitler's territorial expansion of the German Reich, pledging to defend Poland, Greece, and Romania from external aggressors. Yet the invasion of Poland was assured when Hitler eliminated any possible opposition from the Soviet Union through an August 23 Non-Aggression Pact and Secret Protocol. With these agreements, Hitler and Soviet premier Joseph Stalin settled the terms for Poland's conquest, planning to launch invasions from the east and west and to divide Polish territory between them, and soon thereafter to conquer the Baltic states.[1] Now war with the Western Allies was just a matter of time.

The Nazi-Soviet Pact was no traditional diplomatic alliance between friendly nations; it was "a cynical agreement between two despotic nations that gravely distrusted each other."[2] When the pact was announced Winston Churchill wondered publicly which of the two "enemies," Hitler or Stalin, "loathed [the pact] the most."[3] Nonetheless, the agreement served Hitler's imperial vision and allayed Stalin's immediate security concerns on the Soviet Union's European borders. For years, Stalin and his foreign ministers had tried, unsuccessfully, to negotiate an alliance with Britain and France to check the advances of Nazi Germany.[4] When Soviet overtures were ignored, Stalin determined that a calculated agreement with Germany to divide Poland and establish a Soviet sphere in Eastern Europe would protect his nation from German attack. Much too late to be effective, on August 4, President Franklin Roosevelt warned the Soviets not to trust Hitler, that the Nazi Army would eventually turn on them as well.[5]

Following the announcement of the Nazi-Soviet Pact, Europe waited in limbo between war and peace, a "doom-laden state" for Europe and the world, according to Winston Churchill's observations.[6] Helen Kirkpatrick later recalled the last days of August before war broke out as a "slightly mad" moment in time:

> I spent it in the country, not far from London, in a luxurious house with eleven other guests. We swam, we played tennis, we rode horseback in Windsor Great Park, we gathered frequently around the cocktail bar, and we saw the latest films in a complete miniature moving picture theater next to the squash courts in one wing of the house. The company ranged from stockbrokers to film magnates, from movie actors to two other exceedingly depressing and serious newspaper people like myself. The whole atmosphere was slightly mad, tinged with the same undercurrent that must have pervaded the court of Louis XVI. "Après nous le deluge" might well have been the toast proposed in the excellent champagne we drank each evening.[7]

On August 30, the German government made its case to justify war on Poland, expecting British-French acquiescence once again: former German territory that had been transferred to Poland following the Great War – a corridor of land providing Germany access to the Baltic Sea, and the port city of Danzig – must be restored to safeguard the lives and property of German peoples suffering under "disorganized" Polish rule.[8] The Nazi *Wehrmacht* invaded Poland on September 1. Prime Minister Neville Chamberlain's government mobilized the British Naval Fleet and began evacuating children from London in preparation for war. Chamberlain also phoned Winston Churchill, inviting him into Britain's War Cabinet as First Lord of the Admiralty while simultaneously pledging him to secrecy, not yet ready to formally declare war on the German Reich.[9] Both Chamberlain and his Foreign Secretary, Lord Halifax, made one final offer to Hitler: withdraw German forces from Poland by a September 3 deadline, or go to war. The delay outraged Parliament and confounded reporters like Helen Kirkpatrick who waited to cable the declaration of war that they knew was coming back to the United States.[10]

Churchill's supporters gathered at his London flat and fumed at Chamberlain's weak response to Germany's hyper-masculine aggression, "all in a state of bewildered rage."[11] Germany advanced further into Poland and, finally, on September 3, at 11:00 am, the deadline Britain set for German withdrawal passed. Neville Chamberlain solemnly addressed Parliament and the nation; "the sadness in his voice and his choice of words betrayed his own feelings of deep, personal grief"[12]:

> This morning the British Ambassador in Berlin handed the German Government a final note stating that unless we heard from them by 11 o'clock, that they were prepared at once to withdraw their troops from Poland, a state of war would exist between us. I have to tell you now that no such undertaking has been received, and that consequently this country is at war with Germany.
>
> You can imagine what a bitter blow it is to me that all my long struggle to win peace has failed. Yet I cannot believe that there is anything more or anything different that I could have done and that would have been more successful.[13]

2.1 Winston Churchill leaving 10 Downing Street after a War Council Meeting, *c.* 1939

Winston Churchill, whose elevation to the War Cabinet could now be announced – to the nation's "immense relief and satisfaction," according to Britain's anti-appeasement press[14] – "answered the call with relish." He later recalled being "instantly fearless at the call of honor."[15] Delivering his war speech to Parliament on September 3, Churchill laid out for the British people and the world the "true" nature of the war and the necessity to wage war to restore Britain's manhood. Churchill called upon the British people to show the world what international relations scholar Joshua Goldstein has identified as "warrior values ... closely linked with concepts of masculinity ... physical courage, ... endurance, ... strength and skill, ... honor."[16] This was a manly call to arms that Churchill would repeat in many rousing addresses throughout the war:

> This is not a question of fighting for Danzig or fighting for Poland. We are fighting to save the whole world from the pestilence of Nazi tyranny and in defense of all that is most sacred to man. This is no war of domination or imperial aggrandizement or material gain; no war to shut any country out of its sunlight and means of progress. It is a war, viewed in its inherent quality, to establish, on impregnable rocks, the rights of the individual, and it is a war to establish and revive the stature of man.[17]

Churchill's words, forceful as they were, could not translate into an Allied military campaign that put boots on the ground quickly enough to rescue Poland. On September 27, Poland surrendered to Nazi Germany. British and French armies had done nothing to prevent the catastrophe and Hitler taunted the emasculated Allies: "not a shot fired in the western front,"[18] and "This is how I can deal with any European city." Churchill biographer Carlo D'Este concluded that the defeat was a failure of manly will: "It hardly mattered that between them Britain and France had larger military forces at their disposal than the German army of 1939. Of greater significance was that German success had everything to do with the inability of both France and Britain to put teeth into their pledges of mutual security and support."[19] While the German victors marched through Warsaw, Churchill pushed forward with his accelerated British rearmament plan. He also acknowledged Britain's mistaken appeasement policy of the past, but vowed that Britain would now fight:

> Our reluctance to fight was mocked at as cowardice. Our desire to see an unarmed world was proclaimed as the proof of our decay. Now we have begun. Now we are going on. Now with the help of God, and with the conviction that we are the defenders of civilization and freedom, we are going to persevere to the end.[20]

These were messages that President Franklin Roosevelt needed to hear as he navigated the fickle political climate in the United States at a time when most Americans rejected any military involvement in European (or Asian) wars[21] even as they denounced Germany's "unjust" invasion of Poland.[22] Roosevelt had realized the dangers that the fascist dictators posed to U.S. national security and to global security in the 1930s, and he had privately railed against Chamberlain's appeasement policy, but a vocal isolationist political bloc that rallied around aviation hero Charles Lindbergh and other popular advocates of "America First" prevented him from pushing forward too quickly with his plan to prepare the country for its inevitable role as a belligerent.[23] Throughout the 1930s U.S. military strength was pitifully weak, certainly no match for Germany's state-of-the-art war machine.[24] While recognizing the political and practical realities, in November 1938 FDR had initiated plans to build up a modern air force, the branch of the military that he hoped could beat back any transatlantic attack that the formidable German *Luftwaffe* might launch against the United States.[25]

In the meantime, as soon as the Western Allies declared war on Germany on September 3, President Roosevelt spoke to the American people, announcing the United States' neutrality policy:

> The overwhelming masses of our people seek peace – peace at home and the kind of peace in other lands which will not jeopardize our peace at home ...
>
> This nation will remain a neutral nation, but I cannot ask that every American remain neutral in thought as well. Even a neutral has a right to take account of facts. Even a neutral cannot be asked to close his mind or close his conscience.
>
> I have said many times that I have seen war and I hate war. I say that again and again. I hope the United States will keep out of this war. I believe that it will. And ... every effort of your government will be directed toward that end.[26]

FDR intended to comfort the American people, but he also worried about the fate of "victim" nations under attack. Seeking a politically acceptable way to aid the anti-fascist allies, on September 13, Roosevelt initiated a campaign to amend the 1935–1937 Neutrality Laws that prevented the U.S. Government and U.S. manufacturers from selling any weapons or war materials to nations at war and prohibited American citizens from traveling in war zones.[27] Roosevelt proposed amending the Neutrality Laws, adding "Cash and Carry" provisions for sales of U.S.-made weapons or materials to nations at war, that is, "pay cash, and transport the materials to war zones on your own ships."[28] Congress repealed the arms embargo and adopted Cash and Carry legislation on October 27; Roosevelt signed the bill into law on November 4. Chamberlain's government informed reporters of the good news at its November 3 press briefing.[29]

Roosevelt also reached out directly to Winston Churchill on September 11 to establish a private two-way correspondence between the two like-minded Anglo-American anti-fascists. FDR circumvented diplomatic channels of communication through his own ambassador to London, Joseph Kennedy, not wanting to hear Kennedy's defeatism. And not trusting Chamberlain's past pro-appeasement stance to keep the Western Allies strong in the anti-fascist fight, FDR approached Churchill before suggesting his plan to Britain's prime minister.[30] Roosevelt pursued the personal relationship, sure that Churchill's anti-fascist declarations were in sympathy with his own views – even if, at this stage, he harbored his own reservations about Britain's abilities to defeat the Axis Powers:[31]

> My dear Churchill,
> It is because you and I occupied similar positions in the World War that I want you to know how glad I am that you are back again in the Admiralty. Your problems are I realize complicated by new factors but in the essentials not very different. What I want you and the Prime Minister to know is that I shall at all times welcome it if you will keep me in touch personally with anything you want me to know about. You can always send sealed letters through your [diplomatic] pouch or my pouch. ....[32]

Churchill and Roosevelt had met briefly in London during the Great War and reportedly Churchill had snubbed Roosevelt at that time.[33] Nevertheless, their shared understanding of the fascist threat to their nations' survival and, as they both fervently believed, to the continuation of Western civilization, served as the foundation for their wartime alliance and for their personal friendship that developed over the next five and a half years. Churchill and Roosevelt shared similar backgrounds in class, race, and upbringing. They were both imbued with an "ideology of elite masculinity" that shaped the boys born into their privileged worlds into men beginning in their early years, raised in families headed by powerful fathers, and doted on by loving mothers. They both adhered to an Anglo-American "patrician manhood script," indoctrinated by their prestigious all-male boarding school educations, Churchill at Harrow School and Roosevelt at Groton, "separate from the world of women." Their similar upbringings laid out their lives' pathways that included military and political service to their nations, and asserted their destiny to greatness.[34]

Winston Churchill went through military training as a cadet at Sandhurst Royal Military Academy, in the early 1890s. As a journalist, Churchill saw action in the Boer War, and was appointed First Lord of the Admiralty in charge of Britain's Navy preparations in 1911. When the First World War broke out, Churchill oversaw Britain's naval campaigns. Following two costly naval defeats in the Dardanelles and Gallipoli, however, he resigned his post, only to join the British Army to fight the Germans on the Western Front in Belgium. As the war neared its end, Churchill joined David Lloyd George's Conservative government, serving as Secretary of State for War. After the war ended, he was appointed Secretary of State for the Colonies. During that tenure he earned Irish nationalists' enmity for his role negotiating the Anglo-Irish Treaty that partitioned the country. In and out of government service during the 1920s, Churchill served as Chancellor of the Exchequer 1924–1929, and then spent the 1930s mostly out of power as Prime Ministers Stanley Baldwin and Neville Chamberlain led the Conservative Party and directed British foreign policy. While Churchill was an upper-class conservative in his social outlook, he was eccentric in his personal style. His friends appreciated his passion, the rousing eloquence of his wartime speeches, and his shrewd, realistic political assessments. To his critics, Churchill was unjustifiably vain and bellicose: "capricious and meddlesome, inclined toward dynamic action in every direction at once."[35] They asserted that he had no moral reservations when it came to wartime policies and he was willing to use any means necessary to defeat his enemies and ensure Britain's survival.

Franklin Roosevelt's adolescence spent at Groton was followed by his undergraduate studies at Harvard University, then marriage, and then law school at Columbia University. After passing the bar exam, Roosevelt launched his political career in New York State legislature at the suggestion of his cousin Theodore Roosevelt. Following Woodrow Wilson's election as president in 1912, FDR was appointed Assistant Secretary of the Navy in 1913, and during the First World War he was responsible for building up U.S. naval strength. Although Roosevelt wanted to serve on the fighting front during the war, he was convinced by others that his service in Washington was necessary. Following the war, he was struck down by a crippling attack of polio in 1921. FDR fought the disease and regained some of his strength during the 1920s, although he never walked again without braces. He demonstrated manly fortitude and perseverance and returned to politics, winning the governorship of New York in 1928. When the Great Depression devastated the U.S. economy, he launched his Democratic Party candidacy for the presidency with the promise of a "New Deal." FDR was elected president in 1932, and was re-elected in 1936, 1940, and 1944. Roosevelt's biographers and his contemporary friends and critics have focused on deciphering his complex political personality. In the most generous descriptions, his charismatic leadership skills, and his ability to convey stoic calmness and wisdom in the face of the greatest economic crisis the nation had faced in the 1930s, through the most destructive attack on U.S. territory in Hawaii in 1941, and through the highs and lows of the Allied Powers' fortunes during the Second World War during the 1940s, won the popular support of the majority of his fellow American citizens.[36] His critics have characterized him as a calculating political manipulator, a "juggler" or a "seducer," who had no fixed moral compass.[37]

Although Roosevelt made the first overture to Churchill when the war broke out in Europe, Churchill set the intimate tone for their fraternal friendship, adopting an insider language for their frequent correspondence, dubbing himself the "Former Naval Person," calling on the brotherhood of shared backgrounds and histories of service to their nations during the First World War as the foundation for their common world view.[38] Their ever-growing fraternal bond was especially crucial during the chaotic first two years of war as Churchill appealed to FDR for military aid and moral support to prevent Britain's collapse. And their bond sustained the two leaders after the United States formally entered the Western Alliance to defeat their common enemies.[39]

The shared understandings that developed into an easy friendship were never present in the relationships that either Franklin Roosevelt or Winston Churchill formed with Ireland's Taoiseach Eamon de Valera. De Valera's family's poverty, his participation in the armed revolution against Britain during the 1916 Rising, and his adherence to the cause of Irish independence from the 1920s onward, all established an ideological divide between the Anglo-Americans and the Irishman that none of the national leaders were able to overcome during the Second World War. Roosevelt and Churchill, members of the Anglo-American male elite, represented the "hegemonic masculinity" of their era, with all other national masculinities, especially "colonized" masculinities, rendered "subordinate" to the hegemonic "ideal."[40] In Sikata Banerjee's gender analysis of the historic iteration of Irish Catholic manhood that emerged as de Valera came of age, his generation was compelled to assert its opposition to the British imperial manhood that enslaved it, and to rejuvenate its masculine identity through a nationalist "brotherhood."[41] De Valera's personality also clashed with those of the Anglo-American leaders. In the view of de Valera's friends, he was a charismatic and tough survivor of Ireland's nationalist struggles. They believed he was a superlative leader, a tremendous tactician, and even a great statesman who demonstrated his own moral certainty and diplomatic skills that enabled him to resist heavy-handed Anglo-American pressure campaigns during the war.[42] De Valera's opponents, conversely, described him as ruthless and doctrinaire, malignant, vain, dictatorial, and divisive. Those opponents, Roosevelt and Churchill included, believed de Valera was petty and narrow-minded, and that his rigid neutrality policy during the Second World War was ignorant and amoral, if not pro-Nazi.[43]

For his part, de Valera believed that Nazi Germany was better cultivated as a friend of neutral Ireland than opposed as an enemy of a belligerent

Ireland. The imminent outbreak of the war in summer 1939 persuaded de Valera to assure the Nazi government of Southern Ireland's neutrality, and to explain how Ireland's unique relationship with Great Britain would, in fact, serve Germany's national interest in time of war. With this outreach, de Valera sought to avoid the physical destruction of Ireland, a likely outcome if Ireland became an active war zone.

On August 25, de Valera sent his Secretary for External Affairs, Joseph Walshe, to clarify Ireland's neutral status with the German Minister in Dublin, Eduard Hempel. Joseph Walshe (1886–1956) began his career with the Irish Foreign Service in 1922, when he became the Irish Free State's founding foreign secretary.[44] When the Fianna Fáil government came to power in 1932, Eamon de Valera filled the roles of both President of the Executive Council and Minister for External Affairs; Joseph Walshe was named Secretary for External Affairs, advising de Valera on Ireland's foreign policy and representing de Valera in relations with other foreign ministers in Dublin and with the British Dominions Office. De Valera relied on Walshe's counsel, and Walshe always deferred to de Valera regarding the conduct of Ireland's international affairs, supporting de Valera's wartime policy of neutrality.[45] Walshe was not particularly well liked by his External Affairs staff or his government peers;[46] those who worked with him described him as a "prickly" personality, who "blew hot and cold" in his relationships.[47] While some historians have described Walshe as a realist in terms of Irish foreign policy making, others believed he did not fully understand the nuances of international diplomacy.[48]

In Walshe's report on his August meeting with Hempel, he stressed that Ireland, while still member of the British Commonwealth and linked through history, geography, and economy to Great Britain, was, in fact, independent of the British government and would "not ... participate in any active form in the war against Germany," or allow Britain to use Irish territory to wage war. Germany could retain its Legation in Dublin and its formal diplomatic relations with Ireland, as Ireland would maintain its diplomatic residence in Berlin, as long as "the German Legation [did] not allow itself to be used in any way as part of the machinery for the prosecution of the war."[49]

In Eduard Hempel's account of his meeting with Walshe at the German Foreign Ministry, he emphasized several different points: Ireland would remain neutral, except if it were directly attacked. Walshe had also explained that Irish American opinion was opposed to an alliance with Britain, and Irish American political pressure on Washington would keep the Americans out of the war. The British would not violate Irish neutrality for fear of upsetting the Americans and because Britain relied on regular trade with Ireland. Then:

> He [Walshe] repeated the suggestion that in the case of German acts of war against Britain involving Ireland, any suffering incurred should be kept to a minimum, and at the same time a formal declaration should be made that Germany has no aggressive aims in Ireland, but on the contrary has sympathy for Ireland and Irish national aims [such as the restoration of the Six Counties of Northern Ireland] ...[50]

In reply on August 29, Germany's Foreign Minister, Joachim von Ribbentrop, directed Hempel to settle the following terms with de Valera's government "without delay," as Germany was about to attack Poland:

> In accordance with the friendly relations between ourselves and Ireland we are determined to refrain from any hostile action against Irish territory and to respect her integrity, provided that Ireland, for her part, maintains *unimpeachable neutrality towards us in any conflict*. ...
>
> You are requested to deliver this statement in clear yet definitely friendly terms and in doing so you can refer (without expressly mentioning Northern Ireland) to the wide sympathy felt in Germany for Ireland and the national aspirations of the Irish people.[51] (emphasis added)

Hempel delivered Ribbentrop's message to de Valera, and then reported back to Ribbentrop about their subsequent meeting on August 31, that: "My general impression was one of a sincere effort to keep Ireland out of the conflict, but also of great fear, which de Valera discussed in the usual doctrinaire fashion which betrays his real weakness. Nevertheless, our demarche has made a definitely favorable impression." De Valera also asked Hempel for a formal statement from the German Reich, promising "to respect Irish neutrality," – thus publicly establishing "friendly German-Irish relations" as the war commenced.[52] On September 3, De Valera announced to the Dáil: "Germany would respect Ireland's neutrality."[53]

On September 2, de Valera's private promise of neutrality to the German government was matched by his public address to the nation officially announcing Ireland's neutrality policy:

> Back in February last, I stated in a very definite way that it was the aim of Government policy, in a case of European War, to keep this country, if at all possible, out of it. ...
>
> We of all nations, know what force used by a stronger nation against a weaker one means. We have known what invasion and partition means; we are not forgetful of our own history and, as long as our own country, or any part of it, is subject to force, the application of force, by a stronger nation, it is only natural that our people, whatever sympathies they may have in a conflict like the present, should look at their own country first and should, accordingly, in looking at their own country, consider what its interests should be and what its interests are.[54]

De Valera also introduced the Emergency Powers Act to the Dáil, an Act that ascribed extraordinary powers to the government or, as some have described them, "draconian," "dictatorial" powers.[55] In order to preserve Irish neutrality and "public order" in time of war, the government claimed the power to take any action it deemed "necessary," including taking absolute control over all military and police power, and over all transportation systems, and rationing food, fuel, and other supplies.[56] The Act also empowered the government to enforce a strict censorship law over the wartime press and over public speech that prevented circulation of news that expressed "preference" for any belligerent power and squashed public debate about the war.[57] The censorship law allowed the government to monitor private correspondence passing into and out of the country, as well. De Valera asserted that Ireland's Emergency Powers Act was supported with "virtual unanimity" in the Dáil as it was voted into law on September 3. De Valera also announced that the government's Emergency Powers were accepted by the Irish people, who, he claimed, harbored "a passionate desire in the Irish heart to be neutral."[58]

Yet Irish neutrality policy was not accepted with "unanimity" by the legislature or by the public. Anglo-Irish Senator Sir John Keane, for one, expressed his "Sympathy with the Democracies" in the Senate on September 3, "voicing the opinion of a substantial section unhappy about this attitude of neutrality" and asserting that "there was a very thin dividing line between our national interests and our national honor."[59] Moreover, in practical terms neither their nation's neutrality policy nor the Emergency Powers Act prevented Irish men and women from volunteering to serve in British forces or from working in British industries or from traveling to or from nations at war, practices that violated the government's neutrality policy, as the government's own legal counsel, Michael Rynne, spelled out in a memorandum when the war began.[60] Nevertheless, de Valera's neutrality policy allowed the Irish people to deny many of the political and moral realities of the war. According to Irish journalist Tony Gray's memoirs, "While Britain was blacked out and blitzed, life in Ireland went on in an almost defiantly normal way."[61]

For all the reasons that Joseph Walshe had laid out in his eve-of-war meeting with German Minister Hempel – Ireland's history, geography, and economy – Ireland was not like other neutral powers. This was abundantly clear to Winston Churchill and Franklin Roosevelt and to their nations' diplomats who served in Dublin during the war, Sir John Maffey and David Gray, even though de Valera's government often argued, disingenuously, that Irish neutrality was no different from U.S. neutrality. This claim was made even as a minority of the most ardent – and armed – Irish nationalists had declared war on British imperialism and openly sympathized with

Adolf Hitler's crusade to "restore" the German Reich and to "rescue" Germanic peoples who lived in nations delineated by the "unfair boundaries" drawn up by the victorious powers at the end of the Great War. The new war in 1939, like the last Great War, was, in their view, a contest between two imperial powers. And, if Germany prevailed, it might destroy the British Empire and unify Ireland, an outcome the militant nationalists openly welcomed.[62] To be sure, these views were not the official position of de Valera's government, which in fact provided significant covert security assistance to the British throughout the war.[63] But, these anti-British views circulated among disaffected Irish peoples and Irish Republican Army confrères, as historian Richard English has explained:

> Eire ... adopted a neutral stance in the war, but the IRA took a pro-German (at times, anti-Jewish) approach. The army was committed to aiding the German war effort, and their leader Sean Russell (1893–1940), in Germany in 1940 as a guest of the Nazis, urged his hosts to use the IRA to attack British forces in Northern Ireland as part of a broader German attack on Britain. ... Nor was it just the IRA which displayed such instincts. Many Irish nationalists (including Maude Gonne and Dan Breen) were sympathetic to the Nazis, and numerous other Irish nationalists were clearly anti-Jewish in their thinking during this period.[64]

At times, these anti-British, pro-Nazi views poisoned Anglo-American diplomatic interactions with Taoiseach de Valera and Joseph Walshe, and with de Valera's Minister for the Coordination of Defense Measures, Frank Aiken, and they inspired Anglo-American challenges to Irish neutrality policy.

Frank Aiken (1898–1983), de Valera's Minister for Defense (1932–1939) and Minister for the Coordination of Defensive Measures (1939–1945), was responsible for strengthening Ireland's national army as well as for enforcing Ireland's strict censorship policy in the interest of preserving Ireland's neutrality throughout the wartime Emergency. Aiken had a long history of militant nationalism, begun during the revolutionary era of the 1910s and 1920s. Although he missed the 1916 Easter Rising, soon afterward he joined the IRA and became known as an "IRA Big Man." He commanded an IRA division during the 1920–1923 civil war and served as IRA Chief of Staff in the early 1920s.[65] Like de Valera, Aiken was raised in rural Ireland, with few material advantages. Orphaned at a young age, he took on responsibility for running his family's farm, which never allowed him to pursue a formal education.[66] Robert Fisk wrote about the challenges of his upbringing and its consequences in terms of how others perceived him:

> Aiken was certainly no intellectual. A tall, outwardly diffident man, he often concealed his shyness by adopting a gruff manner that was easily mistaken

2.2 Eamon de Valera and members of the Irish Diplomatic Service, c. 1939. P150/3818. Seated, front row, left to right: John Dulanty, Joseph Walshe, Eamon de Valera, Robert Brennan, Thomas Kiernan. Standing, back row, left to right: John Hearne, Frank Gallagher, Frederick (F. H.) Boland, Michael McWhite, Seán Murphy, Leo Kearney, Michael Rynne

for rudeness. He was deeply suspicious of the British – he had been burnt out of his boyhood home in County Armagh – and his republicanism still had the rough edges of a man who had been forced to experience defeat. ... He provided the muscle for de Valera's nationalism and [was] the firm if not always comprehending Samson upon whom de Valera could lean in his physical infirmity.[67]

When Irish neutrality was announced to the world at the outbreak of war, de Valera's minister in Washington, Robert Brennan, had to make a difficult argument justifying Irish policy, because most Americans – like most Britons[68] – believed that Ireland, as part of the British Commonwealth, would and should automatically join the Western Allies' anti-fascist fight.[69] Irish Americans, of course, took exception to this majority view. Irish Americans, many of whom were staunch Irish Catholic nationalists, supported de Valera's neutrality policy and his right as democratically elected leader of what they considered to be the sovereign Irish state to determine national policy. De Valera trusted Brennan to make the case for Irish neutrality policy to the American public on moral grounds, as neutrality preserved the peace in Ireland, and to focus the attention of America's elected officials, especially President Roosevelt's attention, on supporting Irish neutrality in order to serve their own political interests. That is, Irish Americans who voted as a bloc could determine American politicians' electoral fates. Brennan did not disappoint de Valera; he had established his loyalty to the Taoiseach as well as his skills as Ireland's public relations manager and diplomat during his tenure at the Irish Legation in Washington since 1934.[70]

The British government also needed a trusted diplomat on site in Dublin, hopefully one who could guide Britain's wayward Irish Dominion back into line with the other Commonwealth countries, which had all followed Great Britain and declared war on Germany after September 3.[71] The new Dominions Secretary in Chamberlain's War Cabinet, Chamberlain's former anti-appeasement critic and Churchill's ally Anthony Eden, appointed veteran colonial officer Sir John Loader Maffey to fill the post of Britain's 'Representative' in Dublin. De Valera may have initially frowned on Sir John Maffey's appointment. With Maffey's long record of diplomatic appointments in Britain's colonies in India and the Sudan and his aristocratic class background, Maffey might have been expected to bring some high-handed imperialist attitudes to his interactions with the Irish.[72] Moreover, de Valera and Joseph Walshe, whom de Valera sent to London as his emissary to settle the terms of Maffey's appointment with Eden on September 6, lobbied for the appointment of a British diplomat at the ambassadorial rank to be sent to Dublin as a sign of respect and acknowledgment of Eire's independent (if not yet formally sovereign) status. That argument was rejected, and Maffey was dispatched to Dublin on Eden's (and Winston Churchill's) recommendations.[73] Emissary Walshe delivered messages to Eden that there were "the possibilities of real cooperation" between Britain and Ireland if partition was ended and if the British (and the United States) issued statements "guaranteeing" Irish neutrality. Additionally, Walshe asserted, Northern Ireland's Prime Minister, Lord Craigavon, should be kept "out of mischief," the British should refrain from pro-war propagandizing in Ireland, and de Valera's government "should be left to look after our own public opinion."[74]

De Valera and Walshe were determined to set the tone for Eire's wartime relations with Britain as an equally distinguished and equal-in-sovereign-status "mother country," that would not beg for Britain's favors.[75] They did not need to worry about Sir John Maffey (1877–1969), who treated the Irish leaders with respect and earned their respect in return. Maffey's long career as a diplomat served him well in Dublin during the Second World War. He was known as a consummate diplomat, praised for his tact,

2.3 Sir John Loader Maffey, Lord Rugby, January 1931

integrity, and sympathetic understanding by all his Dublin-based counterparts, as well as by de Valera and Churchill – no one spoke ill of him. Loyal to the British Empire, Maffey followed the directives of his superiors and worked hard to secure Ireland's wartime alliance with Britain, a feat never accomplished. Nonetheless, Maffey maintained friendly diplomatic relations with de Valera's government and reported fully and faithfully to the British Foreign Office when he saw opportunity for Britain to press its advantage and gain concessions from Ireland.[76]

Winston Churchill, however, now returned to an influential position in Chamberlain's War Cabinet, could sabotage de Valera's neutrality policy. Churchill considered de Valera to be a "hater" of England and a perpetrator of "foolish" independence policies.[77] Churchill and de Valera shared a long and acrimonious history, dating back to de Valera's leading role in the 1916 Easter Rising and his subsequent denunciation of the postwar settlements – most notably, de Valera's rejection of the 1920 Government of Ireland Act and 1921 Anglo-Irish Treaty that had partitioned the island and led to a bloody Irish civil war, and exacerbated by the terms of the 1938 Anglo-Irish Treaty, when Neville Chamberlain, in Churchill's words, "cast ... away real and important means of [Britain's] security and survival" and returned the treaty ports at Berehaven, Cobh, and Lough Swilly to Irish control. Churchill believed that Chamberlain's government "caved" under pressure from perfidious de Valera, who, Churchill predicted, "would demand the surrender of Ulster as the price for any friendship or aid [during war with Germany]. This fell out exactly. For Mr. de Valera has recently declared that he cannot give us any help or friendship while any British troops remain to guard the Protestants of Ulster."[78] According to historian Eunan O'Halpin, "There is no doubt that Churchill regarded Irish neutrality almost as a personal affront."[79]

Churchill rejected Eire's right to claim neutrality as "odious,"[80] and in the first weeks of war pushed forward the argument in Cabinet meetings that Irish neutrality policy was not "legal": "What is the international judicial status of Southern Ireland? It is not a Dominion. They themselves repudiate this idea. It is certainly under the Crown. Nothing has been defined. Legally I believe they are 'At war but Skulking.' Perhaps Sir William would explore this thesis."[81]

On September 5, First Lord of the Admiralty Churchill asked for an intelligence report from his naval chiefs, directing them to investigate "various considerations":

> (1) What does intelligence say about possible succoring of U-boats by Irish malcontents in west of Ireland inlets? If they throw bombs in London, why should they not supply petrol to U-boats? Extreme vigilance should be practiced, and the closest contact maintained between the D.N.I. and "C".
>
> Secondly, a study is required of the addition to the radius of our destroyers through not having the use of Berehaven or other south Irish anti-submarine bases; showing also the advantage to be gained by our having these facilities.
>
> The Board must realize we may not be able to obtain satisfaction, as the question of Eireish neutrality raises political issues which have not yet been faced, and which the First Lord is not certain he can solve. But the full case must be made for consideration.[82]

Churchill often raised the question of Britain's use of the surrendered Irish ports during the war. At several points he floated the idea that England would be justified in retaking the ports by force if Ireland would not voluntarily open them to the British Navy.[83] Cooler heads prevailed and no such plans were put in place, but the rumors that Britain might invade Eire to retake the ports or to achieve other military objectives kept relations with de Valera's government on the brink of turning hostile at any moment.[84]

De Valera, Walshe, and Aiken were always conscious of Ireland's precarious position as a neutral power adjacent to the European war zone.[85] They feared that Britain or Germany might attack Ireland at any time, if either belligerent power determined that control of Irish territory would serve their strategic or military purposes.[86] One potentially dangerous episode occurred in late September, when a German U-boat sunk the Irish ship *Inver Liffey*. De Valera quickly excused the German attack, acknowledging that the ship was carrying "contraband," and therefore German actions were justified: "De Valera was bending over backwards, so as not to provoke the Germans."[87] De Valera, Walshe, and Aiken established wartime practices that alternately aided or enraged the two powerful adversaries, with the twin goals of keeping Ireland out of the line of fire and persuading the Irish people at home and abroad that they had adopted the most morally defensible position. Ireland's pendulum-like neutrality policy never fully satisfied either the Allied or Axis Powers and they had to develop convoluted justifications for Ireland's wartime foreign relations and silence the critics among their own populations. Postwar histories have established the nature and extent of the assistance de Valera's government offered to the warring nations; accounts by Western historians have generally emphasized Southern Ireland's helpful contributions to the Allied cause that could not be made public during the war for fear of German reprisals. And even though the aid Ireland provided to the British during the war was significant,[88] at the time it never satisfied either British or American leaders.

Britain's Representative Sir John Maffey, while never openly antagonistic to the Irish perspective in conversations with de Valera or Walshe, never understood de Valera's stubborn insistence on lobbying for the end of partition at every opportunity, when the British Foreign Office believed other matters, such as the dangers posed by German submarines patrolling off the coast of Ireland when British ships were barred from using Irish naval ports, were far more urgent.[89] Nevertheless, in the first months of war, Maffey followed the lead of Prime Minister Chamberlain[90] who reasoned with his friend de Valera in the gentlest of terms to cooperate with Britain's strategic imperatives:

[At this time of crisis] the need for closer contact will grow more and more pressing. You may rely on us to operate in such a manner as to cause you as little difficulty as possible and, having that assurance from me, I greatly hope you will be able to agree to my suggestion.

On the more general questions which are of immediate concern I think it better to leave it to Sir John Maffey to explain to you what we have in mind. The submarine menace is at the present time one of the outstanding problems engaging our thoughts and energies. So far as we can judge we have no reason to be dissatisfied with the success of our counter measures. ... In this sphere of activity problems may suddenly arise the solution of which would be of vital moment to this country and which would also naturally involve the interests of Eire. For that reason, I attach great importance to full mutual understanding of the special problems which the war has created for both of us, and to reaching some line of agreement as to how these difficulties can best be dissolved and adjusted. Kind regards, Yours sincerely, Neville Chamberlain[91]

According to Maffey's account of de Valera's justification for his anti-partition/pro-neutrality stance, de Valera was bound to act in the country's best interests to keep the country out of war, even though his own personal "sympathies were with the Allies, [and] ... there was on the whole, perhaps, a vague majority sentiment in favor of the Allies, [but] any encroachment upon on Irish interest would create a swift swing over of opinion. ... [De Valera's] goal had been to maintain neutrality and to help us within the limits of that neutrality to the full extent possible."[92] Maffey reported in October that although de Valera would not permit British use of the ports, "in so many ways the Government of Eire has been helpful to me since I came here, and this setback over the ports has obscured the bright side of the picture," that is, the Irish provided some valuable intelligence to British forces.[93]

Eduard Hempel also believed that "The personal attitude of the Government toward me is definitely friendly." Hempel explained to Germany's Foreign Ministry that there were "pro-British elements" among the Irish people, but there were also "certain pro-German trends" and the Irish Army, following their government's policy, "is supposedly ready to defend neutrality in all directions."[94] Assured of de Valera's sincerity, Hempel advised his superiors to respect neutrality while he vigilantly monitored the Irish government's actions.[95] De Valera and Walshe also urged Ireland's Minister in Berlin, William Warnock, to monitor the mood in the Nazi capital, looking for additional assurances of Germany's friendly attitudes toward Ireland's neutrality policy. Warnock provided generally favorable reports, but also explained that German attitudes were based on Ireland's traditional opposition to British rule and German support for the IRA.[96]

Roosevelt's Minister in Dublin, John Cudahy, also advised Roosevelt to respect Irish neutrality and to maintain U.S. neutrality, as well. Irish American Cudahy sympathized with de Valera, whom he considered to be a great statesman.[97] Cudahy, who had served as U.S. ambassador to Poland from 1933 to 1937 before his posting to Dublin, sympathized with conquered Poland, too, but he counseled Roosevelt to follow a pragmatic course: "we must face the disagreeable fact that Poland is now a memory and our business is primarily to stay out of war."[98] And, Cudahy shared de Valera's worry that Churchill might order the British Navy to reoccupy the Irish ports by force, warning FDR that would be a "great mistake" as Ireland would go to war with Britain if that transpired.[99] Roosevelt may have bristled at Cudahy's advice; nonetheless, Cudahy left Ireland at his own request at the end of 1939, and was reassigned to the U.S. embassy in Belgium from January to May 1940.[100] David Gray, FDR's uncle-by-marriage and a staunch Anglophile, replaced Cudahy as U.S. Minister at the Legation in Dublin in March 1940. Regarding U.S. neutrality, during fall 1939 FDR closely watched U.S. public opinion polls to gauge the nation's readiness for war. According to an October 22 Gallup poll, most Americans, 95 percent, still opposed U.S. military involvement in the European conflict. Sixty-two percent of Americans polled, however, agreed that "the United States should do everything possible to help England and France win the war except go to war themselves."[101]

American reporters in Europe, including London-based Helen Kirkpatrick, continued the anti-fascist crusade in their war reporting throughout the first months of the war. In early October, Hitler had issued one final offer of "peace" to the Allies, if they accepted German occupation of Poland.[102] Kirkpatrick and other American reporters denounced the Nazi Führer's Polish *blitzkrieg* campaign that slaughtered many Jewish peoples in the Warsaw ghetto and broadcast their enthusiastic support for Neville Chamberlain's uncharacteristically "venomous" speech that rejected German peace terms and forcefully condemned Germany's "grievous crime against humanity."[103] At the end of October Chamberlain's government also released "a remarkable document," duly published by Kirkpatrick, describing the despicable treatment of Jews and other political prisoners that the Nazis imprisoned in concentration camps at Buchenwald, Dachau, and Sachsenhausen. Kirkpatrick asserted that reporters from neutral nations – "and your correspondent is one of them" – had personally seen and talked to the victims of German brutality.[104] Evidence of these camps and the torture that took place within them had also reached Franklin Roosevelt by late fall 1939, "through many sources, including photographs and newspaper cuttings."[105]

Among her other published reports on widespread Allied anti-fascist resistance, Kirkpatrick also reported that there was "Increasing anti-Nazi feeling in Eire ... causing many Irish to become discontented with Eire's neutrality." Irish resistance to Nazi Germany, she speculated, was due to a theory that she would pursue with greater zeal in summer 1940: that Germany was planning clandestine operations in Ireland, and Nazi intervention would generate Irish resentment.[106] Here, she was not entirely mistaken; factions in Germany were making plans to invade Ireland and had sent spies ahead to scout the territory, but she may have misread the nature of the reception the Nazis would receive. Although German Minister Hempel cautioned his Foreign Ministry superiors to respect Irish neutrality, Germany's *Abwehr* advocated for using the IRA to perpetrate anti-British sabotage, if not to launch an outright coup to unseat de Valera's government.[107]

During the war years, the IRA was a wild card that de Valera could not control.[108] The IRA's attack on the Irish government's arsenal in Dublin's Phoenix Park on December 23, 1939 made this abundantly clear.[109] In December, de Valera wrote to Neville Chamberlain again urging an end to partition, followed by a warning:

> A free Ireland would have every interest in wishing Britain to be strong, but when Britain's strength appears to be used to maintain the division of our island no such consideration can have any force. ... The intensification of feeling here and amongst our people in the United States makes it imperative to act quickly lest it be too late to save the situation.[110]

De Valera referred to the IRA in Ireland, and to significant anti-British, anti-Semitic, pro-Nazi public opinion in the United States, evidenced by the growing popularity of Catholic Father Charles Coughlin's radio broadcasts that incited a mass movement with "upwards of forty million listeners" at its peak, many working-class Irish American Catholics among them.[111]

Threats to de Valera's neutrality policy from whatever quarter were opposed with as much force as his government could muster.[112] Frank Aiken's contribution to defending neutrality came in the form of aggressive assertions of the government's emergency powers and strict application of censorship of any public speech or written communications that seemed biased in favor of any belligerent. Aiken quickly shut down all challenges to the government's "undemocratic" censorship policies with the justification that "neutrality" in the age of total warfare did not guarantee "peace" to the neutral power. According to Aiken, neutrality in the modern sense was, in fact, a condition of "limited warfare," and Ireland had to recognize that fact and take drastic measures to defend and preserve it.[113] Aiken's arguments, as Robert Fisk has explained them, were "remarkable":

There was ... a simplistic element in his analysis. Eire was not being physically attacked and her people were not being killed; thus the "limited warfare" of neutrality could not possibly coincide with the condition of total warfare in which the belligerents existed. But there was a tough, pragmatic determination to Aiken's arguments. Contained within them was the fiber that would resist the pressures of Britain and America to participate in the war. Aiken not only defended neutrality, he raised it to a high, almost exalted plane. He described neutrality in an entirely new way, not as a symbol of national independence but as an active, decisive and coherent policy. It was – according to his own lights – honorable, even courageous. More to the point, it was realistic.[114]

Joseph Walshe also provided guidance to his foreign service officers about how to present Irish neutrality policy to skeptical Western allies. He advised the Irish government's diplomat in Ottawa, John Hearne, not to apologize publicly to the Canadian Dominion for Ireland's position. Hearne could explain privately, if necessary, that:

> The countries at war are fighting for their own immediate material interests. Spiritual evils cannot be cured by the supreme evil of war. All this will be admitted when the war is over as it was after the last war and Canada as well as other countries will admit that the Irish Government was right. For the present we have to be patient under adverse criticism. Even attempts to explain our neutrality publicly would cast some doubt on our conviction of its inherent necessity.[115]

Throughout fall 1939, Kirkpatrick had continued to write for the *Whitehall Letter* and to freelance for U.S. newspapers. She returned to the United States at the end of December to promote her just-published book, *Under the British Umbrella*, and to secure a salaried position as a correspondent for a U.S. paper so that she could return to London and continue her war reports. In early 1940, Kirkpatrick was speaking at Chicago Palmer House hotel to the Council on Foreign Affairs when she ran into Carroll Binder, the *Chicago Daily News* foreign editor whom she had previously met in London. Binder introduced her to the editor of the paper, Paul Scott Mowrer, and she made her pitch for a job. As she later recalled, he told her: "I like your stuff, but we don't have women on the foreign staff." Mowrer, however, arranged a meeting for Kirkpatrick with *Daily News* publisher Colonel Frank Knox, a Republican who would join the Roosevelt Administration as Secretary of the Navy in June 1940. Again, Kirkpatrick heard the same response when she asked Knox for a job:

> "I like your stuff, but we don't have women on the foreign staff." Carroll Binder interjected, "Well Colonel, you know the UP [United Press] is trying to get her." I think he just made it up. I don't know. But the Colonel said, "Well we can't have that. Let's have lunch." ...

[Kirkpatrick remembered the argument that won Knox over]: "I can't change my sex, but you can change your policy." And that was the end of the discussion. And it never came up again.[116]

Kirkpatrick returned to London in March 1940,[117] just as David Gray was also arriving in Europe. In February 1940, President Roosevelt had appointed Gray (1870–1968) as U.S. Minister to Dublin, replacing John Cudahy. Gray and FDR shared family connections as well as Roosevelt's democratic values and strong support for Great Britain's fight against the fascist powers.[118] In 1914, Gray had married Maude Livingston Hall Waterbury, the youngest sister of Eleanor Roosevelt's mother, and Eleanor's aunt. Maude and Eleanor were born only seven years apart and were close to one another growing up. The couples, Maude and David, and Eleanor and Franklin, also maintained close relationships and referred to each other as "cousins." When the United States entered the First World War, Gray, who had been working as a writer and journalist, enlisted, fought in France, and was wounded in action. Assistant Secretary of the Navy Roosevelt arranged Gray's transport back to the States.[119] In 1940, even though he was "an amateur in the world of diplomacy,"[120] Gray's appointment as Minister to Dublin was confirmed by the Senate. Appointing a personal emissary such as David Gray was thoroughly in character for FDR, who "distrusted career diplomats in the State Department." Roosevelt selected his ambassadors the way he conducted foreign policy, following instincts that were "intuitive, idiosyncratic, and highly personalized."[121]

When Gray began his post in Ireland, he supported FDR's foreign policy as he understood it, that is, to give as much aid to Britain as possible in order to fortify Britain's fight against the Germans.[122] To achieve these aims, Gray tried to persuade Ireland to abandon its neutrality policy and join the Allied war efforts. Gray later recalled that the State Department initially gave him no introduction to Irish politics:

> No one in the West European Division, which conducted Irish affairs, seemed interested in the realities of Irish politics which involved Irish neutrality. No one mentioned the state of Anglo-Irish relations, the significance of the Coal–Cattle Pact, and the surrender of the ports. No one mentioned the "Gentleman's Agreement" in London. No one told me anything about the conflict going on in the Irish Societies in the United States between the de Valera supporters and the Irish Republican Army which now opposed him. Nobody told me that the IRA financed with American funds had declared war on England as of January 1939, and was the avowed ally of Germany and the enemy of de Valera.[123]

To be sure, what Gray picked up on his own was tainted by his own biases, and his lack of historical knowledge may explain why he believed at the

2.4 David and Maude Gray in Dublin, *c.* 1940

outset of his tenure in Dublin that the major cause of Anglo-Irish enmity – the partition of Ireland – could be easily resolved, and Anglo-Irish differences could be put in the past. Most of Gray's initial encounters with de Valera, Walshe, and Aiken were focused on his proposals to trade Irish unity (and eventual full independence for the island nation) for a wartime alliance with Britain, which included expelling Axis diplomats from Dublin and granting the British Navy immediate access to Irish ports.

En route to Dublin, Gray stopped in Rome where he met with the Irish Minister to the Vatican and had an audience with the Pope.[124] He then stopped in London where he met with Winston Churchill and members of Chamberlain's Foreign Office and floated his plans to the foreign leaders. Whatever these men may have thought about Gray's naivety, Gray believed he had the Foreign Office's support for his efforts to negotiate the alliance, if not Winston Churchill's – Gray reported that Churchill adamantly rejected any "bribes" to "sell out Ulster for any kind of American support," as Churchill was "sick of the Irish" who had been made a "generous settlement" by the British but were now "stabbing England in the back."[125] Gray wrote to Alfred Duff Cooper – a British Conservative and Churchill ally whom he had also met in London – after he arrived in Dublin:

> I had a very interesting time with the First Lord [Churchill]. He caught me out the first thing holding out a bait for the coercion of Ulster and gave me merry hell for which I love him. There are so few people left in this world who haven't a price for everything. Mr. De Valera at this end of it has a high disdain for the tempter with the main chance so it looks bad for Gray the peacemaker. God knows I mean well …[126]

Despite the forewarning, Gray believed that all he had to do was to persuade Eire's Taoiseach de Valera and Northern Ireland's Prime Minister Lord Craigavon to go along with the compromises he proposed to the Anglo-Irish parties.[127] From the time he arrived in Dublin, Gray cooperated with British officials in efforts to convince de Valera's government to join the Allies in war against the fascists, or at least to give the British Navy control of Ireland's strategic ports in exchange for an end to partition of Ireland at an unspecified future date.[128] He was not an effective negotiator because he quickly changed tactics from persuasion to intimidation, never respecting de Valera's "moral" arguments for neutrality or accepting de Valera's suspicions of British motives, and never appreciating how pressures from Germany and the IRA also affected Eire's foreign policy.[129]

Soon after he arrived and settled into the U.S. Legation, Gray dined with de Valera and "Dev's" longtime friends in Dublin, the brothers-in-arms who against the odds had survived the bloody trials of the fight for independence from the British and the Irish civil war – Frank Aiken, Sean

T. O'Kelly, and Sean McEntee – and who served together on de Valera's governing Cabinet. The sentimental bond these men shared cemented their conviction that they knew best how to lead the Irish nation, and their fraternal friendships moved Gray.[130] Yet he never fully understood that their convictions, forged in battle, barred any possibility of compromise of their nation's sovereignty that might also weaken their own hold on governing power, to the point where de Valera's government was preparing to execute his countrymen – several imprisoned IRA men – for crimes against the state soon after Gray's arrival.

The parents of one of the condemned IRA men came to see David Gray, hoping that Gray could intercede on behalf of their son with de Valera, and plead for clemency. At the time, Gray tried to explain to the distraught parents, "Colonel and Countess Plunkett," that their son had broken the law established by the legally elected government of Ireland. The mother tried to argue back that the IRA in fact represented the majority Irish opinion, but had been kept from the voting polls. Gray grew frustrated as they continued to argue back and forth. He said:

> "You people are worse than the Americans who have been hiding their head in the sand like ostriches and not looking at the danger that faces them. If I were an Irishman I would fight on the side of the English till Germany is beaten, then if I wanted to fight the English, well and good." Colonel Plunkett said "I would take a chance myself with the Germans. We are friendly with them." I said "what about Denmark and Norway. Have you been more friendly than these countries?" He had nothing to say to that.[131]

The course of the war had changed dramatically soon after Gray arrived in Dublin. On April 9, the German *Wehrmacht* overran neutral Denmark and then turned its attack on Norway. The British launched a counterattack, but "a sorry display of military humiliation ... followed."[132] Fifth columnists in Norway led by Vikdun Quisling aided the Germans who quickly established control over the country.[133] Winston Churchill delivered a frustrated speech to Parliament asserting that Norway's neutrality policy had prevented the Allies from providing any military protection until it was too late – clearly, he was sending a message to other neutral powers that they could not trust German avowals of friendship and should join the Western Alliance before they, too, were overrun.[134]

Churchill's message was lost on Eamon de Valera. De Valera was treading a fine line, trying to sustain "friendly" relations with both Britain and Germany in April and May 1940, as Germany's conquests of neutral Holland, Luxembourg, and Belgium followed the invasions of Denmark and Norway. Joseph Walshe, dispatched on another mission to London to secure Anglo-Irish trade relations, met with Foreign Secretary Eden on

May 6 and delivered messages from Taoiseach de Valera: he conveyed Ireland's continued sympathy for the Allies and reminded Eden about Ireland's "benevolent neutrality." But Walshe also protested against stories that appeared in the British press reporting on "Nazi Activities in Ireland" that inspired international criticisms of Irish policy, and warned that "any interference by [the British Government] with our neutrality would be a disaster for them as well as for us." Walshe ended his meeting with Eden with the familiar refrain: "I told him that you [de Valera] were constantly thinking of the unity of Ireland and that you earnestly hoped that he would give his serious attention to the restoration of the Six Counties."[135] The Foreign Office expected these messages, even if they weren't welcomed. But several events were about to occur in the following weeks that upset the equilibrium neutral Ireland was trying so hard to maintain.

On May 10, Germany launched its invasions of the Low Countries and France. Chamberlain, "shaken and gray," according to Helen Kirkpatrick's account,[136] was forced to resign. Chamberlain had presided over British war policy as the Allies suffered these major setbacks and his own Conservative Party joined the coalition that turned against him following the loss of Norway. Conservative MP Leo Amery gave an impassioned speech in Parliament, "roaring" out against Chamberlain's ineffective leadership: "You have sat here too long for any good you have been doing. Depart, I say, and let us have done with you! In the name of God, GO!"[137]

Winston Churchill, elevated to Prime Minister, was ready to meet his "destiny" and anxious to direct a vigorous anti-fascist resistance: "all my past life had been but preparation for this hour and this trial."[138] Churchill put all doubters on notice as he declared in the House Commons on May 13:

> We have before us an ordeal of the most grievous kind. We have before us many, many long months of struggle and of suffering. You ask, what is our policy? I will say: It is to wage war, by sea, land and air, with all our might and with all the strength that God can give us: to wage war against a monstrous tyranny, never surpassed in the dark, lamentable catalogue of human crime. That is our policy. You ask, what is our aim? I can answer in one word: Victory – victory at all costs, victory in spite of all terror, victory, however long and hard the road may be; for without victory, there is no survival.[139]

Germany's attack on Britain was sure to follow. Now Prime Minister, Churchill reached out to President Roosevelt to assure him personally of Britain's determination to fight the noble anti-fascist fight: "If necessary, we shall continue the war alone, and we are not afraid of that."[140] After establishing British resolve, Churchill appealed for American aid in the form of "forty or fifty of 'your older' destroyers, several hundred 'of the latest types' of aircraft, … antiaircraft equipment and ammunition, and steel."

And, he asked Roosevelt for a "visit of a United States Squadron to the Irish Ports,"[141] as he also refocused his war planners' attention on the strategic value of Berehaven, Cobh, and Lough Swilly.[142] In readying Britain for the coming German invasion, Churchill did not forget the dangers posed by neutral Ireland.

Chamberlain's resignation came as a blow to de Valera and he wrote a warm personal note to Chamberlain on hearing the news: "I would like to testify that you did more than any former British Statesman to make a true friendship between the peoples of our two countries possible, and, if the task has not been completed, that it has not been for want of good will on your part."[143] Appeasing Germany, however, soon dominated de Valera's concerns. On May 11, following Germany's march into Holland and Belgium, de Valera had made a speech in Galway commiserating with the neutral powers that were "fighting for their lives." This was, as David Gray reported to Roosevelt, "Mr. de Valera's first condemnation of Germany."[144] De Valera asserted:

> I was at Geneva [at the League of Nations] on many occasions ... the representatives of Belgium and of the Netherlands were people I met frequently, because we cooperated not a little with the northern groups of nations. Today these two small nations are fighting for their lives, and I think it would be unworthy of this small nation, on an occasion like this, if I did not protest against the cruel wrong done to them.[145]

De Valera followed this mild rebuke with a call to the people in Ireland: "We have to see to it that if there should be any attack of any kind upon us from any quarter they would find us a united people ready to resist it."

German Foreign Minister Ribbentrop directed Eduard Hempel to immediately protest about de Valera's "unneutral" words: "Germany's view was [that] taking sides was not permissible in neutral countries and [Ireland] should remain silent. ... Holland and Belgium had not adhered to strict neutrality. And it was not in accordance to strict neutrality that Mr. de Valera should have protested."[146] Hempel had already protested to the Irish Ministry for External Affairs on May 12, and Frederick Boland, Walshe's deputy secretary, had tried to explain de Valera's perspective: "de Valera, in his unprepared speech, had not mentioned Germany and had not wanted to commit himself on the question of guilt. In addition, he had established extensive good political connections with small northern nations as had been made known to him in sympathetic understanding."[147] On May 14, Joseph Walshe went again to Eduard Hempel to "clarify" de Valera's words, that were certainly not "intended ... as a gratuitous judgement on the rights and wrongs of the German actions."[148] William Warnock in Berlin was also dispatched to placate the German Foreign Ministry. Warnock reported back to Walshe: "the Taoiseach's remarks on the invasion were not too well received," but they weren't printed in the German press, which relieved Warnock.[149] Hempel met with de Valera at the end of May, following Holland's and Belgium's surrender to Germany, and de Valera again scrambled to "clarify once more his point of view that was directed against any aggressor." Hempel repeated Germany's warning, and years later wrote that "I had the impression ... that the Irish Government did not want to have any doubts in Berlin about Irish neutrality."[150]

Germany's threat had alarmed de Valera and he immediately sought out U.S. protection. De Valera asked David Gray to request a statement from Washington to the effect that preservation of Irish neutrality, the "*status quo*," was in the United States' vital interests, and to ask for assistance in buying weapons from the Allies to build up the Irish Army's defenses.[151] Denying the aid, Secretary of State Cordell Hull told Gray pessimistically that the U.S. government was not sure what good the statement would do to dissuade German advances, but he directed Gray to "please tell [de Valera] that his country enjoys a very special position in the hearts of our people and that we hope and pray that Ireland will be spared from the conflagration now raging."[152] With regard to any weapons forthcoming from U.S. sources, that was also unlikely. Franklin Roosevelt was sounding the alarm in Congress and he gained support for a huge increase in military spending that greatly accelerated U.S. rearmament plans, but any available military weapons or equipment would go to Britain.[153]

The end of May 1940 brought one more challenge to Irish neutrality, again coming from Germany. On May 4, a German spy named Hermann Goertz parachuted into Ireland. His mission: to contact IRA cells to plan for a German invasion of the island in preparation for an attack on Britain. Goertz's mission, however, quickly went off course. He lost his radio transmitter on his descent and landed seventy miles from his planned drop site. He made contact with some nationalist sympathizers who took him to meet up with IRA collaborator Stephen Held at his home in Dublin, but one of Held's servants tipped off the police and the Irish Garda raided Stephen Held's home on May 22. Goertz escaped capture, but Held was arrested. Although Held made up a fantastic tale to confuse the authorities, Germany's involvement in dispatching an agent to Ireland was indisputable. De Valera now had proof that the German government was collaborating with his enemies, the subversives in the IRA.[154] Hempel tried to deny the German government's role, but de Valera and the British were convinced that with German spies landing in Ireland, a German military invasion would soon follow. At the end of May, with their French allies about to be overpowered and Germany's war machine on the march, the British, led by Winston Churchill, were about to make some bold and desperate moves.

Notes

1 "Treaty of Nonaggression Between Germany and the Union of Soviet Socialist Republics," The Avalon Project Documents in Law, History and Diplomacy, Yale Law School online, https://avalon.law.yale.edu/20th_century/nonagres.asp (accessed 1 December 2020); "Secret Additional Protocol," https://avalon.law.yale.edu/20th_century/addsepro.asp (accessed 1 December 2020).
2 Carlo D'Este, *Warlord: A Life of Winston Churchill at War, 1874–1945* (New York: HarperCollins, 2008), 325.
3 Blanche Wiesen Cook, *Eleanor Roosevelt: The War Years and After*, vol. 3: *1939–1962* (New York: Viking, 2016), 114.
4 *Ibid.*, 113.
5 *Ibid.*, 115; Robert Dallek, *Franklin D. Roosevelt: A Political Life* (New York: Penguin, 2017), 351.
6 Winston Churchill, "At the Eleventh Hour," *Daily Mirror*, 24 August 1939, CHAR 8/650/60, Winston Churchill Archive online, The Chartwell Trust.
7 Helen Kirkpatrick quoted in Nancy Caldwell Sorel, *The Women Who Wrote the War* (New York: Arcade Publishing, 1999), 66.
8 The German perspective explained by Joseph Walshe to Eamon de Valera, 31 August 1939, P150/2571, Eamon de Valera Papers (on microfilm), University College Dublin (hereafter: EdV Papers, UCD). See also "German Territorial Losses, Treaty of Versailles, 1919," United States Holocaust Memorial Museum, https://encyclopedia.ushmm.org/content/en/map/german-territorial-losses-treaty-of-versailles-1919 (accessed 1 December 2020). "In the 1919 Treaty of Versailles, the victorious powers (the United States, Great Britain, France, and other allied states) imposed punitive territorial, military, and economic provisions on defeated Germany. ... German forfeited 13 percent of its European territory (more than 27,000 square miles) and one-tenth of its population (between 6.5 and 7 million)."
9 D'Este, *Warlord*, 331; Martin Gilbert, *Churchill: A Life* (New York: Henry Holt, 1991), 619.
10 Sorel, *The Women Who Wrote the War*, 68.
11 D'Este, *Warlord*, 331–332.
12 Brian Barton, *Northern Ireland in the Second World War* (Belfast: Ulster Historical Foundation, 1995), 4.
13 Neville Chamberlain, Prime Minister, "Radio Address September 3, 1939," The Avalon Project Documents in Law, History and Diplomacy, Yale Law School, https://avalon.law.yale.edu/wwii/gb3.asp (accessed 1 December 2020).
14 "The War Cabinet," *Daily Telegraph* (4 September 1939), 8. See also Sonia Purnell, *Clementine: The Life of Mrs. Winston Churchill* (New York: Viking Penguin, 2015), 224.
15 Anthony J. Jordan, *Churchill: A Founder of Modern Ireland* (Dublin: Westport Books, 1995), 170.

16 Joshua S. Goldstein, *War and Gender* (New York: Cambridge University Press, 2001), 266–267.
17 Winston Churchill, "War, a Speech Delivered to the House of Commons," 3 September 1939, in Winston S. Churchill, *Into Battle, 1941* (RosettaBooks, 2013), 119–120.
18 Cook, *Eleanor Roosevelt*, 132, 135–136.
19 D'Este, *Warlord*, 330.
20 Churchill, "The First Month of War, An Address Broadcast October 1, 1939," in Churchill, *Into Battle, 1941*, 126.
21 Robert Cole, *Propaganda, Censorship and Irish Neutrality in the Second World War* (Edinburgh: Edinburgh University Press, 2006), 8: "[I]n September 1939, roughly 90 percent of Americans favored neutrality."
22 Washington Embassy Confidential Reports 1938–1939, Doc. No. 8 NAI DFA, Robert Brennan to Joseph P. Walshe, 5 September 1939, *Documents on Irish Foreign Policy* vol. VI, 1939–1941.
23 Dallek, *Franklin D. Roosevelt: A Political Life*, 349; Nicholas J. Cull, *Selling War: The British Propaganda Campaign Against American 'Neutrality' in World War II* (Oxford: Oxford University Press, 1996), 28; Jean Edward Smith, *FDR* (New York: Random House, 2008), 436–437.
24 Lynne Olson, *Those Angry Days: Roosevelt, Lindbergh, and America's Fight Over World War II* (New York: Random House, 2013), 29.
25 John A. Thompson, "Conceptions of National Security and American Entry into World War II," *Diplomacy & Statecraft* 16: 4 (December 2005), 673–674, 676.
26 Cook, *Eleanor Roosevelt*, 123–124.
27 Smith, *FDR*, 436.
28 Cook, *Eleanor Roosevelt*, 137.
29 Helen Kirkpatrick, "Lifting of Ban Puts Arsenal at Allies' Disposal: Shortage of Materials to be Filled in U.S., London Says," *Chicago Daily News* (3 November 1939), box 2, Helen Paull Kirkpatrick Papers, CA-MS-01132, Sophia Smith Collection, Smith College Special Collections, Northampton, Massachusetts (hereafter: HPK Papers). See also Kirkpatrick, "Britain Hails Embargo's End; See Unfair Discrimination Against Sea Power Removed," *Chicago Daily News* (4 November 1939), box 2, HPK Papers.
30 Dallek, *Franklin D. Roosevelt: A Political Life*, 357–358. See also Cook, *Eleanor Roosevelt*, 140–141.
31 Purnell, *Clementine*, 224–225.
32 Printed copies of telegrams and letters exchanged between Winston Churchill and Franklin Roosevelt, 11 September 1939, CHAR: 20/15/13, Winston Churchill Archives online.
33 Purnell, *Clementine*, 225.
34 Robert D. Dean explains these early twentieth-century Anglo-American elite masculine affinities as "factors" in foreign policy making in his study: *Imperial Brotherhood: Gender and the Making of Cold War Foreign Policy* (Amherst, MA: University of Massachusetts Press, 2001), 3–40.

35 Erik Larson, *The Splendid and the Vile: A Saga of Churchill, Family, and Defiance during the Blitz* (New York: Crown, 2020), 21.
36 See Smith, *FDR*; David Gray, *Behind the Emerald Curtain*, in *A Yankee in De Valera's Ireland: The Memoir of David Gray*, ed. Paul Bew (Dublin: Royal Irish Academy, 2012).
37 Frank Costigliola, "Pamela Churchill, Wartime London and the Making of a Special Relationship," *Diplomatic History* 36: 4 (September 2012), 754, 761; Frank Costigliola, *Roosevelt's Lost Alliances: How Personal Politics Helped Start the Cold War* (Princeton, NJ: Princeton University Press, 2012), 83.
38 Jon Meacham, *Franklin and Winston: An Intimate Portrait of an Epic Friendship* (New York: Random House, 2004), 45.
39 D'Este, *Warlord*, 498.
40 Charlotte Hooper, *Manly States: Masculinities, International Relations, and Gender Politics* (New York: Columbia University Press, 2001), 72, 220–222.
41 Sikata Banerjee, *Muscular Nationalism: Gender, Violence and Empire in India and Ireland, 1914–2004* (New York: New York University Press, 2012), 26–52.
42 David McCullagh, *De Valera: Rule*, vol. II: *1932–1975* (Dublin: Gill Books, 2018), 169; T. Ryle Dwyer, *Irish Neutrality and the USA, 1939–47* (Dublin: Gill & Macmillan, 1977), 221; Robert Fisk, *In Time of War: Ireland, Ulster and the Price of Neutrality, 1939–1945* (London: Andre Deutsch, 1983), 360–361.
43 Diarmaid Ferriter, *Judging Dev: A Reassessment of the Life and Legacy of Eamon de Valera* (Dublin: Royal Irish Academy, 2007), 3–7; Dwyer, *Irish Neutrality and the USA*, 1–2; Fisk, *In Time of War*, 362; Brian Girvin, *The Emergency: Neutral Ireland 1939–45* (London: Pan Macmillan, 2007), 31; McCullagh, *De Valera*, 110–112.
44 Royal Irish Academy, "New Exhibition on Joseph Walshe (1886–1956): The Founding Father of the Irish Foreign Service." Online exhibition, co-curated with the National Archives of Ireland, 13 February 2019, www.ria.ie/ga/node/97858 (accessed 1 December 2020).
45 McCullagh, *De Valera*, 23–24.
46 Elizabeth Bowen, *"Notes on Eire": Espionage Reports to Winston Churchill 1940-2*, 3rd ed., With a review of Irish Neutrality in World War 2 by Jack Lane and Brendan Clifford (Cork: Aubane Historican Society, 2009), 33.
47 John P. Duggan, *Herr Hempel and the German Legation in Dublin* (Dublin: Irish Academic Press, 2003), 30.
48 Fisk, *In Time of War*, 366; Aengus Nolan, "'A Most Heavy and Grievous Burden': Joseph Walshe and the Establishment of Sustainable Neutrality, 1940," in *Ireland in World War Two: Neutrality and Sustainability*, ed. Dermot Keogh and Mervyn O'Driscoll (Cork: Mercier Press, 2004), 126–128.
49 Joseph Walshe, Minister for External Affairs to Eamon de Valera, 25 August 1939, P150/2571, EdV Papers, UCD.
50 The Minister in Eire [Hempel] to the Foreign Ministry, 26 August 1939,

Doc. 303, *Documents on German Foreign Policy, 1918–1945*, vol. 7: *The Last Days of Peace, 1939*, (Washington, DC: Government Printing Office, 1956).
51 The Foreign Minister [Ribbentrop] to the Legation in Eire, 29 August 1939, Doc. 428, *Documents on German Foreign Policy, 1918–1945*, vol. 7.
52 The Minister in Eire to the Foreign Ministry, 31 August 1939, Doc. 484, *Documents on German Foreign Policy, 1918–1945*, vol. 7.
53 *Irish Examiner*, 4 September 1939: 7.
54 "Neutrality Declared, September 2, 1939, de Valera's address to the Dáil," *Being a Selection of the Speeches of Eamon de Valera During the War, 1939–1945* (Dublin: McGill & Son, 1946), P104/3808, Frank Aiken Papers (on microfilm), University College Dublin (hereafter: FA Papers, UCD).
55 Tony Gray, *The Lost Years: The Emergency in Ireland, 1939–1945* (London: Warner Books, 1998), 5.
56 Ronan Fanning, *Eamon de Valera: A Will to Power* (Cambridge, MA: Harvard University Press, 2016), 190–191.
57 "Re: Censorship of foreign periodicals, illustrated and otherwise," 27 October 1939, P104/3436, FA Papers, UCD.
58 Eunan O'Halpin, *Defending Ireland: The Irish State and Its Enemies Since 1922* (New York: Oxford University Press, 2000), 151.
59 "Arrangements for the trade to go On, Taoiseach States View in Seanad, National Emergency Motion, Sympathy with the Democracies," *Irish Press* (3 September 1939), 10; see also "Eire to Maintain Neutrality, But with Difficulty," *Belfast Newsletter*, 3 September 1939: 3.
60 Legal Adviser's Papers, Memorandum "Ireland's Neutrality in Practice" from Michael Rynne to Joseph P. Walshe, 1 September 1939, Doc. No. 1 NAI DFA, *Documents on Irish Foreign Policy* vol. VI, 1939–1941.
61 Gray, *The Lost Years*, 6, 8: "during the course of the war about 50,000 young Irish people volunteered to join the British forces … In all about 250,000 young Irishmen and women enrolled in the Irish defense forces. [Between] 25,000 and 50,000 men and women (again mainly the younger ones) left Ireland each year of the Emergency to find jobs in England, and few of them returned after the war. Many tens of thousands more went to the United Kingdom to work for short periods to earn a bit of extra money."
62 O'Halpin, *Defending Ireland*, 152.
63 See Eunan O'Halpin, ed., *MI5 and Ireland, 1939–1945* (Dublin: Irish Academic Press, 2003).
64 Richard English, *Irish Freedom: The History of Nationalism in Ireland* (London: Pan Macmillan, 2007), 340.
65 Biographical History, FA Papers UCD, www.ucd.ie/archives/collections/depositedcollections/items/collectionname,234399,en.html#accordion1 (accessed 2 December 2020).
66 Girvin, *The Emergency*, 32.
67 Fisk, *In Time of War*, 264.
68 Clair Wills, *That Neutral Island: A Cultural History of Ireland During the Second World War* (London: Faber & Faber, 2007), 5: "British people believed

Neutral states in a world at war 75

that Ireland had deliberately cut itself off, and had betrayed its neighbor. Many Britons were simply unable to absorb the fact that the country was no longer part of the United Kingdom. Ireland's neutrality was regarded by the Allies as the nadir of national protectionism, an extension of the economic isolationism of the 1930s. Ireland had cut itself off not only from the war but from the vital flow of ideas that was shaping the new world. Rather than being active, sovereign and independent, its neutral stance was negative: defensive, distrustful and inward-looking."

69 Eunan O'Halpin, "The Second World War and Ireland," in *The Oxford Handbook of Modern Irish History*, ed. Alvin Jackson (Oxford: Oxford University Press, 2014), 711–712.
70 John Day Tully, *Ireland and Irish-Americans, 1932–1945: The Search for Identity* (Dublin: Irish Academic Press, 2010), 76.
71 McCullagh, *De Valera*, 169.
72 Announcement of the Appointment of Sir John Maffey as British Representative to Dublin, *Nationalist and Leinster Times*, 30 September 1939: 5: "Sir John Maffey (Grand Cross of the Order of St. Michael and St. George; Knight Commander of the Bath; Knight Commander of the Victorian Order, Companion of the Order of the Star of India, and Companion of the Order of the Indian Empire, Order of the Rising Sun, Grand Cordon of the Crown of Italy, Grand Cordon of the Egyptian Order of Ishmail, Grand Cordon of the Star of Ethiopia) would appear to be distinguished in the service of the British Empire ... He is a Governor of Rugby School and a student of Christ Church, Oxford. With the British Undersecretary for Air he flew 14,000 miles in 1937. He was a member of the Executive Committee which made arrangements for the Coronation of George VI of England."
73 Fisk, *In Time of War*, 91.
74 Joseph Walshe, Minister for External Affairs, Report on Visit to London September 6–10, 1939, P150/2571, EdV Papers, UCD.
75 Ibid.
76 Fisk, *In Time of War*, 380.
77 Jordan, *Churchill*, 163.
78 Ibid., 167.
79 O'Halpin, *Defending Ireland*, 173.
80 Jordan, *Churchill*, 171; McCullagh, *De Valera*, 174.
81 Fisk, *In Time of War*, 103.
82 "The First Lord's Minutes," First Lord of the Admiralty's Printed minutes September 1939 [multiple documents]. September 1939, CHAR: 19/3/1, Winston Churchill Archives online.
83 Jordan, *Churchill*, 171–172; Fisk, *In Time of War*, 99–101, 118; Paul Bew, *Churchill and Ireland* (Oxford University Press, 2016), 141–142. See also "Memorandum: The Need for Berehaven [Ireland]" by Deputy Chief of Naval Staff [Rear Admiral Tom Phillips], with attached note by Winston Churchill, 18 October 1939, CHAR: 19/4/25–28, Winston Churchill Archives online.
84 Bowen, *Notes on Eire*, 7–8. The Anglo-Irish writer Elizabeth Bowen, who

traveled back and forth between Dublin and London during the war, spied on Ireland and wrote reports of her impressions of Irish public opinion for the British government. According to her account, "Churchill wanted to know how Irish people would respond to a British invasion and takeover of Irish ports. As it happened, Miss Bowen was able to warn that it would be a disastrous mistake, and militarily counterproductive. If, however, she had found any substantial element in Ireland that was eager to participate on Britain's side in the war, she would have let Churchill know that an invasion was practical." According to Terry de Valera, Eamon's son, and his *A Memoir* (Curragh Press; illustrated edition, 2004), Churchill authorized a plan to use poison gas on Ireland if Germany landed an invasion force and the British launched a counter-invasion.

85 "Eire to Maintain Neutrality, But with Difficulty," *Belfast Newsletter*, 3 September 1939: 3: "In the Chamber of Deputies, Mr. de Valera referred to the difficulty of maintaining neutrality. 'It is not sufficient for us to indicate our attitude to the desire of our people,' he said. 'It is necessary at every step to protect their interest in that regard to avoid giving any of the belligerents cause for complaint. A neutral state, if it is a small state, is always open to considerable pressure.'"

86 Max Hastings, *The Secret War: Spies, Ciphers, and Guerrillas 1939–1945* (New York: HarperCollins, 2016), 329. From 1939 and up to 1943, Ireland was infiltrated by British and German spies as both belligerents gathered intelligence on their enemies, and gauged the possibilities of using Irish territory to attack one another.

87 Duggan, *Herr Hempel*, 78.

88 For example, Dwyer, *Irish Neutrality and the USA*, 17–19. De Valera's government monitored and radioed information about German submarines, radio transmissions which the British could intercept; British aircraft were also allowed to fly over Southern Ireland's air space, en route to Northern Ireland bases; Irish nationals were never prohibited from serving in British Armed Forces or working in British war industries throughout the war years. Other accounts noted cooperation between Irish Army and British forces in terms of sharing information collected by Irish coastal watch stations and other military intelligence agencies, and maintaining open borders for "civilian" travel between Southern and Northern Ireland.

89 Fisk, *In Time of War*, 93.

90 Fanning, *Eamon de Valera*, 191.

91 Neville Chamberlain to Eamon de Valera, 19 September 1939, P150/2548, EdV Papers, UCD.

92 Fisk, *In Time of War*, 105–106.

93 Letter from Sir John Maffey, on Use of Berehaven, 26 October 1939, CAB 66/2/47, British National Archives.

94 Girvin, *The Emergency*, quoting Hempel's dispatches to Berlin, 288.

95 Duggan, *Herr Hempel*, 79. See also The Minister in Eire [Hempel] to the Foreign Ministry, 7 October 1939, Doc. 216; The Minister [Hempel] to the Foreign

Ministry, 13 November 1939, Doc. 355, *Documents on German Foreign Policy, 1918–1945*, vol. 8: "The War Years, September 4, 1939 – March 18, 1940," (Washington, DC: Government Printing Office, 1954).
96 Confidential Report from William Warnock to Joseph P. Walshe, 21 October 1939, Doc. No. 60 NAI DFA 219/4, *Documents on Irish Foreign Policy* vol. VI, 1939–1941.
97 Minister John Cudahy to Franklin Roosevelt, 19 August 1939, box 40, President's Secretary's Files, Ireland 1938–1939, Franklin Delano Roosevelt Papers, Franklin Roosevelt Presidential Library, Hyde Park, NY (hereafter: FDR Papers).
98 Minister John Cudahy to Franklin Roosevelt, 2 October 1939, box 40, President's Secretary's Files, Ireland 1938–1939, FDR Papers. See also Minister John Cudahy to R. Walton Moore, Counselor of the Department of State, 29 November 1939, box 40, President's Secretary's Files, Ireland 1938–1939, FDR Papers.
99 US Minister to Ireland John Cudahy to President FDR, 27 October 1939, box 40, President's Secretary's Files, Ireland 1938–1939, FDR Papers.
100 Dwyer, *Irish Neutrality and the USA*, 23.
101 Meacham, *Franklin and Winston*, 50.
102 Fisk, *In Time of War*, 100.
103 Kirkpatrick, "Scorns 'Peace' on Nazi Terms; Blasts Regime," *Chicago Daily News* (12 October 1939), box 2, HPK Papers.
104 Kirkpatrick, "No Peace Offer by Hitler or Any Nazi to Succeed, British Government Indicates," *Chicago Daily News* (31 October 1939), box 2, HPK Papers.
105 Cook, *Eleanor Roosevelt*, 150, 199: On December 5, 1939, Hitler's decrees regarding Nazi policy to imprison and execute Jews were published: "Mass public executions of Jews and Poles were ongoing, as William Shirer reported in his amazing broadcasts from Berlin and Helsinki: Hitler was engaged in 'a holy struggle against the Jews ... an ideological struggle against world Jewry.' According to Nazi propaganda, Shirer continued, England was 'spiritually, politically and economically at one with the Jews ... England and the Jews remain the common foe.'"
106 Kirkpatrick, "Neutrality Irks Irish as Hate of Nazis Grows," *Chicago Daily News* (27 October 1939), box 12, HPK Papers. See also Kirkpatrick, "Eire's Desire for Neutrality. Population Anti-Nazi," *The Whitehall Letter* (27 October 1939), CHAR: 2/362, 01, Winston Churchill Archives online.
107 The Minister in Eire [Hempel] to the Foreign Ministry, 13 November 1939, Doc. 355; The Minister in Eire to the Foreign Ministry, 16 December 1939, Doc. 465; Memorandum by the Director of the Political Department [Woermann] Berlin, 10 February 1940, Doc. 605, *Documents on German Foreign Policy, 1918–1945*, vol. 8. See also Duggan, *Herr Hempel*, 80–81, 87–88, 138–139; Fisk, *In Time of War*, 294–295.
108 O'Halpin, *Defending Ireland*, 248.
109 Girvin, *The Emergency*, 75–76: "The real threat to Irish neutrality and

sovereignty between September 1939 and May 1940 came from the IRA, rather than from Britain or Germany, with the most explosive expression of this occurring just before Christmas in 1939 … [on Saturday December 23], when the IRA attacked the Magazine Fort in Phoenix Park, where the Irish army stored most of its ammunition." And p. 78: "Between 1935 and 1945 the IRA was linked directly with a series of deadly attacks on the state, most of which occurred between 1939 and early 1941 and which included ten murders, including those of a number of policemen."

110 McCullagh, *De Valera*, 163.
111 Olson, *Those Angry Days*, 239–241. See also Cook, *Eleanor Roosevelt*, 156.
112 See for example: Hastings, *The Secret War*, 330: "… when the Republicans staged a spectacular raid on the Irish army's magazine at Phoenix Park, the exasperated de Valera rounded up every IRA man his policemen could catch, and introduced internment without trial. If the prime minister hated the British, he now disliked his erstwhile fellow-freedom fighters almost as much. The Phoenix Park raid was a turning point, because it made Ireland's government explicit foes of Germany's Republican allies"; Tim Pat Coogan, *Eamon de Valera: The Man Who Was Ireland* (New York: HarperCollins, 1993), 523–524.
113 Fisk, *In Time of War*, 141. See also Wills, *That Neutral Island*, 163–166.
114 Fisk, *In Time of War*, 142.
115 Telegram from Joseph P. Walshe to John J. Hearne (Ottawa), 26 February 1940, Doc. No. 128 NAI DFA 219/49, *Documents on Irish Foreign Policy* vol. VI, 1939–1941.
116 Interview with Helen Kirkpatrick Milbank by Anne Kasper, Women in Journalism, Oral History Project of the Washington Press Club Foundation, April 3–5, 1990, 46–48.
117 Sorel, *The Women Who Wrote the War*, 76.
118 Girvin, *The Emergency*, 181.
119 Bernadette Whelan, "Biography of David Gray," in Bew, *A Yankee in De Valera's Ireland*, 305–308.
120 *Ibid.*
121 Smith, *FDR*, 417. See also Dallek, *Franklin D. Roosevelt: A Political Life*, 367.
122 Dwyer, *Irish Neutrality and the USA*, 48–49.
123 Gray, *Behind the Emerald Curtain*, in Bew, *A Yankee in De Valera's Ireland*, 3–4.
124 Confidential report from William J. B. Macaulay [the Vatican] to Joseph P. Walshe, 20 March 1940, Doc. No. 140 NAI DFA 218/55, *Documents on Irish Foreign Policy* vol. VI, 1939–1941; Dwyer, *Irish Neutrality and the USA*, 49; Tully, *Ireland and Irish-Americans*, 81.
125 Bew, *Churchill and Ireland*, 145.
126 David Gray to Duff Cooper, 10 April 1940, box 3, David Gray Papers, Coll. 03082, University of Wyoming American Heritage Center, Laramie, Wyoming (hereafter: Gray Papers, AHC).
127 US Minister to Ireland David Gray to Franklin Roosevelt, 8 April 1940, box 40,

President's Secretary's File: Ireland, 1940, FDR Papers. Referring to his meeting with Churchill, Gray told FDR: "I had asked him what he thought Craigavon would do if de Valera were ready to throw out the Hitler Legation and throw in Berehaven. That was something else he said but it was all up to Ulster. I asked him whether in the case that Mr. de Valera was willing that I should see Craigavon in order to get firsthand this third side to this tragic triangle he would arrange it. He said yes and it should be in London because then no one would hear of it. This last of course was all off the record. All the other ministers I have spoken of expressed great hope that something could be arranged to improve relations, spoke with respect and liking of Mr. de Valera, wanted not to embarrass him in his present troubles but like Churchill, though not as emphatically, said that Ulster could not be coerced. It is clearly up to Mr. de Valera and Craigavon." See also Dwyer, *Irish Neutrality and the USA*, 50–51.

128 US Minister to Ireland David Gray to FDR, 19 April 1940, box 40, President's Secretary's File: Ireland, 1940, FDR Papers.

129 Memorandum from Joseph P. Walshe to Eamon de Valera, 30 April 1940, Doc. No. 164 NAI DFA 205/4, *Documents on Irish Foreign Policy* vol. VI, 1939-1941: "During the last three or four weeks it has been persistently rumoured that in the course of one of his talks, the German announcer known as 'Lord Haw-Haw' [William Joyce 'Lord Haw-Haw' (1906-1946), was a British Fascist who had grown up in Ireland and who made radio propaganda broadcasts to Britain from Germany from 1939 to 1945. Executed for treason in 1946.] made a statement to the effect that 'Ireland is at present a garden of roses, but she will very soon become a garden of tombstones if by trying to increase her exports of food to Britain, she involves herself in the war.'"

130 David Gray to Franklin Roosevelt, 15 April 1940, box 40, President's Secretary's File: Ireland 1940, FDR Papers.

131 David Gray Memorandum re Count and Countess Plunkett, 19 April 1940, box 3, Gray Papers, AHC.

132 Cull, *Selling War*, 67.

133 Dwyer, *Irish Neutrality and the USA*, 66. See also Joseph Walshe, Minister for External Affairs, Report on Visit to London, 1 April 1940, P150/2571, EdV Papers, UCD: "There is very real pessimism about the present state of the war operations. The defeat in Norway is regarded as a blow of the first magnitude, not merely to the British naval power, which is primarily affected, but to the prestige of Great Britain all over the world ... There is a feeling amounting to a conviction that Hitler will take over all of the Balkans and perhaps Holland and Belgium in the next few months, and the Allies have little or no hope of being able to stop him."

134 Winston Churchill, "Norway, A Speech Delivered to the House of Commons, 11 April 1940, in Churchill, *Into Battle, 1941*.

135 Report from Joseph P. Walshe [in London] to Eamon de Valera (Most Secret), 6 May 1940, Doc. No. 169 UCDA P150/2571, *Documents on Irish Foreign Policy* vol. VI, 1939-1941.

136 Sorel, *The Women Who Wrote the War*, 76.

137 Amery quoted in Purnell, *Clementine*, 232.
138 David Dilks, *Churchill and Company: Allies and Rivals in War and Peace* (London: I. B. Tauris 2012), 38.
139 Winston Churchill, "Prime Minister, A Speech delivered in the House of Commons," 13 May 1940, in Churchill, *Into Battle, 1941*, 191.
140 Churchill's 15 May 1940 letter to Roosevelt quoted in Meacham, *Franklin and Winston*, 48.
141 *Ibid.*, 48–49. In the same letter, Churchill also asked Roosevelt to "keep that Japanese dog quiet in the Pacific. ..."
142 O'Halpin, *Defending Ireland*, 172–173; Fisk, *In Time of War*, 121–122.
143 Letter from Eamon de Valera to Neville Chamberlain, 15 May 1940, Doc. No. 176 UCDA P150/2459, *Documents on Irish Foreign Policy* vol. VI, 1939–1941; Neville Chamberlain to de Valera, 18 May 1940, P150/2548, EdV Papers, UCD.
144 David Gray to Franklin Roosevelt, 12 May 1940, box 40, President's Secretary's File: Ireland 1940, FDR Papers.
145 "Invasion of Low Countries," de Valera's Speech at Galway during a by-election, 12 May 1940, in *Being a Selection of the Speeches of Eamon de Valera During the War (1939–1945)*, Dublin: McGill and Son, 1946, P104/3808, FA Papers, UCD.
146 Fisk, *In Time of War*, 149.
147 Confidential Telegram from Hempel to German Foreign Ministry, No. 239, 14 May 1940, box 3, Gray Papers, AHC.
148 Bew, *A Yankee in De Valera's Ireland*, "Introduction," xvi.
149 Confidential Report from William Warnock [Berlin] to Joseph P. Walshe, 18 May 1940, Doc. No. 179 NAI DFA 219/4, *Documents on Irish Foreign Policy* vol. VI, 1939–1941.
150 Fisk, *In Time of War*, 149.
151 The Minister in Ireland (Gray) to the Secretary of State, 18 May 1940, Doc. 147, *Foreign Relations of the United States Diplomatic Papers* (hereafter: *FRUS*), 1940 vol. III (Washington, DC: US Government Printing Office, 1958); Cordell Hull to Franklin Roosevelt, 21 May 1940, Official Files, File 218, Ireland, Government of, 1939–1945, FDR Papers.
152 The Secretary of State (Hull) to the Minister in Ireland (Gray). 22 May 1940, Doc. 148, *FRUS* 1940 vol. III.
153 Washington Embassy Confidential Reports from Robert Brennan to Joseph P. Walshe, 21 May 1940, Doc. No. 181 NAI DFA, *Documents on Irish Foreign Policy* vol. VI, 1939–1941.
154 Hastings, *The Secret War*, 331–332; Fisk, *In Time of War*, 302; Dwyer, *Irish Neutrality and the USA*, 70–71; Girvin, *The Emergency*, 96.

3

"Unstoppable" Germany, "unbeatable" Britain, June to December 1940

The May 10 Nazi invasion of Belgium, Holland, and France and the seemingly unstoppable advance of the German *blitzkrieg* stunned the Western democracies. The British government, believing that the nation was next in line for the German onslaught, called on their Warlord, Winston Churchill, to lead them through the coming trials. That Britain prevailed against the greater military might that the Nazis marshaled in the summer and fall of 1940 was due in large part to the collective resistance that Churchill inspired, as he defined those trying times for posterity as Britain's "finest hour."[1]

In mid-May, the German military machine broke through what was supposed to be an impregnable defense, France's Maginot Line. After Holland's surrender on May 15, the Germans quickly defeated the French and Belgian armies, forcing them and the British Expeditionary Force (BEF) that had come to their aid to retreat to the French coastline under cover from the British Royal Air Force (RAF) that slowed, but could not stop, Germany's forward momentum. They faced a German assault that was "advancing and breaking all opposition at an incredible pace, ... at last in a position to set about the accomplishment of one of their most intense desires – a thrust at the heart of Britain."[2] Churchill called on the United States for "more aeroplanes, more tanks, more shells, more guns"[3] and approved a desperate evacuation plan that he hoped would save at least 40,000 soldiers from slaughter. Germany's victories incited "feverish activity" on the part of the Roosevelt Administration, as well. President Roosevelt lobbied Congress to approve a billion dollar increase in defense spending to build 50,000 new aircraft immediately and "rushed [the proposals] through Congress at record speed."[4] Roosevelt followed up his Congressional appeal calling for the unprecedented defense build-up with a radio address to the American people. FDR concluded his remarks by describing the "noble task" that confronted Americans – pray for peace but prepare to defend America's political values and the future of humankind: "We defend the foundations laid down by our fathers. We build a life for generations yet unborn.

We defend and we build a way of life, not for America alone, but for all mankind. Ours is a high duty, a noble task."[5]

To be sure, none of the proposed military equipment could be produced to arrive in time to meet the immediate needs of the Allies. In May and June 1940, it appeared to many Americans including the U.S. Ambassador in London, Joseph Kennedy, that "only a miracle" would save the British forces from "annihilation."[6] The miracle came in the form of the evacuation of the BEF and their French allies from the beaches of Dunkirk. "Operation Dynamo" was a dramatic salvage operation of heroic magnitude,[7] passing into the realm of British national myth almost instantaneously. The British Royal Navy, assisted by "a handful of civilian volunteers,"[8] conducted a rescue that swelled the nation's pride and faith in the righteousness of their fight. American newspapers also seized on the drama of the moment to eulogize the lifesaving mission:

> So long as the English tongue survives, the word Dunkirk will be spoken with reverence. For in that harbour, in such a hell as never blazed on earth before, at the end of a lost battle, the rages and blemishes that have hidden the soul of democracy fell away. There, beaten but unconquered, in shining splendour she faced the enemy.[9]

The British evacuation saved over 200,000 British troops and over 100,000 French Allied forces.[10] What they left behind in military equipment, arms, and ammunition, however, left Britain nearly "naked before her foes."[11] Churchill acknowledged that the defeat was "a colossal military disaster,"[12] but he also pivoted the narrative to revive Britain's spirits with words that ever after shaped the popular memory of "Dunkirk," the name spoken as shorthand for Britain's invincibility:[13]

> Even though large tracts of Europe and many old and famous States have fallen or may fall into the grip of the Gestapo and all the odious apparatus of Nazi rule, we shall not flag or fail. We shall go on to the end, we shall fight in France, we shall fight on the seas and oceans, we shall fight with growing confidence and growing strength in the air, we shall defend our island, whatever the cost may be, we shall fight on the beaches, we shall fight on the landing grounds, we shall fight in the fields and in the streets, we shall fight in the hills; we shall never surrender, and even if, which I do not for a moment believe, this island or a large part of it were subjugated and starving, then our Empire beyond the seas, armed and guarded by the British Fleet, would carry on the struggle, until, in God's good time, the new world, with all its power and might, steps forth to the rescue and the liberation of the old.[14]

David Gray recalled a conversation he had with Sir John Maffey following the Dunkirk debacle. Maffey had gone back to England to see his son who had been among the rescued wounded soldiers. Gray asked Maffey about the mood in London and Maffey answered, "'Pretty grim,' ... Then he laughed, 'Everybody is saying Thank God! Now we are on our own!'"[15] Gray interpreted Maffey's bravado as signaling Britain's distinctly proud national character, proof that "England had only begun to fight." And Gray explained what he understood to be the key distinction between politically evolved and principled "friends" and tribalistic "enemy" peoples:

> The Sinn Féin Irish [militant IRA nationalists] could not understand this. They resented it the way the Vichy French did. England ought to know when she was beaten. ... The Sinn Féin never understood Churchill. They never grasped the meaning of the Magna Carta, ... They had nothing to rally about but leaders; no central idea except tribal loyalty to a person, no appreciation of "Civility", of government by law. ...[16]

Britain had its principles and democratic traditions, but the German war machine seemed poised to overrun the Western world.[17] Italy's Il Duce, Benito Mussolini, finally made good on the "Pact of Steel" he forged with Führer Adolf Hitler in 1938 and formally entered the war as an Axis Power belligerent on June 10. The French government under its new collaborationist prime minister Marshal Pétain capitulated to Germany and signed an armistice on June 22. Now Hitler turned his attention to Britain and began mustering his forces for the next step: attack and occupation of England.[18] Both the British and Irish governments believed that Germany would launch the attack through Ireland.

The arrest at the end of May of IRA collaborator Stephen Held,[19] who had hidden the German spy Hermann Goertz in his Dublin home, and the discovery of proof in the raid on Held's home that the IRA colluded with German spies, convinced de Valera that a German invasion of Ireland was imminent.[20] In fact, Stephen Held had visited Germany in April 1940 and had delivered a proposal for the invasion, "Plan Kathleen," to the *Abwehr* chiefs in Berlin that involved parachute landings and amphibious landings of German troops, who would meet with friendly IRA forces, take control of Ireland, and then launch an attack on England.[21] While the Dublin-based German Minister Eduard Hempel never put much stock in the IRA's strength or reliability to facilitate such an invasion and advised the German Foreign Ministry to be cautious, the *Abwehr* believed that the IRA's anti-British sympathies were worth exploiting and sent various covert agents into Ireland to assess the situation during the course of the war. The *Abwehr*'s spying operations and collusion with the IRA nevertheless panicked de Valera's government and the Anglo-Americans who believed that the German spies posed security threats, especially in summer 1940.[22] Sir John Maffey reported to the Foreign Office that after Held's arrest, the Irish "Government departments were burning secret papers on a large scale." De Valera also met with leaders in the Fine Gael party, and "offered to include them in consultations and promised to set up a defence council which would include members of the opposition."[23] Although historians have not uncovered evidence that the spies collected much information to aid Germany, or information that the Irish Army intelligence force was not aware of, or that affected the outcome of the war,[24] in May and June 1940, de Valera tried to allay British fears of German collusion with the IRA to prevent Britain from launching a "pre-emptive" strike on Ireland, and to secure German promises, again, to respect Irish neutrality.[25]

Meeting with de Valera immediately after Held's arrest, Eduard Hempel offered de Valera assurances of Germany's friendly intentions. Hempel was initially in the dark about the *Abwehr*'s connections to the spy Hermann Goertz, or to Held and the IRA,[26] but he made the case for supporting de Valera's leadership rather than trying to undermine de Valera's authority with his superiors in Berlin.[27] When the Foreign Ministry brought Hempel into their confidence regarding Held's assistance to Goertz, they directed Hempel to share the following message with de Valera:

> The Irish Government must be clearly aware that the struggle between the German Reich and England was now entering its decisive stage. We were conscious of the fact that the measures we had to take for carrying out this struggle against England which had been forced upon us might also affect Irish interests. Just because of this, however, we considered it important to inform the Irish Government once again that our sole objective in the struggle was England. We believed that Ireland, whose enemy through history was known to be England, was fully aware that the outcome of this struggle would be of decisive importance for the Irish nation and the full realization of its national demands. Given this situation, we believed that we could also count on the greatest possible understanding from the Irish Government, despite its neutral attitude, even if Ireland might in some ways be affected by our measures.[28]

At a subsequent meeting, Joseph Walshe accepted Hempel's explanations and noted that "The German Minister was very friendly." Hempel said that he understood de Valera's concerns for Ireland's safety, but could not make assurances that Germany would not use Irish territory in Germany's fight with Great Britain, because "that would be tantamount to a partial revealing of their plans to the enemy."[29] In June and July 1940 both Joseph Walshe[30] and Frank Aiken[31] were telling de Valera that Britain's defeat (and Germany's victory) was "inevitable," and that Britain's male leaders were "too soft, too class prejudiced (they are almost all of the wealthy Tory family type) to be able to win a war against men of steel like Hitler, Stalin and their followers."[32] Consequently, they advised de Valera not to negotiate with Britain or join the Western

Alliance at that time – even when British leaders were desperate enough to discuss the end of partition as an enticement for use of Irish naval bases, and even though Walshe was hedging Ireland's bets and offering some cooperation and information sharing with the British Foreign Office and Military Intelligence.[33]

With the Western Allies' defenses crumbling across the European continent at the end of May, Neville Chamberlain suggested to the British War Cabinet that they should reach out to de Valera with new proposals to secure use of the Irish ports. He also made a personal appeal to de Valera to meet him in London, an invitation that de Valera declined.[34] This must have mortified Winston Churchill who had long predicted Britain would regret the return of the ports to Irish control that Chamberlain acceded in 1938. Adding to the irony, Chamberlain's chief negotiator in the 1938 Anglo-Irish treaty deliberations that reached the Irish ports settlement, Malcolm MacDonald, was dispatched to Dublin to revive his personal friendship with de Valera and to initiate the bilateral talks. According to historian Paul Bew, "The fact that Churchill allowed MacDonald, whom he despised for his role in the concession of the treaty ports, to take up this mission, speaks volumes."[35] Churchill reportedly considered MacDonald to be "rat poison" after the Irish ports were surrendered,[36] but he buried his ego to ensure Britain's survival. Although it took MacDonald a few conversations with de Valera to put the possibility of an end to partition onto the negotiating table, Sir John Maffey had previously suggested this move to the Foreign Office, reporting in April that partition "was the only real cause of conflict between Britain and Ireland."[37] Even so, Maffey was not hopeful of success, and offered his view that de Valera was not a strong enough leader to stand up to the inevitable outcry from the IRA and other Irish nationalists if he allowed Britain to use the ports: "[De Valera] seems incapable of courageous or original thought ... in every matter he lives too much under the threats of the extremists."[38]

Nevertheless, in mid-June, the British War Cabinet decided to offer up resolution of Irish partition in trade for the use of the ports. On his return from visiting his wounded son in London on June 6, Maffey told David Gray that his government was laying the ground work for the deal by putting pressure on Northern Ireland Prime Minister Lord Craigavon, giving him "merry hell," and "all but ordering him to make up with de Valera and end Partition on the best terms he could."[39] Again, these developments must have been anathema to Winston Churchill, who had always considered Ireland to be a vital, if wayward, member of the British Empire, and who prized Ulster's consistent loyalty to the British Crown. At a June 20 Cabinet meeting Chamberlain advocated strong-arming Northern Ireland into accepting the end of partition and seizing Eire's ports by force if necessary, a "curious reversal of roles"[40] for Chamberlain, who rarely played the part of the belligerent man of action.

MacDonald's mission to Dublin went forward on June 17. MacDonald's patrician background as the son of former prime minister Ramsay MacDonald, and his service heading Neville Chamberlain's Dominions Office in the 1930s, made him the British government's "establishment" choice to meet with de Valera. He represented a certain "ideal type" of British masculinity that gender and media studies scholar Gill Plain has used to describe a popular British actor of the 1930s and 1940s, John Mills, that is, an Englishman who was "restrained, determined, honorable, good-humored and capable."[41] At his initial meeting with de Valera, MacDonald sought to reason with him, stressing the dangers of neutrality. War was coming to Ireland and neutrality had "saved nobody" among the European powers. MacDonald appealed for Britain's use of the ports and proposed a meeting between de Valera and Craigavon to form a Joint Irish Defence Council. MacDonald also warned de Valera about the dangers of IRA "Fifth Columnists" who acted on behalf of Germany's interests, preparing the way for a German invasion.[42]

Receiving no joy from de Valera, MacDonald arranged a second meeting on June 21.[43] He now asserted that Britain accepted the "principle" of a united Ireland, and explained that a Joint Defence Council comprised of Northern and Southern representatives could be the first step toward ending partition. The promise of a future united Ireland, however, would not satisfy de Valera; moreover, "Great Britain had no right to attempt to barter the unity of the Irish nation for the blood of her people" that would surely be shed in a civil war if Ireland entered the European war.[44] De Valera countered with his terms: immediate end to partition, all of Ireland to remain neutral, no British access to Irish ports but the U.S. Navy could come into the ports to "guarantee" Irish neutrality and offer protection from German or British invasion. "MacDonald thought this 'entirely impracticable.'" It seemed like an irrational response to Britain's reasonable proposals, and de Valera seemed to be displaying traits that were the opposite of the masculine ideology that the model Englishman adhered to, a masculinity that "idealizes the life of the rational mind, fetishizing organized activity: moving forward, making progress, thrusting with force into the future, untrammelled by emotion."[45] MacDonald managed only to wrench a grudging concession from de Valera that Ireland "might" enter the war as a British ally if partition were ended, but Ireland wanted British guns to defend itself.[46] However, even if de Valera had been sincere in stating that Ireland "might" join the British alliance, Joseph Walshe and Frank Aiken rejected the alliance unequivocally. Aiken responded to questions about the possibility of aligning with the

British at the time: "Get this clear ... we are never going to abandon our neutrality."[47]

Lord Craigavon of Northern Ireland was just as adamant that Ulster would never agree to ending partition if it meant leaving the British Empire and succumbing to rule by a majority Irish Catholic government. When he heard rumors of MacDonald's negotiations with de Valera on June 26, Craigavon railed in a letter to Chamberlain: "I am profoundly shocked and disgusted by your letter making suggestions so far reaching, behind my back and without preconsultation. To such treachery to loyal Ulster, I will never be a party."[48] Craigavon sped to London to enlist Churchill's support for Northern Ireland. Craigavon achieved his mission; Churchill insisted that Ulster *must not* be coerced into ending partition and Ireland *must* agree to join the British alliance – Irish neutrality would not be accepted.[49] In the meantime, MacDonald made one more pitch in a meeting with de Valera, Aiken, and the government's Minister of Supplies, Sean Lemass, on June 27. He asserted that:

> The present was the best opportunity that had yet offered itself of a union of the whole of Ireland against the Nazi attack, then that union would not be broken afterwards. But if the leaders of Eire now stayed out of the war and, perhaps contributed to German strength while doing so, whilst the people of Northern Ireland and the United Kingdom were joined in the supreme struggle against the Nazis, then none of us in Britain would be very concerned to create a united Ireland afterwards. My private, most sincere advice to them was to seize this opportunity which might never recur.[50]

Again, de Valera rejected MacDonald's plea and his implied ultimatum. MacDonald reported to the Cabinet that de Valera sensed Ireland's relative strength as a neutral power and Britain's relative weakness vis-à-vis the outcome of the war: "I felt ... that one of the decisive influences on Mr de Valera's mind now is his view that we are likely to lose the war."[51] To be sure, pragmatism dictated de Valera's actions as it seemed that German victory was assured in 1940.[52] But Joseph Walshe reminded de Valera of the symbolic value of Ireland's neutral stance, as well. Neutrality was an assertion of Ireland's "muscular Catholic manhood": "Neutrality has given the people more faith in what the Government has achieved for the independence of this country more than any other act. ... If it goes, they will believe – and rightly – that our independence has gone with it."[53] De Valera shut down negotiations with a final rejection of the British proposals in a letter he penned to Neville Chamberlain on July 4, unable to resist moralizing once more:

> I regret that my proposal that the unity of Ireland should be established on the basis of the whole country becoming neutral is unacceptable to your

government. On the basis of unity and neutrality we could mobilise the whole of the manpower of this country for the national defence. That, with the high morale which could thus be secured and the support of the Irish race throughout the world, would constitute the most effective bulwark against attack, and would provide the surest guarantee against any part of our territory being used as a base for operations against Britain. ....[54]

De Valera defended his neutrality policy publicly in a July 9 interview with the *New York Times* that was also reported in the *Irish Independent*.[55]

As the Anglo-Irish negotiations sputtered to a stand-off, on June 28 Maffey finally shared details of the unhappy saga of MacDonald's mission with David Gray[56] who, on his own initiative, had been urging de Valera, throughout the month of June, to open the ports to the British (or to the Americans), and to join Britain's righteous fight against Nazi Germany.[57] Gray had been kept in the dark regarding the particulars of Anglo-Irish negotiations. Throughout June and July 1940, Gray, acting on his own, supported the Irish government's efforts to obtain weapons and ammunition from the United States for its volunteer army, and he generally reported favorably on de Valera's national leadership in his letters to Franklin Roosevelt.[58] However, Gray's good opinion of de Valera's government, and the government's good opinion of him, eroded over the course of summer and fall 1940 as German bombing of Britain began in earnest and the Irish continued to close their ports to the British Navy.[59] One year later, by summer 1941, relations between Gray and de Valera, Walshe, and Aiken were openly antagonistic. In his post-ministerial memoir written in the 1950s, Gray bitterly denounced the "immoral" neutrality policy that de Valera's government followed in 1940, and Ireland's refusal to fight the fascists throughout the war:

> After the publication of Mr de Valera's Galway speech on May 12th, the Irish censorship allowed no condemnation of Hitler or Mussolini, nor any generous word of praise of the Allies whose wheat was feeding half the Irish people and whose coal was supplying Dublin with the gas to bake the bread. If that June was England's finest hour, it was not Eire's. Neither was it one of the finest hours of my own country, [the United States was also a neutral power at the time]. ... What was left of the forces of Law and Morality had been thrown back to the British island. ... To play no part in this drama, save pass the ammunition from the rear, seemed not only ignoble but stupid. This our isolationists were shortly to discover. As the days passed it became clearer that in situations where there is a moral issue, to be neutral not only indicates a disease of the spirit but of the intelligence. No one has ever outwitted the moral order.[60]

Helen Kirkpatrick met David Gray in Ireland in June 1940, as negotiations for British use of the Irish ports were underway. She had traveled from London, escorting the children of two of her American colleagues to Galway where an American passenger liner, the SS *Roosevelt*, was docked to collect American citizens who were fleeing the European war zone. Gray was on site to oversee the evacuation.[61] At the time of their meeting in mid-June, revelations about German spies landing in Ireland were coming to light. Kirkpatrick recalled that Gray gave her:

> lots of stories of things that were going on, including the fact – "the fact" – he said, that the German submarines were surfacing in bays on the west coast of Ireland ... and that the Germans had a wireless station which they used to get news to Germany – picking up information and intelligence on what happened in Britain. And, of course, Ireland was ablaze with lights – southern Ireland was ablaze with lights – whereas the north was blacked out, as the whole of the British Isles were. And the Germans were using triangulation from the south of France to Ireland, to fix on bombing targets in Britain.[62]

Malcolm MacDonald was also making these accusations during his negotiations with de Valera in mid-June,[63] suggesting that Britain intelligence shared information with the Americans, and David Gray then passed it on to Kirkpatrick. Kirkpatrick filed stories on Germany's covert activities in Ireland with the *Chicago Daily News* in summer 1940, defying the Irish government's efforts to silence her "biased" war reporting.[64] Under instructions from Joseph Walshe in mid-July, Irish Minister in Washington Robert Brennan registered his government's protest with the *Daily News* for publishing "lying reports against us"[65] – among other claims, Kirkpatrick's reporting included the incendiary charge that "some [Catholic] priests were pro-Nazi."[66] Gray had identified Kirkpatrick as an anti-fascist ally, and encouraged her to return to Dublin to report on German activities in stories that would get through to the Irish people via their Irish American relatives reading U.S. newspapers – with this plan he intended to put public pressure on de Valera's government to support the British cause. In August, Gray wrote to Franklin Roosevelt and explained his thinking:

> The Government has got to get over its panic of being invaded by the British. I have been mostly engaged with Joe Walshe Permanent Under Secretary for External Affairs trying to get him straightened out about American correspondents and giving him a little straight talk about American sentiment and what is profitable for the USA. He has become de Valera's eyes and is personally a defeatist on the war and not a good influence though personally a very nice fellow.[67]

Gray's opinion of Joseph Walshe's character deteriorated over the next year while his friendship with Helen Kirkpatrick blossomed as she filed reports criticizing Irish neutrality with her newspaper from London, Belfast, and Dublin. In an oral history recorded years later, Kirkpatrick recalled that after her critical reports appeared in print,

> De Valera denounced me and said it was absolutely untrue – the Germans were not doing the things that I had alleged they did. ... David Gray, the Minister, phoned me and said, "You know, if you get thrown from a horse, climb right back on. Come on over." I said, "Well, I think I'm *persona non grata*." He said, "Never mind. Come over and stay with us." That's when I first came to know them [David Gray and his wife Maude], and staying with them [at the American Legation in Phoenix Park] became a habit. So I would go at regular intervals. I would go either north across Stranraer [ferry port town in Scotland] to Belfast and stay there for a couple of days and do pieces about what was going on in Ulster, Northern Ireland. Then take the train down to Dublin and stay there.[68]

As the ports negotiations with de Valera unfolded, Churchill expressed his frustration: "The fact that we cannot use the south and west coasts of Ireland to refuel our flotillas and aircraft, and thus protect the trade by which both Britain and Ireland live, that fact is a most grievous and burdensome one, which should never have been placed on our shoulders, broad though they be." He wrote to President Roosevelt, "We are denied the use of ports or territory of Eire in which to organize our coastal patrols by air or sea."[69] In June and July 1940, Britain was shaken by the fall of France and Churchill focused on securing Roosevelt's moral support and America's military aid for the British war effort.[70] Roosevelt's sympathies lay with Britain, but FDR gave off mixed signals regarding any concrete expressions of support. When Italy entered the war on June 10, Roosevelt condemned Italy's alliance with Nazi Germany and staked out America's future course during a commencement address he delivered at the University of Virginia:

> In our American unity, we will pursue two obvious and simultaneous courses: we will extend to the opponents of force the material resources of this nation; and, at the same time, we will harness and speed up the use of those resources in order that we ourselves in the Americas may have the equipment and training equal to the task of any emergency and every defence. ... Signs and signals call for speed – full speed ahead.[71]

Churchill interpreted FDR's remarks as the promise of military aid that the Western Allies desperately needed. He wrote to Roosevelt on June 11:

> We all listened to you last night and were fortified by the grand scope of your declaration. Your statement that the material aid given to the Allies in their struggle is a strong encouragement in a dark but not unhopeful hour. Everything must be done to keep France in the fight. The hope with which you inspired them may give them the strength to persevere. ... I send you my

heartfelt thanks and those of my colleagues for all you are doing and seeking to do for what we may now indeed call a common cause.[72]

From Washington, Irish Minister Robert Brennan reported back to Walshe that Roosevelt's speech was "universally recognized here as making the United States a non-belligerent ally of Britain and France," and it seemed to be a precursor to the United States' formal entry into the war.[73] In Dublin, the *Irish Press* also reported that the United States was moving from the policy of strict neutrality to "friendly non-belligerency" with the Western Allies.[74] Roosevelt, however, would not accede to Churchill's request for U.S. entry into the war to save France at the last minute – or even issue a public statement of support for France with words that might inspire the French to keep on fighting in the anti-fascist war.[75] Roosevelt also rejected Churchill's request for a U.S. Navy squadron to make a show of Western strength and solidarity at the Irish ports.[76] However, following France's capitulation to the Nazis on June 22, Roosevelt reconstituted his Cabinet and brought in pro-Allied interventionists, including Kirkpatrick's boss Colonel Frank Knox as his new Secretary of the Navy and Henry Stimson to head the War Department, to silence some of the internal resistance to his plans to increase aid to Britain and mobilize the nation's defense.[77] Moreover, Roosevelt agreed with Churchill that the French naval fleet must not fall to the Germans following the French surrender.

In early July, Churchill approved a bold and controversial plan of action, "Operation Catapult," to prevent the Germans from taking control of the French battleships off the coast of North Africa. Britain presented French fleet commanders with an ultimatum: sail their ships to British or U.S. harbors and turn them over to the Allies, or the British Navy would sink them. When the French commanders did not comply, the British Navy attacked the French ships and destroyed them. At Mers-El-Kébir, and at the nearby port of Oran, Algeria, Britain sank the French battleship *Bretagne* and several other destroyers. Nearly 1,300 French sailors and officers lost their lives.[78] The Nazi government condemned Winston Churchill who had issued the order and pronounced him to be "the greatest criminal in history." Churchill, however, took full responsibility for the decision. He addressed a shocked British Parliament and nation and insisted he could not let the French fleet fall under control of Britain's enemies, who would use the ships to inflict a "mortal injury" on Britain.[79]

Churchill biographer Carlo D'Este explained the impact that the sinking of the French fleet had in Britain and in the United States. The act restored Churchill's (and Britain's) manhood:

> Mers-el-Kébir had other incalculable, unintended consequences, the most important of which was that it forcefully established, perhaps once and for

all, Churchill's position as the unmistakeable political and military leader of Britain. He had done what a Halifax-led government would never have dared, and in so doing Churchill established just how utterly ruthless and determined he could be in prosecuting the war, even if it meant attacking what had been, until the creation of the Vichy government, his nation's closest ally. ... Those who had underestimated him could now hardly be in doubt over who was in charge.

In Washington the message from London was loud and clear: Britain would fight to the bitter end. "Immense relief spread through the high government circles in the United States," Churchill later wrote. "Henceforth there was no talk about Britain giving in."[80]

In the aftermath of the French fleet's destruction, Churchill and Roosevelt together crafted a plan that would provide Britain with some needed naval destroyers without a long production delay, that is, a transfer of "old" U.S. destroyers of the First World War vintage that could be sent immediately into British war service, in exchange for long-term leases on British colonial bases in the Western hemisphere awarded to the U.S. Navy.[81] The "destroyers for bases" deal provided political cover for Roosevelt, who had announced his intention to run for a third presidential term in July while also pledging to keep the United States from active belligerency.[82] And, it promised aid to Britain that was now under attack from an incessant German *Luftwaffe blitzkrieg* campaign focused on destroying British resistance and paving the way for a planned German invasion of the British Isles.[83]

As the destroyers for bases deal was being worked out, American journalists based in London, including Helen Kirkpatrick, reported chilling firsthand accounts of the raging battles waged by the *Luftwaffe* and the RAF in the skies over Dover and London, with the goal of inspiring more active U.S. support for the British war effort. According to the journalists, Britain was now engaged in a "People's War."[84] Once again, Churchill's words defined the "true" nature of the war for the British people and for American reporters like Helen Kirkpatrick. In his July 14 broadcast to the nation, Churchill noted that Britain was "alone in the breach":

> But all depends now upon the whole life strength of the British race in every part of the world and of all our associated peoples and of all our well-wishers in every land, doing their utmost day and night; giving all; daring all; enduring all – to the utmost – to the end. This is no war of dynasties or national ambition: it is a war of peoples and causes. There are vast numbers not only in this island but in every land, who will render faithful service in this War, but whose names will never be known; whose deeds will never be recorded. This is a War of the Unknown Warriors but let us all strive without falling in faith or in duty; and the dark curse of Hitler will be lifted from our age.[85]

American reporters documented the devastating costs of war as the rain of bombs on Britain's cities and countryside destroyed homes, businesses, and government offices, killing hundreds of civilians and combatants – the "unknown warriors" in Churchill's words – with indiscriminate cruelty. In summer and fall 1940, U.S. journalists gained widespread notoriety as they told the war stories that helped to shape the American public's response to the "European" and "Asian" wars and as they defined what was at stake for humanity depending on whether the Allied or Axis Powers prevailed.[86] Like other American war reporters, mostly men and a few independent and courageous women, Kirkpatrick put herself in the line of fire, lying in the fields atop the cliffs of Dover to feel the earth shake and hear the roar of the swarm of German planes flying in low to drop their bombs over London.[87] One of Kirkpatrick's colleagues, Vincent Sheehan, wrote about an instance when he observed Kirkpatrick's daring exploits, saying she "outmanned" the male reporters on the scene:

> Helen Kirkpatrick of the *Chicago Daily News*, a tall, slender girl with a humorous glint in her eyes, is the only other American woman (besides Virginian Cowles – war correspondent in Europe since Spanish Civil War) who does this bomb-dodging work. At one moment this week on the cliffs, when all hell was breaking loose, every man in sight had taken some sort of cover under projecting roofs or trees but Virginia and Helen were lying out on a meadow flat on their backs counting aeroplanes.[88]

Kirkpatrick took risks willingly in order to describe in vivid detail the sights and sounds and feel of war and share the immediacy of the experience with her readers:[89]

> Germany's *blitzkrieg* on Great Britain appears to have begun in earnest during the end of last week, culminating in an all-day attack yesterday in which about 400 German bombers hurtled through the skies all along Britain's coast.
>
> Sixty-one German planes are known to have been shot down, while 26 British Spitfires were lost in their efforts to drive off the Nazis. The main battle raged around Dover and farther southwest, at Fortland and Weymouth, but the Germans covered a wide area, even taking in Wales.
>
> The sky in almost every part of southern England yesterday was alive with planes – German British and the noise in some parts was almost deafening. It was a perfect day for a raid, with a fairly high wind and masses of clouds and patches, here and there, of a blue sky. ...[90]

The air battles, Kirkpatrick noted, felt unreal, like watching a prize fight in the air.[91] However, Kirkpatrick's firsthand experiences of air raids in London reported to *Chicago Daily News* readers[92] were all too real. She later recalled the raids being both "scary and fascinating":

> I went down river with the fire brigade during the bombing of the docks and the huge fires down there. That was scary and fascinating. These two young officers who were in charge of the river part of the fire brigade – one of them said as we got down there, he said, "You know, last night I almost struck my head as I was getting out and I rather wish that I had and could have passed out and then I wouldn't have had to go and cope with it." Because it was monstrous. It was so enormous. I remember getting home that night, and I lived out in the West End, just beyond Hyde Park Corner, and I could have read a newspaper by the light of the fire, and it was way down at the docks. It lit the whole of London. And, of course, they used that to guide planes in and drop more bombs. It was pretty bad.[93]

Kirkpatrick shared heart-rending stories to convey the human consequences of the indiscriminate bombing campaigns that flattened large sections of the city and targeted London's citizens and to build sympathy for Britain among her fellow Americans. Kirkpatrick's reporting gave names to the "unknown warriors," such as "Nurse Thomas" who was trapped in her room in her collapsed apartment building, "pinned in her bed forty feet above a London street":

> Throughout the day, from the early hours of the morning, even before the Nazis had left, the six men working from the top to hoist the beams and bricks, while others tried to burrow through the shaky and dangerous wall. They managed to get a tube through, and a matron reached for the nurse's arm to give her morphine. They could hear her voice telling them not to bother about her, but to get her four companions in the next room, whom she did not know were already dead.
>
> Working madly against time and the inevitable nightly visit of the Nazi planes, the men did not take time off even for food, and when I was there in mid-afternoon, they thought they would succeed in a few hours. As they lifted a big beam off the girl, allowing the doctor to crawl into her, the shrieking sirens gave her the last shock she could stand.[94]

At times, the unbelievable absurdity of the situations she witnessed triggered her wry, self-deprecating humour:

> Next to my house is a stable, most of the inmates have been called up for service in the army, but three remain. So, we moved into a box stall of fighting horses – seven of us who live in the mews houses – each of us with our sleeping accommodation. Mine consisted of two easy chairs which, with a blanket, made an excellent bed.
>
> It seemed strange to emerge from a West End house, clad in dressing gown and woollen stockings, with a blanket over the arm, and enter a stable for the night, but it looks as if that might become routine procedure. Already bombers had been overhead for about four hours, and the crump of bombs could be heard in the various districts of London, while our guns let go

occasionally. From that time, to the all-clear in the early dawn, I heard little more.[95]

For the most part, the British government welcomed the vivid and detailed reports on the war that the Americans shared with their newspaper readers and radio audiences. In some instances, though, the government's desire to control sensitive information and prevent its publication clashed with reporters' desires to share war news; this was the case in one incident involving Helen Kirkpatrick. Churchill believed that Kirkpatrick had learned some classified information about Vichy government operations at a dinner that he had hosted for Eve Curie, daughter of the physicist Marie Curie, at one of the British great houses outside London in fall 1940. When he heard that Kirkpatrick published the information in the *Chicago Daily News*, Churchill wrote to Foreign Secretary Anthony Eden: "Miss Helen Kirkpatrick has betrayed the confidence for journalistic profit. Both these women should be questioned by MI5 at the earliest moment, and their explanations obtained." And, Churchill continued: "It is very undesirable to have a person of this kind scouting about private houses for copy regardless of British interests."[96] The incident also upset Kirkpatrick, who recalled it years later in an oral history interview:

> I never wrote anything that I had heard on a social occasion at someone's house, in spite of what Mr. Churchill said. That, to me, was unethical. Or if it was something that I thought was important, then I would try to get at it from another source. And I also never wrote anything that was told us off the record – and there were occasions when that happened – and I always made every attempt to see that whatever I wrote was accurate as best one could. ... I liked the British. I thought they were admirable. I couldn't stand the Nazis or the Fascists. I thought they were a menace and that if they conquered the whole of Europe that we would be the next. ... from back at the time Hitler came to power it was clear to me that this was going to be a fight to the end.[97]

Kirkpatrick also recalled that the British people "adored Churchill," as she admired him, too.[98] In part, this was because Winston Churchill put himself in the line of fire and displayed his manly courage for all to see. He monitored the "ferocious" air battles from RAF command centers, and strode through the streets of London in the aftermath of the battles to survey the damage and show his solidarity with the British people who lost so much in the Blitz – the fifty-seven straight nights of German bombardment of the nation's capital that began September 7. Britons lost their sons and daughters who served the nation's military, as well as their neighbors and relatives who died in their homes or in the underground shelters that could not always protect them from harm.[99] Churchill publicly praised the

London citizens, the heroic air raid wardens, and the fire brigades, rallying the people's resolve and defining Britain's national character:

> These cruel, wanton, indiscriminate bombings of London are, of course, a part of Hitler's invasion plans. He hopes, by killing large numbers of civilians, and women and children, that he will terrorise and cow the people of this mighty imperial city, and make them a burden and an anxiety to the Government and thus distract our attention unduly from the ferocious onslaught he is preparing. Little does he know the spirit of the British nation, or the tough fibre of the Londoners, whose forbears played a leading part in the establishment of Parliamentary institutions and who have been bred to value freedom far above their lives. This wicked man, the repository and embodiment of many forms of soul-destroying hatred, this monstrous product of former wrongs and shame, has now resolved to try to break our famous island race by a process of indiscriminate slaughter and destruction. What he has done is to kindle a fire in British hearts, here and all over the world, which will glow long after all traces of the conflagration he has caused in London have been removed.[100]

Soon after the London Blitz began, on September 17, Adolf Hitler postponed Germany's plans to invade England, the Nazis' "Operation Sea Lion."[101] Nonetheless, the nightly bombing went on for another forty-seven days. Less frequent but equally devastating bombing of London continued throughout 1940 and 1941. During the Blitz, 27,000 bombs and incendiaries were dropped on London and more than 40,000 people, including an estimated 5,000 children, were killed.[102] Witnessing the bitter attacks and their aftermath, de Valera's Minister in London, John Dulanty, reported back to Joseph Walshe that:

> The British press is eloquent upon the "chin-up" attitude of the people. My own observation confirms this. ... Tired, hungry and worried, the people show miraculous calm – cheerful acceptance of things which they are powerless to alter. In their morning journeys you can see listlessness and weariness borne of sleepless nights but you hear no "grousing". Whether this will continue in the winter and possible epidemics of influenza remains to be seen. As yet, the food distribution is good, there are no queues, and leaving out of account the East End, which is horror piled on horror, the social system appears to work more or less normally.[103]

De Valera's government feared that a German invasion of Ireland was coming in August and September 1940, too. The Germans had drawn up plans for "Operation *Grün*" to land German troops along the southeastern Irish coast and establish air bases for the *Luftwaffe*, as part of the planned Sea Lion offensive.[104] When German planes bombed Ireland's County Wexford on August 25, killing three young girls, Irish fears escalated. David Gray reported to Roosevelt that de Valera didn't want "to tangle with Hitler and is soft pedalling indignation."[105] The Irish government still walked a careful line by issuing a mild but "formal" protest that allowed the German government to deny that any attack or intimidation were intentional.[106]

In the meantime, Roosevelt focused on his re-election campaign while also walking a careful line between aiding Britain and placating isolationist critics among the American people, from his political rivals, and even from within his own administration. U.S. Ambassador to Britain Joseph Kennedy, for example, criticized the "destroyers for bases" deal and other U.S. aid to Britain that moved the United States away from its neutral status and closer to active belligerency than he considered prudent. Roosevelt worried that Kennedy could turn Irish American voters away from him if Kennedy endorsed FDR's Republican Party opponent Wendell Willkie.[107] With Kennedy and his former Minister to Ireland John Cudahy, as well as his Republican rivals in Congress, mobilizing Irish American voters who opposed active U.S. involvement in the war, Roosevelt declared in a campaign speech in Boston in September, "I have said this before … but I shall say it again and again and again, your boys are not going to be sent into any foreign wars."[108] FDR made this pledge even as he ordered a peacetime draft, following up his promise of "no American soldiers deployed to fight in foreign wars" with the words: "They [America's "boys"] are going into training to form a force so strong that by its very existence, it will keep the threat of war away from our own shores."[109] The peacetime draft in fact trained "massive numbers of troops" and, by "December 1941, the War Department had on its roster thirty-six divisions, numbering some 1.65 million men."[110] Nonetheless, in the fall 1940 run-up to the election, Roosevelt convinced Americans of the sincerity of his pledge to keep the country out of the war. He convinced Joseph Kennedy as well, gaining Kennedy's endorsement for his presidential bid. In November, voters "overwhelmingly" re-elected Roosevelt. FDR won 55 percent of the popular vote and 449 electoral votes.[111] Following his victory at the polls, Roosevelt replaced Kennedy as Ambassador to Britain with John Gilbert Winant, another strong anti-fascist Anglophile who, after his arrival in London in March 1941, quickly won the friendship of Winston Churchill and his wife Clementine.[112]

Roosevelt's electoral victory thrilled Winston Churchill.[113] Churchill believed that Anglo-American relations would be strengthened and that his personal relationship with Roosevelt would move into a new, more intimate phase; he expressed these views in a warm note of congratulations to FDR.[114] Now that Roosevelt's re-election was no longer in danger of being sabotaged by angry Irish-American voters,[115] Churchill also felt emboldened to once again publicly and harshly criticize de Valera's government for denying Britain the use of its ports and for allowing German U-boats to patrol freely in Irish coastal waters.[116] Churchill's effusive letter to Roosevelt, however, fell flat, and he never received a reply or even an acknowledgment from Roosevelt.[117] Moreover, de Valera pushed back hard against Churchill's provocations with a defiant declaration in the Dáil:

> It is a lie to say that German submarines or any other submarines are being supplied with fuel or provisions on our coasts. A most extreme system of coast observation has been established here since the war. I say it is a lie, and I say further that it is known as a fabrication by the British Government itself. Having said that I now come to the question of our ports. There can be no question of the handing over of these ports so long as this State remains neutral. They are ours. They are within our sovereignty.[118]

De Valera also dispatched his Minister in Washington, Robert Brennan, to the State Department to deny Churchill's charges that Ireland was aiding the Germans and to gain U.S. government support for Ireland's neutrality policy, established "to preserve its independence, its peace and its democratic institutions."[119] The outcome of the diplomatic brouhaha soon became clear to all parties: Britain would never gain access to the Irish ports unless they were occupied by force, and any British occupation would likely cause civil war within Ireland and international war with Britain.[120] Roosevelt remained on the sidelines throughout the post-election Anglo-Irish controversy, giving David Gray free rein to remind de Valera that there were costs associated with neutrality in terms of Ireland's deteriorating moral standing in the world and in worsening relations with the United States, if not other more tangible consequences if Germany attacked Ireland.[121]

Although Churchill was still floating proposals to pressure Ireland into opening the ports to the British Navy,[122] he was making a separate case with Roosevelt that the United States' continued neutrality also came at great cost to Britain. On December 7, Churchill sent Roosevelt a long telegram detailing the precarious state of Britain's military forces, to make clear the threats to Britain's national survival. German submarines were cutting off supply lines from North America across the Atlantic, and Britain could no longer pay for these critically needed arms, artillery, tanks, aircraft, and ammunition with its dwindling cash reserves, in any case. These factors were crippling Britain's abilities to fight on against the fascist forces in Mediterranean and East Asian theaters of war. Churchill pleaded for relief from the Cash and Carry restrictions of the U.S. Neutrality Laws, urging Roosevelt to extend credit so that Britain could buy the quantities of U.S. weapons, aircraft, and war materials that it desperately needed. He also called on Roosevelt to order U.S. naval convoys to protect the supply ships as they crossed the Atlantic. Again, Churchill asked FDR to put pressure on de Valera to open Irish naval ports to British ships so that they could better defend the North Atlantic approaches from German submarine warfare.[123] Justifying his big ask, Churchill wrote "… it seems to me that the vast majority of American citizens have recorded their conviction that the safety of the United States as well as the future of our two democracies and the kind of civilization for which they both stand are bound up with the survival and independence of the British Commonwealth of Nations."[124] Churchill continued his pitch: "Even if the United States was our Ally instead of our friend and indispensable partner we should not ask for a large American expeditionary army."[125] Rather, Churchill wanted an extension of U.S. credit to buy more weapons, more military equipment and aircraft, and armed U.S. convoys to escort these necessary infusions of aid across the Atlantic.

Franklin Roosevelt, accompanied by his close friend and political adviser Harry Hopkins, was on a post-election cruise recovering his health when he received Churchill's long telegram – almost 4,000 words long. Reportedly, Roosevelt sat alone on the ship's deck reading and rereading Churchill's appeal. When he returned to Washington, he held a press conference on December 17 and introduced his idea for a lifeline to Britain that would become the "Lend–Lease" legislation Congress adopted in March 1941. In folksy, non-threatening terms, Roosevelt explained his plans to aid Britain, making the analogy that when your neighbor's house is on fire, you lend him your garden hose: "Now what do I do? I don't say to him, 'Neighbour, my garden hose cost me fifteen dollars, now you have to pay me fifteen dollars for it.' No! I don't want fifteen dollars. I want my garden hose back after the fire is over. What I am trying to do is eliminate the dollar sign, and that is something new … get rid of the foolish old dollar sign."[126] Hopkins recalled that FDR hadn't thought through any concrete details for the Lend-Lease program in December: "He didn't seem to have any clear idea how it could be done legally. But there wasn't a doubt in his mind that he'd find a way to do it."[127]

Roosevelt also spoke to the nation in a radio address on December 29, calling on the United States to redefine its purpose, to become the "great arsenal of democracy," to produce the weapons that could defeat the fascist powers that were united in "a program aimed at world control," which included "ultimate action against the United States." Roosevelt debunked isolationist delusions that the United States could escape the war with declarations of neutrality or through its geographic separation from the European war zones. FDR warned:

> The experience of the past two years has proven beyond doubt that no nation can appease the Nazis. No man can tame a tiger into a kitten by stroking it.

> There can be no appeasement with ruthlessness. There can be no reasoning with an incendiary bomb. We know now that a nation can have peace with the Nazis only at the price of total surrender.

Britain and its allies were at war with the "unholy alliance" of Axis Powers. The British were calling on the United States to provide the "implements of war," not American soldiers – "no demand for sending an American expeditionary force outside of our own borders." But the vast quantity of materials the Allies needed could not be supplied if the U.S. industries and American workers followed "business as usual." And so, Roosevelt called on America to "be the great arsenal of democracy. For this is an emergency as serious as war itself. We must apply ourselves to the task with the same resolution, the same sense of urgency, the same spirit of patriotism and sacrifice as we would show were we at war."[128]

Roosevelt rallied the nation with his December 29 address, and he continued his campaign to aid Britain in its anti-fascist fight in his January 1941 addresses to Congress and to the American people. In language that was "less ornate" than that of Winston Churchill[129] but in ways that were just as effective, Roosevelt explained the stakes of war, identifying America's friends and defining its enemies to mobilize the collective response of the wartime generation. Roosevelt's words would also shape the collective memories of the war for succeeding generations of American people.[130]

Notes

1. Winston Churchill, Speech to the House of Commons, "Their Finest Hour," 18 June 1940 (The International Churchill Society, 2020), https://winstonchurchill.org/resources/speeches/1940-the-finest-hour/their-finest-hour/ (accessed 3 December 2020).
2. Confidential Report from William Warnock to Joseph P. Walshe, 28 May 1940, Doc. No. 185 NAI DFA 219/4, *Documents on Irish Foreign Policy* vol. VI, 1939–1941.
3. Winston Churchill, "Be Ye Men of Valor," A Radio Address, 19 May 1940, in Winston Churchill, *Into Battle, 1941* (RosettaBooks, 2013).
4. Washington Embassy Confidential Reports from Robert Brennan to Joseph P. Walshe, 21 May 1940, Doc. No. 181 NAI DFA, *Documents on Irish Foreign Policy* vol. VI, 1939–1941.
5. Franklin Roosevelt, "Fireside Chat 15: On National Defense," 26 May 1940, Presidential Speeches, Franklin D. Roosevelt Presidency (University of Virginia Miller Center, 2019), https://millercenter.org/the-presidency/presidential-speeches/may-26–1940-fireside-chat-15-national-defense (accessed 3 December 2020).

"Unstoppable" Germany, "unbeatable" Britain   101

6 Nicholas J. Cull, quoting Joseph Kennedy to U.S. Secretary of State Cordell Hull, in *Selling War: The British Propaganda Campaign Against American 'Neutrality' in World War II* (Oxford: Oxford University Press, 1996), 70.

7 Winston Churchill, "Dunkirk," A Speech delivered in the House of Commons, 4 June 1940, in Churchill, *Into Battle, 1941*, 199–200. Churchill noted that the evacuation of Dunkirk involved "the Royal Navy, [which] with the willing help of countless merchant seamen, strained every nerve to embark the British and Allied troops; 220 light warships and 650 other vessels were engaged," as well as the Royal Air Force that "engaged the main strength of the German Air Force, and inflicted upon them losses of at least four to one."

8 Cull, *Selling War*, 71.

9 *Ibid.*, 71, Cull quoting a contemporary *New York Times* editorial.

10 Numbers of soldiers rescued vary in sources. See Robert Dallek, *Franklin D. Roosevelt: A Political Life* (New York: Penguin, 2017), 378, who reported that "220,000 British troops and another 120,000 French infantry" were recovered from Dunkirk beach on June 4, 1940.

11 Jean Edward Smith, *FDR* (New York: Random House, 2008), 447.

12 Brian Girvin, *The Emergency: Neutral Ireland 1939–45* (London: Pan Macmillan, 2007), 107.

13 Carlo D'Este, *Warlord: A Life of Winston Churchill at War, 1874–1945* (New York: HarperCollins, 2008), 445. D'Este includes an account related by the commanding officer of the British "Home Guard," the volunteer force that formed to resist a German invasion of the home island. "Lord Willis" described the effect of Churchill's "Dunkirk" speech: "You could almost measure it. We would have gone down to the beach at the Germans and beat them with broom-handles. Such was the magic effect of Churchill. It was thrilling. It was absolutely thrilling. Before we'd been ambling along under Chamberlain, this funny old man, who seemed to us to represent a past age, and here suddenly was a man talking with vigour and energy and courage. It was remarkable. The effect on morale was unbelievable."

14 Churchill, "Dunkirk," in Churchill, *Into Battle, 1941*, 203–204.

15 David Gray (unpublished memoir), *Behind the Emerald Curtain*, in *A Yankee in de Valera's Ireland*, ed. Paul Bew (Dublin: Royal Irish Academy, 2012), 180–181.

16 *Ibid.*

17 John P. Duggan, *Herr Hempel and the German Legation in Dublin, 1937–1945* (Dublin: Irish Academic Press, 2003), 92.

18 Cull, *Selling War*, 72.

19 Stephen Held was the son of an Irish mother and German father who sympathized with the IRA.

20 T. Ryle Dwyer, *Irish Neutrality and the USA, 1939–47* (Dublin: Gill & Macmillan, 1977), 70. The spy was later identified as Hermann Goertz, who remained at large in Ireland until November 1941, when he was captured and imprisoned for the duration of the war.

21 Carolle J. Carter, *The Shamrock and the Swastika: German Espionage in Ireland in World War II* (Palo Alto, CA: Pacific Books, 1977), 149.
22 David McCullagh, *De Valera: Rule*, vol. II, *1932–1972* (Dublin: Gill Books, 2018), 189: A June MI6 report to the British Cabinet predicted that the Germans were preparing an attack on Southern Ireland and "some 2000 German troops could probably capture the whole country."
23 Girvin, *The Emergency*, 96. See also Clair Wills, *That Neutral Island: A Cultural History of Ireland During the Second World War* (London: Faber & Faber, 2007), 156; T. Ryle Dwyer, *Behind the Green Curtain: Ireland's Phoney Neutrality During World War II* (Dublin: Gill & Macmillan, 2009), 63–65.
24 Girvin, *The Emergency*, 159–160; Eunan O'Halpin, *Defending Ireland: The Irish State and Its Enemies Since 1922* (New York: Oxford University Press, 2000), 204, 229–230, 243. See also Mark M. Hull, "A Tale of German Espionage in Wartime Ireland," in *Ireland in World War Two: Neutrality and Survival*, ed. Dermot Keogh and Mervyn O'Driscoll (Cork: Mercier Press, 2004), 92: "espionage operations were doomed to failure because the Germans failed to take even elementary steps to ensure a minimum level of success. This effectively threw the agents to the winds of chance, a dangerous prospect considering the low quality of the personnel deployed on the missions. This combination of poor agent selection, lack of knowledge and a non-functioning support system made attainment of even minimal goals impossible. By contrast, Britain and Ireland's highly efficient counter espionage organization helped make this into one of the great mismatches in espionage history – a happy result in the larger war against Hitler's Germany."
25 Dwyer, *Irish Neutrality and the USA*, 71; Girvin, *The Emergency*, 96.
26 The Minister in Eire [Hempel] to the Foreign Ministry, 24 May 1940, Doc. 314, *Documents on German Foreign Policy, 1918–1945*, vol. 9, "The War Years, March 18–June 22, 1940," (Washington, DC: Government Printing Office, 1956).
27 The Minister in Eire [Hempel] to the Foreign Ministry, 23 May 1940, Doc. 310 and 17 June 1940, Doc. 473, *Documents on German Foreign Policy, 1918–1945*, vol. 9.
28 Document German Foreign Ministry Director of the Political Department [Woermann] to the Minister in Eire [Hempel], 15 June 1940, quoted in Robert Fisk, *In Time of War: Ireland, Ulster and the Price of Neutrality, 1939–1945* (London: Andre Deutsch, 1983), 303.
29 Secretary's Files P3 Memorandum from Joseph P. Walshe to Eamon de Valera, 17 June 1940, Doc. No. 191 NAI DFA, *Documents on Irish Foreign Policy* vol. VI, 1939–1941.
30 Secretary's Files A2 Memorandum from Joseph P. Walshe to Eamon de Valera, 21 June 1940, Doc. No. 196 NAI DFA, *Documents on Irish Foreign Policy* vol. VI, 1939–1941: "Britain's defeat has been placed beyond all doubt … Neither time nor gold can beat Germany." See also Memorandum Joseph P. Walshe to Eamon de Valera, 11 July 1940, Doc. No. 221 NAI DFA Secretary's Files A2, *Documents on Irish Foreign Policy* vol. VI, 1939–1941: "England is

already conquered. That is also an elementary fact for everyone who has not allowed himself to be overcome by Britain's belief in her permanent invincibility. The moment Germany and Russia (even without Italy and Japan) proposed to act together against England, her fate was sealed. To the sane looker-on, Chamberlain's announcement of England's declaration of war on Germany in his radio talk on 3rd September 1939, sounded the death knell of the British Empire."

31 Fisk, *In Time of War*, 184: Fisk quoting Malcolm MacDonald's recollections of negotiations with de Valera's government in June 1940, offering to trade an end to partition for an Irish alliance with Britain: "Aiken felt fairly certain that there would be an Axis victory. ... When he was on his own, Dev would say: 'My Cabinet won't agree with me.' I think he meant Aiken, who was very strong in the belief that Britain would lose." See also McCullagh, *De Valera*, 194.

32 Aengus Nolan quoting Joseph Walshe, "'A Most Heavy and Grievous Burden': Joseph Walshe and the Establishment of Sustainable Neutrality, 1940," in *Ireland in World War Two: Neutrality and Survival* ed. Dermot Keogh and Mervyn O'Driscoll (Cork: Mercier Press, 2004), 127. See also Girvin, *The Emergency*, 124–126.

33 Nolan, "A Most Heavy and Grievous Burden," 135. See also McCullagh, *De Valera*, 186: "Towards the end of May 1940 [May 23–24] Walshe and the director of intelligence Colonel Liam Archer travelled to London for secret discussions on military cooperation in the event of a German attack." See also Francis M. Carroll, "Ireland Among the Nations of the Earth: Ireland's Foreign Relations from 1923–1949," *Irish Studies* (2016), 14.

34 McCullagh, *De Valera*, 188. Neville Chamberlain to Eamon de Valera, 12 June 1940, P150/2548, Eamon de Valera Papers (on microfilm), University College Dublin (hereafter: EdV Papers, UCD).

35 Paul Bew, *Churchill and Ireland* (Oxford: Oxford University Press, 2016), 147.

36 Tim Pat Coogan, *Eamon de Valera: The Man Who Was Ireland* (New York: HarperCollins, 1993), 520.

37 Girvin, *The Emergency*, 97.

38 Dwyer, *Behind the Green Curtain*, 59.

39 U.S. Minister to Ireland David Gray to Franklin Roosevelt, 6 June 1940, box 40, President's Secretary's Files: Ireland 1940, Franklin Delano Roosevelt Papers, Franklin Roosevelt Presidential Library, Hyde park, NY (hereafter: FDR Papers).

40 Fisk, *In Time of War*, 167. See also Anthony J. Jordan, *Churchill: A Founder of Modern Ireland* (Dublin: Westport Books, 1995), 174.

41 Gill Plain, *John Mills and British Cinema: Masculinity, Identity and Nation* (Edinburgh: Edinburgh University Press, 2006), 1–2, 43.

42 Résumé of Talks between Taoiseach and Mr. Malcolm MacDonald, 28 June 1940 [on talks that took place June 17, 21, 26, and 27], P150/2594, EdV Papers, UCD. See also, for MacDonald's account of the June 17 meeting: Notes of a conversation between Eamon de Valera and Malcolm MacDonald,

17 June 1940, Doc. No. 193 TNA PREM 3/131/1, *Documents on Irish Foreign Policy* vol. VI, 1939–1941.
43 Notes of a conversation between Eamon de Valera and Malcolm MacDonald, 23 June 1940, Doc. No. 198 TNA PREM 3/131/1, *Documents on Irish Foreign Policy* vol. VI, 1939–1941.
44 Résumé of Talks between Taoiseach and Mr. Malcolm MacDonald, 28 June 1940, P150/2594, EdV Papers, UCD. See also Fisk, *In Time of War*, 163–169.
45 Plain, *John Mills and British Cinema*, 72, quoting Stephen Frosh, *Sexual Difference: Masculinity and Psychoanalysis* (London: Routledge, 1994), 103.
46 Fisk, *In Time of War*, 169. See also Notes of a conversation between Eamon de Valera and Malcolm MacDonald, 23 June 1940, Doc. No. 198 TNA PREM 3/131/1, *Documents on Irish Foreign Policy* vol. VI, 1939–1941.
47 Bew, *Churchill and Ireland*, 147.
48 Jordan, *Churchill*, 174.
49 Fisk, *In Time of War*, 177, 187.
50 MacDonald quoted in Bew, "Introduction," *A Yankee in De Valera's Ireland*, xxvii. The quote also appears in Fisk, *In Time of War*, 176.
51 MacDonald quoted in Fisk, *In Time of War*, 174. Girvin, *The Emergency*, 134–135: Chamberlain also asserted that de Valera based his rejection of the British proposals on the belief that Britain would be defeated.
52 Duggan, *Herr Hempel*, 102.
53 McCullagh, *De Valera*, 194: quoting a memo from Joseph Walshe to de Valera, dated 1 July 1940.
54 Letter from Eamon de Valera to Neville Chamberlain, 4 July 1940, Doc. No. 213 UCPDA P150/2548, *Documents on Irish Foreign Policy* vol. VI, 1939–1941.
55 "Neutrality of Eire, Mr. De Valera States Nation's Attitude," *Irish Independent*, July 9, 1940: 8; Harold Denny, "The National Position, Taoiseach Interviewed," *New York Times* (9 July 1940), P150/2596, EdV Papers, UCD.
56 U.S. Minister to Ireland David Gray to Franklin Roosevelt, 28 June 1940, box 40, President's Secretary's Files: Ireland, 1940, FDR Papers.
57 Dwyer, *Irish Neutrality and the USA*, 59.
58 David Gray to Franklin Roosevelt, 19 June 1940, box 40, President's Secretary's Files: Ireland 1940, FDR Papers. David Gray quoting from letter to Franklin Roosevelt, 22 June 1940, in Gray, *Behind the Emerald Curtain*, 212–213, 215. See also Girvin, *The Emergency*, 183–185.
59 U.S. Minister to Ireland David Gray to Franklin Roosevelt, 28 June 1940, box 40, President's Secretary's Files: Ireland 1940, FDR Papers. See also Dwyer, *Irish Neutrality and the USA*, 63, 79–80; John Day Tully, *Ireland and Irish Americans 1932–1945: The Search for Identity* (Dublin: Irish Academic Press, 2010), 87–88; McCullagh, *De Valera*, 187–188.
60 Gray, *Behind the Emerald Curtain*, 181–182.
61 Franklin Roosevelt to David Gray, 19 June 1940, box 3, Coll. 03082 David Gray Papers, 1857–1960, University of Wyoming American Heritage Center, Laramie Wyoming (hereafter: Gray Papers, AHC).

62 Interview with Helen Kirkpatrick Milbank by Anne Kasper, Women in Journalism oral history project of the Washington Press Club Foundation, April 3–5, 1990, p. 52, in the Oral History Collection of Columbia University and other repositories.
63 Notes of a conversation between Eamon de Valera and Malcolm MacDonald, 17 June 1940, Doc. No. 193 TNA PREM 3/131/1, *Documents on Irish Foreign Policy* vol. VI, 1939–1941.
64 Joseph Walshe to David Gray, *c.* July–August 1940, box 3, Gray Papers, AHC. Joseph Walshe also gave David Gray a memorandum with excerpts of U.S. newspaper stories critical of Ireland's neutrality or that spread rumors about German activities in Eire, including excerpts from two stories published in the *Chicago Daily News* and republished in the *New York Post* and *Boston Evening Transcript* that were written by Kirkpatrick.
65 Code telegram from Joseph P. Walshe to Robert Brennan (Personal) (Most Secret), 21 July 1940, Doc. No. 234 NAI DFA Secretary's Files P2, *Documents on Irish Foreign Policy* vol. VI, 1939–1941: "Kirkpatrick and [Virginia] Cowles reported to be in this country again. Could you ask friends in New York, Chicago and San Francisco to form small strong committees to watch Press and Radio which are apparently so bad that Ministry of Information officials London are advising their Government that America is ready to accept British reoccupation of Ireland? ... Could you inspire all Irish papers to launch campaign against pro-British American journalists who are misleading American public about Ireland and preparing opinion for a British invasion of Ireland? ..."
66 Kirkpatrick, "Nazi 'Blitz' to Hit Eire Next, Belief," *Chicago Daily News* (12 June 1940), box 12, and also "German Plans for 'Victory' Startle Irish," *Chicago Daily News* (5 June 1949), box 12; "Situation in Eire Continues to be Very Serious," *Chicago Daily News* (6 June 1940), box 12, Helen Paull Kirkpatrick Papers, CA-MS-01132, Sophia Smith Collection, Northampton, Massachusetts (hereafter: HPK Papers).
67 David Gray to Franklin Roosevelt, 14 August 1940, box 3, Gray Papers, AHC.
68 Interview with Kirkpatrick by Kasper, Women in Journalism oral history project, 53.
69 Jordan, *Churchill*, 176.
70 Girvin, *The Emergency*, 107.
71 Jon Meacham, *Franklin and Winston: An Intimate Portrait of an Epic Friendship* (New York: Random House, 2004), 60.
72 Smith, *FDR*, 449.
73 Washington Embassy Confidential Report from Robert Brennan to Joseph P. Walshe, 11 June 1940, Doc. No. 189 NAI DFA, *Documents on Irish Foreign Policy* vol. VI, 1939–1941.
74 "US War Secret for Allies?" *Irish Press* (12 June 1940).
75 Meacham, *Franklin and Winston*, 61–63.
76 Warren F. Kimball, ed., *Churchill and Roosevelt, The Complete Correspondence*, vol. 1, *Alliance Emerging, October 1933–November 1942* (Princeton, NJ: Princeton University Press, 1984), 45; Tully, *Ireland and Irish Americans*, 87.

77 Blanche Wiesen Cook, *Eleanor Roosevelt: The War Years and After*, vol. 3: *1939–1962* (New York: Viking, 2016), 280; Smith, *FDR*, 449; David Kaiser, *No End Save Victory: How FDR Led the Nation into War* (New York: Basic Books, 2014), 19.
78 Erik Larson, *The Splendid and the Vile: A Saga of Churchill, Family, and Defiance during the Blitz* (New York: Crown, 2020), 122–123.
79 Winston Churchill, "The Tragedy of the French Fleet," A Speech delivered in the House of Commons, 4 July 1940, in Churchill, *Into Battle, 1941*, 218–223.
80 D'Este, *Warlord*, 471.
81 Smith, *FDR*, 468.
82 Dallek, *Franklin D. Roosevelt: A Political Life*, 391; Kaiser, *No End Save Victory*, 50, 76, 392. See also Dwyer, *Irish Neutrality and the USA*, 32.
83 D'Este, *Warlord*, 466–467.
84 Cull, *Selling War*, 98–100, 104; Lynne Olson, *Citizens of London: The Americans Who Stood with Britain in Its Darkest, Finest Hour* (London: Random House, 2011), 43, 50.
85 Winston Churchill, "Alone in the Breach," radio broadcast, 14 July 1940.
86 See Frederick S. Voss, *Reporting the War: The Journalistic Coverage of World War II* (Washington, DC: Smithsonian Institution Press, 1994).
87 Interview with Kirkpatrick by Kasper, Women in Journalism oral history project, 51.
88 Vincent Sheehan, "Covering Hell's Corner: While Bombers Hurl their Deadly Loads, Correspondents Dig In," *Current History*, 22 October 1940: 18–20.
89 Nancy Caldwell Sorel, *The Women Who Wrote the War* (New York: Arcade Publishing, 1999), 96–97.
90 Helen Kirkpatrick, "Mass Attacks Launch Blitz in Earnest, Observer Writes," *Chicago Daily News* (12 August 1940), box 3, HPK Papers.
91 Helen Kirkpatrick, "Air War Like a Prize Fight, Observer Finds," *Chicago Daily News* (16 August 1940), box 3, HPK Papers.
92 Helen Kirkpatrick, "London Stands, to Surprise of Alarmed Writer," *Chicago Daily News* (9 September 1940), box 3, HPK Papers; "Heart of London Gets Full Brunt of Nazi Attacks," *Chicago Daily News* (11 September 1940), box 2, HPK Papers.
93 Interview with Kirkpatrick by Kasper, Women in Journalism oral history project, 48.
94 Helen Kirkpatrick, "Signal of New Raid Kills Trapped Girl," *Chicago Daily News* (10 September 1940), box 2, HPK Papers.
95 Helen Kirkpatrick, "A Good Nap, Even in a Barn, A Treat During Air Raids: Writer Moves in on Stall of Fighting Horses for a Night of Rest," *Chicago Daily News* (10 September 1940), box 2, HPK Papers.
96 Larson, *The Splendid and the Vile*, 341–342.
97 Interview with Kirkpatrick by Kasper, Women in Journalism oral history project, 57–58.
98 Ibid.
99 Cook, *Eleanor Roosevelt*, 314.

"Unstoppable" Germany, "unbeatable" Britain 107

100 Winston Churchill, "Every Man to His Post," An Address Broadcast 11 September 1940, in Churchill, *Into Battle, 1941*, 249.
101 Duggan, *Herr Hempel*, 113; Kaiser, *No End Save Victory*, 87.
102 D'Este, *Warlord*, 477; Meacham, *Franklin and Winston*, 73.
103 Confidential report from John W. Dulanty to Joseph P. Walshe, 5 October 1940, Doc. No. 308 NAI DFA 219/2A, *Documents on Irish Foreign Policy* vol. VI, 1939–1941.
104 Fisk, *In Time of War*, 189–193; Duggan, *Herr Hempel*, 116.
105 U.S. Minister to Ireland David Gray to Franklin Roosevelt, 25 August 1940, box 40, President's Secretary's File: Ireland 1940, FDR Papers.
106 Telegram from External Affairs (via Geneva) to William Warnock (Berlin), 26 August 1940, Doc. No. 276 NAI DFA Secretary's Files P3; and Statement by External Affairs on the Campile Bombing, 8 October 1940, Doc. No. 309 NAI DFA 221/147, *Documents on Irish Foreign Policy* vol. VI, 1939–1941.
107 Dallek, *Franklin D. Roosevelt: A Political Life*, 395; Cook, *Eleanor Roosevelt*, 347.
108 Dwyer, *Irish Neutrality and the USA*, 34–36.
109 Cook, *Eleanor Roosevelt*, 332.
110 Lynne Olson, *Those Angry Days: Roosevelt, Lindbergh, and America's Fight Over World War II, 1939–1941* (New York: Random House, 2013), 219.
111 Kaiser, *No End Save Victory*, 109.
112 See Olson, *Citizens of London*; Cook, *Eleanor Roosevelt*, 390.
113 Winston Churchill, "We Will Never Cease to Strike," Speech Delivered in the Mansion House, 9 November 1940, in Churchill, *Into Battle, 1941*, 280.
114 Meacham, *Franklin and Winston*, 76.
115 McCullagh, *De Valera*, 199; Dwyer, *Irish Neutrality and the USA*, 85–86.
116 Raymond Daniell, "Churchill Sees Rising U-Boat Peril; Urges Ireland to Modify Neutrality: All Parties in Commons Back Plea for Bases," *New York Times* (6 November 1940); "U-Boats Peril 'Life of State', Churchill Says: Nation is Warned to Expect 'Heavier Attack' Next Year," *New York Times* (6 November 1940).
117 Meacham, *Franklin and Winston*, 77.
118 "Question of the Ports," de Valera's speech to the Dáil, 7 November 1940, in *Being a Selection of the Speeches of Eamon de Valera During the War (1939–1945)* (Dublin: McGill & Son, 1946), F P104/3808, Frank Aiken Papers (on microfilm) University College Dublin (hereafter: FA Papers, UCD).
119 Memorandum of Conversation [with Robert Brennan] by Under Secretary of State (Welles), and Addendum "The Irish Legation to the Department of State," 9 November 1940, Doc. 161, *Foreign Relations of the United States Diplomatic Papers* (hereafter: *FRUS*), 1940 vol. III (Washington, DC: US Government Printing Office, 1958).
120 The Minister in Ireland (Gray) to the Secretary of State (Hull). November 10, 1940, Doc. 162, *FRUS* 1940 vol. III. See also Elizabeth Bowen, *"Notes on Eire": Espionage Reports to Winston Churchill 1940–2*, 3rd ed., With a review of Irish Neutrality in World War 2 by Jack Lane and Brendan Clifford (Cork:

Aubane Historical Society, 2009), 36–38; "Bases Mean War, De Valera Insists: Even End of Irish Partition Would Not Sway Him, He Says, in Explaining Position," *New York Times* (11 November 1940).
121 Tully, *Ireland and Irish Americans*, 93; Paraphrase of a telegram dated 19 November 1940, received by the American Minister [Gray] from the United States Under-Secretary of State, P150/2604; and U.S. Minister David Gray to PM de Valera, 21 November 1940, P150/2589, EdV Papers, UCD; The Minister in Ireland (Gray) to the (Acting) Secretary of State (Welles), 24 November 1940, Document 166, *FRUS* 1940 vol. III.
122 McCullagh, *De Valera*, 203; Jordan, *Churchill*, 98–99.
123 Kaiser, *No End Save Victory*, 117–118.
124 Telegram, Churchill to Roosevelt, 7 December 1940, in Kimball, *Churchill and Roosevelt, The Complete Correspondence*, 102.
125 *Ibid.*, 103.
126 Smith, *FDR*, 485. See also Dallek, *Franklin D. Roosevelt: A Political Life*, 403–404; Kaiser, *No End Save Victory*, 118.
127 Smith, *FDR*, 484.
128 Franklin Delano Roosevelt, "The Great Arsenal of Democracy," delivered December 29, 1940, www.americanrhetoric.com/speeches/fdrarsenalofdemocracy.html (accessed 3 December 2020).
129 Meacham, *Franklin and Winston*, 78.
130 Smith, *FDR*, 487.

4

In pursuit of America's friendship, January to June 1941

Prime Minister Winston Churchill and Taoiseach Eamon de Valera each held a clear vision of what "America's friendship" meant to their nations in 1941. Their visions, however, were difficult to reconcile. To Churchill, America's friendship must be demonstrated through greatly increased quantities of war aid, which in the immediate term meant more weapons, ships, planes, tanks, and an extension of credit to pay for the materials. America's friendship also meant that the U.S. government, personified by Franklin Roosevelt, would condemn Britain's enemies and stand side by side with Britain, personified by Winston Churchill, in principled solidarity, proclaiming that the fight against the fascist powers was a fight *for* "civilization," "human dignity," "freedom," and "democratic values." To de Valera, America's friendship meant respect for Ireland's decision as a sovereign nation to stay out of the fight in what de Valera defined as the ongoing "imperialist war." De Valera sought America's friendship in the form of U.S. government pledges to defend Ireland's rights to remain neutral and to protect the Irish nation from an attack originating from *any* belligerent power. A friendly America would defend Ireland from either Germany or Britain, Axis or Allied Power, with equal strength and speed, with both military aid and proclamations of moral support for Ireland's sovereign rights and its sincere desire for peace.

As 1941 began, the version of American friendship on offer from President Franklin Roosevelt was much more closely aligned with Churchill's vision, and Roosevelt was ready to advocate energetically for aid to Britain in order "to save the American way of life."[1] Roosevelt defined the meaning of the war for the American people in terms that were reminiscent of Churchill's emotional declarations. These messages were evident in Roosevelt's State of the Union address to Congress delivered on January 6. Broadcast on radio and short wave from the White House Oval Office to Congress, to the American people, and to the world, Roosevelt denounced isolationism and past practices of appeasing the fascist "enemies" – Germany, Italy, and Japan.[2] He praised the "gallant," "armed defense of democratic existence" that the British-led allies were waging. Roosevelt promoted his Lend-Lease aid proposals, committing the United States "to full support of those resolute peoples, everywhere, who are resisting aggression and thereby keeping war from our hemisphere." He called for more speed in production of war materials, more loans to the anti-fascist allies to purchase the materials, and for personal sacrifices from the American people, who should expect to pay more taxes and work longer hours in order to produce the promised aid. Along with these appeals, Roosevelt ended his address by explaining what Americans were sacrificing their labor and treasure for – to protect "four essential human freedoms":[3]

> The first is freedom of speech and expression – everywhere in the world.
>
> The second is freedom of every person to worship God in his own way – everywhere in the world.
>
> The third is freedom from want – which, translated into world terms, means economic understandings which will secure to every nation a healthy peacetime life for its inhabitants – everywhere in the world.
>
> The fourth is freedom from fear – which, translated into world terms, means a world-wide reduction of armaments to such a point and in such a thorough fashion that no nation will be in a position to commit an act of physical aggression against any neighbor – anywhere in the world.

By supporting these freedoms, Americans would be declaring their faith in a righteous moral order, "the very antithesis of the so-called new order of tyranny which the dictators seek to create with the crash of a bomb." Roosevelt ended his address with a claim that must have cheered Churchill and Britain's allies as they engaged in a life-and-death struggle with the fascist powers:

> This nation has placed its destiny in the hands and heads and hearts of its millions of free men and women, and its faith in freedom under the guidance of God. Freedom means the supremacy of human rights everywhere. Our support goes to those who struggle to gain those rights or keep them. Our strength is our unity of purpose. To that high concept there can be no end save victory.[4]

Roosevelt followed up these stirring words with a budget proposal to Congress that included an increase in defense spending that vastly exceeded his funding requests of the previous summer. In his Third Inaugural Address, delivered two weeks later, on January 20, FDR returned to the high-minded language designed to appeal to Americans' pride in their nation's mythical origin story and its divine mission to preserve freedom for all, a mission laid out by America's premier "founding father," President George Washington:

The destiny of America was proclaimed in words of prophecy spoken by our first President in his first Inaugural in 1789 – words almost directed, it would seem, to this year of 1941: "The preservation of the sacred fire of liberty and the destiny of the republican model of government are justly considered ... deeply, ... finally, staked on the experiment entrusted to the hands of the American people."

If you and I in this later day lose that sacred fire – if we let it be smothered with doubt and fear – then we shall reject the destiny which Washington strove so valiantly and so triumphantly to establish. The preservation of the spirit and faith of the Nation does, and will, furnish the highest justification for every sacrifice that we may make in the cause of national defense.[5]

If American isolationists recalled Washington's Farewell Address to the nation in 1796 that warned the nation against forming "entangling alliances" with foreign powers[6] – as Eamon de Valera did when he recalled Washington's words to justify Irish neutrality during his St. Patrick's Day address later in March 1941[7] – Roosevelt recast Washington as the author of America's Manifest Destiny: to preserve liberty and democracy in the world.

By January 1941, de Valera realized that Ireland needed to work much harder to secure America's friendship, as Roosevelt's pro-Allied addresses to the American people were preparing the nation for entry into the war to fight side by side with Britain. If that occurred, de Valera believed that Ireland's neutrality would certainly be challenged, if not destroyed. Roosevelt's December 29 radio address that called on the American nation to become "the great arsenal for democracy" included a swipe at Eamon de Valera's neutrality policy. In making his pitch for the Lend-Lease aid program, Roosevelt also issued a warning reference to Nazi Germany's record of overrunning "neutral" powers:

> Belgium today is being used as an invasion base against Britain, now fighting for its life. And any South American country, in Nazi hands, would always constitute a jumping-off place for German attack on any one of the other republics of this hemisphere.
>
> Analyze for yourselves the future of two other places even nearer to Germany if the Nazis won. *Could Ireland hold out? Would Irish freedom be permitted as an amazing pet exception in an unfree world?* Or the Islands of the Azores which still fly the flag of Portugal after five centuries?[8] (emphasis added)

Roosevelt was challenging de Valera and Ireland (and António Salazar and Portugal) to step up to the fight: Which side are you on? Do you support fascism or freedom?

De Valera got the message. His government had been pushing back against the Roosevelt administration's criticisms of Irish neutrality policy since Roosevelt's November re-election with its own public relations campaign that targeted Irish Americans. De Valera and his policy advisers believed Irish neutrality policy was threatened by Roosevelt's victory, and with good reason.[9] U.S. Minister David Gray was saying this very thing openly in conversations with Joseph Walshe: If Britain seized the ports by force (as Churchill was suggesting in his post-election remarks to the British press), the United States would support Britain.[10] In private letters to Roosevelt, Gray told FDR he was supporting de Valera's Fine Gael political rival, James Dillon, who denounced the neutrality policy in the Dáil,[11] and who, according to German Minister Eduard Hempel, was "a 'German hater', a 'Jew' and 'a bitter enemy of de Valera.'"[12]

The Irish Minister in Washington Robert Brennan's November 9 conversation with Under Secretary of State Sumner Welles did not quell de Valera's fears. Welles criticized Ireland's shortsighted neutrality policy and warned Brennan that a victorious Germany would surely overrun Ireland, too.[13] On November 19, de Valera gave a widely published interview to Wallace Carroll of the United Press defending Irish neutrality as a sovereign right, and claiming that press reports about Irish aid offered to the Germans were false, misleading, or greatly exaggerated.[14] On November 24, de Valera's Irish American supporters, including elected politicians and Irish Catholic clergy mobilized by Brennan,[15] formed a new organization, "the American Friends of Irish Neutrality" (AFIN). The AFIN convened a mass meeting in New York City and formed chapters in cities across the United States where large concentrations of Irish Americans resided.[16]

By early January 1941, Eamon de Valera and Joseph Walshe began to rail against David Gray to one another and to Robert Brennan, as their conversations with Gray became more and more contentious as a result of the divergence of American and Irish national interests. In one instance, de Valera and Gray bickered with one another over whether Gray had said that the Irish government was "pro-German." Gray retorted:

> "I never said that, but I may have said there were certain members of the Irish Government who were pro-German." ... [De Valera replied], "Anti-British, but not pro-German." ... [Then] some reference was made by one of us to the growing volume of public opinion in the United States in favor of aid to Britain, and [Gray] said, "That's what I've been telling you all along and you wouldn't believe me." "Not at all," [de Valera] said. "You were telling us that America would be in the war, perhaps within two weeks." "I told you," [Gray] said, "in early summer that America was already morally in the war and that an 'incident' ... might bring us in any day."[17]

And so they went round and round.

Joseph Walshe, too, was increasingly exasperated with Gray's repeated assertions that if Britain's survival required the use of the Irish ports, Ireland *must* see reason and agree to their use:

One of the things which is maintaining an anti-Irish campaign in America is the easy assumption that the possession of a few Irish ports would in itself win the war for the British. The sacrifices which are still open to America to make before she reaches the magnitude of those involved for us in the handing over of the ports is enormous, and we are getting tired of America's vicarious heroism at our expense.[18]

While the British and Americans leaned on de Valera to open its ports to British ships, Germany was also pressuring de Valera's government to take some unneutral steps that de Valera's government also resisted. At the end of November 1940, German Foreign Minister von Ribbentrop instructed Eduard Hempel to make several overtures to the Irish Taoiseach, designed to establish Ireland's bias toward the Axis Powers. The Germans offered captured British rifles to the Irish government to arm its defense forces in case the British should attack the Irish ports or try to violate Irish territory in other ways.[19] The Germans must have been aware that de Valera's government had been trying to buy U.S. guns and ships since summer 1940, and that the Roosevelt administration put them off, selling all weapons America did not reserve for its own defense to the British. Following Hempel's advice, the German Foreign Office offered de Valera's government the weapons and protection from British attack to the Irish government, rather than offering the guns to the illegal IRA. De Valera rejected the German offer with the assertion that Ireland would not "get away" with accepting the captured guns, that Britain would find out and would launch a justified attack on Ireland.[20] The German offer, of course, was not disinterested; even though Operation Sea Lion was on hold, if the Germans launched an invasion of England through Ireland in the future, they wanted to be assured of a welcome reception.[21]

Germany made a further 'request' to de Valera's government in December 1940. The Foreign Ministry wanted to send additional personnel to staff the Dublin Legation, and they wanted to land German aircraft transporting these Germans at Dublin Airport. De Valera's government again refused, realizing the provocative nature of the request. De Valera explained to Hempel that continued operations of the Axis missions in Dublin already threatened Britain's security, and the arrival of additional Germans would breach the limits of British tolerance. Hempel reported to the Foreign Ministry that he "did not speak about possible concrete consequences of a negative Irish [response]," but Hempel knew these consequences were coming. He was told to inform de Valera that the "attitude of the Irish Government was incomprehensible" to the Germans.[22] Nonetheless, de Valera and Walshe were steadfast in their refusal. They asserted that the number of German staff at the Legation was "adequate," and increases in staff would only "aggravate the delicate situation created by the American and British press campaign" that was pressuring Ireland to open its ports. In Hempel's further conversation with Walshe's deputy, Frederick Boland, Hempel said again that "he was very worried as to what the reactions would be" if Ireland continued to resist German plans.[23] Hempel didn't have to wait too long; on January 2, German bombs were dropped on County Kildare, County Carlow, and County Louth, killing three people and injuring seven.[24] On January 3, Germany bombed County Wexford and Dublin City. Walshe contacted the Irish Minister in Berlin, William Warnock, with the Irish government's message: "We expect an early apology, which we would wish to publish on receipt, and we must of course hold the German Government liable for damage caused. For the moment, however, the most important thing is that there should be no recurrence."[25] At first Germany denied responsibility,[26] but the evidence was incontrovertible. Even Frank Aiken, who insisted at the time that he "feared an attack from both Britain and Germany, and that 'his mind switched from one to the other from day to day,'" asserted that "he had not 'the slightest doubt' that the bombs were German."[27]

In spite of David Gray's energetic interventions on behalf of British interests in Dublin – well known and approved by Franklin Roosevelt – and in spite of Roosevelt's public speeches that highlighted the close, sentimental alignment of British and American democratic and anti-fascist values, FDR's personal relationship with British Prime Minister Churchill was still superficial. The leaders had not yet met face to face and the level of trust that must exist in a true friendship had not been established. Churchill's effusive letter of congratulations following Roosevelt's re-election in November was never answered, and Congress had not yet approved the Lend-Lease aid that Roosevelt called for in his December and January addresses to the nation. In order to better assess the British leader's character, as well as the British War Cabinet's ability to fight back against the German military machine and against Germany's Axis allies, FDR sent a series of emissaries to London to meet with Winston Churchill, beginning with his most trusted adviser and close personal friend, Harry Hopkins.

Harry Hopkins, who worked at several social service agencies early in his career, joined New York State Governor Franklin Roosevelt's administration in 1931, administering the state's emergency relief program during the Great Depression. When Roosevelt was elected president in 1932, Hopkins went to work in Roosevelt's presidential administration as a New Deal agency administrator and he served in Roosevelt's Cabinet as Commerce Secretary from 1938 to 1940. During these years, he and FDR developed a close fraternal friendship as their professional relationship grew, so close that Hopkins moved into the White House as Roosevelt's personal adviser in 1940.[28] Hopkins deeply admired Roosevelt. In early 1941, he shared his analysis of Roosevelt's sometimes opaque character with Robert Sherwood, one of Roosevelt's speechwriters who later wrote a book about Hopkins's and FDR's friendship:[29]

> "You and I are for Roosevelt," Hopkins had told Sherwood ..., "because he's an idealist, like [President Woodrow] Wilson, and he's got the guts to drive through against any opposition to realize those ideals. Oh – he sometimes tries to appear tough and cynical and flippant, but that's just an act he likes to put on, especially at press conferences. ... Maybe he fools some of them, now and then – but don't ever let him fool you, or you won't be any use to him. You can see the real Roosevelt when he comes out with something like the Four Freedoms. And don't get the idea that those are any catch phrases. He believes them! He believes they can be practically attained."[30]

Churchill had appealed to Roosevelt for a face-to-face meeting, and, in January, Roosevelt decided to send Harry Hopkins to represent him in London even though Hopkins was in poor health and travel wore him down. FDR needed the opinion of someone he could trust.[31] Initially Hopkins was skeptical of Churchill's leadership[32] and Hopkins had a reputation for being blunt – he could "be disagreeable and say hard and sour things."[33] But during Hopkins's stay in England from January 10 to February 8, Winston Churchill and Churchill's wife Clementine won him over completely.[34] In turn, Hopkins convinced Churchill (for the moment at least) that "the President is determined that we shall win the war together. Make no mistake about it. ... At all costs and by all means he will carry you through. ... There is nothing he will not do so far as he has human power."[35] One evening at dinner with Churchill and Clementine, Hopkins opened the conversation:

> "I suppose you wish to know what I am going to say to President Roosevelt on my return," ... They sat in agonized suspense while a blizzard roared outside, until he finally resumed. "Well, I'm going to quote you one verse from that Book of Books. 'Whither thou goest, I will go; and where thou lodgest, I will lodge: thy people shall be my people, and thy God my God.'" He added very quietly, "Even to the end." Tears poured down Winston's face; Clementine, too, was sobbing. "The words," recalled Winston's doctor Lord Moran, who was present at Clementine's insistence, "seemed like a rope to a drowning man."[36]

Hopkins also shared his glowing appraisal of Churchill in a letter to Roosevelt:

> *Churchill* is the gov't here is every sense of the word – he controls the grand strategy and often the details – labor trusts him – the army, navy, and air force are behind him to a man. The politicians and upper crust pretend to like him. I cannot emphasize too strongly that he is the one and only person over here with whom you need to have a full meeting of the minds.

Churchill wants to see you – the sooner the better – but I have told him of your problem until the [Lend-Lease] bill is passed. I am convinced this meeting between you and Churchill is essential – and soon – for the battering continues and Hitler does not wait for Congress. ...[37]

In February, Hopkins returned to Washington to help FDR persuade Congress to accept the Lend-Lease bill and to get aid to Britain as quickly as possible.

Although Roosevelt trusted Hopkins implicitly, he also sent several other emissaries who weren't afraid to challenge Roosevelt's opinions. Colonel William J. (Bill) Donovan, an "old Republican adversary"[38] and veteran of the First World War who had been awarded a Medal of Honor for his heroic service, accompanied Hopkins and stayed on in London after Hopkins returned to the United States. FDR sent Donovan on an intelligence-gathering mission, specifically to assess Britain's military capacity. Donovan would later become the first head of the Office of Strategic Services in 1942, the precursor to the postwar Central Intelligence Agency (CIA).[39] In spring 1941, Donovan visited Ireland to consult with Irish Army officers who shared information on German activities in Ireland with their British Army counterparts, and to confer with Northern Ireland's military forces about building bases for U.S. troops that might be stationed there in the future.[40] He also met Helen Kirkpatrick during his mission in London and they exchanged information on Irish leaders, including their mutual suspicions about Frank Aiken's political loyalties.[41]

FDR sent a third emissary to meet with Churchill in February, his Republican Party opponent in the 1940 presidential election, Wendell Willkie. Although he was FDR's political rival, Willkie shared FDR's conviction that the fascist powers must be defeated, and the British must be kept in the fight against Hitler.[42] Willkie also supported the Lend-Lease aid program and testified before Congress to make his views known, using his political reputation to establish the credibility of the aid program, even when the powerful isolationist lobby – including Joseph Kennedy, Charles Lindbergh,[43] and his Republican Party cohorts in Senate – all opposed him.[44] Before Willkie embarked on his mission to London, FDR invited him to the White House and wrote out a verse from Henry Wadsworth Longfellow's poem, "The Building of the Ship," and asked Willkie to deliver the message to Churchill:

Dear Churchill,
Wendell Willkie will give you this. He is truly helping to keep politics out over here.
I think this verse applies to your people as it does to us.

    Sail on, O Ship of State!
    Sail on, O Union, strong and great!

Humanity with all its fears,
With all the hopes of future years,
Is hanging breathless on thy fate!

As ever yours,
Franklin D. Roosevelt[45]

After meeting Willkie and receiving Roosevelt's encouraging message, Churchill addressed the nation on February 9, five months since his last national radio address, noting that, "In wartime, there's a lot to be said for the motto: 'Deeds, not words.'" He recounted Britain's battles and the Allies' fierce resistance. He talked about his visits with Roosevelt's envoys, Harry Hopkins and Wendell Willkie, and their promises of American aid. He also shared the lines from the Longfellow poem with the British people, and its message of Anglo-American solidarity. He answered FDR's message with assurances of British resolve to prevail in the anti-fascist fight:

> What is the answer that I shall give, in your name, to this great man, the thrice-chosen head of a nation of a hundred and thirty millions? Here is the answer which I will give to President Roosevelt: Put your confidence in us. Give us your faith and your blessing, and, under Providence, all will be well.
>
> We shall not fail or falter; we shall not weaken or tire. Neither the sudden shock of battle, nor the long drawn battles of vigilance and exertion will wear us down. Give us tools and we will finish the job.[46]

Churchill's words anticipated the passage of the controversial Lend-Lease Act in U.S. Congress that finally occurred on March 11, 1941. The Lend-Lease bill gave President Roosevelt "sweeping powers ... to make or procure 'any defense article for the government of any country whose defense the President deems vital to the defense of the United States.'" The terms of the transfer, exchange, lease, or lending of any military aid was also left to the President's discretion.[47] Churchill wrote to Roosevelt: "The Former Naval Person has expressed to the President his heartfelt gratitude on the passing of the Bill, which is so great an event in the history of our two nations."[48]

In March 1941, just prior to the passage of the all-important Lend-Lease aid bill, Roosevelt's hand-picked ambassador to Britain, John Gilbert Winant, arrived in London. Unlike former ambassador Joseph Kennedy, Winant's progressive politics and anti-fascist, pro-Allied sympathies were well established. Winant had served in Roosevelt's New Deal Cabinet as the first head administrator of the Social Security program in the mid-1930s, and FDR appointed him as the U.S. representative to the International Labour Organization (ILO) in 1939. At the time, the ILO was headquartered in Geneva. When the Germans occupied Czechoslovakia in

March 1939, Winant went to Prague "as a gesture of solidarity and sympathy." He also went to France in June 1940, when the Germans marched triumphantly into Paris, and to London in fall 1940, when the Battle of Britain raged. He sent a message back to Roosevelt from London insisting the British would fight on, even though Joseph Kennedy expressed the opposite opinion. Winant had also urged FDR to send more military aid to the Allied forces.[49] After his appointment as U.S. ambassador to Britain in spring 1941, Winant immediately endeared himself to King George VI, who personally met Winant's train as he arrived in London, and to the Churchills, to the Foreign Office, and to the British people.[50] Winant recognized Britain's desperate situation as he toured the devastated country. He appealed to Washington officials on Britain's behalf when delays in sending Lend-Lease aid frustrated Churchill's War Cabinet no end, even as London was once again under a barrage of German bombs in April and May 1941.[51] Helen Kirkpatrick reported on John Winant's "maiden speech" on arriving in London, when Winant expressed his anti-fascist sympathies in no uncertain terms, as well as his affirmations of Anglo-American friendship:

> John G. Winant, at a luncheon given today by the Pilgrim Society, told Great Britain that the "policies which draw your country and mine more closely together in the face of common peril are policies to which the American people as a whole have solemnly committed themselves."
>
> Speaking to a record crowd in the Savoy Hotel, Winant paid tribute both to the "great mass of the American people, working in factories and shipyards and on the farms, who are building the arsenals and granaries for democracy's defense," and "to all those here and everywhere ... who defend with their lives freedom's frontiers."
>
> Ambassador Winant's deliberate manner of speaking made his speech one of the most impressive delivered here in some time by anyone but Prime Minister Winston Churchill. His vigorous denunciation of Nazi tyranny and the assumption throughout his speech that Britain and the United States are finally and irretrievably committed to the Nazi defeat brought home to people here what they have been finding it hard to believe – that the United States is really backing them in their fight against the Axis.[52]

Kirkpatrick's journalistic investigations had taken her back to Ireland at the end of January and beginning of February 1941, where she reported carefully – to avoid Irish censure – but critically on Irish neutrality.[53] Like the British and American officials before her, she could not understand Ireland's "unreasonable" clinging to its neutrality. She interviewed dozens of Dubliners to ask them *why* Ireland remained neutral, "when less than thirty miles to the east, Britain is fighting for her life, and, as the British believe, for the freedom and independence not only for herself but all small nations – Eire included?" The answers she received continued to confound her:

When they affirm their belief in neutrality, you've heard the last affirmation you're likely to hear in the discussion. Perhaps I've been unlucky, but every conversation I've had with Irishmen has been largely devoted to negatives on their part. You hear mainly what the British shouldn't have done; what Eire won't do; what isn't likely to happen; but try your best, it's difficult if not impossible to find out what the British should do, what Eire will do and what may happen. And then before you really get down to discussion of present day affairs, you'll go back to Cromwell, the troubles, and the Black and Tans.

Even the Anglo-Irishmen, and, to their credit, let it be said that intelligent and well-informed Englishmen as well, have little good to say of British policy towards Ireland up to 1923. For stupid handling and some say terrorization, it's generally agreed to rank pretty high.

"Yes," you agree, "but that's over. The British have no desire to rule Ireland. They haven't interfered with you in recent years, and if they win the war, you'll be free and independent. If the Germans win, will you be?"

"Ah no, who can say? Do you think the Germans would find us easier to manage than the British did? And it's by no means sure that the British will win. Where would we be, and Germany winning, if we were to come into the war on the British side?"[54]

Kirkpatrick pressed on: And what of America's support for Great Britain? Her interviewees insisted that the United States was able to proclaim its support and speak out against Germany because it was 3,000 miles from the war zones. If Eire offered aid to Britain, the Germans would bomb Ireland (again), as Kirkpatrick had reported on the bombings of January 2–3, when she had noted: "from the German point of view, the bombings accomplished one good thing. It stiffened the resolution of the Irish against altering their policy of neutrality. No more bombs for them if they can help it."[55] She even resorted to taunting the emasculated Irish government for its weak response to continued German aggression when she reported that a "Nazi Bombing of Irish Boat Stirs Dublin. Eire Not Strong Enough to Protect Neutral Status," asserting that de Valera could not even get Germany to accept responsibility for sinking Irish ships in Ireland's territorial waters in early February.[56] Fine Gael's James Dillon joined her in voicing the opinion that de Valera was afraid of the German reaction if he criticized Germany too vigorously.[57]

Irish government censors blocked Kirkpatrick's reports and Dillon's critiques from appearing in Irish papers, but they couldn't restrict content printed in U.S. newspapers.[58] Nonetheless, the government tried to silence Kirkpatrick as it monitored all journalists who worked in Ireland during the Emergency.[59] Joseph Walshe also composed arguments to counter attacks on Irish neutrality in the American press for Frank Aiken, who, at the end of February 1941, was preparing for his mission to the United States seeking U.S. military aid for Ireland's self-defense. Walshe had met with Kirkpatrick when she was in the country in early February,[60] and Walshe's instructions for Aiken read like a direct response to stories that Kirkpatrick was writing for the *Chicago Daily News* at the time:

> The general line adopted by anti-Irish writers and speakers in America is that we are standing aside from the great fight which is being made by the democratic countries against dictatorship and all its evils. These people chide us for attaching excessive importance to grievances of the remote past. They try to make it appear that our main reason for staying out of the war is based on historic hatred of England. They generally avoid the issue of what would happen if we handed over the ports to Great Britain or otherwise joined in the war against Germany. They pretend to assume that no particular evil for us would follow the surrender of the ports to Great Britain.
>
> In fact, the anti-Irish propagandists in America show a particular cleverness in avoiding the real issues for the purpose of drawing facile conclusions likely to depreciate us in the minds of gullible people. They avoid most carefully any reference to the continued occupation by Great Britain of a substantial part of our territory, and most of them avoid any reference to the period between 1916 and 1922. They assume that, if Germany wins the war, Ireland will be taken over and run by the Nazis. This assumption is intended to make their propaganda more effective. It is unfortunately also for us the most difficult point to answer owing to the anti-German atmosphere in America and the child-like belief that England is fighting for exclusively selfless aims. However, the problem has to be faced, and the only way we have discovered of answering without provoking the accusation of pro-Nazism is to say that there is no certainty of a German occupation of this country should we remain neutral and Germany win the war.[61]

De Valera had decided to make another appeal to the American government. At the end of March, he sent Frank Aiken to Washington to make Ireland's case, once again, for the moral and practical necessity of Irish neutrality, and to obtain American guns and ships to defend its territory from all attackers, as well as food to make up for blockade-imposed shortages.[62] Earlier in January, Sir John Maffey had sent de Valera's request for guns to the Dominions Office. The Dominions Secretary, Lord Cranborne, had passed on the request to Churchill with the note: "Will we provide Eire with further arms for her defense?" Churchill's response in the margins of the document: "*No.*"[63]

De Valera's subsequent appeal to Roosevelt for arms, as he probably realized, was also doomed to disappointment. Roosevelt and his official emissaries were avowedly pro-British – this included not only the U.S. Minister David Gray, but also Wendell Willkie who made a brief visit to Dublin on February 4 and who tried, and failed, to persuade de Valera to open Irish ports to the British Navy.[64] Nonetheless, de Valera still counted on the

4.1 Eamon de Valera and Frank Aiken at Dublin Airport, as Aiken begins journey to the United States, March 1941

pressure that Irish American politicians and voters could bring to bear that might weaken the Roosevelt administration's resistance to aiding Ireland. According to Sir John Maffey, "These Irish Americans are the pillars of de Valera's temple. They created him, preserved him, and endowed him."[65]

Frank Aiken's mission to the United States was as much about cultivating public support for Irish neutrality as it was about gaining U.S.

weapons,[66] even though Ireland desperately needed the weapons for its own defense force.[67] Although de Valera's government professed to believe that either Britain or Germany might attack them,[68] it was Germany that had sent agents to collaborate with the government's IRA enemies, and Germany, not Britain, that had dropped bombs on Eire and sunk Irish ships. At the end of February, the German Foreign Ministry renewed its efforts to press captured British guns on de Valera's government, the offer rejected once again.[69] Aiken's March mission to obtain arms from the United States vexed Ribbentrop, who "continued to smolder at the incomprehensible attitude of the Irish," who would not accept guns from Germany and continued to deny Germany permission to increase its Legation staff in Dublin.[70]

The selection of Frank Aiken to make the appeal for arms was not a wise one as far as the U.S. government was concerned. Aiken's background in the IRA and his previous statements regarding Germany's likely victory in the war wouldn't have endeared him to Roosevelt administration officials who were conducting inquiries to determine Aiken's loyalties. Maffey's assessment of Aiken – that Aiken was "anti-British but certainly not pro-German. He is not impressive and rather stupid"[71] – was known to David Gray, who passed it on to the State Department, along with what Gray knew of Aiken's IRA background and Aiken's personal relationship with de Valera.[72] Gray shared James Dillon's snide description of Aiken with FDR: "… a mind halfway between that of a child and an ape … a physically huge man with a mentality of a boy gang leader playing at war with real soldiers."[73] Gray also wrote a letter of introduction for Aiken to Eleanor Roosevelt, although Aiken never met the First Lady on his visit to the United States, which lasted from March to June 1941. In the letter to Eleanor, Gray shared "a favorable though not uncritical view of the proposed visit by Aiken," but Gray did not support Ireland's request for U.S. arms.[74]

Colonel Bill Donovan, FDR's emissary in London, met with Aiken and Irish Minister John Dulanty on March 6, when Aiken was en route to the United States. Donovan "'interrogated', as Aiken put it, John Dulanty about Irish neutrality, the ports, and the charge that Aiken was pro-German."[75] The day before this meeting, Helen Kirkpatrick had written out her own assessment of Aiken for Donovan: "Aiken is stupid, probably pro-German but with considerable influence owing to his former IRA connections." She also told Donovan: "With the approval of the American Minister [Gray], I put up to both Aiken and de Valera the proposition that the US Government would supply Eire with arms and ammunition if Britain were permitted to use the [naval] bases. Both rejected it out of hand because of lack of defense for Cork, Waterford, Limerick, and Dublin."[76] Donovan went on his own fact-finding trip to Ireland on March 10 to consult with Northern Ireland's

Army officers, and he sent his warning back to Washington: "Aiken is possibly in America for other reasons [than meeting with U.S. government officials]; he is of the extreme left."[77]

In addition to all the troubling intelligence regarding Aiken coming from the Roosevelt administration's own sources, Taoiseach de Valera had not prepared the ground for a positive reception for his hand-picked emissary in Washington, either. In de Valera's March 1941 St. Patrick's Day address, he restated the claim that Ireland was facing blockades and threats to its national security "equally" from Germany and Britain. These remarks incensed David Gray, who vented his frustrations in a letter to President Roosevelt: "I have just been reading Mr. De Valera's broadcast to America which goes on tonight. It will do him no good over there. He cannot get out of this self-centered dream world and realize that the Irish will be goose-stepping if Britain goes down." In Gray's opinion, De Valera "wants England to win" the war against Germany, but "his parochial estimate of the importance of considerations of Irish pride blind him to enlightened self-interest, Christian principle, and all sense of reality."[78] According to Gray, a "rational" man would ally with Britain in exchange for the promise of a future end to partition. Gray still believed this offer to be floating in the ether, even though de Valera personally had "alienated Ulster so that no settlement can come about while he is in power."[79]

Aiken arrived in Washington on March 20 for a series of meetings Robert Brennan had arranged with the State Department and with the President. Aiken, "Ireland's towering, 210-pound minister of defense," entered Washington with his own combative male attitude on display. According to a *Washington Post* account:

> Ireland, [Aiken] said, is ready to pay cash for weapons, and is prepared to buy ships to carry them across the Atlantic. If he can persuade the United States Government to deal with Ireland, he said, it will be fine; If not, Ireland will fight off an invasion, anyway, whether the invader be British or German.
>
> "If anybody attacks us," he said confidently, "I think they'll get a severe blow on the nose." ...
>
> Aiken, a broth of a man from Armagh who stands 6 feet 3 inches was a general in Ireland's war against the British Black and Tans. However, he doesn't use the military title now and asks that you not get him started talking about "the past." Ireland's policy, he says, is based on self-interest and not on antipathy for the British.[80]

Aiken made it clear in interviews with the Washington newspapers that Ireland was not making any deals to compromise its neutrality. He told reporters: "Our country has declared herself neutral after mature consideration ... and to give bases to England would be entering into the war at once – and by the back door. If Ireland goes to war she will come in by the front door."[81]

Aiken's first meeting with Under Secretary of State Sumner Welles took place the first night he arrived in Washington. Welles did not hold out much hope for Eire's request for arms: "I said, ... that I must make it emphatically clear that assistance to Great Britain came first and foremost in our program, in complete harmony with our own efforts at rearmament."[82] Welles also noted his impressions of Aiken following the meeting: "Aiken has the narrowest point of view – no cooperation with England while the Ulster question remains unsettled." Welles criticized Aiken's "rather extraordinary diatribe" against Britain, which was wildly out of sync with the administration's sympathies. Congress had just passed Roosevelt's Lend-Lease plan and it rankled the State Department that "the Irish refused to lift a finger to assist the British in their attempts at self-defense nor to cooperate with the British in this common endeavor."[83] Aiken's representations of the Irish point of view, arguments that Joseph Walshe had laid out for him, only alienated the State Department as Aiken insisted that Britain's threats to take over Irish ports and its colonial occupation of Northern Ireland had put Britain, not Germany, in the role of the aggressor.[84]

Aiken also alienated President Roosevelt at their meeting on April 7, although this was hardly a surprise. De Valera's biographer Tim Pat Coogan observed that the Irish leaders and the American president were from different worlds: "Neither Aiken nor de Valera was a potential entrant to Roosevelt's charmed circle. They would not have been at home sailing off Newport with FDR in the company of Henry Morgenthau Jr."[85] Robert Brennan, who accompanied Aiken on the Oval Office visit, reported at the time that the meeting with the President was "cordial," although he acknowledged that Aiken and Roosevelt clearly disagreed about whether Ireland's neutrality was justified. Aiken and Roosevelt clashed about whether Britain planned to attack Ireland (as Aiken asserted was likely and Roosevelt laughed off), and whether a German victory posed a threat to Irish sovereignty and security (Roosevelt asserted that Aiken had said Ireland had "nothing to fear" from Germany and Aiken vigorously denied it).[86] In a memoir written ten years later, Brennan told another version of the Aiken–Roosevelt meeting that other sources have repeated. In this version, Brennan reported that Roosevelt grew so enraged by Aiken's insistence that Britain and Germany posed equal threats to Ireland that he swept the dishes and cutlery from his lunch table onto the floor and abruptly ended the meeting.[87] In Aiken's account of the meeting with FDR that he recorded in August 1941, he reported that he "had to interrupt the President and keep talking against his attempts to interrupt me in what would be a boorish way in dealing with an ordinary individual. I did, however, succeed in giving him clearly to understand that neutrality is supported by 99.9% of our people, that it was decided upon in their own interests and that the Government would take no step leading our people towards involvement in the war and that we were determined to resist aggression from any quarter." And while the President insisted that Britain had no plans to attack Ireland, Aiken challenged him to "ask Mr. Churchill" to publicly confirm it.[88] Historian John Day Tully adds: "Years later, Aiken said he knew right after the meeting he would not be able to persuade Roosevelt: 'Churchill had been at him to put the screw to us.'"[89]

Franklin Roosevelt wrote a brief, fairly innocuous note to Eamon de Valera soon after meeting with Frank Aiken: "… may I say that I was glad to receive Mr. Aiken and have the opportunity of an interesting discussion with him. I am sure Mr. Aiken has informed you on this discussion."[90] President Roosevelt made an announcement to the press regarding his decision to sell two transport ships to Ireland while the Red Cross would provide food aid. American guns would be spared only for "those nations which are actively waging war on behalf of the maintenance of Democracy, and there isn't anything left over."[91]

FDR's official response to Ireland's request for arms, relayed personally to the Taoiseach by David Gray on April 28 following the State Department's specific instructions, was that Ireland could purchase two cargo ships from the United States to transport food to the island nation. No guns would be sold to Ireland. Gray added the following message, criticizing Frank Aiken and, by implication, scolding de Valera:

> My Government has noted, regretfully, as a result of several conferences which officials of the United States Government have had with Mr. Aiken, that his point of view has appeared to be one of blind hostility to the British people. It seems to my Government that the holding of such a point of view is wholly lacking in appreciation of the fact which seems completely clear to my Government – that is, that the future security and safety of Ireland inevitably rests upon the success of the British cause. …
>
> The United States Government does not question the determination or the right of Ireland to preserve its neutrality, but it holds that there is a clear distinction between such a policy and one which, at least potentially, affords real encouragement to the Government of Germany.[92]

De Valera, not surprisingly, angrily rejected the American ships offered up along with Gray's "impertinent" "lectures."[93] According to Gray's account of their meeting, de Valera defended Aiken and insisted that:

> he was at a loss to understand how Mr. Aiken had been understood as expressing a hostile attitude to Great Britain; that he was one of the clearest headed members of the Irish Government and that he very well understood

the probable significance of a German victory for Ireland, and that, though he had taken the field against England, his intelligence made him understand the desirability of letting anti-British feeling die down as quickly as possible.[94]

De Valera's protestations were hard to believe, given that Aiken had repeatedly challenged the Roosevelt administration's material and moral support for Britain's anti-fascist war in meetings with the President and State Department officials. Moreover, Aiken had taken his arguments public, appealing directly to the American people. In April and continuing through May and June, Aiken toured the United States and spoke to AFIN rallies, to the press, to isolationist politicians – all the "anti-British elements" that opposed FDR's domestic and foreign policies.[95] On April 23, Aiken appeared at an anti-war rally in New York City with Charles Lindbergh, whose isolationist views and "star power" brought out an audience of 25,000, with many Irish Americans in attendance. Aiken gave a press conference before the rally and asserted that British shipping blockades caused Irish suffering: "England has not been giving us a fair share of goods from overseas," and "There is no acute shortage of petrol in England," feeding into the crowd's anti-British sentiments.[96] Historian Brian Girvin has written about these months when Aiken traveled across the country,[97] promoting the "Irish position":

> ... whether expressed by Aiken, Brennan, or their supporters inside the USA, [their message] was to continually condemn the British and insist that nothing should be done to help Britain's defense unless partition was ended. In this Aiken was echoing de Valera's longtime strategy of giving nothing away and waiting for the other side to concede, but this had little impact on Roosevelt, who was drawing ever closer to Britain. If Aiken had genuinely wanted to accomplish something while in the United States it would have been relatively simple to nuance his comments and to provide the Americans with various assurances about Irish good faith. Instead, his belligerent behavior, his openly anti-British attitudes and his association with isolationists alienated not only the administration but also some of Ireland's supporters.[98]

Aiken's continued complaints about the British blockade of Ireland and insistence that the U.S. government was being "pressured" by Great Britain or by some pro-British lobby implied that Franklin Roosevelt was weak, challenging FDR's masculine autonomy. On May 20, de Valera's Fine Gael political opponent, Richard Mulcahy, demanded that Aiken be reined in to stop him from further antagonizing the U.S. government:

> If the Minister [Aiken] can get supplies, he should abstain from public pronouncements and get on with his job; if he can't get supplies he should come home and leave the interpretation of Irish Government policy to the Irish Minister in Washington, whose communications to the American people will

be made through the correct channel, i.e. the American Government. It is intolerable and highly dangerous for any member of the Executive Council of Eire to leave himself open to the charge of campaigning in America against the American Government, and that is what the Minister's San Francisco speech amounts to.[99]

Irish neutrality was a hard sell in America, especially after the German *Luftwaffe* unleashed its *blitzkrieg* bombing attacks and dropped explosive landmines on Belfast, Northern Ireland on April 7–8, 15–16, and again on May 4–5, causing widespread damage to a poorly defended city. All told, almost 3,000 people were killed in these assaults. Belfast had never imposed a strict blackout policy, it had few anti-aircraft guns, inadequate fire brigade responders, and spotty distribution of gas masks. The lack of preparation was especially hard on Belfast's slum-dwelling impoverished citizens whose government didn't have any formal evacuation plans in place to get them out of the targeted city center when the attacks began.[100] Belfast's major shipbuilding industry, concentrated at the Harland and Wolff factory and dockyards, also suffered crippling blows from the incendiary bomb blasts and the ensuing fires. However, rather than concentrating on these military targets, "German records show that 180 aircraft were over the Belfast target area – were dropping all their high explosive bombs onto civilian districts. Instead of pouring onto the harbor and shipyards, well over a hundred tons of bombs were unloaded in sticks across thousands of back-to-back terraced homes where the poor of Belfast lay unprotected."[101] In a show of Irish solidarity, de Valera sent Dublin fire crews north to help Belfast put out the fires that were consuming the city in mid-April,[102] but the renewed attack in May turned Belfast into "a great ring of fire, the whole city was ablaze." A German radio broadcaster who was permitted to fly with the *Luftwaffe* during the May raid provided a firsthand witness of the attacks to his listeners:

> ... I revised all my ideas about the effects of German bombing. I can really say that I could not believe my eyes. When we approached the target at half-past two we stared silently into a sea of flames such as none of us had seen before. Then after some time our squadron leader, who has already made more than 100 flights, said "One would not believe it" ... in Belfast there was not a number of conflagrations, but just one enormous conflagration which spread over the entire harbor and industrial area. ...[103]

The Belfast Blitz was followed by another fierce *Luftwaffe* attack on London on May 10, "the worst day" in terms of damage inflicted on London's landmarks, which included the British Museum, Westminster Abbey, Big Ben, and the House of Commons. Even more devastating, 1,436 civilians were killed.[104] Historian James MacGregor Burns recounted that the following day, "Churchill stood in the wreckage and cried."[105] Throughout the months of April and May 1941, the Nazi armies had raged across Central Europe and the Middle East, launching "thunderous" attacks on Greece, Yugoslavia, and North Africa, forcing the British armies to retreat and evacuate Allied positions.[106] Crete, Syria, and Iraq were about to fall under German control, and the allegiance of the nominally neutral nations of Portugal, Spain, and Turkey were also suspect; the Allies anticipated that these countries might join the Axis Powers at any time. On May 3, Churchill pleaded with Roosevelt to intervene: "Mr. President, I am sure you will understand me if I speak to you exactly what is on my mind. The one counterweight I can see would be if the United States were to immediately range herself with us as a belligerent power." Roosevelt replied to Churchill with a promise of thirty more ships to be sent to the Middle East and an expression of moral support for Britain's determination to hold the front.[107]

With Britain's war-making capacity stretched to the limits, Winston Churchill made an announcement in Parliament on May 20 that the War Cabinet had decided to extend military conscription to Northern Ireland. Eamon de Valera immediately protested: "The conscription of the people of one nation by another, revolts the human conscience. No fair-minded man anywhere, can fail to recognize in it an act of oppression upon a weaker people and it cannot but do damage to Britain herself."[108] To be sure, the IRA and other militant Irish Catholic nationalists would have resisted the draft and split the country in civil war. Northern Ireland's Cardinal MacRory, the Catholic Primate for All Ireland who was known for sympathizing with the IRA, also raised the alarm to incite Irish Catholic resistance. Forced conscription would be "an outrage to the national feeling and an aggression on our national rights ... an ancient land was partitioned by a foreign power against the vehement protests of its people ... [that foreign power] would not seek to compel those who still writhe under this grievous wrong to fight on the side of its perpetrators."[109]

Irish objections to conscription infuriated Churchill who reportedly told Irish Minister John Dulanty: "It makes my blood boil to think of your position. Ireland has lost its soul."[110] Churchill met with Dulanty in London on May 22, who asserted that Irish Catholics in the North would surely cross the border into Eire to avoid the British government's conscription order, and the following clash of Anglo-Irish manhood ensued:

> "If" [Churchill] said, "they want to run away we will put no obstacle in their path." I retorted with some heat that we [Irishmen] had not anywhere shewn a disposition to run away, least of all when in his own day our small forces had fought the might of the British.

Mr. Churchill instantly agreed that in the past we had never run away. He spoke vehemently about our fame all over the world for valour – we were "one of the world's finest fighting races" – and how lamentable it was that we had put ourselves out of the world fight for freedom through the ignoble fear of being bombed. He had always shewn a warm friendship for Ireland. He was conscious of what Ireland had suffered in the past, but it was heartbreaking to him to see us with our glorious record standing aside from this life and death fight for freedom. He had always been in favour of a united Ireland. He was still in favour of it. What chance was there now when their friends in the North of Ireland were fighting with them and we were standing aside? He was afraid we were perpetuating Partition. ...

"You should tell your Government that we are fighting for our lives, and owing to the imprudence of Mr. Chamberlain we are denied the use of the ports which were given to you." I enquired whether "given" was the correct expression, when in fact they were merely restoring to us what was our own. To this he made no answer but referred again to his support of our cause in the British Parliament, how he and others had taken a great risk in securing the passage of a Treaty [in 1921] only to find it later so unjustifiably repudiated. ...

Mr. Churchill said that we were keeping out of the war because we thought the British would lose. They would not lose. It would be a long fight, but they would win.[111]

The views these men held regarding the meaning of the war and their nations' competing warrior values were worlds apart. At the time, they were irreconcilable. De Valera pressed the Irish case opposing conscription with David Gray,[112] and with the Canadian Prime Minister through the Irish Minister in Ottawa.[113] Sir John Maffey also cautioned the British Dominions Office about the serious repercussions in Northern Ireland if conscription were enforced: "draft riots, the escape of draft dodgers to Southern Ireland who will be acclaimed as hero martyrs by three fourths of the population, and fermenting of trouble by representatives and fifth columnists. ... [And, De Valera] will raise anti-British feeling and call a Holy War."[114] In the face of these apocalyptic predictions, caution prevailed. The message went out: "although there could be no dispute about [Britain's] rights, or about the merits, it would be more trouble than it was worth to apply conscription in Northern Ireland."[115] On May 27, Churchill announced in the House of Commons that conscription for Northern Ireland had been dropped.

Churchill lost the fight to impose conscription in Northern Ireland, but Roosevelt made another public expression of U.S. support for Britain during his May 27 "Fireside Chat" radio address. Proclaiming that *America* now faced an "unlimited national emergency," the U.S. government would provide for Britain's military needs by whatever means were necessary, and Roosevelt pledged to "give every possible assistance to Britain and to all who, with Britain, are resisting Hitlerism."[116] Despite FDR's sweeping statement, supplies from the United States were slow in coming. Lend-Lease shipments of food had begun to arrive in Britain in late May, but weapons were not yet being produced in large quantities, and ships were not yet available to transport the armaments.[117]

Ireland maintained its neutrality, even when, three days later on May 30, the *Luftwaffe* bombed Dublin's North Strand Road with a 500-pound bomb that killed thirty-four people and injured eighty more, and dropped another bomb on Phoenix Park near the American Legation and the Irish President Douglas Hyde's residence.[118] Gray reported on the damage to the Legation that it was "but a little broken glass and the loss of an hour's sleep. ... I haven't found out whether there is much indignation or whether excuses will be made for the Germans as there have been previously."[119] Joseph Walshe met with German Minister Hempel on May 31 and provided the line that de Valera's government wanted the Germans to take in order to defuse any anti-German public outcry among the Irish people that would force the government to abandon its neutrality policy: don't try to blame the British, take responsibility and apologize.[120] The Germans responded to the Irish government with the following disingenuous statement on June 5:

> ... [the] German Government is deeply concerned at the incident, which he [the Under Secretary of State] described as terrible, and is making all possible investigations to determine whether German aircraft could have been involved. He stated Air Force is confronted with [a] "puzzle". He assured me [Irish Minister William Warnock in Berlin], if German aircraft were responsible, German Government would not hesitate to give us full satisfaction, and he asked that we should, on our part, furnish them with all available evidence which would assist in clearing up the matter as early as possible.
> He said they wish to make it clear that there could be absolutely no question of German aircraft having bombed Dublin on purpose.[121]

Ireland's official protests to Germany following the bomb attack were distinctly milder than the protests issued following Britain's proposed conscription policy. In David Gray's view, the reasons for the difference were clear: "I think this means a very lively fear of the Germans, also a definite unwillingness to make any sacrifice to help England. ... I don't think de Valera is going to change his line unless forced to do so. He has deliberately passed up the chance to excite anti-German feeling over the recent bombing. He has in fact clamped down on expression of anti-German feeling."[122] Walshe's telegram to Robert Brennan on June 19 confirmed the government's desire to avoid German reprisals: "Promptness of German apology and offer of compensation ... affords proof that bombing was not deliberate and constitutes satisfactory settlement of incident."[123]

The focus of the Anglo-American officials involved took a sharp turn away from Ireland on June 22. Germany attacked the Soviet Union, violating the 1939 Nazi-Soviet Non-Aggression Pact. With the new military campaign, the chances of Germany invading Ireland in order to launch an attack on Britain dropped significantly[124] – at least, so long as the Russian Army engaged the German *Wehrmacht* and kept the German forces concentrated on the Eastern Front. Winston Churchill, adhering to a classic rule of war, that "the enemy of my enemy is my friend," embraced the Soviet Union as an anti-fascist ally. He openly acknowledged the charges of hypocrisy that the new alliance with a Communist Party-run state elicited from his many critics, in Ireland and elsewhere. He had defined Britain's war against Germany as a war *for* democracy, freedom, and preservation of Christianity and Western civilization. Following Germany's attack on the Soviet Union, Churchill addressed his critics and the British people: "No one has been a more consistent opponent of Communism than I have for the last twenty-five years. I will unsay no word that I have spoken about it. But all this fades away before the spectacle which is now unfolding. The past, with its crimes, its follies, and its tragedies, flashes away."[125] He asserted, "We are resolved to destroy Hitler and every vestige of the Nazi regime. ... It follows, therefore, that we shall give whatever help we can to Russia and the Russian people."[126] Britain now had an ally that was actively fighting the German war machine and he told the beleaguered British people: "We are no longer alone" in the fight.[127] Roosevelt was slower to voice his support for the Soviets' anti-fascist resistance,[128] but he soon came around. And despite the Soviet alliance, Churchill and Roosevelt kept the focus on their nations' principled democratic aims throughout the war, in their public speeches and in their private communications.[129] They defined these goals, voiced in their common language, when they met face to face for the first time in August 1941, off the coast of Newfoundland.

Notes

1 Robert Dallek, *Franklin D. Roosevelt: A Political Life* (New York: Penguin, 2018), 409.
2 "The President Speaks," *Time Magazine* 37: 1 (6 January 1941), 11–14.
3 Franklin Roosevelt, "State of the Union (Four Freedoms)," 6 January 1941, Presidential Speeches, Franklin D. Roosevelt Presidency (University of Virginia Miller Center, 2019), https://millercenter.org/the-presidency/

presidential-speeches/january-6-1941-state-union-four-freedoms (accessed 4 December 2020).
4 David Kaiser, *No End Save Victory: How FDR Led the Nation into War* (New York: Basic Books, 2014), 126.
5 Franklin Roosevelt, "Third Inaugural Address," 20 January 1941, Presidential Speeches, Franklin D. Roosevelt Presidency (University of Virginia Miller Center, 2019), https://millercenter.org/the-presidency/presidential-speeches/january-20-1941-third-inaugural-address (accessed 4 December 2020).
6 "George Washington's Farewell Address, 1796," Milestones 1784–1800, U.S. Department of State Office of the Historian, https://history.state.gov/milestones/1784-1800/washington-farewell (accessed 4 December 2020).
7 John Day Tully, *Ireland and Irish Americans 1932–1945: The Search for Identity* (Dublin: Irish Academic Press, 2010), 97.
8 Franklin Roosevelt, "Fireside Chat 16: On the 'Arsenal of Democracy,'" 29 December 1940, Presidential Speeches, Franklin D. Roosevelt Presidency (University of Virginia Miller Center, 2019), https://millercenter.org/the-presidency/presidential-speeches/december-29-1940-fireside-chat-16-arsenal-democracy (accessed 4 December 2020).
9 Brian Girvin, *The Emergency: Neutral Ireland 1939–45* (London: Pan Macmillan, 2007), 186.
10 T. Ryle Dwyer, *Irish Neutrality and the USA, 1939–47* (Dublin: Gill & Macmillan, 1977), 86. See also "The Minister in Ireland (Gray) to the (Acting) Secretary of State (Welles), November 24, 1940, Document 166, *Foreign Relations of the United States Diplomatic Papers* (hereafter: *FRUS*) 1940 vol. III (Washington, DC: U.S. Government Printing Office, 1958); Code Telegram from Joseph P. Walshe to Robert Brennan, 4 December 1940, Doc. 359 NAI DFA Secretary's Files P2, *Documents on Irish Foreign Policy* vol. VI, 1939–1941.
11 U.S. Minister to Ireland David Gray to Franklin Roosevelt, 30 November 1940, box 40, President's Secretary's File: Ireland 1941, Franklin Delano Roosevelt Papers, Franklin Roosevelt Presidential Library, Hyde Park, NY (hereafter: FDR Papers).
12 Maurice Manning, *James Dillon, A Biography* (Dublin: Wolfhound Press, 1999), 162.
13 "Memorandum of Conversation by Under Secretary of State Welles," 9 November 1940, Document 161, *FRUS* 1940 vol. III.
14 "Interview with US Journalist," de Valera interviewed by Wallace Carroll, United Press, 19 November 1940, P104/3808 "Being a Selection of the Speeches of Eamon de Valera During the War (1939–1945)" (Dublin: McGill & Son, 1946), Frank Aiken Papers (on microfilm), University College Dublin (hereafter: FA Papers, UCD).
15 Girvin, *The Emergency*, 186–187.
16 Dwyer, *Irish Neutrality and the USA*, 89–90. See also "Irish Neutrality Lauded: Meeting Here Protests Any Attempts to Jeopardize Nation," *New York Times* (9 December 1940).

17 U.S. Minister David Gray, Memorandum of Conversation with PM de Valera, 6 January 1941, P150/2589, Eamon de Valera Papers (on microfilm), University College Dublin (hereafter: EdV Papers, UCD). See Gray's report of this conversation to U.S. Secretary of State Cordell Hull: "The Minister in Ireland (Gray) to the Secretary of State (Hull), 7 January 1941, Document 161, *FRUS 1941* vol. III (Washington, DC: US Government Printing Office, 1959).

18 Joseph Walshe, Minister for External Affairs, Notes on Meeting with David Gray, 17 January 1941, EdV Papers, UCD. See also Memorandum by Joseph Walshe (Personal), 17 January 1941, Doc. No. 398 NAI DFA Secretary's Files P48/A, *Documents on Irish Foreign Policy* vol. VI, 1939–1941: "Mr. Gray knows perfectly well that, if he or the members of his Government were in charge of Ireland's destiny at this precise moment in history, they would be absolutely obliged to follow the policy of neutrality, at least until that moment when a defeat of Germany became a certainty."

19 The Foreign Minister [Ribbentrop] to the Legation in Ireland, 5 December 1940, Doc. 455, *Documents on German Foreign Policy, 1918–1945*, vol. 11: "The War Years, September 1 – December 31, 1940" (Washington, DC: Government Printing Office, 1957).

20 The Minister in Ireland [Hempel] to the Foreign Minister [Ribbentrop], 17 December 1940, Doc. 523, *Documents on German Foreign Policy, 1918–1945*, vol. 11; John P. Duggan, *Herr Hempel and the German Legation in Dublin, 1937–1945* (Dublin: Irish Academic Press, 2003), 126–129.

21 Robert Fisk, *In Time of War: Ireland, Ulster and the Price of Neutrality, 1939–1945* (London: Andre Deutsch, 1983), 193–194.

22 The Minister in Ireland [Hempel] to the Foreign Minister [Ribbentrop], 29 December 1940, Doc. 576, *Documents on German Foreign Policy, 1918–1945*, vol. 11.

23 "Memorandum by the Department of External Affairs on the German Request to Provide Extra Staff for the German Legation in Dublin," 3 January 1941, Doc. No. 379 NAI DFA Secretary's Files A21, *Documents on Irish Foreign Policy* vol. VI, 1939–1941.

24 Telegram from Joseph P. Walshe to William Warnock (Berlin), 2 January 1941, Doc. No. 378 NAI DFA 221/147A, *Documents on Irish Foreign Policy* vol. VI, 1939–1941.

25 Telegram from Joseph Walshe to William Warnock (Berlin), 3 January 1941, Doc. No. 381 NAI DFA 221/147/A, *Documents on Irish Foreign Policy* vol. VI, 1939–1941.

26 Code Telegram from William Warnock to Joseph Walshe (Personal), 30 January 1941, Doc. No. 415 NAI DFA 221/14/A, *Documents on Irish Foreign Policy* vol. VI, 1939–1941.

27 Aiken quoted in Fisk, *In Time of War*, 317.

28 Carlo D'Este, *Warlord: A Life of Winston Churchill at War, 1874–1945* (New York: HarperCollins, 2008), 499.

29 Robert E. Sherwood, *Roosevelt and Hopkins: An Intimate History* (New York: Grosset & Dunlap, 1948).

30 Hopkins quoted in Kaiser, *No End Save Victory*, 140.
31 Dallek, *Franklin D. Roosevelt: A Political Life*, 410: "Aside from Eleanor, no public figure was seen as representing the president more faithfully than Hopkins."
32 D'Este, *Warlord*, 500.
33 June Hopkins, "Churchill and Three Presidents – Churchill and Hopkins: The Main Prop and Animator of Roosevelt Himself," *Finest Hour* 160 (Autumn 2013), https://winstonchurchill.org/publications/finest-hour/finest-hour-160/churchill-and-three-presidents-3-churchill-and-hopkins-the-main-prop-and-animator-of-roosevelt-himself/ (accessed 4 December 2020).
34 Sonia Purnell, *Clementine: The Life of Mrs. Winston Churchill* (New York: Viking Penguin, 2015), 264–265.
35 Hopkins quoted in Dallek, *Franklin D. Roosevelt: A Political Life*, 412.
36 Hopkins quoted in Purnell, *Clementine*, 266.
37 Jon Meacham, *Franklin and Winston: An Intimate Portrait of an Epic Friendship* (New York: Random House, 2004), 93. See also D'Este, *Warlord*, 500–501.
38 James MacGregor Burns, *Roosevelt: The Soldier of Freedom, 1940–1945* (Open Road media, e-book, 2012), 186.
39 Dallek, *Franklin D. Roosevelt: A Political Life*, 411.
40 Dwyer, *Irish Neutrality and the USA*, 105. See also The Minister in Ireland (Gray) to the Secretary of State (Hull), 10 March 1941, Doc. 169, *FRUS* 1941 vol. III.
41 Helen Kirkpatrick, "Confidential: Memorandum on Eire to Col. Donovan," 5 March 1941, box 2, Helen Paull Kirkpatrick Papers, Sophia Smith Collection, SSC-MS-00103, Smith College Special Collections, Northampton, Massachusetts (hereafter: HPK Papers).
42 Lynne Olson, *Those Angry Days: Roosevelt, Lindbergh, and America's Fight over World War II, 1939–1941* (New York: Random House, 2013), 280.
43 Burns, *Roosevelt*, 124.
44 Olson, *Those Angry Days*, 274–277.
45 Meacham, *Franklin and Winston*, 95.
46 "Text of Radio Broadcast by Prime Minister Winston Churchill," 9 February 1941, box 190, John Gilbert Winant Papers, Franklin Roosevelt Presidential Library (hereafter: JGW Papers, FDR Library).
47 Burns, *Roosevelt*, 120.
48 "Telegram from Winston Churchill to John Winant, thanking him for personal message from FDR about the passage of the Lend-lease Act," 11 March 1941, CHAR: 20/21B/140, Winston Churchill Archives online, The Chartwell Trust.
49 Lynne Olson, *Citizens of London: The Americans Who Stood with Britain in its Darkest, Finest Hour* (New York: Random House, 2011), 21–22.
50 Purnell, *Clementine*, 269–270.
51 Olson, *Citizens of London*, 72–78. See also Olson, *Those Angry Days*, 291–292.
52 Helen Kirkpatrick, "Winant Assails Nazi Tyranny in Maiden Speech: British Impressed by U.S. Speed in Implementing Lend-Lease," *Chicago Daily News* (18 March 1941), box 2, HPK Papers.

53 Helen Kirkpatrick to David Gray, 25 February 1941, box 4, David Gray Papers, 1857–1960, Coll. 03082, University of Wyoming American Heritage Center, Laramie, Wyoming (hereafter: Gray Papers, AHC).
54 Helen Kirkpatrick, "Typed Notes for Article 'Why is Eire Neutral?', Dublin, January 1941," box 2, HPK Papers. See also Kirkpatrick, "Neutrality is Only Choice, Eire Contends; Ninety Pct. Of Irish Back De Valera's Policy of Isolation," *Chicago Daily News* (30 January 1941), box 12, HPK Papers.
55 Helen Kirkpatrick, "Eire Asks if Nazi Bombing was a Mistake or Deliberate," *Chicago Daily News* (1 February 1941), box 12, HPK Papers. See also Kirkpatrick, "Typed Notes for Article 'Why is Eire Neutral?'"; Kirkpatrick, "Civil War Seen if Britain Takes Ports from Eire; Irish Fear Nazis Will Bomb Cities and that British Won't Leave," *Chicago Daily News* (31 January 1941), box 2; Kirkpatrick, "20,000 Soldiers Guard Eire Against Germans or British, Hope to Escape Invasion," *Chicago Daily News* (3 February 1941), box 12, HPK Papers.
56 Kirkpatrick, "Nazi Bombing of Irish Boat Stirs Dublin. Eire Not Strong Enough to Protect Neutral Status," *Chicago Daily News* (6 February 1941), box 12, HPK Papers.
57 Manning, *James Dillon*, 163.
58 Michael Knightly, Chief Press Censor, "Press Censor's Report for January 1941," P104/3477, FA Papers, UCD.
59 Helen Kirkpatrick, "Freedom of Press Killed by Eire's 'Neutral' Policy," *Chicago Daily News* (4 February 1941), box 12, HPK Papers.
60 Helen Kirkpatrick to Joseph Walshe, Under Secretary for External Affairs, 10 March 1941, box 2, HPK Papers.
61 Memorandum by Joseph Walshe for Frank Aiken, "Anti-Irish Propaganda in the United States: Our Counter Propaganda," 28 February 1941, Doc. No. 15 NAI DFA Washington Embassy File 121, *Documents on Irish Foreign Policy* vol. VII, 1941–1945.
62 Girvin, *The Emergency*, 191; Fisk, *In Time of War*, 264.
63 Lord Cranborne [Dominions Secretary] to Winston Churchill [Prime Minister], 30 January 1941, PREM3/131/3, Talks between de Valera and John Maffey, British National Archives. See also "Prime Minister's Personal Minutes. Note from Winston Churchill to Lord Cranborne (Dominions Secretary), 31 January 1941, PREM3/131/3, Talks between de Valera and John Maffey, British National Archives, Kew, Richmond, Surrey, UK.
64 U.S. Minister to Ireland David Gray to Franklin Roosevelt, 4 February 1941, David Gray Papers, 1855–1962, Franklin Roosevelt Presidential Library, Hyde Park, NY (hereafter: DG Papers, FDR Library), box 6; Dwyer, *Irish Neutrality and the USA*, 104–105; Girvin, *The Emergency*, 189–190.
65 January 20 Report from Sir John Maffey to the Dominions Office quoted in Dwyer, *Irish Neutrality and the USA*, 101.
66 Memorandum by Joseph Walshe for Frank Aiken, "Attitude of the State Department Towards Us," 28 February 1941, Doc. No. 16 NAI DFA Secretary's Files P35, *Documents on Irish Foreign Policy* vol. VII, 1941–1945.

67 Fisk, *In Time of War*, 255–256.
68 "Memorandum by Joseph P. Walshe (Most Secret)," 14 March 1941, Doc. No. 24 NAI DFA Secretary's Files A2, *Documents on Irish Foreign Policy* vol. VII, 1941–1945.
69 The Foreign Minister [Ribbentrop] to the Legation in Ireland [Hempel], 24 February 1941, Doc. 79, *Documents on German Foreign Policy, 1918–1945*, vol. 12, "The War Years, February 1 – June 22, 1941" (Washington, DC: Government Printing Office, 1962). See also "Telegram Eduard Hempel to Foreign Secretary [Ribbentrop], 11 March 1941, and German Foreign Office memorandum, *c*. mid-March, 1941, box 4, Gray Papers, AHC.
70 Duggan, *Herr Hempel*, 132–133. See also "Memorandum by Ambassador Ritter," March 13, 1941, Doc. 164, *Documents on German Foreign Policy, 1918–1945*, vol. 12: "Captured British arms as follows have been collected and made ready for a possible shipment to Ireland: 46 field guns, 550 machine guns, some 10,000 rifles, 1,000 anti-tank rifles, all with the necessary ammunition."
71 Maffey quoted in Fisk, *In Time of War*, 264.
72 The Minister in Ireland (Gray) to the Secretary of State (Hull), 24 February 1941, Document 164, *FRUS* 1941 vol. III. See also U.S. Minister David Gray Memorandum of Conversation with PM de Valera, 28 February 1941, P150/2589, EdV Papers, UCD: "[de Valera] asked me to believe him when he told me that Mr. Aiken was in no wise pro-German, as, he said, a newspaper correspondent had told him (the Prime Minister) that Mr. Aiken was generally reputed to be. The Prime Minister said that very definitely it was not so."
73 Tim Pat Coogan, *Eamon de Valera, The Man Who Was Ireland* (New York: HarperCollins, 1993), 574.
74 Girvin, *The Emergency*, 194–195, 209. See also The Minister in Ireland (Gray) to the Secretary of State (Hull), 7 March 1941, Doc. 168, *FRUS* 1941 vol. III.
75 Girvin, *The Emergency*, 198. See also Memorandum by Frank Aiken of a Meeting with Colonel Bill Donovan (London), 6 March 1941, Doc. No. 21 NAI DFA Secretary's Files P35, *Documents on Irish Foreign Policy* vol. VII, 1941–1945.
76 Kirkpatrick, "Confidential: Memorandum on Eire to Col. Donovan," 5 March 1941, box 2, HPK Papers.
77 Donovan in a March 11 telegram passed on by Ambassador Winant, "From Colonel Donovan for the Secretary of the Navy [Knox]," 11 March 1941, box 3, President's Secretary's File: Ireland, FDR Papers.
78 David Gray to Franklin Roosevelt, 18 March 1941, box 6, DG Papers, FDR Library.
79 *Ibid*. See also Girvin, *The Emergency*, 205–206; Dwyer, *Irish Neutrality and the USA*, 122.
80 Edward T. Pollard, "Irish Minister Here to Persuade U.S. to Sell Arms," *Washington Post*, 20 March 1941, P150/2615, EdV Papers, UCD. "A broth of a man" is a phrase used to praise a virile man.

81 "Eire Needs Aid But Won't Give Bases for It, Co-ordinator Says," *Washington Times-Herald* (20 March 1941).
82 Memorandum of Conversation, the Acting Secretary of State (Welles), 20 March 1941, Doc. 170, *FRUS* 1941 vol. III.
83 Girvin, *The Emergency*, 206–207.
84 Extract from a letter from Robert Brennan to Joseph P. Walshe, 26 March 1941, Doc. No. 31 NAI DFA Washington Embassy File 119, *Documents on Irish Foreign Policy* vol. VII, 1941–1945. See also Memorandum of Conversation, the Assistant Secretary of State (Acheson), 2 April 1941, Document 170, *FRUS* 1941 vol. III; Memorandum by Denis Devlin of a Meeting between Frank Aiken and Dean Acheson, 2 April 1941, Doc. No. 37 NAI DFA Washington Embassy File 119, *Documents on Irish Foreign Policy* vol. VII, 1941–1945; Dwyer, *Irish Neutrality and the USA*, 113.
85 Coogan, *Eamon de Valera*, 576.
86 Telegram from Robert Brennan to Joseph Walshe concerning a meeting between Frank Aiken and President Franklin D. Roosevelt, 7 April 1941, Doc. No. 38 NAI DFA Secretary's Files P35; and Letter from Robert Brennan to Joseph Walshe (Confidential), 10 April 1941, Doc. No. 40 NAI DFA Secretary's Files P 35, *Documents on Irish Foreign Policy* vol. VII, 1941–1945. "From Mr. Brennan on Mr. Aiken's Interview with President Roosevelt of 7th April 1941, P150/2604, EdV Papers, UCD.
87 Dwyer, *Irish Neutrality and the USA*, 112–113; David McCullagh, *De Valera: Rule, Volume II 1932–1975* (Dublin: Gill Books, 2018), 210; Girvin, *The Emergency*, 211: Girvin writes: "This is a good story, but the problem is it does not seem to have happened."
88 Dictated Memorandum by Frank Aiken of his Mission to the United States of America (March–June 1941), 5 August 1941, Doc. No. 114 UVDA P104/3585, *Documents on Irish Foreign Policy* vol. VII, 1941–1945.
89 Tully, *Ireland and Irish Americans*, 99.
90 Franklin Roosevelt to Eamon de Valera, 15 April 1941, P150/2615, EdV Papers, UCD.
91 Dwyer, *Irish Neutrality and the USA*, 116–120.
92 The Secretary of State (Hull) to the Minister in Ireland (Gray), April 25, 1941, Document 174, *FRUS* 1941 vol. III; Memorandum dated 26 April 1941, handed to the Taoiseach by the American Minister on 28 April," P150/2604, EdV Papers, UCD.
93 Memorandum by Eamon de Valera of a Meeting with David Gray, 28 April 1941, Doc. No. 49 UCDA P150/2589, *Documents on Irish Foreign Policy* vol. VII, 1941–1945; The Minister in Ireland (Gray) to the Secretary of State (Hull), 1 May 1941, Document 177, *FRUS* 1941 vol. III; Dwyer, *Irish Neutrality and the USA*, 114–116.
94 US Minister David Gray Memorandum of Conversation with PM de Valera, 28 April 1941, P150/2589, EdV Papers, UCD. See also Blue Code Telegram from Joseph Walshe to Robert Brennan (Washington) (No. 111), 13 May 1941, Doc. No. 69 NAI DFA Secretary's Files P35, *Documents on Irish Foreign*

Policy vol. VII, 1941–1945: "They [the Irish Government] cannot agree that the estimate of Mr. Aiken's attitude and the criticism directed against him is just."

95 Cablegrams received from Washington Legation, 19 April 1941, P150/2615, EdV Papers, UCD; "Irish Here Offer Prayers for Peace: If Forced into War Eire would become 'a Mass of Ruins,' Says Father Flanagan," *New York Times* (20 April 1941); "Eire Will Stay Firm on Refusing Bases to Britain, Envoy Says Here: Gen. Aiken Tells Rally There is No Chance of Changing Attitude – Despite Need for Food He Sees No 'Bartering' of Neutrality," *New York Times* (26 April 1941).

96 Dwyer, *Irish Neutrality and the USA*, 117–118. See also Girvin, *The Emergency*, 213.

97 Tully, *Ireland and Irish Americans*, 110, n.101: Aiken's major stops included New York, Boston, Philadelphia, Minneapolis, Seattle, and Los Angeles.

98 Girvin, *The Emergency*, 215.

99 Typescript, "handed in by Mulcahy, The Minister was sent to America to get supplies," P150/2615, EdV Papers, UCD.

100 Brian Barton, *Northern Ireland in the Second World War* (Belfast: Ulster Historical Foundation, 1995), 21–22; Jonathan Bardon, "The Belfast Blitz," in *Ireland in World War Two: Neutrality and Survival*, ed. Dermot Keogh and Mervyn O'Driscoll (Cork: Mercier Press, 2004), 259–273. These raids were recorded in pictures taken by the *Belfast Telegraph*, "Bombs on Belfast 1941," D3038/3/2 Public Records Office of Northern Ireland (PRONI).

101 Fisk, *In Time of War*, 418. See also Ian S. Wood, *Britain, Ireland and the Second World War* (Edinburgh: Edinburgh University Press, 2010), 174–176.

102 Fisk, *In Time of War*, 430.

103 *Ibid.*, 431.

104 Blanche Wiesen Cook, *Eleanor Roosevelt: The War Years and After*, vol. 3, *1939–1962* (New York: Viking, 2016), 392. See also Olson, *Citizens of London*, 93.

105 Burns, *Roosevelt*, 196.

106 *Ibid.*, 219. See also Memorandum from Denis R. McDonald (London) to Joseph Walshe, 24 June 1941, Doc. No. 102 NAI DFA Secretary's Files P12/14/1, *Documents on Irish Foreign Policy* vol. VII, 1941–1945.

107 Jean Edward Smith, *FDR* (New York: Random House, 2008), 492.

108 Fisk, *In Time of War*, 447.

109 Anthony J. Jordan, *Churchill: A Founder of Modern Ireland* (Dublin: Westport Books, 1995), 178.

110 Tully, *Ireland and Irish Americans*, 101. See also Coogan, *Eamon de Valera*, 589.

111 Confidential Report from John W. Dulanty to Joseph Walshe, 22 May 1941, Doc. No. 68 NAI DFA Secretary's Files P12/14/1, *Documents on Irish Foreign Policy* vol. VII, 1941–1945. A second meeting took place between Dulanty and Churchill on May 26, and similar arguments were made by each man. See Confidential Report from John W. Dulanty to Joseph Walshe (No. 15) (Secret),

26 May 1941, Doc. No. 78 NAI DFA Secretary's Files P12/14/1, *Documents on Irish Foreign Policy* vol. VII, 1941–1945.
112 "David Gray Notes on Phone Conversation with de Valera," 24 May 1941, and "draft of Telegram to Washington," 24 May 1941, box 9, DG Papers, FDR Library; Letter from Eamon de Valera to David Gray, 25 May 1941, Doc. No. 77 NAI UCDA P150/2589, *Documents on Irish Foreign Policy* vol. VII, 1941–1945.
113 Jordan, *Churchill*, 179.
114 Application of Conscription to Northern Ireland, Telegram from United Kingdom Representative to Eire (Maffey) to Dominions Office, 25 May 1941, CAB 66/2/47, British National Archives.
115 McCullagh, *De Valera*, 208–209.
116 Cook, *Eleanor Roosevelt*, 393; Smith, *FDR*, 493.
117 Olson, *Citizens of London*, 115.
118 Fisk, *In Time of War*, 434; Tony Gray, *The Lost Years: The Emergency in Ireland, 1939–1945* (London: Warner Books, 1998), 127–130.
119 David Gray to Hugh [last name unknown], 3 June 1941, box 5, Gray Papers, AHC.
120 Memorandum by Joseph Walshe (Secret), 31 May 1941, Doc. No. 86 UCDA P150/21/1, *Documents on Irish Foreign Policy* vol. VII, 1941–1945.
121 Telegram from William Warnock to Joseph Walshe, 5 June 1941, Doc. No. 91 NAI DFA 221/147E, *Documents on Irish Foreign Policy* vol. VII, 1941–1945.
122 David Gray to Franklin Roosevelt, June 9, 1941, box 6, DG Papers, FDR Library.
123 Personal Code Telegram from Joseph Walshe to Robert Brennan (No. 157), 19 June 1941, Doc. No. 101 NAI DFA Secretary's Files P12/8, *Documents on Irish Foreign Policy* vol. VII, 1941–1945.
124 Memorandum from Denis R. McDonald (London) to Joseph Walshe, 24 June 1941, Doc. No. 102 NAI DFA Secretary's Files P12/14/1, *Documents on Irish Foreign Policy* vol. VII, 1941–1945.
125 Churchill quoted in Burns, *Roosevelt*, 239–240.
126 *Ibid.*, 252.
127 D'Este, *Warlord*, 504.
128 Kaiser, *No End Save Victory*, 202. See also Frank Costigliola, *Roosevelt's Lost Alliances: How Personal Politics Helped Start the Cold War* (Princeton, NJ: Princeton University Press, 2012), 88.
129 Girvin, *The Emergency*, 283.

5

British friend, Irish foe, July to December 1941

Winston Churchill's long courtship of Franklin Roosevelt and his concerted efforts to engage the United States as an active ally and belligerent power in the anti-fascist war were finally starting to bear fruit by mid-summer 1941. In a major move toward war with Nazi Germany, Roosevelt agreed to Churchill's request to send U.S. Navy ships to protect neutral Iceland, the island nation that Britain had occupied in May 1940 when Germany overran neutral Denmark. At the time, Iceland was united with Denmark through a shared monarch. Since May 1940, the British Navy had guarded Iceland's coastline and Canadian Allied forces had set up garrisons on the island to resist a German attack. On July 7, 1941, President Roosevelt announced that the U.S. Navy would relieve British ships and conduct protective patrols around Iceland. This naval deployment also extended the American zone of protection for supply ships that were transporting aid to Britain across the North Atlantic.[1] It was not lost on Roosevelt's domestic political rivals or on the Axis Powers that the U.S. President had taken a "great step" toward war, as FDR also announced that U.S. warships would fire on any German submarines impeding their paths "without warning."[2] Any of these actions might cause an "incident" that could prompt a German declaration of war on America.[3] In the immediate term, Churchill told his War Cabinet that U.S. Naval commitments "would free enough British warships for action in the Atlantic to guarantee victory over German U-boats."[4]

Roosevelt also ordered the U.S. military to take two additional steps to aid Britain in July. First, on July 13, orders went forward to the British and U.S. Army chiefs to arrange for joint military exercises to be held in August and September on U.S. bases. The goal was to share knowledge of military operations and procedures, as the two nations could soon be fighting side by side.[5] Second, plans that had been made in spring 1941 to send U.S. Army corps into Northern Ireland to improve naval and army bases and to construct new air bases also went into operation in July 1941, as newspapers in Eire and in the United States reported.[6] David Gray shared the Irish government's alarmed reactions with Franklin Roosevelt, as Taoiseach Eamon de Valera objected to *any* foreign troops stationed on Irish soil as violations of Irish sovereignty and challenges to its neutrality policy.[7] But Gray also knew that there were some Irish politicians who were questioning the government's foreign policies and its censorship of dissenting views.[8]

James Dillon, then deputy leader of the Fine Gael party, for one, had already made his views known to Gray. After reaching a "crisis point" of conscience, Dillon delivered a bold speech in the Dáil on July 16 challenging the government's neutrality policy,[9] claiming it was "not in the true interest, moral or material, of the Irish people,"[10] and arguing that "it was wrong for Ireland to 'sell its honor and stake its whole material future on the vain hope that it might be spared the passing pain of effort now.'"[11] While the government censored Dillon's speech and it did not appear in Irish newspapers to inform the public's view, his words caused a "sensation" in the Dáil.[12] Dillon's sympathies were with the Western democratic allies in the anti-fascist war, and he believed that Ireland should "declare, in no uncertain way, on the side of liberty, decency and freedom."[13] He criticized de Valera's amoral neutrality policy in his shocking speech to the assembled Dáil, opening himself up to Fianna Fáil's outcry when he asserted:

> At present we act the part of Pontius Pilate in asking, as between the Axis and the Allies, "What is truth?" and washing our hands and calling the world to witness that this is no affair of ours. I say we know, as between those parties, what the truth is – that on the side of the Anglo-American alliance is right and justice and on the side of the Axis is evil and injustice.[14]

Political scientist Ben Tonra has argued that Irish foreign relations can be understood as being directed by four "constructed narratives" that compete with one another for dominance in policy making and in the discourse that rationalizes Ireland's foreign affairs. Tonra suggests that Ireland defines "itself" and its foreign policies in relation to the rest of the world as either: (1) the Irish Nation, (2) the Global Citizen, (3) the European Republic, or (4) the Anglo-American State.[15] In analyzing the conflict between the majority perspective of Eamon de Valera and his Fianna Fáil cohorts in the 1930s and 1940s, and the minority opinion of James Dillon within the minority party Fine Gael, according to Tonra's scheme de Valera espoused the narrative of Ireland as "Irish Nation," and Dillon subscribed to the narrative of Ireland as "Anglo-American State." According to de Valera and the narrative of the Irish Nation:

> Where England was Protestant, Ireland was Catholic, where it was urban, Ireland was rural, where it was industrial, Ireland was agrarian and where it was Anglo-Saxon, Ireland was Gaelic ...

> The state's earliest foreign policy efforts were thus directed towards defining the precise relationship [and boundaries] between the new Irish Free State and the British Empire ...[16]

And according to Dillon and the narrative of the Anglo-American State:

> This narrative looks to the English-speaking world as being Ireland's natural political and cultural hinterland ...
>
> From the arrival of the Anglo-Normans in the twelfth century the history of the peoples on the island of Ireland may be seen as having been completely intertwined with that of the broader cultural family both within these islands and further abroad ... In this context this narrative also redefines the bilateral relationship with Britain as it focuses upon the shared and common experiences. ....[17]

For Dillon, during the Second World War, "neutrality" represented a betrayal of "Ireland-as-Anglo-American-State's" values and interests. To be sure, Dillon expressed a minority opinion, and even as he sympathized strongly with the Anglo-American anti-fascist fight, he was advocating for more cooperation with the Allies, not a declaration of war on the Axis Powers. Nonetheless, he was censured by his own party colleagues for his speech in July 1941, and, in 1942, Fine Gael leadership expelled Dillon from his party for publicly denouncing the government's neutrality policy.

President Roosevelt didn't escape criticism from his domestic political rivals, either. Like de Valera and his government in Eire, America First advocates in the United States questioned the "legality" of building U.S. bases on "foreign" soil. Roosevelt responded that the British government employed American "workmen," drawing on Lend-Lease aid to contract with U.S. laborers to build bases within the United Kingdom's domain. But FDR was clearly skating the truth; the U.S. Army was constructing these bases in Northern Ireland.[18] At the end of June, Roosevelt had also misrepresented the Irish government's commitment to resist a German invasion with an offhand response to a reporter's question at a press conference. When Roosevelt stated that he "never received" Irish assurances regarding their intention to fight back if Germany attacked Eire, he started a flurry of diplomatic cables back and forth across the Atlantic that went on for weeks as the Irish government sought an official retraction of the president's false claims.[19]

As Irish-American relations worsened, Anglo-American relations strengthened as Franklin Roosevelt and Winston Churchill planned their first wartime face-to-face meeting. The national leaders understood better than any of their political or military advisers that their first meeting would define their nations' wartime alliance from that point forward. They each attempted to stage the meeting to achieve the maximum benefits that would further their national interests and enhance their personal political reputations. Moreover, they each understood the wartime security imperatives that required subterfuge and enthusiastically joined in the preparations. Churchill personally inspected the British warship *Prince of Wales* that would escort him across the Atlantic and was assured that the ship could steer clear of any German U-boat attacks. For his part, Roosevelt devised a complicated plan that involved sending a second cruise ship to anchor off the shores of Cape Cod, staged with a "double" playing the part of FDR on board deck to fool the American press who might try to follow the president on his "fishing vacation" at sea, as he sailed north, undetected, on the *Augusta* to Placentia Bay off the coast of Newfoundland to rendezvous with Churchill.[20] According to historian Frank Costigliola, "each saw the meeting as an occasion to display his manly resolve and their common values"; "both regarded theatrics and personal bonding as vital in constructing an alliance"; and both leaders "were also alike in approaching the conference as boys setting off on an adventure."[21]

Roosevelt and Churchill had already established roles in their political relationship.

The President was more aloof in his demeanor and cautious in making commitments of military support for the Allied Powers. The Prime Minister was more emotional, vigorously representing his nation's unwavering resolve to carry on as the embattled underdog to convince "America," Roosevelt, and "the world" that Britain would ultimately prevail against the evil and tyrannical fascist powers. Roosevelt was willing to make important but at this point largely symbolic expressions of unity with Britain's anti-fascist crusade; Churchill sought definitive plans and solid commitments for a formal military alliance with the United States.[22] In summer 1941, Britain was struggling to hold onto oilfields in the Middle East, and to ports in Singapore and in the Canary Islands. The War Cabinet was also worried about a German invasion of Spain and threats to capture Gibraltar. The United States' entry into the war could bring relief to British forces on all these fronts.[23] While Roosevelt achieved many of his objectives at Placentia Bay, Churchill's hopes to elicit a formal declaration of war from the United States were disappointed.[24] Nonetheless, the meeting produced a document, the Atlantic Charter, that articulated common Anglo-American values and shared political goals to be pursued in the postwar world, as well as additional consequential results. It established the fraternal friendship between Roosevelt and Churchill[25] and cemented the wartime Anglo-American "special relationship" through the creation of national myths of brotherhood and shared warrior values – major achievements for the two leaders' first encounter, to be sure.

The stories that emerged following the August shipboard meetings have often been repeated in contemporary and historic accounts.[26] Testimonies

5.1 Prime Minister Winston Churchill and President Franklin Roosevelt seated on the quarterdeck of the HMS *Prince of Wales* following the Sunday religious service, Atlantic Conference, August 1941

that highlighted the significance of the first words the two men exchanged: "At last we have gotten together," said Franklin Roosevelt; "Yes we have," replied Winston Churchill. Tales of the first lunch meeting that put the two "great men" on a first-name basis. Fabled accounts of the Sunday, August 10, religious service held on board the *Prince of Wales* for the American and British leaders, naval commanders, and sailors, that recounted how the scene was set with the two national flags flying together, the military band playing the two national anthems, the sailors turned out in their dress uniforms standing at attention. Emotional accounts of Roosevelt's legendary walk across the deck to attend the service, enduring the pain of walking in braces that stiffened his crippled legs. Memories of singing message-laden Christian hymns: "O God, Our Help in Ages Past" and "Onward Christian

Soldiers." Roosevelt's stoic words to his son Elliott, who stood by his side throughout the meetings, after the ceremony: "'Onward Christian Soldiers.' We *are*, and we *will* go on, with God's help."[27] Churchill, moved to tears at the time, recalled the religious service in his postwar memoirs, far more effusively than FDR had done, as:

> a deeply moving expression of the unity of faith of our two peoples, and none of us who took part in it will forget the spectacle presented that sunlit morning ... the symbolism of the Union Jack and the Stars and Stripes draped side by side on the pulpit ... and the close packed ranks of the British and American sailors, completely intermingled, sharing the same books and joining fervently together in the prayers and hymns familiar to both ... Every word seemed to stir the heart. It was a great hour to live. Nearly half those who sang were soon to die. ...[28]

All these war stories, told and retold, created a unified memory shared by the two Western powers. Although Roosevelt's and Churchill's first meeting had proceeded with "a planned emotionalism ... that could appear uncalculated,"[29] accounts of the meeting denied any differences between themselves or their nations, and affirmed and justified the pre-eminence of the two nations' warlords.

The meeting's document, the Atlantic Charter, promoted a "Wilsonian" vision: a future world of democratic sovereign states, that cooperated to forge free trade agreements to keep the peace, reduced the need for great armies and stores of weapons, and that sought "no aggrandizement, territorial or other," as the spoils of war. It allowed the Allied Powers to claim the moral high ground and justified the war to defeat utterly and completely the fascist powers and the ideologies that fueled them. In eight clauses, the charter affirmed these "certain common principles in the national policies of [Britain and the United States] ... on which they base their hopes for a better future for the world."[30] From the perspective of many of the world's still-colonized peoples, the Atlantic Charter signaled the end of the British Empire, although Winston Churchill kept the faith in the British upper class's "White Man's Burden" and its pledge to spread the British version of Christian civilization to "enlighten" the rest of the world.[31] Nonetheless, the Charter was an "enduring result" of the conference,[32] articulating high-minded ideals that both leaders would use to mobilize their nations' peoples, who, in turn, could claim the righteousness of their fight. Churchill soon addressed his nation, applying his "rhetorical splendor" to illuminate the meaning of the Atlantic Charter: "Would it be presumptuous of me to say that is symbolizes something more majestic – namely: the marshalling of the good forces of the world against the evil forces which are now so formidable and triumphant and which

5.2 Prime Minister Winston Churchill looks out from deck of HMS *Prince of Wales* as the USS *Augusta* sails away following the Atlantic Conference with U.S. President Franklin Roosevelt on board the vessel, August 1941

have cast their cruel spell over the whole of Europe and a large part of Asia?"³³

In the aftermath of the August meeting, Franklin Roosevelt wrote to David Gray in Dublin to profess that he believed the Atlantic conference with Churchill "had done good," and that "it may make a few more people in Ireland see the light." Roosevelt also dismissed "my old friend Dev," and de Valera's claims that Eire was strong enough to mount an effective self-defense against a German invasion.³⁴ Roosevelt and Gray had been goading de Valera regarding Ireland's defense capabilities since the end of June, even as the administration denied most of the requests for guns and other materials that de Valera's government had been making throughout the spring of 1941.³⁵ These jibes were intended to mount a public pressure campaign on the Irish government to grant the British access to Irish ports, with the goal of building pro-British opinion in both the United States and Ireland as the Roosevelt administration increased its military support for Britain. Gray had continued to advise Roosevelt that access to the Irish ports was valuable to the British Navy, and would also "eventually" benefit the American Navy, too.³⁶ Access to Irish airfields would also benefit Allied forces, aiding them in protecting ships crossing the Atlantic from German U-boat attacks, providing refueling stations for Allied attacks on the Continent, and reducing if not eliminating the substantial security risks that Germany posed to the Allies through their foothold in Ireland.³⁷ Gray was not only troubled by the presence of the German Legation in Dublin and the intelligence that it passed on to Berlin, he was convinced that German spies and Irish government officials were collaborating with IRA nationalists. He was making these claims in private letters to Roosevelt, and in conversations with Irish opposition politicians and American reporters, casting aspersions on Frank Aiken in particular, who, Gray asserted, was aiding the Germans, or, the pro-German IRA, from within de Valera's government.³⁸

On July 20, Gray supplied American reporters, including Helen Kirkpatrick, with his "Notes on Axis Activities in Ireland," which began with a caveat: "OFF the record I am making the following answers according to my best information and belief." Gray was careful not to slur de Valera, who, Gray asserted, "is neutral and pro-Irish," but he also shared what he suspected about German subversion in Eire. German agents, he asserted:

> *probably* finance such IRA groups and activities as have escaped internment by the government: they stir up anti-British feeling whenever possible. They were *probably* active at the time of the last German bombing of Dublin when, until the government announcement of the German origin of the bombs, word was passed through the Dublin masses that the English had done it. A very intelligent IRA woman whom I know met me in the street at the time and told me it would be proved that the English did it, possibly with captured German bombs. At the time of the recent crisis over conscription in the North, there was great activity on the part of the German agents stirring up anti-British feeling.³⁹ (emphasis added)

Gray did not accuse the German Minister Eduard Hempel of involvement: "I doubt if he directs any Nazi activities in Ireland or whether his Nazi Secretary does either." But, he asserted, "The head of the German spy system is presumably some agent, unknown to the public." In this statement, Gray may have been referring to Hermann Goertz, the German spy who parachuted into Ireland in the midst of the German *blitzkrieg* attacks on Western Europe in May 1940 and who was still at large.[40] To the question of whether the German spy network was effective in gathering useful intelligence about the Allies, Gray replied:

> I have no means of knowing. There is every reason why it should be efficient and extremely important. It must be impossible to prevent the sending of information useful to Germany out of England with the hundreds of people travelling back and forth. Once it arrives here, the German Legation has cable communication with Washington. Everything of importance could be passed along very quickly and fully.[41]

How much Gray knew about German spying and collusion with Irish nationalists, versus what was conjecture or was deliberately manufactured misinformation, came under Irish government scrutiny in August 1941. Gray's loose tongue and an accidental leak of a report written by Helen Kirkpatrick based on their shared suspicions of pro-German sympathizers within the Irish government might have caused a diplomatic incident, if the U.S. and British foreign offices' attentions were not focused elsewhere.

Gray's reports back to Washington and his whisper campaign in Ireland gained some credibility when another German agent was captured after he parachuted into Ireland at the end of July.[42] Moreover, although Gray most likely did not know the extent of it, the German Foreign Ministry was, in fact, drafting plans in August 1941 for a possible invasion of Ireland to take place in mid-September.[43] The plans were speculative, but they were detailed. The Foreign Ministry noted that "The landing will take place only if the landing place can be definitely identified and no particular risks are present." Several German agents accompanied by an IRA operative, Frank Ryan, who had been stranded in Berlin for over a year, were to parachute into Northern Ireland with a radio transmitter. The plans were to make contact with the local IRA, begin sabotage operations of British bases in Northern Ireland, and begin transmitting "military information, including weather reports, since at de Valera's demand radio traffic of the Legation with the Foreign Ministry has to be cut down to the very minimum." According to the German intelligence, "With the progress of war in the east, Ireland is becoming more and more a focus of English-American interests."[44] The Germans, as well as the Southern Irish, were well aware that the U.S. Army was constructing military bases in the North.

Gray probably didn't know about Berlin's August/September invasion plans, nor did de Valera's government. But de Valera and Walshe *did* know that the German Embassy had a "secret transmitter" and were using it to send intelligence reports – primarily weather reports that could aid German bombers – back to Germany, against international agreements that restricted belligerent activities in neutral states. De Valera protested to German Minister Hempel about these transmissions in mid-August, and hinted that the British were aware of this breach, which was very likely since David Gray possessed a report of this meeting.[45] Even so, the Irish leaders were outraged when Gray mistakenly sent a report written by Kirkpatrick that was based on Gray's "Notes on Axis Activities in Ireland," and that included their shared suspicions of "anti-American" elements in de Valera's government (i.e. Frank Aiken *and* Joseph Walshe), in a note to Joseph Walshe.

When Walshe read Kirkpatrick's report that was intended for the U.S. Ambassador in London, John Winant,[46] he and de Valera were determined to stop Gray from spreading stories that were, as Walshe and de Valera believed, either figments of Gray's imagination or malicious gossip intended to malign the Irish government. Kirkpatrick's report described the "dangerous" level of German spying going on in Eire and suggested that the U.S. and British governments "put the screws on" de Valera's government by rationing food and fuel until de Valera opened Irish ports to the Allies, put a stop to the anti-British press campaign in the United States, and lifted press restrictions on American reporters in Ireland. The anti-Irish-government sentiments expressed in Kirkpatrick's report surprised Ambassador Winant, and Kirkpatrick wrote to Gray to let him know Winant's reaction: "I hope I have accurately conveyed your views, and the general situation in Eire. I told him last night that you had taken me into your confidence, and that I thought I had a pretty good idea of how matters stand between you and Dev."[47]

Kirkpatrick also filed stories that were published in the *Chicago Daily News* at the end of August. An article titled "Alarmed Irish Looking to U.S. for Protection Against Nazis; Dublin Group Seeking Action" focused on the minority politicians in the Dáil and Irish Senate who were criticizing the Irish neutrality policy.[48] "Eire Facing Hardest Winter Since the Famine of 1847" asserted that rationing of key foods and supplies was linked to the government's stubborn adherence to its neutrality policy.[49] Fianna Fáil Director of the Government Information Bureau Frank Gallagher lashed out at Kirkpatrick after the first article appeared in print,[50] taking "violent exception" to Kirkpatrick's characterization of de Valera's government as being "anti-American." Kirkpatrick wrote to Gray that "I shall answer [Gallagher's] letter coolly and calmly point out one or two things which Frank Aiken and Joe Walshe said to me. He [Gallagher] also breathed fire and threats about what the Irish in America would think and do about people like me who try to stir up trouble between the two countries." Gallagher also accused Kirkpatrick of knowing "nothing about Irish history," which insulted her. Nonetheless, she stood up to Gallagher's attempt to bully her and planned to file other stories she wrote about Nazi

5.3 Helen Kirkpatrick [far left] with David and Maude Gray on United States Legation grounds, Phoenix Park, *c.* 1941

activities in Ireland, as she and Gray had agreed.[51] Another angry missive from Gallagher followed:

> I find it at least a little curious that somebody who seems so concerned that goodwill should exist between two peoples should herself write contrary to the truth, the only effect of which can be to make ill will. As I had already denied to you the "information" which you probably got from Mr. Gray that there was a scintilla of anti-American feeling in our Government, and as you nevertheless accepted it and used it in what you sent your paper, I feel it is no use arguing the question and explaining that there could not be any "anti-American" feeling here.[52]

Kirkpatrick again pushed back, rejecting Gallagher's characterization of her motives, and asserted she got her information from Irish government sources that regretted the fallout from Frank Aiken's belligerent anti-British statements during his visit to the United States in the spring.[53] Kirkpatrick could clearly stand up for herself, even as Gray offered to fall on his sword to defend her.

David Gray received an alarming shock after Walshe read a copy of Kirkpatrick's report to Ambassador Winant.[54] Gray wrote to Kirkpatrick on September 2 to explain his diplomatic gaffe, and warned her that she might suffer repercussions in terms of access to sources in Ireland:

> I just got back after a talk with Maffey in town and found your article which Joe W. returned to me. Now prepare yourself for a shock. I am jolted alright. I thought I had your confidential memorandum for Mr. Winant in a separate envelope in my locked drawer. Instead it was fastened to your article which I gave to Joe yesterday. As I see it now there is only one thing to do, that is to pretend you wanted him to see it and that I passed it over to him by design and without comment; that we both wanted him to know just what was going on and just what we thought about it. How I can ever square myself with you I don't know. Usually I am pretty careful, but this was about as bad a slip as could be made. I am terribly sorry for you but do not regret having him know my own inside thoughts. I have got to capitalize on it in some way that isn't very clear yet. ... However, be assured that I will take full responsibility for everything in the memorandum, that is, that I inspired it. We must assume he has copied it but as it was given to him confidentially for his private ear he can't very well use it.[55]

After several days elapsed and Gray had not heard from Walshe, he consulted with Sir John Maffey. What should he do? Apologize and admit his mistake? Maffey advised Gray to "do nothing": "He said the best thing to do was to let Joe puzzle what it meant and make no admissions."[56]

Finally, Walshe wrote to David Gray on September 11: "As you were good enough to let me know quite frankly the line you were taking with visiting American correspondents, I feel I owe it to you to write in the frankest possible manner what I think." Walshe accused Gray of spreading baseless rumors about German espionage in Ireland, and exaggerating the size of the IRA and the extent of its connections with the Germans: "If I didn't know your good intentions and your friendly feelings toward this country, I would have described it [Gray's 'Notes on Axis Activities in Eire'] as a poison carrier." Walshe dissected and disputed all the points Gray had speculated about in his "Notes," and ended with the "suggestion" that Gray should consider whether he could continue in his diplomatic post:

> If you really feel that your interest in this – not the least of the motherland of the American people – is limited by the passions and prejudices of the present moment, perhaps you ought – in fairness to both countries – review your position. This is, of course, a purely personal suggestion, but the whole character

of your notes forces the conviction upon me that your prejudices make it impossible for you to be the instrument through which a proper balance of goodwill can be established between our two Governments. You have fallen into the fatal error of believing that the interests of a small nation are less sacred than those of countries great in size and population. Such a philosophy holds no future for the world, and I can't see how it can be made a basis for friendship and co-operation between us.[57]

Walshe hoped for Gray's resignation, but Gray had President Roosevelt's support and the Irish government knew it.[58] Following Walshe's dressing down, Gray wrote to Roosevelt on September 12, affirming that support. Gray also indicated in his letter to FDR that he would fight back against Walshe's assertions that he was fabricating stories and was not acting in the best interests of friendly Irish-American relations:

Many thanks for your letter of August 21. It was good of you to write when you have thousands of important matters on your mind. Dev is still grim and obstinate and blind. I keep pounding away on the idea that we do not like to be pressure-grouped by ANY hyphenated minority. It is a good deal of a blow to them for they have come to take playing politics in our backyard as a right. I have asked Sumner Welles please to find out for me from the FBI if they have anything on Aiken. I don't want to know details, but it would strengthen my hand if they had connected him with subversive activities [when Aiken was in America during his March–June mission to America]. As I wrote you, it is reported to me by enemies of his in his own party that he has boasted that "he had everything lined up." If he could be mentioned in some sabotage file it would be a good thing and have a good effect here.[59]

Walshe, in turn, urged de Valera to issue an official objection to the presence of "American bases" in Northern Ireland, and to chastise David Gray, as well.[60] In fall 1941, however, U.S. Army construction of bases in Ulster proceeded without any breaks, and Colonel Bill Donovan, now based in Washington with a new title, "Coordinator of Military Intelligence" for the War Department, launched a new propaganda effort and covertly funded a new organization, the "Committee for American Irish Defense" (CAID), to build up popular support for American bases in Northern Ireland. A CAID petition campaign also gathered signatures from Irish Americans who backed Roosevelt's pro-British foreign policy. America First Senator Burton Wheeler exposed Donovan's role in forming CAID in November. The American Friends of Irish Neutrality (AFIN) organized a rally of 4,000 people in New York City[61] to denounce Roosevelt's actions to undermine Irish neutrality, but a majority of Americans favored Roosevelt's actions, and support for the Irish was dimming throughout the fall.[62] In October, German U-boats torpedoed American merchant ships off the coast of Iceland, and most Americans now favored repeal of the last vestiges of the U.S. Neutrality Acts. Over the course of the last two years, Roosevelt had successfully prepared a predominantly isolationist nation to support America's entry into the war.[63]

The United States became an active belligerent following the Japanese surprise attack on the U.S. Naval Fleet stationed in Pearl Harbor, Hawaii, on December 7. The crippling attack – more than 2,300 American casualties, two battleships destroyed, twelve ships sunk or beached, nine other ships damaged, 160 aircraft destroyed and 150 additional aircraft damaged[64] – "stunned Americans."[65] Secretary of Labor Frances Perkins observed the scene in the administration's emergency Cabinet meeting, when President Roosevelt shared the news with his Cabinet secretaries and Congressional leadership:

> He [FDR] admitted a "very confused story coming in. Navy didn't know exactly what or how." Pressed on the failure in U.S. intelligence, he repeated, "We don't know." A bit later, Senator Tom Connally of Texas banged his fist on the table demanding, "How did it happen that our warships were caught like tame ducks in Pearl Harbor?" He seemed to feel that the nation's manhood had been exposed and found wanting. "How did they catch us with our pants down?" With bowed head FDR muttered, "I don't know, Tom. I just don't know."[66]

Roosevelt and his military advisers expected that an assault on some Allied territory in the Asia-Pacific region was coming. Intelligence reports from early November revealed that Japan was planning a major attack, maybe on the Philippines, maybe on British Malaysia, but the exact target wasn't known.[67] It was no secret, however, that U.S.-Japanese relations had been deteriorating throughout the 1930s, and that Japan's imperial ambitions and territorial expansion had advanced beyond the abilities, or the will, of the United States or the European colonial powers to stop them. Throughout the 1930s, Japan advanced its imperial expansion into China and into territories previously dominated by European colonial powers in Southeast Asia. As Nazi Germany had promoted a doctrine of racial superiority and defined itself as a "master race" to justify its subjugation of Jewish, Slavic, and Roma peoples in Europe, Japan justified its domination of non-Japanese Asian peoples with a racist ideology and styled itself as a "liberator" of Asia from European colonial overlords, creating a "Greater East Asian Co-Prosperity Sphere."[68]

The Roosevelt administration objected to Japan's imperial aggression that shut U.S. businesses out of Asian markets, and sympathized with Asian "victim" nations, overrun and dominated by a ruthless Japanese Army. The administration imposed economic sanctions and issued diplomatic protests, but these measures failed to halt Japan's expansion. However, the pressures imposed by the U.S. government sanctions – freezing Japanese assets in U.S.

banks and enforcing an embargo on oil sales to the Empire – finally inspired the Japanese military to launch a surprise attack on the U.S. Naval Fleet at Pearl Harbor on December 7. This devastating blow to U.S. military presence in the Pacific was followed by Japanese attacks on other U.S. territories in the Philippines and South Pacific islands, and attacks on British colonial holdings in Malaysia and Hong Kong.

On December 8, Franklin Roosevelt addressed a Joint Session of U.S. Congress to ask for a declaration of war on Japan. He defined Japan's "treachery" and asserted the "righteousness" of the American people's war of self-defense:

> Yesterday, December 7, 1941 – a date which will live in infamy – the United States of America was suddenly and deliberately attacked by naval and air forces of the Empire of Japan. ... With confidence in our armed forces – with the unbounding determination of our people – we will gain the inevitable triumph, so help us God. I will ask that the Congress declare that since the unprovoked and dastardly attack by Japan on Sunday, December 7, 1941, a state of war has existed between the United States and the Japanese Empire.[69]

Roosevelt left the chamber with the cheers of the representatives ringing out: "Vote! Vote! Vote!"[70] The U.S. Senate voted to declare war 82 to 0; the House of Representatives passed the declaration of war 382 to 1.

On December 9, Roosevelt spoke directly to the American people in his "Fireside Chat" national radio address. Again, he defined the Japanese enemies as treacherous gangsters who were in league with Europe's fascist dictators:

> The course that Japan has followed for the past ten years in Asia has paralleled the course of Hitler and Mussolini in Europe and in Africa. Today, it has become far more than a parallel. It is actual collaboration so well calculated that all the continents of the world, and all the oceans, are now considered by the Axis strategists as one gigantic battlefield.[71]

Roosevelt laid out the chronology of Japanese, Italian, and German offenses during the 1930s and in the first two years of war in Europe, and declared: "It is all of one pattern." Moreover, "We are now in this war. We are in it – all the way." The United States must fight with its arsenal of weapons and military equipment and with its warriors. It could no longer appease dictators, nor believe it was protected from aggression by its ocean borders. Finally, Roosevelt explained what the American people would be fighting for, and who they would be fighting against:

> We are now in the midst of a war, not for conquest, not for vengeance, but for a world in which this nation, and all that this nation represents, will be safe

for our children. We expect to eliminate the danger from Japan, but it would serve us ill if we accomplished that and found that the rest of the world was dominated by Hitler and Mussolini.[72]

It did not take long for the Axis Powers to respond. On December 11, Nazi Germany declared war on the United States, criticizing the United States' faux neutrality policy that favored Britain, and charging the U.S. government with open acts of military aggression, especially in the North Atlantic due to Roosevelt's convoy policy.[73] Italy's declaration of war soon followed. Adolf Hitler also delivered a war address to the German people that emphasized Germany's resentments against the Western democracies, the victor nations in the Great War, and their privileged leaders who had profited from that war. In Hitler's version of history, Germany was justified in its imperialist campaign:

> I understand only too well that a world-wide distance separates Roosevelt's ideas and my ideas. ... Roosevelt comes from a rich family and belongs to the class whose path is smoothed in the democracies. I was the only child of a small, poor family and had to fight my way by work and industry. When the Great War came Roosevelt occupied a position where he got to know only its pleasant consequences, enjoyed by those who do business when others bleed. ... As for the German nation, it needs charity neither from Mr. Roosevelt nor from Mr. Churchill. ... It wants only its rights! It will secure for itself this right to live even if thousands of Churchills and Roosevelts conspire against it.[74]

Upon hearing of the Japanese attack on Pearl Harbor, Winston Churchill immediately seized on what was for him the salient point – the United States was now fighting with Britain and against the fascist powers. To him, that meant one thing: the Allies would prevail. He recorded his thoughts of that momentous night:

> The United States was in the war, up to its neck and to the death. So, we had won after all. ... England would live; Britain would live; the Commonwealth of Nations and the Empire would live. ... Many disasters, immeasurable cost and tribulation lay ahead, but there was no more doubt about the end. ... Being saturated and satiated with emotion and sensation, I went to bed and slept the sleep of the saved and the thankful.[75]

Churchill heard the news at Chequers, the country house and retreat of Britain's prime ministers. He was dining with several advisers and family members, including U.S. Ambassador John Winant and U.S. Lend-Lease administrator Averill Harriman. In his great relief, and now bounding with energy, Churchill was anxious to visit Roosevelt in Washington and launch their joint war plans.[76] Winant and others persuaded him to wait for Roosevelt's invitation and accept the Americans' timetable, and Churchill's call to Roosevelt was restrained and brief:

"Mr. President, what's this about Japan?"

"It's quite true," Roosevelt replied. "They have attacked us at Pearl Harbor. We are all in the same boat now."

"That certainly simplifies things," said Churchill. "God be with you."[77]

Churchill reluctantly agreed when FDR delayed his trip to Washington for several weeks.[78] But he could not refrain from sending a message to Eamon de Valera, believing that with America in the war against the Axis Powers, the Irish Taoiseach must now declare that Ireland would enter the anti-fascist alliance. If Eire had not joined their former enemy, Britain, in the righteous war, it surely could not deny the alliance with its historic friend, the United States. Churchill sent de Valera an impetuous telegram on December 8: "Now is your chance, now or never, 'A Nation once again.' Am very ready to meet you at any time."[79] Churchill understood the message to mean that Eire and de Valera had the chance to do the right thing and regain Ireland's national honor, or, in Churchill's view, recover Ireland's "lost soul."[80] Churchill also shared his message to Ireland with Roosevelt, who was "Delighted to know of message to de Valera," indicating that Roosevelt also understood that now was the time to press for Ireland's alliance with the Western Powers.[81]

The Irish, however, were not so sure about the message Churchill sent. Was the message in fact a threat? Would the British take the opportunity to invade Eire and re-establish its semi-colonial status within the United Kingdom? Or, was this another offer to end partition of Ireland? Was this cryptic message a renewal of the offer made in 1940, to promise a future restoration of the Six Counties of Ulster to Irish rule if Eire provided access to the naval ports, expelled the Germans from the country, and joined the anti-fascist united front as the Anglo-Americans desired?[82]

Eamon de Valera met with Sir John Maffey who delivered Churchill's telegram to him at four in the morning. Joseph Walshe, who arranged the pre-dawn meeting, later recalled that "Our opinion ... was that Churchill had been imbibing heavily that night after the news of Pearl Harbor, ... and that his effusion flowed into his message."[83] De Valera, who neither liked nor trusted Churchill,[84] was advised by Walshe, who interpreted the message as yet another call for the surrender of Irish neutrality that would surely result in a German attack,[85] as a promise that the action "would ultimately lead to the unification of the country."[86] De Valera refused the offer again. He told Maffey:

> I saw no opportunity at the moment of securing unity, that our people were determined on their attitude of neutrality, etc. I pointed out that it was not because I did not wish to meet Mr. Churchill, that I was not in favour of going. I was not in favour of it because I considered it unwise; that I didn't see

any basis of agreement and that disagreement might leave conditions worse than before and that my visit in any case would have the results that I had already indicated.[87]

A few days later, de Valera responded directly to Winston Churchill and suggested that Churchill send his Dominions Secretary, Lord Cranborne, to Dublin to meet with de Valera so that he could get "a fuller understanding of our position here."[88] Churchill agreed and the visit was arranged.[89] Nonetheless, "the British despaired of changing de Valera's mind"[90] as de Valera held fast to Irish neutrality even when Cranborne hinted that Ireland's postwar international standing would be compromised if they were not present at the future Peace Conference.[91]

On December 14, de Valera delivered a "fuller explanation" of Eire's decision to remain a "friendly neutral" in a speech aimed at an American audience:

> ... The part that American friendship played in helping us to win the freedom that we enjoy in this part of Ireland has been gratefully recognized and acknowledged by our people.
>
> It would be unnatural then if we did not sympathize in a special manner with the people of the United States and if we did not feel with them in all the anxieties and trials which this war must bring upon them.
>
> For this reason, strangers who do not understand our conditions have begun to ask how America's entry into the war will affect our State policy here. We answered that question in advance. *The Policy of the State remains unchanged. We can only be a friendly neutral.* ...
>
> We are fully aware that, in a world at war each set of belligerents are ever ready to regard those who are not with them as against them, but the course we have followed is a just course. God has been pleased to save us during the years of war that have already passed. We pray that He may be pleased to save us to the end; but we must do our part.[92] (emphasis added)

Robert Brennan delivered a copy of the Taoiseach's speech to the State Department for the President's review,[93] and Roosevelt replied to de Valera, the "friendly neutral," with his own advice, offered in the "duty of deep friendship":

> Your expressions of gratitude for the long interest of the United States in Irish freedom are appreciated. The policy of the American Government now, as in the past, contemplates the hope that all free institutions, liberties, and independence which the Irish people now enjoy may be preserved for full enjoyment in the future. If freedom and liberty are to be preserved, they must now be defended by the human and material resources of all free nations. Your freedom, too, is at stake. No longer can it be doubted that the policy of Hitler and his Axis associates is the conquest of the entire world and the enslavement of all mankind.

I have every confidence in the Irish Government and the Irish people, who love liberty and freedom as dearly as we, will know how to meet their responsibilities in the present situation.[94]

Those responsibilities might include opening Irish naval bases "to offset [U.S.] naval losses," as Kirkpatrick suggested in an article published in the *Chicago Daily News* on December 15,[95] or listening to the "will" of the "majority of the Irish *people*" who sympathized with the United States, even if their leaders did not.[96] They might also include a scaling back on Irish Americans' public support for Irish neutrality in order to demonstrate their patriotism and support for the U.S. war effort. With those considerations in mind, the AFIN, which had held mass rallies in Boston and New York earlier in the year, quickly and quietly disbanded.[97]

Churchill's mind was now focused, however, on his trip to Washington to meet with Roosevelt and not on the recalcitrant Eamon de Valera or the rebellious Irish nation. Churchill and Roosevelt needed to work out details for the Anglo-American Combined Chiefs of Staff who would coordinate the anti-fascist war in Europe and in Asia, and would bring American troops and bomber squadrons into the theaters of war as quickly as possible.[98] Churchill arrived in Washington, DC on December 22, triumphant at last in his long quest to gain the United States as a fighting partner in the war against the Axis Powers. As Jon Meacham, who chronicled the "epic friendship" of the two great warlords, noted:

> They now shared largely identical interests and would treat the world, and themselves, to a pageant of personal diplomacy. Mutual admiration can be seductive – if you are one of the people being admired. These weeks at the White House belong to a vanished age, but the human forces shaping the time Roosevelt and Churchill spent together – affection, shared drama, and hints of tension – almost always play some role in high politics.[99]

Living at the White House, Churchill shocked the staff and First Lady Eleanor Roosevelt with his eccentric personal habits and late night hours – "She thought he was dogmatic and chauvinistic, stayed up far too late at night, drank too much, and was having an adverse effect on her husband"[100] – but Churchill was unfazed and held nothing back.[101] One day, Eleanor looked in on the War Map Room that Roosevelt had installed at the White House to match the room Churchill had constructed at his London headquarters, and she observed: "They looked like two little boys playing soldier. They seemed to be having a wonderful time, too wonderful in fact."[102] Yet, as Churchill biographer Carlo D'Este has written about Churchill's unique character, his "genius and his imperfections ... went hand in hand."[103] Churchill wrote to Deputy Prime Minister Clement Atlee that "We live together as a big family in the greatest intimacy and informality, and I have formed the highest regard and admiration for the President."[104] Together, Roosevelt and Churchill held a press conference on December 23, and Churchill disarmed reporters with praise for the United States industries that produced the weapons and machinery that had kept Britain in the war, fighting the great anti-fascist fight, and he responded eagerly to the barrage of questions the press corps threw at him. He also joined Roosevelt and addressed the American people on Christmas Eve during FDR's broadcast from the White House, emphasizing the unity of values and the "fraternal association" that he felt for the United States and its leader:

> I spend this anniversary and festival far from my country, far from my family, yet I cannot truthfully say that I feel far from home. Whether it be the ties of blood on my mother's side, or the friendships I have developed here over many years of active life, or the commanding sentiment of comradeship in the common cause of a great peoples who speak the same language, who kneel at the same altars and, to a very large extent, pursue the same ideals, I cannot feel myself a stranger here in the centre and at the summit of the United States. I feel a sense of unity and a fraternal association which, to the kindliness of your welcome, convinces me that I have a right to sit at your fireside and share your Christmas joys.[105]

On December 26, Churchill addressed a Joint Session of Congress in a speech intended again to highlight the unity of the two Allied nations. He spoke lovingly of his American mother, Jennie Jerome, and quipped, "If my father had been American and my mother British, instead of the other way 'round, I might have got here on my own." But then he added, "I am a child of the House of Commons. I was brought up in my father's house to believe in democracy. ... Therefore I have been in full harmony all my life with the tides which have flowed on both sides of the Atlantic against privilege and monopoly, and have steered confidently towards the Gettysburg ideal of 'Government of the people, by the people, for the people.'"[106] He condemned the Axis Powers with fire and passion, the tyrannical states that were "enormous, bitter and ruthless," ruled by "wicked men ... that will stop at nothing." Then, he referenced the Christian Bible, quoting from the Book of Psalms: "He shall not be afraid of evil tidings; His heart is fixed, trusting in the Lord,"[107] and called up the image of his mother waving an American flag on the 4th of July with tears in his eyes. He flashed his "V for Victory" sign as he exited the floor, and won a rave response from the assembled dignitaries for his dramatic performance.[108] Later, Churchill wrote about what the address to Congress had meant to him:

> The occasion was important for what I was sure was the all-conquering alliance of the English-speaking peoples. I had never addressed a foreign parliament before. Yet to me, who could trace the unbroken male descent

on my mother's side through five generations from a lieutenant who served in George Washington's army, it was possible to feel a blood right to speak to the representatives of the great Republic in our common cause. It certainly was odd that it should all work out this way; and once again I had the feeling, for mentioning which I may be pardoned, of being used, however unworthy, in some appointed plan.[109]

Churchill and Roosevelt also concluded some key military agreements during Churchill's visit to Washington: that Germany would be defeated before Japan, and that the allies would focus their first coordinated campaign on an Anglo-American invasion of North Africa.[110] They also "made an unprecedented decision: to bring their forces together under a unified command," with a "Combined Chiefs of Staff Committee ... [based] in Washington to coordinate Anglo-American strategy." Additionally, they created joint "US-British agencies ... to control munitions, shipping, raw materials, food and production." These decisions represented "'the most complete unification of military effort ever achieved by two allied nations,'" according to U.S. General George Marshall.[111] The meeting and the grand alliance were, as Helen Kirkpatrick and her fellow reporters opined at the time, a "great stride forward – from the strategical viewpoint, in permitting closer cooperation and unity of command, and in the material sense of pooling resources,"[112] even as General Marshall would later concede that there were major disagreements regarding some of the strategic decisions made at this December–January Anglo-American conference, including the timing of both the North African campaign and the invasion of France.[113]

Roosevelt and Churchill also settled on the name of the anti-Axis alliance: the "United Nations," the name proposed by FDR. And, they organized an official signing ceremony on January 1, 1942, for the twenty-six nations that were pledged to fight together, led by the United States, Great Britain, the Soviet Union, and China.[114] They declared their common purpose: that a "complete victory over their enemies is essential to defend life, liberty, independence and religious freedom, and to preserve human rights and justice in their own lands," and that together they were "now engaged in a common struggle against savage and brutal forces seeking to subjugate the world."[115]

Eire remained outside the righteous fraternal alliance, neither ally nor enemy, by its leader's choice.

Notes

1 James MacGregor Burns, *Roosevelt: The Soldier of Freedom, 1940–1945* (Open Road media, e-book, 2012), 258–260.

2 "Mr. Roosevelt's War," *Time Magazine* 38: 2 (14 July 1941), 13–15.
3 Martin Gilbert, *Churchill: A Life* (New York: Henry Holt, 1991), 706.
4 David Kaiser, *No End Save Victory: How FDR Led the Nation into War* (New York: Basic Books, 2014), 209.
5 "Attachment of British Officers to the American Army, Memorandum by Chief of the Imperial General Staff," 13 July 1941, CAB/80/29, War Cabinet Meeting Minutes, Chief of Staff Committee, British National Archives.
6 Clear Cablegram from Washington Legation, 11 July 1941, P150/2635, Eamon de Valera Papers (on microfilm), University College Dublin (hereafter: EdV Papers, UCD).
7 David Gray to Franklin Roosevelt, 18 July 1941, box 6, David Gray Papers, Franklin Roosevelt Presidential Library, Hyde Park, NY (hereafter: DG Papers, FDR Library). See also US Minister to Ireland David Gray to Franklin Roosevelt, 28 July 1941, box 40, President's Secretary's File: Ireland 1941, Franklin Roosevelt Papers, Franklin Roosevelt Presidential Library, Hyde Park, NY (hereafter: FDR Papers).
8 David Gray to Franklin Roosevelt, 11 July 1941, box 6, DG Papers, FDR Library.
9 Maurice Manning, *James Dillon, A Biography* (Dublin: Wolfhound Press, 1999), 165.
10 David McCullagh, *De Valera: Rule, 1932–1972* (Dublin: Gill Books, 2018), 212.
11 John Day Tully, *Ireland and Irish Americans 1932–1945: The Search for Identity* (Dublin: Irish Academic Press, 2010), 102.
12 McCullagh, *De Valera*, 212. See also T. Ryle Dwyer, *Irish Neutrality and the USA, 1939–47* (Dublin: Gill & Macmillan, 1977), 131.
13 Ben Tonra, *Global Citizen and European Republic: Irish Foreign Policy in Transition* (Manchester: Manchester University Press, 2007), 74.
14 *Ibid.*, 75; Manning, *James Dillon*, 166.
15 Tonra, *Global Citizen and European Republic*, 14.
16 *Ibid.*, 16.
17 *Ibid.*, 66–67.
18 Excerpts from U.S. and Irish press stories re American bases being built in Northern Ireland, 12 July 1941, P150/2635, EdV Papers, UCD.
19 Dwyer, *Irish Neutrality and the USA*, 129; "Press report of remarks made by President Roosevelt at a Press Conference on 27 June 1941," P150/2604, EdV Papers; Personal Code Telegram from Joseph Walshe to Robert Brennan (Washington) (No. 183), 11 July 1941, Doc. No. 109 NAI DFA Secretary's Files P53, *Documents on Irish Foreign Policy* vol. VII, 1941–1945; The Irish Minister (Brennan) to the Acting Secretary of State (Welles), July 15, 1941, Doc. 186, *Foreign Relations of the United States* (hereafter: *FRUS*), 1941 vol. III (Washington, DC: Government Printing Office, 1959).
20 Frank Costigliola, *Roosevelt's Lost Alliances: How Personal Politics Helped Start the Cold War* (Princeton, NJ: Princeton University Press, 2012, 91–92. See also Burns, *Roosevelt*, 306–309.

21 Costigliola, *Roosevelt's Lost Alliances*, 91.
22 Burns, *Roosevelt*, 309. See also Robert Dallek, *Franklin D. Roosevelt: A Political Life* (New York: Penguin, 2018), 430.
23 Kaiser, *No End Save Victory*, 209.
24 Blanche Wiesen Cook, *Eleanor Roosevelt: The War Years and After*, vol. 3, *1939–1962* (New York: Viking, 2016), 396. See also Telegram from Winston Churchill to Harry Hopkins, 28 August 1941, CHAR: 20/42A/35, Winston Churchill Archives online, The Chartwell Trust: "Prime Minister to Mr. Hopkins, ... I ought to tell you that there has been a wave of depression through the Cabinet and other informed circles here about the President's many assurances about no commitments and no closer to war, etc. I fear this will be reflected in Parliament. ..."
25 Gilbert, *Churchill*, 706. Carlo D'Este, *Warlord: A Life of Winston Churchill at War, 1874–1945* (New York: HarperCollins, 2008), 507: "While much has been made of their special relationship and their partnership as allies, Robert E. Sherwood offered a caveat. 'It would be an exaggeration to say that Roosevelt and Churchill became chums at this conference or at any subsequent time. They established an easy intimacy ... and also a degree of frankness in intercourse, which, if not quite complete, was remarkably close to it.' However, both men were politicians first and friends second, and the interests of their respective nations came first. From their frank person-to-person appraisal of each other they achieved 'a degree of admiration and sympathetic understanding of each other's personal problems that lesser craftsmen could not have achieved.' Roosevelt later gave Churchill the ultimate compliment when, during a particularly dismal time, he ended a cable with, 'It is fun to be in the same decade with you.'"
26 "Home from the Sea," *Time Magazine* 38: 8 (25 August 1941), 13–17; Dallek, *Franklin D. Roosevelt: A Political Life*, 431; Jean Edward Smith, *FDR* (New York: Random House, 2008), 500–501; D'Este, *Warlord*, 506; Kaiser, *No End Save Victory*, 208; Jon Meacham, *Franklin and Winston: An Intimate Portrait of an Epic Friendship* (New York: Random House, 2004), 107–116.
27 Meacham, *Franklin and Winston*, 116.
28 Churchill quoted in Dallek, *Franklin D. Roosevelt: A Political Life*, 431. See also D'Este, *Warlord*, 506.
29 Costigliola, *Roosevelt's Lost Alliances*, 96–97.
30 "Atlantic Charter, August 14, 1941," The Avalon Project, Documents in Law, History and Diplomacy (New Haven, CT: Lillian Goldman Law Library, Yale Law School, 2008), https://avalon.law.yale.edu/wwii/atlantic.asp (accessed 7 December 2020).
31 Kaiser, *No End Save Victory*, 212. See also Costigliola, *Roosevelt's Lost Alliances*, 95.
32 Smith, *FDR*, 502. See also Burns, *Roosevelt*, 323.
33 Churchill's August 24 radio address to the British people quoted in Meacham, *Franklin and Winston*, 121.
34 Brian Girvin, *The Emergency: Neutral Ireland 1939–45* (London: Pan Macmillan, 2007), 283–284, citing document dated 21 August 1941.

35 U.S. Minister to Ireland David Gray to Franklin Roosevelt, 26 June 1941, box 40, President's Secretary's File: Ireland, 1941, FDR Papers. Dwyer, *Irish Neutrality and the USA*, 129; Press Report of Remarks made by President Roosevelt at a Press Conference on 27 June 1941, P150/2604, EdV Papers, UCD; The Acting Secretary of State (Welles) to the Minister in Ireland (Gray), 31 July 1941, Doc.188, *FRUS* 1941 vol. III.

36 David Gray to Franklin Roosevelt, 11 August 1941, box 5, David Gray Papers, 1857–1960, Coll. 03082, University of Wyoming American Heritage Center, Laramie Wyoming (hereafter: Gray Papers, AHC).

37 U.S. Minister to Ireland David Gray to Franklin Roosevelt, 10 and 11 July 10 1941, box 40, President's Secretary's File: Ireland 1941, FDR Papers. See also Tully, *Ireland and Irish Americans*, 102–103.

38 David Gray to Franklin Roosevelt, [recounting conversation with Eamon de Valera], 18 July 1941, box 6, DG Papers, FDR Library; U.S. Minister to Ireland David Gray to Franklin Roosevelt, 28 July 1941, box 40, President's Secretary's File: Ireland 1941, FDR Papers; "Press Censor's Report for July 1941," Michael Knightly, Chief Press Censor, P104/3482, Frank Aiken Papers, University College Dublin (hereafter: FA Papers, UCD); Dwyer, *Irish Neutrality and the USA*, 133.

39 David Gray, "Notes on Axis Activities in Ireland," 20 July 1941, box 9, DG Papers, FDR Library. See also "Notes on Axis Activities in Ireland," box 2, Helen Paull Kirkpatrick Papers, CA-MS-01132, Sophia Smith Collection, Smith College, Northampton, MA (hereafter: HPK Papers).

40 Carolle J. Carter, *The Shamrock and the Swastika: German Espionage in Ireland in World War II* (Palo Alto, CA: Pacific Books, 1977), 170–171. Carter reported than in the summer of 1941 Goertz had given up on organizing the IRA against the Irish government, and was trying, unsuccessfully, to leave Ireland and make his way back to Berlin. Nonetheless, IRA collusion with the Irish authorities was suspected because Goertz eluded capture for so long.

41 Gray, "Notes on Axis Activities in Ireland," 20 July 1941, box 9, DG Papers, FDR Library.

42 U.S. Minister to Ireland David Gray to Franklin Roosevelt, 28 July 1941, box 40, President's Secretary's File: Ireland 1941, FDR Papers.

43 "Memorandum by SS Standartenfuhrer Veesenmayer, 24 August 1941, Proposal for the Ireland Operation," Doc. 234, *Documents on German Foreign Policy, 1918–1945*, vol. 11, "The War Years, June 23–December 11, 1941," (Washington, DC: Government Printing Office, 1964). See also McCullagh, *De Valera*, 225.

44 "Memorandum by SS Standartenfuhrer Veesenmayer, 24 August 1941, Proposal for the Ireland Operation," Doc. 234, *Documents on German Foreign Policyi 1918–1945*, vol. 11.

45 Translation of German Embassy Telegram, report from Eduard Hempel German Secretary of State Weizsacker, 18–19 August 1941, box 5, Gray Papers, AHC.

46 "Memorandum on Eire, To: the American Ambassador, From: Helen Kirkpatrick," 25 August 1941, box 2, HPK Papers.
47 Helen Kirkpatrick to David Gray, 25 August 1941, box 4, DG Papers, FDR Library.
48 Helen Kirkpatrick, "Alarmed Irish Looking to U.S. for Protection Against Nazis; Dublin Group Seeking Action," *Chicago Daily News* (26 August 1941), box 12, HPK Papers.
49 Helen Kirkpatrick, "Eire Facing hardest Winter Since the Famine of 1847," *Chicago Daily News* (28 August 1941), box 12, HPK Papers.
50 Frank Gallagher to Helen Kirkpatrick, 29 August 1941, box 2, HPK Papers.
51 Helen Kirkpatrick to David Gray, *c.* 28 August 1941, box 4, DG Papers, FDR Library. Typescript for *Chicago Daily News* sent via cable, 28 August 1941, box 2, HPK Papers: "German propaganda working through news bulletins broadcasts and agents is trying to upstir [sic] anti-American feeling in Ireland and to incite extremist Irish in America against [US] Government. Evidences of this are very apparent in Ireland and according to American official sources in United States. ..."
52 Frank Gallagher to Helen Kirkpatrick, 1 September 1941, box 2, HPK Papers.
53 Helen Kirkpatrick to Frank Gallagher, 15 September 1941, box 5, Gray Papers, AHC: "What I said was: 'The Government is neither more nor less anti-British than it was, but there is clearly discernible anti-American feeling in some government circles. This arises from two things, first, the failure of Frank Aiken, Minister for the Coordination of Defense, to secure a reversal of that decision during his visit to Washington this spring.' ... My assessment of the feeling in the Government was based entirely on my conversations with members of the Government, not on anything David Gray said."
54 Joseph Walshe to David Gray, 2 September 1941, box 5, Gray Papers, AHC.
55 David Gray to Helen Kirkpatrick, 2 September 1941, box 2, HPK Papers.
56 David Gray to Helen Kirkpatrick, 5 September 1941, box 2, HPK Papers.
57 Letter from Joseph Walshe David Gray, 11 September 1941, Doc. No. 125 NAI DFA Secretary's Files P48A, *Documents on Irish Foreign Policy* vol. VII, 1941–1945. See also Tully, *Ireland and Irish Americans*, 104: "Gray's portrayal of German espionage in Ireland was off the mark. ... In the most current and complete review of German intelligence efforts in Ireland during the war, Mark Hull concludes that the entire German espionage effort was an 'absolute failure', primarily because of brilliantly effective counterintelligence operations run by both Ireland and Britain."
58 David Gray to Helen Kirkpatrick, 18 September 1941, box 2, HPK Papers. See also Extracts from a Letter from Joseph Walshe to Robert Brennan (Washington), 14 October 1941, Doc. No. 132 NAI DFA Secretary's Files P48A, *Documents on Irish Foreign Policy* vol. VII, 1941–1945.
59 U.S. Minister to Ireland David Gray to Franklin Roosevelt, 12 September 1941, box 40, President's Secretary's File: Ireland 1941, FDR Papers.

60 Memorandum from Joseph Walshe to Eamon de Valera, 16 September 1941, Doc. No. 128 UCDA P150/2635, *Documents on Irish Foreign Policy* vol. VII, 1941–1945.
61 Extract of article in the *New York Herald Tribune, c.* November 1941, box 6, Gray Papers, AHC.
62 Dwyer, *Irish Neutrality and the USA*, 135–136.
63 Kaiser, *No End Save Victory*, 236–238.
64 "The Japanese Attack on Pearl Harbor, December 7, 1941," United States Library of Congress, America's Story, www.americaslibrary.gov/jb/wwii/jb_wwii_pearlhar_1.html accessed 7 December 2020).
65 Costigliola, *Roosevelt's Lost Alliances*, 101.
66 *Ibid.*, 100.
67 Kaiser, *No End Save Victory*, 250–252.
68 John W. Dower, *War Without Mercy: Race and Power in the Pacific War* (New York: Pantheon, 1986).
69 Franklin Roosevelt, "Address to Congress Requesting a Declaration of War," 8 December 1941, Presidential Speeches, Franklin D. Roosevelt Presidency (University of Virginia Miller Center, 2019), https://millercenter.org/the-presidency/presidential-speeches/december-8–1941-address-congress-requesting-declaration-war (accessed 7 December 2020).
70 "National Ordeal," *Time Magazine* 38: 24 (15 December 1941), 20–21.
71 Franklin Roosevelt, "Fireside Chat 19: On the War with Japan," 9 December 1941, Presidential Speeches, Franklin D. Roosevelt Presidency (University of Virginia, Miller Center, 2019), https://millercenter.org/the-presidency/presidential-speeches/december-9–1941-fireside-chat-19-war-japan (accessed 7 December 2020).
72 *Ibid.*
73 "German Declaration of War Against the United States," 11 December 1941, The History Place, www.historyplace.com/worldwar2/timeline/germany-declares.htm (accessed 7 December 2020).
74 Hitler's war address quoted in Meacham, *Franklin and Winston*, 134.
75 Churchill quoted in Dallek, *Franklin D. Roosevelt: A Political Life*, 441.
76 Smith, *FDR*, 542. See also Meacham, *Franklin and Winston*, 139–140: "'He is a different man since America came into the war,' Lord Moran said of Churchill, 'The Winston I knew in London frightened me. I used to watch him as he went to his room with swift paces, the head thrust forward, scowling at the ground, the somber countenance clouded, the features set and resolute. ... I could see he was carrying the weight of the world, and wondered how long he could go on like that and what could be done about it. And now – in a night it seems – a younger man has taken his place.'"
77 Smith, *FDR*, 536.
78 *Ibid.*, 542–543.
79 Telegram from Winston Churchill to Eamon de Valera, No. 120. Most Immediate. 8 December 1941, Doc. No. 154 TNA DO 130/17, *Documents on Irish Foreign Policy* vol. VII, 1941–1945. See also Dermot McEvoy, "What if

Michael Collins Had Been Irish Leader the Night Pearl Harbor was Bombed?" *Irish Central*, 7 December 2018, www.irishcentral.com/opinion/others/what-if-michael-collins-had-been-irish-leader-the-night-pearl-harbor-was-bombed (accessed 9 December 2020). McEvoy notes that Churchill was referencing a poem by Thomas Davis, with the refrain: "A Nation once again, / A Nation once again, / And Ireland long a province / Be a Nation once again."

80 On 9 December 1941 Lord Cranborne explained to Sir John Maffey in Dublin that Churchill's phrase "a nation once again" "certainly contemplated no deal over partition" and he meant "by coming into the war Ireland would regain her soul." Cranborne to Maffey (No. 121), 9 December 1941, TNA DO 130/17, *Documents on Irish Foreign Policy* vol. VII, 1941–1945.

81 Roosevelt to Churchill, 8 December 1941, in *Churchill and Roosevelt, The Complete Correspondence*, vol. 1, *Alliance Emerging, October 1933–November 1942*, ed. Warren F. Kimball (Princeton, NJ: Princeton University Press, 1984), 282.

82 Paul Bew, *Churchill and Ireland* (Oxford: Oxford University Press, 2016), 150–151.

83 Ronan Fanning, *Eamon de Valera: A Will to Power* (Cambridge, MA: Harvard University Press, 2016), 214.

84 *Ibid*.

85 Eunan O'Halpin, *Defending Ireland: The Irish State and Its Enemies Since 1922* (New York: Oxford University Press, 2000, 182.

86 Memorandum by Eamon de Valera of a meeting with Sir John Maffey, *c.* 9 December 1941, Doc. No. 155 UCDA P150/2632, *Documents on Irish Foreign Policy* vol. VII, 1941–1945.

87 *Ibid*.

88 Telegram from Eamon de Valera to Winston Churchill, 10 December 1941, CHAR: 20/46/73, Winston Churchill Archives online.

89 Telegram from Winston Churchill to Eamon de Valera, 11 December 1941, CHAR: 20/46/102, Winston Churchill Archives online.

90 McCullagh, *De Valera*, 217.

91 Memorandum by Eamon de Valera, General Impression of a Conversation with Lord Cranborne 17 December 1941, Doc. No. 166 UCDA P150/2632, *Documents on Irish Foreign Policy* vol. VII, 1941–1945.

92 Extract from speech made by the Taoiseach at Cork on 14 December 1941, P150/2604, EdV Papers, UCD.

93 The Irish Minister in Washington (Brennan) to the Secretary of State 16 December 1941, Document 195, *FRUS* 1941 vol. III.

94 Personal message from President Roosevelt to the Taoiseach, 22 December 1941, addendum to: The Irish Minister in Washington (Brennan) to the Secretary of State 16 December 1941, Document 195, *FRUS* 1941 vol. III. See also The Secretary of State (Hull) to the Irish Minister in Washington (Brennan) 22 December 22, 1941, Document 196, *FRUS* 1941 vol. III.

95 Helen Kirkpatrick, "Demand Raised for Bases in Ireland to Offset Naval Losses," *Chicago Daily News* (15 December 1941), box 3, HPK Papers.

See also Kirkpatrick, "Northern Bases Built by US Nearly Done," *Chicago Daily Dews* (22 December 1941), box 3, HPK Papers.
96 Helen Kirkpatrick, "People Sympathize with the US but Eire Clings to Neutrality," *Chicago Daily News* (26 December 1941), box 2, HPK Papers.
97 Tully, *Ireland and Irish Americans*, 105.
98 Sir Martin Gilbert, CBE, "Churchill Proceedings; Churchill and Bombing Policy," the fifth Churchill lecture, The George Washington University, Washington, DC, 18 October 2005, *Finest Hour* 137 (Winter 2007–2008), www.winstonchurchill.org/publications/finest-hour/finest-hour-137/churchill-proceedings-churchill-and-bombing-policy/ (accessed 7 December 2020).
99 Meacham, *Franklin and Winston*, 140.
100 D'Este, *Warlord*, 507.
101 Sonia Purnell, *Clementine: The Life of Mrs. Winston Churchill* (New York: Viking Penguin, 2015), 283–284; Cook, *Eleanor Roosevelt*, 409.
102 D'Este, *Warlord*, 508.
103 *Ibid.*, 696.
104 Smith, *FDR*, 543–544.
105 Dallek, *Franklin D. Roosevelt: A Political Life*, 446–447.
106 Winston Churchill's Speech to U.S. Joint Session Congress, 26 December 1941, CHAR: 9/153/29–45, Winston Churchill Archives online.
107 *Ibid.*
108 Costigliola, *Roosevelt's Lost Alliances*, 107; Smith, *FDR*, 545.
109 Churchill quoted in Meacham, *Franklin and Winston*, 154.
110 Smith, *FDR*, 546.
111 Lynne Olson, *Citizens of London: The Americans Who Stood with Britain in Its Darkest, Finest Hour* (New York: Random House, 2011), 149.
112 Helen Kirkpatrick, "Grand Alliance 'Way to Victory' British Assert," *Chicago Daily News* (3 January 1942), box 3, HPK Papers.
113 Kaiser, *No End Save Victory*, 261.
114 Smith, *FDR*, 547.
115 "A Declaration of the United Nations," 1 January 1941, in The United Nations, Section 1: Origin and Evolution. Chapter A, *The Yearbook of the United Nations*, www.unmultimedia.org/searchers/yearbook/page.jsp?volume=1946–47&page=36&searchType=advanced (accessed 7 December 2020).

6

Efforts to "break the backbone" of Irish neutrality, January 1942 to December 1943

When the United States entered the war and joined the United Nations antifascist alliance fighting the Axis Powers, Winston Churchill's and Franklin Roosevelt's roles in their wartime friendship, "pursuer" and "pursued," were transformed. Now, as Churchill returned to Britain from Washington, DC on January 14, Roosevelt bade him to "Trust me to the bitter end."[1] Roosevelt, from that point forward, "continued to be a generous and supportive ally. ... The personal respect and affection between the two leaders would ebb and flow but would never be in danger of collapse."[2] In contrast, Eamon de Valera, Taoiseach of neutral Eire, remained the "odd man out," the stubborn younger brother who refused to play the role of comrade-in-arms that Churchill and Roosevelt had tried to assign to him in the wartime drama.

Sir John Maffey, David Gray, and journalist Helen Kirkpatrick, however, continued to advance Anglo-American interests in Eire. They prodded the Irish government with a combination of carrots and sticks, urging the government to surrender neutrality and join the United Nations now that the Americans, longtime "friends" of the Irish people, had entered the war and American troops were landing in Northern Ireland, but their efforts were frustrated. De Valera and his Dublin advisers Joseph Walshe and Frank Aiken rejected Anglo-American pressures and tried to get their nemesis, U.S. Minister David Gray, recalled from his post and replaced with a friendlier American representative, but they, too, were disappointed.

During the next two years, from January 1942 to December 1943, major theaters of war in North Africa, Italy, and Southeast Asia heated up and drew Churchill's and Roosevelt's attention away from neutral Eire. With Anglo-American bases secured in Northern Ireland, Iceland, Greenland, and the Azores, and as better submarine detection technology increased the Atlantic convoys' success in protecting necessary supply routes, acquiring access to Southern Ireland's naval bases became less important to the Allies from a strategic perspective.[3] Nevertheless, David Gray, aided by British Representative Sir John Maffey, found new avenues to direct their governments' propaganda campaigns to criticize Ireland's neutrality policy and to call into question de Valera's relationship with the fascist enemies.

Germany inadvertently played into the anti-Axis narrative that David Gray, Sir John Maffey, and willing journalists such as Helen Kirkpatrick were spinning in Ireland as the United States entered the war in late 1941. The German spy Hermann Goertz, who had eluded capture by Irish Military Intelligence, the G2, since his ill-fated parachute landing in western Ireland in May 1940, was finally apprehended on November 27, 1941. He had remained at large for eighteen months, aided by IRA agents and Irish nationalist sympathizers. During those months, the G2 and its informants tracked Goertz's whereabouts. The Irish government as well as the British domestic counterintelligence and security agency MI5 monitored Goertz's contacts with the German Legation and German Minister Eduard Hempel, and MI5 shared information with the Americans.[4] The G2 never trusted David Gray or his Legation staff to be discreet; they believed Gray had "spies on the brain" and they knew he was openly hostile to Irish neutrality policy. The British, however, shared their knowledge of German espionage in Ireland with Gray, and, beginning in fall 1942, with an Office of Strategic Services (OSS) agent, Ervin Ross 'Spike' Marlin, who was assigned as a "Special Assistant" to David Gray.[5] Goertz had been trying to leave Ireland and return to Germany for many months, but his attempts to gain passage on boats or submarines never succeeded. During the months Goertz spent hiding out in Ireland, Eduard Hempel worried about the propaganda repercussions and negative attention that would rain down on the German Embassy if Goertz's activities became public, and he kept the agent at arm's length.[6] Hempel's attempts to deflect attention from Goertz were thwarted when the G2 arrested Goertz in November.

According to Irish historian Eunan O'Halpin, among the small number of German agents who operated in Ireland during the war, "the one agent who made a serious impact was Goertz. His mission was essentially to explore the possibility of a reconciliation between the IRA and the Irish state with the object of supporting German operations in Northern Ireland."[7] Nevertheless, he, too, failed in this mission as he lost his transmitter and the cash he was carrying to finance IRA sabotage operations when he first parachuted into Ireland in May 1940.[8] From that point forward, Goertz went into hiding, and "quickly became disillusioned with the IRA."[9] He tried to gather intelligence information that would be useful to the Germans regarding Irish harbors, landing grounds, and military sites without the aid of unreliable IRA collaborators, but he had no way to transmit whatever information he might have collected to the *Abwehr* in Berlin.[10]

When the G2 took Goertz into custody, de Valera and Walshe scrambled to keep the story from attracting unwanted public attention, too.

As they knew, "A public trial, with all its accompanying sensationalism, would at least give an opportunity to American interventionist newspapers to attack all the Irish groups who, at our request, have been defending us against the charge of being an elaborate spy centre."[11] Walshe met with Eduard Hempel on December 4, and while both men agreed that publicity would not serve their nations' interests, Hempel also denied any knowledge of Goertz's activities at that time.[12] Following de Valera's December 14 speech proclaiming Ireland's "friendly neutral" status in regard to relations with the United States, Walshe met with Hempel again. Both men tried to determine whether Irish-German relations would change due to the United States' new belligerent status and Goertz's arrest. Hempel now admitted he knew Goertz, and Walshe warned him to end all radio transmissions from the German Embassy.[13] Evidence of German espionage in Ireland, they both knew, would jeopardize Ireland's neutrality policy if it became public knowledge.[14]

Helen Kirkpatrick, on a weekend visit to Ditchley Park, the country home of Ronald and Nancy Tree, immediately returned to London when she heard the news of the Japanese attack on Pearl Harbor. On December 8, she dined with U.S. Ambassador John Winant, and together they listened to Churchill's broadcast relaying the news to the British people.[15] Kirkpatrick,[16] like David Gray,[17] was convinced that with America's entry into the war de Valera's government could be forced by public opinion in Ireland and America to give up its neutral status and join the United Nations alliance against the fascist powers.

Kirkpatrick traveled to Ireland in mid-December to be on site to report the news she thought would soon be announced – that Ireland was abandoning neutrality to join the Allies. Instead, she broke the story of Goertz's arrest on December 27. She initially got the particulars wrong,[18] asserting that "Goetz" (*sic*) was an officer in the Nazi Gestapo who was the head of an extensive spy ring operating in Ireland that was funded by IRA sympathizers in the United States. A follow-up story asserted that 200–300 IRA men, part of Goertz's Irish spy ring, were still at large in Ireland.[19] Nonetheless, her reports of the arrest were printed in the *Chicago Daily News* along with other accounts that appeared in British newspapers, putting pressure on de Valera to publicly declare his loyalties to the anti-fascist cause.[20] She wrote privately to her *Chicago Daily News* editor, Carroll Binder, that "Dev is doing everything he can to help both the British and ourselves. He shuts his eyes to as much as he can [regarding cooperation between the Irish Army and British military planners], and has proved very helpful in many ways which cannot be made public, even if they were known."[21] But, without a formal renunciation of neutrality, Kirkpatrick kept filing her reports on German intrigues in Ireland to build up popular support for aid to the

Allies. If the Irish people could be "enlightened" about Germany's "unneutral" and provocative actions, Kirkpatrick believed that "the people" would demand that their government join the United Nations alliance.

Kirkpatrick wasn't alone in following this strategy to shame de Valera into breaking his neutrality policy. A special January issue of the U.S. magazine *Nation* also argued that Ireland owed the United States a debt of friendship dating back to de Valera's visit to America in 1920–1921, and if Germany occupied Ireland it would "snuff out" Ireland's hard-won freedom and independence.[22] The publicity surrounding Goertz's arrest put the German Embassy on the defensive and Eduard Hempel scrambled to assure the Irish government that "no action of [the German government] of any kind had been directed against Ireland," and "The German government regret that more importance has been attached to this [Goertz] affair than it deserved."[23] The pressure to renounce neutrality lifted, however, when de Valera was able to rally the Irish people behind another expression of nationalist outrage, triggered by American troops arriving at Northern Ireland bases at the end of January.[24]

Kirkpatrick, along with other Anglo-American officials, misjudged the intensity of de Valera's negative reaction to the U.S. troops and his commitment to neutrality.[25] Although it was widely known in Ireland that American soldiers were building bases "for the British" in the North throughout the summer and fall of 1941, the deployment of tens of thousands of Americans to the military installations in the Six Counties did not take place until after the United States entered the war.[26] Even so, as Kirkpatrick reported, by the time U.S. troops arrived in Belfast on January 26 and "marched down the local streets with the American flag flying," the "Yanks'" arrival was the "Worst Kept Secret of the War."[27] Many of the Northern Anglo-Irish people enthusiastically welcomed the 37,000 American soldiers that disembarked from troopships in January as Kirkpatrick and other observers asserted,[28] but de Valera and his nationalist supporters in the South immediately protested against the violation of "Irish sovereignty," as did several IRA men who tried to intimidate Kirkpatrick when she followed the story into Dublin:

> Then I got back to the hotel [in Dublin] ... and as I went in the man at the desk said that Mr. O'Sullivan, the manager of the hotel, would like me to come into his parlor for a drink. I said, "Well, thank him, but I'm tired and I want to go to bed." He became very agitated and he said, "Oh, he's very insistent," and so on, and called and O'Sullivan came out. "Please would I come in." So, I went in and there were three of the biggest thugs you've ever seen in your life – IRA men – who accused me of being the forerunner of an American invasion of Eire. ... And I must say, I didn't find it very pleasant. I really was rather scared. They were very menacing looking. I said, "Well, you're quite

mistaken. We wouldn't do that. In the first place, we have all the Irish we need in the United States, and we're not interested in acquiring any more." And I dashed out of the door.[29]

When Sir John Maffey officially "informed" Eamon de Valera about the arrival of U.S. troops after the fact, the Taoiseach issued an indignant protest to Washington, London, and the Holy See in Rome on January 27 that was also published in the Irish newspapers, making his case that Ireland's rights as a sovereign power had been abused. In the immediate instance, Ireland's sovereignty was disrespected when de Valera was not consulted about the placement of U.S. troops on Irish soil. In the longer term, Ireland suffered due to partition of the motherland, "one of the cruelest wrongs that can be committed against a people."[30] David Gray's advice to the State Department regarding how to respond to de Valera's angry outburst ran the gamut from offering the Irish government enticements to encourage cooperation with the Allies, such as providing the Irish Army with some guns, shipping some needed foodstuffs into Ireland, paying cash to lease Irish bases in the south, and promising to aid Irish efforts to end partition – after the war ended.[31] He also opined to Ambassador Winant in London that it was time to allow the "inevitable shortages" of food and other needed commodities such as fuel to build up "without any coercive design" and thereby put pressure on de Valera's government to end its "isolationism" from the realities of a world war.[32] Gray also wrote directly to President Roosevelt: "I suspect the British are preparing the situation for an embargo on coal. If these two things can be done without appearing to be coercive measures I would anticipate swift results. ... Why should coal be rationed in Britain and yet be exported to Eire, or why should gasoline that we need be sent to Eire? It's not coercion; it is simple justice."[33] Roosevelt's response to de Valera's protests at a press conference were similarly dismissive. When asked about de Valera's assertion that the Irish isle was one nation, FDR replied: "Live and learn."[34] Sir John Maffey also believed that it was time to take a hard line with de Valera. As needed imports became harder to come by, it would become clear that "The logical consequence of Mr. de Valera's [neutrality] policy is to reduce Eire to a state of friendless beggardom. We shall not move into a happier and saner relationship until this fact is brought home to the people of Ireland."[35]

Relations between David Gray and Eamon de Valera declined further during this episode, as did Irish American government relations, and never fully recovered during the war. Gray and de Valera kept up the diplomatic veneer of faux-polite exchanges when they met face to face, but de Valera did not concede to all the U.S. government's subsequent demands for special consideration for the Allies' wartime needs by any means. A major exception was made by G2 and Irish Army officers who provided covert assistance to Britain's and the United States' militaries, especially regarding the treatment of American and British airmen who were sometimes forced to land their planes on Southern Irish territory. Even so, a telling conversation between Gray and de Valera on January 29 revealed the wide gulf between the American and Irish perspectives, that neither David Gray nor Eamon de Valera made any attempts to disguise:

> I brought up again the question of the Prime Minister's protest and said that I feared it would give the impression of an unfriendly attitude in America, especially in view of the fact that he made no protest to Germany when Germany bombed Belfast. If he claimed sovereignty over the Six Counties, the Germans had violated that sovereignty by killing hundreds of people, Catholic nationalists as well as Protestant Orangemen, and it would seem to the average American a much more flagrant violation of the sovereignty in question than the sending of American troops to reinforce British troops already there. He said the cases were not similar, that the Northern Irish were at war with Germany against their will and that there was a clear distinction.[36]

Anglo-Irish observer Elizabeth Bowen also commented on the disconnect between the Irish and American governments and people at this time:

> Feeling against America does run high. Apart from everything else, I still ... notice a sort of hangover from what must have been a sharp emotional shock. Eire, besides being morally indignant, is *upset*. ... In his present attitude towards America, Mr. de Valera is in perfect touch with popular feeling.[37]

Ireland's sovereign right to determine its own national policy, and its masculine national identity that had been effectively linked to neutrality by de Valera's government, had both been violated. Irish manhood – its autonomy and independence – had been challenged by British colonizers and betrayed by American "collaborators," but Irish manhood would not be compromised.

Historian Robert Fisk has written about this point in the war, that for de Valera's government and for (manly) Irish politicians generally, "To be un-neutral in private was one thing. ... To oppose neutrality in public was quite another."[38] James Dillon, whose speech in the Dáil the previous July earned the wrath of Fianna Fáil and other nationalist politicians and challenged the "muscular" Irish Catholic gender identity, further crossed the line into no man's land when he made an even more vigorous speech criticizing Irish neutrality policy at the annual Fine Gael party conference on February 10. Dillon called on the Irish government to support the United States now that it had entered the fight – in other words, to defer to another nation's war policy. Dillon argued that America was the traditional friend of the Irish people, and Ireland should regain its manhood by taking a stand against the "Nazi-Fascist Powers of Europe," that cuckolded Ireland, or, in Dillon's words, were turning (Germany's colony) Ireland into a "German Gibraltar of the Atlantic": "Whoever attacks America is my enemy, without reservation or qualification, and I say the United States has been treacherously and feloniously attacked by Germany, Italy and Japan. These nations are, therefore, my enemies, and I would to God they were the enemies of a united Irish people."[39]

Dillon's speech had "the effect of a time bomb." Even though Dillon's remarks were "greeted with applause,"[40] as Elizabeth Bowen reported to the British Dominions Office: "[the] applause ... seemed so general that I could have believed for a minute that Mr Dillon had carried the room with him. His shots had been nicely placed. I should say that of the people there one-third were strongly with Dillon; one-third were neutral (temporarily swayed but due to react against him later); one-third definitely hostile." Nonetheless, Dillon had violated de Valera's wartime censorship policy, strictly policed by Frank Aiken, Fianna Fail's muscleman who allowed no criticism of the government's neutrality policy. Dillon was forced to resign from the Fine Gael party ten days later.[41]

Additional American troops arrived in Northern Ireland throughout spring and summer 1942, preparing for "Operation Torch," the Allied campaign in North Africa, reaching a peak of over 100,000 troops occupying bases at Belfast and Londonderry. With the Americans and their planes and weapons on site in the North, Britain's fears of a German landing in Ireland abated.[42] De Valera's government also de-escalated its protests.[43] In the brief moment of calm, David Gray proposed a new propaganda campaign to provoke the Irish government and expose the government's supposedly favorable treatment of the Axis Powers.

In February 1942, Gray and Sir John Maffey decided that the time had come to focus on neutralizing the German and Italian "war news" pamphlets circulating in Dublin. The Axis propaganda, "a campaign of circularized vituperation" against the Allies, according to Gray, should be countered with positive Allied propaganda.[44] He and John Maffey had several contentious and unproductive meetings with Joseph Walshe during spring 1942, when they tried, without success,[45] to persuade the Secretary for External Affairs to put a stop to German and Italian propaganda that encouraged "pro-German sentiments" among the Irish population.[46] Gray also prepared a "Memorandum on Proposed Press Bureau" that he submitted to Washington in February. His proposal would eventually get routed to the Office of War Information (OWI) that formed in June 1942. Gray was ahead of the curve in terms of his ambitious plans for production of war propaganda, so it took many months for his envisioned propaganda project, the *Letter from America*, to become a reality and go into production in

Efforts to "break the backbone" of Irish neutrality

October 1942,[47] but he laid out the "objectives" for the messages that could and should, in his view, be conveyed to the Irish people:

1. To convince the Irish people of the certainty of American victory.
2. To impress on the Irish people the fact of Hitler's hostility to Christianity and especially to the Roman Catholic Church.
3. To explain the basic cause of war, that is the impossibility of relying upon any pact with Hitler by continuously citing his promises and pledges and the historic events which exposed their falseness.
4. As far as possible to suggest to the Irish people that survival of their nationality is bound up with the success of the United Nations.[48]

Gray and Helen Kirkpatrick also began discussing the possibility of her appointment as "press attaché" to the U.S. Legation in Dublin, and they put out feelers with John Winant and other U.S. Embassy officials in London to see if they could get support for their proposals.[49]

Helen Kirkpatrick's reputation for bold and brave war reporting was well established by early 1942. The *Chicago Daily News* bureau chief in London, William Stoneman, and fellow reporter Bill Robertson both praised Kirkpatrick's dedication to getting on-the-spot "scoops" of war news. They shared stories of Kirkpatrick's composure with regard to her own near misses as bombs exploded around her in a wartime supplement printed in the *Chicago Daily News* in July, noting that she had been "nominated as 'one of the six bravest women in London', ... bombed out of her dwelling, ... narrowly escaped being blasted to pieces in the streets and was once blown bodily through a doorway by the explosion of a bomb. ..."[50] She earned "the confidence of many of the most famous figures in the world," was presented to the King and Queen of England,[51] and received recognition,[52] awards from her peers,[53] and high praise from her publisher, Secretary of the Navy Frank Knox.[54] David Gray, however, could not secure Kirkpatrick's appointment as press attaché in Dublin,[55] and she was passed over in favor of *New York Herald Tribune* drama critic Richard Watts.[56] Her reportorial status would soon change, however, when the U.S. military decided to designate official "war correspondents," who were "accredited" to cover stories about U.S. engagements with the enemy. Kirkpatrick became one of the few "exceptional" women who were awarded this status in March 1942.[57] She and other accredited journalists, selected through a stringent application process by the U.S. War Department, agreed to accept government censorship of their news reports in exchange for privileged access to U.S. troops and high-level military officers, and permission to join selected combat missions.[58] Kirkpatrick's new status took her focus away from Ireland, although she did return to Northern Ireland in May 1942,[59] to report on King George and Queen Elizabeth's visit to review the American troops as they trained for deployment in the fall 1942 North African campaign.[60]

Meanwhile, German espionage activities in Ireland had never completely abated, even after Hermann Goertz's arrest came to light in December 1941–January 1942. Joseph Walshe had several meetings with Eduard Hempel to alert him that the Allies had once again detected transmissions emanating from the German Embassy that violated treaty agreements,[61] and Hempel continued to try to warn off his superiors from using the illegal communication channel.[62] In Northern Ireland, the U.S. military focused on the security risks posed by "inadequate border controls" between Northern Ireland and Eire, and the "ever-present danger of the IRA" that was "pro-Nazi chiefly because Germany was an enemy of Britain." The danger of IRA sabotage operations and of leaked military information were constant concerns as "there was little doubt the Nazis knew exactly what took place in Northern Ireland."[63] German reconnaissance planes monitored troop movements in the North; Hempel reported on weather conditions that aided German naval movements in and out of the English Channel. The Anglo-American governments suspected that one of these reports in early February allowed several German battleships and a cruiser to navigate a dash from the occupied French port at Brest, through the Channel, and back to the German port at Kiel, ready for an attack on Soviet Russia.[64] Walshe again registered a protest with Hempel and threatened to confiscate the transmitter since its existence threatened Ireland's neutral status.[65] Hempel denied his involvement: "I replied curtly to Walshe that, as I had explained to him earlier, the imputation to my Embassy of violations of the Hague Convention of 1907 as well as other violations of international law was without foundation."[66]

David Gray did not know the details of this specific transmission at the time, but a conversation with the Brazilian Consul in Dublin on February 16 warned him again that "the German Legation is the center of a very active propaganda effort and controls the Italian Legation." And, that "the Germans have very direct communications with Berlin, presumably by wireless, and a large staff of paid Irish agents."[67] While these reports were much exaggerated, according to Joseph Walshe,[68] they had an element of truth in them and they fed David Gray's indignation and shaped his low opinion of de Valera's government that built throughout 1942: "He [the Brazilian Consul, Nabal Costa] is satisfied that Mr. [Frederick] Boland, the number two in [Eire's Department of] External Affairs, is definitely pro-German and pro-Italian and turns in all information to the Axis Legation which may be of interest to them. ... I have always suspected Boland of this orientation."[69] In May, Gray wrote to Winston Churchill, as Britain had suffered a number of costly

Efforts to "break the backbone" of Irish neutrality

military defeats during the spring of 1942 and Gray wanted to register his support for the Prime Minister's leadership. In this letter, Gray also took the opportunity to tell Churchill that he had been right when he voiced skepticism regarding Eamon de Valera's ability to make compromises or amend Ireland's neutrality policy, as Gray believed was possible when he began his post as U.S. Minister in Dublin in March 1940:

> Since you discussed the Irish situation with me two years ago, when I stopped in London on the way to my post, much has happened and many changes have occurred in Ireland as elsewhere, but it is always the same malign genius that controls. This man is blind to handwriting on walls and deaf to the rumble of approaching catastrophe. ... Economic forces are now operating to dispel the illusions on which Mr. de Valera bases his program for a self-sufficient Ireland. The beauties of isolation are already somewhat dimmed.[70]

De Valera and Joseph Walshe held similarly low opinions of Gray at this time, and Walshe wrote to Ireland's Ambassador, Robert Brennan, in June, "When you hear the details you will realize what a source of bitter poison [David Gray] has been in all our relations with the U.S. Never was there more need of an understanding personality really interested in the welfare of our two countries."[71]

Gray had concluded that de Valera was stubbornly committed to neutrality, but that his pro-German defense minister Frank Aiken kept "crowding Dev to the left whenever he wavers."[72] The German Minister also worried about Irish loyalties and Hempel warned Berlin to keep the demands for transmissions of espionage reports from the Dublin Embassy to a minimum. He explained to his superiors that:

> The British as well as the American Government have, in my opinion, no easier and more popular way of ending Irish neutrality, without even arousing the public opinion of all Irish, than to demand the withdrawal of the German and Italian embassies here under the guise of pointing to their impermissible activities, detrimental to the Anglo-American conduct of the war. With that, the backbone of Irish neutrality would be broken.[73]

This was the advice that Walshe and de Valera also hoped the Germans would heed in order to keep Ireland out of the world war, and avoid a civil war with the IRA if de Valera was forced to join the alliance with Britain.

In the early months of 1942, Winston Churchill's and Franklin Roosevelt's wartime friendship had continued to strengthen as the U.S. President had offered the "Former Naval Person" encouraging words following Britain's major military losses to Japan that included the surrender of Singapore, a costly naval battle in the Java Sea, and Japanese capture of the Dutch West Indies.[74] When Roosevelt wrote to Churchill on March 18, he offered sympathy for Churchill's military and political "troubles," and urged him not to pay attention to the press critics and not to look back and regret past defeats, but to look forward and defend territory that must be protected in South Asia and the Middle East. Roosevelt asserted that he would personally "handle" the criticisms emanating from their Soviet ally, Joseph Stalin, who "thinks he likes me better, and I hope he will continue to do so." Then he offered some personal counsel:

> I know you will keep up your optimism and your grand driving force, but I know you will not mind if I tell you that you ought to take a leaf out of my notebook. Once a month I go to Hyde Park for four days, crawl into a hole and pull the hole in after me. I am called on the telephone only if something of really great importance occurs. I wish you would try it, and I wish you would lay a few bricks or paint another picture. ...[75]

Churchill's and the Allies' troubles continued into the summer months. On June 21, when Churchill was back in the United States for conferences with Roosevelt, German General Erwin Rommel forced another capitulation of British-led Allied troops at Tobruk in eastern Libya. A garrison of over 30,000 men surrendered to Rommel's smaller forces. This was "a

6.1 Winston Churchill and Franklin Roosevelt relax in the grounds of the White House in Washington, DC, prior to the daily meeting with the Joint Chiefs of Staff from the United Kingdom and the United States to discuss war strategy, *c*. June 1942

far greater strategic defeat than the loss of Singapore," as it "cleared the way for a German advance toward Cairo and the Suez Canal, threatening the entire British presence in the Middle East."[76] The defeat at Tobruk "humiliated the British," and the blow to Churchill's masculine pride was compounded as Churchill had to learn the news from his wartime partner. Historian Jon Meacham wrote of this episode that "Churchill believed Tobruk's fall to be 'one of the heaviest blows I can recall during the war. ... I did not attempt to hide from the President the shock I had received.'"[77] But Roosevelt stood by him and offered his fraternal support. Churchill later wrote that this was the measure of a true friend: "'A man loves his friend,' Churchill had noted, because 'he has stood by him perhaps at doubtful moments.'"[78] During their June meeting, Roosevelt also backed Churchill's plan to mount the invasion of North Africa in fall 1942, rather than launching a cross-Channel invasion of Western Europe, as Stalin advocated.[79] In July, U.S. General Dwight D. Eisenhower was sent to London to direct the joint-Anglo-American 'Operation Torch' as well as future Allied operations in the European theater of war.

In August and September, an incident in Ireland briefly commanded the Anglo-American leaders' attention once again. In August, a Northern Ireland court sentenced to death six IRA men who had been convicted of killing an Ulster policeman in Belfast earlier in the summer. The IRA 'men' were in fact boys, aged 18 to 21 years old, and the Ulster government's decision to execute them all incited a nationalist protest from Eamon de Valera and his diplomats Joseph Walshe in Dublin, Robert Brennan in Washington, and John Dulanty in London. American diplomats David Gray in Dublin and Ambassador John Winant in London, and the U.S. Secretary of State Cordell Hull in Washington, were all called on to intervene, and eventually Winston Churchill and Franklin Roosevelt also weighed in.

De Valera's diplomats all argued that the death sentence too harsh and that the IRA boys' "crime" had been committed to protest against the "greater crime" of Ireland's partition. Walshe directed Brennan to appeal to the U.S. Secretary of State to persuade the U.S. government to step in, making the argument that: "The execution of Irishmen on Irish soil by an authority set up contrary to the wishes of the Irish people would recall the unhappy past. It would disturb the relations between the two Islands at a critical time and would thus be a major political blunder. All this is irrespective of the merits of the case, which in themselves would warrant reprieve."[80] After meeting with Brennan, Hull directed John Winant to confer with Britain's Foreign Minister, Sir Anthony Eden, and to gather the facts and send his advice regarding U.S. intervention back to Washington.[81] In Dublin, Gray met with de Valera, who also appealed for U.S. intervention to press the British for a reprieve. Gray reported on the meeting to

Ambassador Winant and expressed his mixed feelings about the situation: "I am honestly undecided which is the right [course] to take, clemency or strict justice. We are going to get nothing from de Valera by kindness but if he dares he can stir up anti-American feeling as well as anti-British feeling on this issue. The Germans are the only people who know how to deal with him. I know I don't."[82] From Germany's perspective, if Eire's relations with Britain deteriorated because Ulster went through with the executions of the IRA boys, that was all to the good. In conversations with de Valera's diplomatic representative in Spain, Leopold Kerney, the German Foreign Office claimed to have no relationship with the IRA and that "Germany would help Ireland militarily, but only if such help were requested; otherwise she would not intervene."[83]

Ultimately, the United States' representatives Gray and Winant counseled clemency, and, at the end of August, Northern Ireland amended the sentencing. Winant reported back to Hull that "four of the six men condemned to death for the murder of the police sergeant in Belfast have had their sentences commuted to life and the fifth to 15 years' imprisonment by the Governor of Northern Ireland. One man is to be executed. We did what we could to help and so did Gray."[84] Following the announcement of the new sentences, Taoiseach de Valera appealed directly to Prime Minister Churchill, to plead for the life of 19-year-old Tom Williams: "The staving at this last moment, through your personal intervention, of the life of young Williams ... would profoundly affect public feeling here. I know the difficulties, but results would justify, and I urge strongly that you do it." Churchill would not intervene, consistent with his longtime position that the British government would not "coerce" Northern Ireland regarding its policies, and Williams was executed in Belfast on September 2.[85]

The results of the whole episode, David Gray reported back to the State Department, "cannot be regarded as satisfactory. Within the past fortnight repeated acts of violence have been committed in Ulster by Irish Republican Army terrorists. On September 7 two new murders of Ulster policemen were reported. The effect on public opinion of the trials of the murderers, if apprehended, is likely to be serious."[86] Not surprisingly, Gray blamed the degeneration of the Allies' relations with Eire first and foremost on Eamon de Valera, who had incited Irish nationalist, anti-Allied agitation when he protested against the stationing of American troops in Northern Ireland. Second, Gray blamed the Germans, who, Gray asserted, were either funding or organizing IRA attacks on the Allies in the North.[87] Railing against de Valera, whose masculine rational thinking lost out to his feminine irrational emotions, Gray reported to the State Department:

Efforts to "break the backbone" of Irish neutrality

[De Valera] condemns the murder [of Ulster policemen], but he is always able to sympathetically understand what motivated the murderers. Similarly, while he has several hundred of the IRA in jail without [due] process of law, he loses no opportunity to identify himself with the nationalistic causes of the organization. ... His mind tells him that his only hope of ending partition is with our help and with the help of British Liberal opinion, but his emotions apparently prevent his acting on this premise. Similarly, his mind tells him that only by the defeat of Germany can Eire be preserved as an independent state, but, again, his nationalistic emotions blind him, and he will exert no leadership in this sense.[88]

Gray also renewed complaints about the Irish government's censorship of the "facts of the Irish situation" – that is, the de Valera government's anti-British and pro-German sympathies – that forbade publication of stories by American reporters, such as Helen Kirkpatrick: "No correspondent can send these out of Eire. If he takes them out with him and sends them from England, he can never come back. In the case of articles that Helen Kirkpatrick wrote the *Chicago Daily News*, I am told the Irish Consulate General in New York organized a protest and a Committee of Irish Americans threatened both the News and the Boston Globe."[89] The same day as he reported to the State Department, September 8, Gray wrote a personal note to the president:

Dear Boss, Things are not very good over here. I am enclosing a memorandum on the situation as I see it. I may be unduly alarmed, but I don't want you caught off base if anything serious should develop. These Germans are not going to miss any bets. This bastard Hempel (the German Minister) was at the great hurling match on Sunday the center of a lot of obsequious Irish and he has recently hoisted the swastika flag on his motorcar. ... I don't know how strong the de Valera Irish are in America now, but it is reported here that they are returning to the support of Eire policies against America. If you can put the heat on in Boston it might do some good. You're the Doctor to write the prescription when the time comes. ...[90]

FDR wrote back to Gray that he and Gray were of one mind regarding their assessment of Irish-American relations, and they agreed on how to deal with de Valera. They were both openly hostile to de Valera and critical of de Valera's leadership and his misguided wartime neutrality policy. FDR shared his thinking with Gray:

Several people who have come back from, or passed through, Ireland have told me what a perfectly magnificent job you are doing. I did not have to be told that because I knew it, for the very simple fact that you have not given me the remote shadow of a headache all these years. I am inclined to think my policy of giving Dev the absent treatment [i.e. silent treatment] is about as effective as anything else. The other day one of his friends over here – a typical professional Irish American – came in to tell me about the terrible starvation among the people of Ireland. I looked at him in a much interested way and remarked quietly "Where is Ireland?" I do wish the people as a whole over there could realize that Dev is unnecessarily storing up trouble because most people over here feel that Dublin, by maintaining German spies and by making all little things difficult for the United Nations, is stirring up a thoroughly unsympathetic attitude toward Ireland as a whole when we win the war. That is a truly sad state of affairs.[91]

De Valera's Army continued its release of Anglo-American pilots and planes that made forced landings in Eire's territory, and allowed them safe passage back into Northern Ireland, which was a great boon to the Allies.[92] Nonetheless, de Valera and Walshe directed Robert Brennan to lodge additional protests with the State Department regarding the American troops stationed in the North. Brennan registered Eire's objections to a few lines in the U.S. Army's "Pocket Guide to Northern Ireland" that was distributed to all U.S. soldiers. The offending passage impugned Irish neutrality policy: "Eire's neutrality is a real danger to the Allied cause. There, just across the Irish Channel from embattled England, and not too far from your own billets in Ulster, the Axis nations maintain large legations and staffs. These Axis agents send out weather reports, and find out by espionage what is going on in Ulster."[93] According to Walshe, these guidebooks misrepresented the numbers of the Axis Legation staffs; Walshe asserted that there were only six staff at each legation. Moreover, Walshe stated: "They do not send out weather reports as they are not allowed to use wireless apparatus and to our certain knowledge do not do so. We have very adequate means of detecting and preventing use of such means of communication. There is no evidence that there are Axis agents at large."[94] In fact, the Anglo-Americans and the Irish government knew the Germans sent transmissions, but they weren't able to decrypt the transmissions they collected until January 1943.[95]

At the end of October, at the same time as Walshe asserted that there were no transmissions, the German Minister was transmitting his report on "Prospects for future incorporation of Ireland into a German-led Europe." In Hempel's opinion,

> the existing conditions are basically not unfavorable for a willingness on the part of the Irish to take a friendly position toward Germany. The recurring assertion in the English papers, that 90 percent of the Irish population is sympathetic to the English and the United States is fabrication, which is designed to partially sweeten for the English the obnoxious fact of Irish participation in the Anglo-Saxon "fight for freedom and Christianity." This does not correspond to the facts.[96]

Efforts to "break the backbone" of Irish neutrality

Hempel based the report on his own observations of the anti-British antipathy he noted among some of the Irish Catholic clergy, most notably the All-Ireland Catholic Primate, Cardinal MacRory, who was based in Northern Ireland and was an avowed "bitter enemy of the British Empire and Anglo-Saxon cant." Nonetheless, Hempel also noted that Irish sympathy for Germany could be undermined by "the consistently renewed reports of alleged unscrupulous German repressive measures in occupied countries, deportations, the fight against the Church, etc." and he urged Berlin to make some settlement with the Catholic Church to secure the loyalties of the Irish Catholic majority.[97] Joseph Walshe was also informed of Hempel's transmission by the head of G2, Colonel Dan Bryan, and Walshe contacted Hempel, warning the German Minister again that exposure of the illicit use of the transmitter would "be a catastrophe," presumably for both governments' national interests.[98]

At this time, in fall 1942 when Irish-American state-to-state relations were at a low point,[99] David Gray's propaganda project, to appeal directly to the Irish people to end neutrality and support the Allied war effort, finally came to fruition. The first issue of the U.S. Office of War Information's *Letter from America* was published on October 30, 1942. An initial circulation of 16,000 in Ireland elicited "500 favorable responses in two days," according to OWI. The first *Letter from America* included many pro-war messages, including one from U.S. Catholic politician Al Smith: "American boys of every faith are fighting today for the same principles that freedom-loving and devout Irishmen themselves have fought for through the years. These American boys are the vanguard of the Armies that will destroy Hitler; they with their comrades of the United Nations are the guarantee that a world will be built wherein all nations can be free to choose their way of life and to preserve their faith."[100] Although Gray would later question the *Letter*'s effectiveness in terms of undermining Irish neutrality,[101] it was published until April 1945, a counterpoint to "lying German propaganda which has endeavored to misrepresent to you [Irish people] every essential fact in recent history."[102]

Rather than the propaganda sheets that the belligerents circulated in Eire, the Anglo-American military successes, including the routing of General Rommel's forces by the British Eighth Army at El Alamein on Egypt's Mediterranean coast in early November 1942, seemed to soften the Irish government's antipathy toward the U.S. government, if not toward David Gray,[103] or toward American reporters such as Helen Kirkpatrick who, according to Robert Brennan, was engaged in an anti-neutrality "propaganda campaign" on her fall 1942 lecture tour in the United States.[104] Robert Brennan had reached out to John Hickerson, Director of the State Department's European Affairs Division, who seemed more receptive to improving relations with Ireland than Secretary Hull.[105] Sir John Maffey also noted, optimistically, that "a great change had been worked in the viewpoint of the Irish Government since the recent Allied victories."[106] Franklin Roosevelt, however, was not convinced that de Valera's government had seen the folly of its neutrality policy, and he wrote to David Gray in December that "It seems to me that during all these years it has been a pity that Ireland has lived in a dream under the rule of a dreamer. They do not know the facts of life and it will take a rude awakening to teach them." Roosevelt projected ahead to a postwar world where Anglo-American interests charted the course for the Ireland: "If and when we clean up Germany, I think that Churchill and I can do much for Ireland and its future – and I think that he and I can agree on the method with due consideration of firmness and justice."[107]

Roosevelt and Churchill were making many decisions together, regarding military strategy[108] and regarding organization of the postwar world. They met together at Casablanca, Morocco, for ten days in mid-January 1943. Their Soviet ally, Joseph Stalin, did not attend this wartime summit, as the fiercely fought Battle of Stalingrad with the German Army was nearing the final days of a six-month-long siege. Against Stalin's wishes, Roosevelt and Churchill determined that the Western Allies would attack the Axis forces through Sicily and Italy, rather than through occupied France. But the "Big Three" United Nations leaders all agreed on another major decision made at Casablanca, proposed by FDR – to fight on until Nazi Germany surrendered unconditionally.[109] There would be no negotiated peace. In early 1943, President Roosevelt was already envisioning that postwar geopolitical power would be concentrated in the hands of the three major wartime allies, and that the "smaller powers" would defer to their guidance.[110] Churchill and FDR shared notions of "Anglo-Saxon superiority" and envisioned an Anglo-American partnership that would bring "the benefit of freedom to the rest of the world,"[111] even as Churchill was less sanguine about a postwar partnership with the Soviet Union.

At this time, Sir John Maffey and David Gray were also thinking ahead to the postwar world, and what would occur in terms of Anglo-Irish and Irish-American postwar relations if de Valera gave up on Irish neutrality policy, allowed the Allies to use Irish ports, and expelled the Axis Legations. Maffey went through a long list of considerations with the Dominions Office: first among them was to gauge whether access to the contested ports would help the Allies defeat Germany faster at this stage of the war. If the Allies approached de Valera again, what would he say? Maffey asserted that, "Whatever his own underlying thoughts may be (and he certainly devoutly desires to see a German defeat), he has lost freedom of action in the international field owing to the fact that the Church and people, scared by fear of bombing, have adopted neutrality as a religion and a virtue."[112] If de Valera was asked about use of the ports again, Maffey advised that President Roosevelt should make the request, on behalf of all the United Nations, with Britain listed as one nation among many. If de Valera said "no," his refusal would be on record with the world and Ireland would be excluded from postwar settlements and international associations. If he said "yes," other problems might arise, such as expressions of resentment from British and American people because Ireland only joined in the war when Allied victory was (almost) ensured. Moreover, if Ireland joined the Allies, Ireland would be in a stronger moral and strategic position to make the case against partition in the postwar era. As Maffey put it to the Dominions Office, "clearly we do not want to run the risk of a 'Yes' from Mr. de Valera if the game is not worth the candle. i.e. if the commitments entailed heavily outweigh the advantages."[113] The Dominions Office decided to "leave matters alone." As they reasoned, "At present we are assured of American sympathy in ignoring Irish complaints, while we do receive certain minor but useful facilities. We might find ourselves in danger of losing these if we provoke a controversy on Irish neutrality."[114] The British decided to leave the Irish alone; David Gray, however, wanted to put de Valera "on record" for refusing a direct request for use of the bases from the United States government.[115] He spent the next year plotting and carrying out his scheme to establish a record of de Valera's refusal to aid the Allies' victory and of the Irish government's unneutral acts that favored the Axis Powers.

Historian John Day Tully has argued that David Gray never understood "how neutrality, for de Valera and increasingly for the Irish people, fostered a fundamental Irish *identity*, separate from Britain."[116] That national identity de Valera envisioned was of a "sovereign, independent, rural and Catholic" Ireland, and de Valera often promoted this vision in his political addresses on national occasions, such as his annual addresses marking St. Patrick's Day.[117] De Valera and his diplomatic representatives made the case in their interactions with the Anglo-Americans that Ireland's justification for neutrality had moral power and the Irish government should not be shut out of postwar planning, but the reception for these arguments among British Foreign Officers was mixed.[118] In May, Winston Churchill wrote to the Dominions Office: "Their [Ireland's] conduct in the war will never be forgiven by the British nation unless it is amended before the end. This in itself would be a great disaster. It is our duty to save these people from themselves. Any proposals you make to terminate the enemy representation in Dublin will be immediately considered by [me]."[119]

In May 1943, David Gray drafted a memorandum for the State Department outlining his vision of continued Anglo-American cooperation regarding policies toward Ireland, for the rest of the war's duration and into the postwar period. He believed that Ireland was already trying to create a rift between the two Allies over the issue of partition and he wanted to shut down what he perceived as Irish manipulations through four joint Anglo-American actions. None of these proposed actions were new, but Gray presented them as a package that would demonstrate Anglo-American solidarity. First, the United Nations should make a unified demand for the lease of Irish naval ports and air bases. Second, the United Nations should demand that the Irish government expel the Axis Missions from Dublin and declare whether Ireland was a member of the British Commonwealth of Nations, or not. Third, if (or, more likely, when) de Valera refused these demands, Britain and the United States should stop shipping any food, raw materials, or other supplies to Ireland, "on the grounds that if Eire chooses to exercise her right to an isolationist position, she must assume responsibility for her own supply." Fourth, Britain should extend its conscription policy to Northern Ireland, as Gray asserted that "There is little doubt that American opinion would support a measure which put an end to the escape of Northern Ireland slackers from duties imposed upon American youth."[120]

Gray presented his ideas to Franklin Roosevelt, and to Irish Catholic clergy, U.S. military chiefs, State Department officials, politicians, and prominent businessmen in Washington and several East Coast cities when he returned to the United States in summer 1943 for several months' "vacation," before returning to his post in Dublin in September.[121] Roosevelt responded favorably to Gray's proposals, but with a few important caveats. Regarding any formal actions such as diplomatic "demands," the State Department in collaboration with the British Foreign Office would write the official document (although Gray and the State Department together produced several drafts based on what Gray envisioned in August and September),[122] and all actions must be approved by Winston Churchill.[123] These conditions and the British government's reticence to move forward[124] slowed the progress of any actions taken along the lines Gray proposed, throughout the remainder of the year.[125] In the meantime, joint Anglo-American military invasions were launched in Sicily and Italy during the summer, and, at their August meetings at Hyde Park and Washington, Roosevelt and Churchill determined that a U.S. general would command the future invasion of France. Fascist Italy's surrender to the Allies in September 1943 (and the subsequent closing of the Italian Legation in Dublin), as well as planning for the November meeting of the Big Three war leaders in Cairo to decide the timing of the Western Front campaign for 1944, all diverted attention away from Ireland. By the end of November, the British Foreign Office decided not to go forward with Gray's proposals.[126]

Efforts to "break the backbone" of Irish neutrality

David Gray, however, persisted. When Edward Stettinius, who had held several key posts in Roosevelt's administration after 1939, became Under Secretary of State in late October, Gray wrote to him to "introduce" him to the "Irish situation." Gray asserted that de Valera stirred up nationalist, anti-British, and anti-American objections to Allied troops in Northern Ireland, and was "fomenting this attack on British-American relations," regarding partition. Gray urged Stettinius to move forward with his proposal to expel the Germans from Ireland and pressure Ireland to give up its neutral status, independently of Britain if necessary.[127] Gray also continued to press for his proposals in personal letters to Franklin Roosevelt.[128]

The Big Three war leaders, Roosevelt, Churchill, and Stalin, met in Tehran from November 28 to December 1, 1943; this was the Western leaders' first joint face-to-face meeting with the Soviet premier since they became wartime allies. Their concerns focused on the wars in East Asia and on the Continent, and on plans for the Allied invasion of France. "Operation Overlord" was set to take place in 1944 at Joseph Stalin's firm insistence and with his pledge that the Soviets would simultaneously attack the Germans from the east.[129] In addition to agreeing that their fascist enemies must surrender unconditionally to end the war, the leaders also began to reconcile their postwar visions.

Ireland was not a topic of conversation with Stalin at the Tehran Conference. A week after the leaders parted, however, Churchill wrote to his Deputy Prime Minister, Clement Atlee, that Britain would go along with an American initiative to put pressure on de Valera to expel the Germans from Ireland and give up the neutrality policy, as the U.S. State Department, advised by Gray, proposed.[130] As Churchill explained, FDR favored Gray's proposal, and Churchill deferred to Roosevelt:

> I spoke to the President about Ireland last night and explained to him the answer which we propose to send to the latest communication of the United States Government. The President said he quite understood our line of thought but believed it would have been a good thing to have the American protest to Ireland on record.[131]

The plans for Operation Overlord and Germany's own actions – another parachute drop of two Irishmen, spies for Germany, in western Ireland was discovered in mid-December[132] – provided more impetus for Gray's scheme to press de Valera's government expel the Axis Powers. The Allies' real security concerns also prompted the British to step in and pressure de Valera to confiscate the radio transmitter in the German Legation that all governments knew existed,[133] and gave Gray the green light to craft an "American Note" that presented the United States' demands to the Irish government.[134] David Gray's long-proposed plan to put "on record" the de Valera government's complicit support of the fascist powers and refusal to aid the "righteous" Anglo-American allies was finally set in motion.

Notes

1 Alonso Hamby, "Democracy's Champions: Churchill and Roosevelt," *Finest Hour* 172 online (Spring 2016), https://winstonchurchill.org/publications/finest-hour/finest-hour-172/churchill-and-roosevelt/ (accessed 7 December 2020). See also Jon Meacham, *Franklin and Winston: An Intimate Portrait of an Epic Friendship* (New York: Random House, 2004), 165.
2 Hamby, "Democracy's Champions."
3 Eunan O'Halpin, *Defending Ireland: The Irish State and Its Enemies Since 1922* (New York: Oxford University Press, 2000), 182; Robert Fisk, *In Time of War: Ireland, Ulster and the Price of Neutrality, 1939–1945* (London: Andre Deutsch, 1983), 455.
4 Donal O' Drisceoil, *Censorship in Ireland, 1939–1945* (Cork: Cork University Press, 1996), 4–5.
5 O'Halpin, *Defending Ireland*, 227–229.
6 Carolle J. Carter, *The Shamrock and the Swastika: German Espionage in Ireland in World War II* (Palo Alto, CA: Pacific Books, 1977), 171.
7 O'Halpin, *Defending Ireland*, 244.
8 T. Ryle Dwyer, *Irish Neutrality and the USA, 1939–47* (Dublin: Gill & Macmillan, 1977), 197.
9 O'Halpin, *Defending Ireland*, 244.
10 Carter, *The Shamrock and the Swastika*, 155–158.
11 Memorandum by Joseph Walshe to Eamon de Valera, "The Case of Mr X" (Secret) 28 November 1941, Doc. No. 150 NAI DFA Secretary's Files A34, *Documents on Irish Foreign Policy* vol. VII, 1941–1945.
12 Memorandum by Joseph Walshe to Eamon de Valera, "The Case of Hermann Görtz" (Most Secret), 4 December 1941, Doc. No. 152 NAI DFA Secretary's Files A34, *Documents on Irish Foreign Policy* vol. VII, 1941–1945.
13 These transmissions were known to British intelligence. Eunan O'Halpin, "'According to the Irish Minister in Rome …': British Decrypts and Irish Diplomacy in the Second World War," *Irish Studies in International Affairs* 6 (1995), 99. The information was passed on to David Gray at the American Legation in Dublin. See David Gray to Franklin Roosevelt, 1 January 1942, box 40, President's Secretary's Files: Ireland, January – April 1942, Franklin Delano Roosevelt Papers, Franklin Roosevelt Presidential Library, Hyde Park, NY (hereafter: FDR Papers). See also Translation of Telegram sent from German Embassy (Dublin) to the German Foreign Ministry (Berlin), via Bern, Switzerland, 16 January 1942, box 6, David Gray Papers, 1857–1960, Coll. 03082, American Heritage Center, University of Wyoming, Laramie, Wyoming (hereafter: Gray Papers, AHC).

14 Memorandum by Joseph Walshe for Eamon de Valera (Dublin) (Secret) 15 December 1941, Doc. No. 165 UCDA P150/2571, *Documents on Irish Foreign Policy* vol. VII, 1941–1945.
15 Nancy Caldwell Sorel, *The Women Who Wrote the War* (New York: Arcade Publishing, 1999), 148–149.
16 Helen Kirkpatrick, "People Sympathize with US but Eire Clings to Neutrality," *Chicago Daily News* (26 December 1941), box 2, Helen Paull Kirkpatrick Papers, CA-MS-01132, Sophia Smith Collection, Smith College, Northampton, MA (hereafter: HPK Papers).
17 John Day Tully, *Ireland and Irish Americans 1932–1945: The Search for Identity* (Dublin: Irish Academic Press, 2010), 111; David Gray to Franklin Roosevelt, 17 December 1941, box 40, President's Secretary's Files: Ireland, 1941, FDR Papers; The Minister in Ireland (Gray) to the Secretary of State (Hull), 23 December 1941, Doc. 197, *Foreign Relations of the United States* (hereafter: *FRUS*), 1941 vol. III (Washington, DC: Government Printing Office, 1959).
18 Helen Kirkpatrick, "Eire Imprisons Masterminds of German Spy Ring; Gestapo Leader Goetz Admits Getting Funds from IRA in U.S.," *Chicago Daily News* (27 December 1941), box 12, HPK Papers.
19 Helen Kirkpatrick, "Nazi Spy Ring in Ireland," *Chicago Daily News* (27 December 1941), box 12, HPK Papers.
20 Confidential report from John Dulanty (London) to Joseph Walshe (No. 2) (Secret) 21 January 1942, Doc. No. 171 NAI DFA Secretary's Files P12/14/1, *Documents on Irish Foreign Policy* vol. VII, 1941–1945.
21 Helen Kirkpatrick to Carroll Binder, Foreign News Editor, *Chicago Daily News* (29 December 1941), box 2, HPK Papers.
22 Suzanne LaFollette, "America's Role in Irish Independence," and William Shirer, "Will Hitler Take Ireland?" in "Ireland and America: A Special Supplement on Ireland's Position in the Battle of the Atlantic," *Nation* 154: 5, part 2 (31 January 1942), 126–128, 132–133.
23 Memorandum by Joseph Walshe for Eamon de Valera, "The Görtz Affair: German Assurances" (Secret), 5 January 1942, Doc. No. 169 NAI DFA Secretary's Files A 34, *Documents on Irish Foreign Policy* vol. VII, 1941–1945.
24 Helen Kirkpatrick, "De Valera Brands A.E.F. Aggression Against Ireland," *Chicago Daily News* (30 January 1942), box 3, HPK Papers.
25 Dwyer, *Irish Neutrality and the USA*, 143: "Churchill and Roosevelt had decided to station three divisions of United States troops in the Six Counties, where they could complete their training, while British soldiers stationed in the areas could be used elsewhere. It was hoped that replacement of British troops by Americans might even help to further improve Anglo-Irish relations. But such was not to be the case."
26 *Ibid.*; Helen Kirkpatrick to Carroll Binder, Foreign News Editor, *Chicago Daily News* (29 December 1941), box 2, HPK Papers. See also Kirkpatrick, Notes for Newspaper Article on American use of military bases in the North and South of Ireland, *c.* January 1942, box 2, HPK Papers; Kirkpatrick, "British to Pass

Buck to U.S. on Eire Bases," *Chicago Daily News* (12 January 1942), box 3, HPK Papers.

27 Helen Kirkpatrick, "Yanks are Coming to Ireland Called Worst Kept Secret of the War," *Chicago Daily News* (26 January 1942), box 12, HPK Papers: (subtitle): "All of Ulster is Prepared for Arrival; Even Nazi Consul is Said to Have Jitters Days Before Landing."

28 Helen Kirkpatrick, "Gen. Chaney, Air Expert, Heads Yanks in Britain," *Chicago Daily News* (27 January 1942), box 3, HPK Papers. See also Anthony J. Jordan, *Churchill: A Founder of Modern Ireland* (Dublin: Westport Books, 1995), 180.

29 Interview with Helen Kirkpatrick Milbank by Anne Kasper, Women in Journalism oral history project of the Washington Press Club Foundation, April 3–5, 1990, 54, in the Oral History Collection of Columbia University and other repositories.

30 Clear telegram from the Department of External Affairs to the Irish Legations at Washington (No. 24) and the Holy See (No. 10) and to the High Commission in London (No. 11) 27 January 1942, Doc. No. 173 NAI DFA Secretary's Files P43, *Documents on Irish Foreign Policy* vol. VII, 1941–1945. See also Official Statement issued in Dublin on 27th January 1942, P150/2604, Eamon de Valera Papers (on microfilm), University College Dublin (hereafter: EdV Papers, UCD).

31 The Minister in Ireland (Gray) to the Secretary of State (Hull), 27 January 1942, Doc. 638, *FRUS* 1942 vol. I (Washington, DC: Government Printing Office, 1960). See also David Gray to Sean T. O'Kelly (Tanaiste, Irish Government), 17 February 1942, box 7, Gray Papers, AHC.

32 David Gray to U.S. Ambassador John Winant (London), 27 January 1942, box 6, Gray Papers, AHC.

33 David Gray to Franklin Roosevelt, 27 January 1942, box 40, President's Secretary's File, Ireland, January – April 1942, FDR Papers.

34 *New York Times* report of remarks made by President Roosevelt at a Press Conference, 27 January 1942, P150/2604, EdV Papers, UCD.

35 Memorandum by Sir John Maffey to the British Dominions Office, quoted in David McCullagh, *De Valera: Rule, 1932–1972* (Dublin: Gill Books, 2018), 219.

36 "Memorandum of Conversation with Prime Minister de Valera [by David Gray]," 29 January 1942, P150/2638, EdV Papers, UCD.

37 Elizabeth Bowen, *Notes on Eire: Espionage reports to Winston Churchill 1940-2*, 3rd ed., With a review of Irish Neutrality in World War 2 by Jack Lane and Brendan Clifford (Cork: Aubane Historical Society, 2009), 47–48.

38 Fisk, *In Time of War*, 286.

39 Maurice Manning, *James Dillon, A Biography* (Dublin: Wolfhound Press, 1999), 173.

40 Press Censor's report for February 1942, Michael Knightly, Chief Press Censor, P104/3486, Frank Aiken Papers on microfilm, University College Dublin (hereafter: FA Papers, UCD).

41 Manning, *James Dillon*, 174–175; Bowen, *Notes on Eire*, 53.
42 Michael Kennedy, *Guarding Neutral Ireland: The Coast Watching Service and Military Intelligence, 1939–1945* (Dublin: Four Courts Press, 2008), 200–202.
43 Letter from Joseph Walshe to Sean Murphy (Vichy) 12 February 1942, Doc. No. 182 NAI DFA Paris Embassy P48/2, *Documents on Irish Foreign Policy* vol. VII, 1941–1945.
44 David Gray to Brendan Bracken, MP, British Cabinet Minister for Information, London, 10 February 1942, box 7, Gray Papers, AHC.
45 Memorandum of Conversation with Sir John Maffey and Joseph Walshe, 31 March 1942, box 7, Gray Papers, AHC. Gray concluded: "Absolutely no progress was made toward modifying the present propaganda situation and both Sir John Maffey and myself are entirely free to recommend to our respective Governments such courses as may seem best."
46 Memorandum by Joseph Walshe of a conversation with Sir John Maffey and David Gray, 31 March 1942, Doc. No. 195 NAI DFA Secretary's Files A 2, *Documents on Irish Foreign Policy* vol. VII, 1941–1945; Memorandum by Joseph Walshe of a Conversation with David Gray, 17 April 1942, Doc. No. 199 NAI DFA Secretary's Files P 48 A, *Documents on Irish Foreign Policy* vol. VII, 1941–1945.
47 Dwyer, *Irish Neutrality and the USA*, 150–151.
48 "Memorandum for Proposed Press Bureau," *c.* February 1942, box 7, Gray Papers, AHC.
49 Helen Kirkpatrick to David Gray, box 4, David Gray Papers, 1855–1962, Franklin Roosevelt Presidential Library, Hyde Park, NY (hereafter: DG Papers, FDR Library); David Gray to Major General William Donovan, Coordinator of Information, Department of State, 5 June 1942, box 8, Gray Papers, AHC.
50 William H. Stoneman and Helen Kirkpatrick, Special Section of *Chicago Daily News*, "In the Air Raids: Experience is the Best Teacher," Air Raid Guide (11 July 1942), box 3, HPK Papers.
51 "Helen Kirkpatrick Writes Under Fire," *Chicago Daily News* (13 January 1942), box 1, HPK Papers.
52 Inez Whitely Foster, "Guts and Glamour," *Mademoiselle* magazine (March 1942), box 1, HPK Papers.
53 Carolyn M. Edy, *The Woman War Correspondent, the U.S. Military, and the Press, 1846–1947* (Lanham, MD: Lexington Books, 2017), 58. Edy quotes a February 15, 1941, *New York Times* article, "Two News Women Honored for Work; Mrs. Roosevelt presents $100 Prizes of their Club at Front Page Ball; War Reporters Hailed": "Among the coterie of women under fire, turning out their daily dispatches as competently as the men beside whom they work, we who envy their assignments and admire their achievements tonight honor Eleanor Packard of the United Press in Rome; Helen Kirkpatrick of the *Chicago Daily News* … They have all done us proud."
54 Frank Knox to Helen Kirkpatrick, 19 January 1942, box 2, HPK Papers.
55 David Gray to Helen Kirkpatrick, 10 March 1942, box 2, HPK Papers.

56 T. Ryle Dwyer, *Behind the Green Curtain: Ireland's Phoney Neutrality During World War II* (Dublin: Gill & Macmillan, 2009), 218.
57 "With AEF," *Chicago Daily News* (25 March 1942), box 3, HPK Papers: "Two American women reporters who lived in London through its worst air attacks became today the first woman correspondents formally accredited to the United States Army." [Helen Kirkpatrick and Mary Welsh of *Time* and *Life* magazines.]
58 Edy, *The Woman War Correspondent*, 50–52.
59 Helen Kirkpatrick, "Somewhere in Northern Ireland with the United States Army," *Chicago Daily News* (19 May 1942), box 3, HPK Papers.
60 Sorel, *The Women Who Wrote the War*, 174. Helen Kirkpatrick, "King, Queen, Find AEF is 'Colossal'," and "With the United States Armed Forces," *Chicago Daily News* (27 June 1942), box 3, HPK Papers.
61 O'Halpin, *Defending Ireland*, 191: "The British also had to worry about Axis diplomatic traffic. All such cables were, like all other cables to and from Ireland, automatically routed through London. They were delayed for reasons for a few days, to lessen the value of any operational intelligence they might contain, before being passed on to Berne and thence to Berlin and Rome respectively. The British evidently broke the Italian cables. So too did the Americans, who read Italian traffic between Dublin and Italian missions in neutral South American states. However, German diplomatic traffic remained impervious to Allied cryptanalysts until January 1943. The British were then able to read some earlier Dublin/Berlin exchanges of which they had records."
62 Translations of Telegrams Sent from German Legation in Dublin [Hempel], back to German Foreign Ministry, 11 January 1942, and 16 January 1942, box 6, Gray Papers, AHC.
63 "A History of United States Army Forces Northern Ireland (USANIF), From January 1, 1942 to May 31, 1942," CAB/3/A/125, U.S. War Department Adjunct General's Office, War Department Records Branch, Historical Records Section, 194, Public Records Office for Northern Ireland, Belfast, Northern Ireland (hereafter: PRONI).
64 McCullagh, *De Valera*, 221–222; O'Halpin, "'According to the Irish Minister in Rome …'," 99.
65 Memorandum from Joseph Walshe to Eamon de Valera (Dublin) (Most Secret) 17 February 1942, Doc. No. 186 NAI DFA Secretary's Files A25, *Documents on Irish Foreign Policy* vol. VII, 1941–1945.
66 Translation of Intercepted German legation (Hempel) report to Under Secretary of State Woermann, sent via Bern, Switzerland, Dublin No. 105 sent 19 February, arrived 24 February 1942, box 7, Gray Papers, AHC.
67 Memorandum of Conversation Senor Narbal Costa, Brazilian Consul, and David Gray, American Minister, Dublin, 16 February 1942, box 7, Gray Papers, AHC.
68 Memorandum by Joseph Walshe of a conversation with David Gray (Secret) 17 April 1942, Doc. No. 199 NAI DFA Secretary's Files P48A, *Documents on Irish Foreign Policy*, vol. VII, 1941–1945.

69 Memorandum of Conversation Senor Narbal Costa, Brazilian Consul, and David Gray, American Minister, Dublin, 16 February 1942, box 7, Gray Papers, AHC.
70 David Gray to Winston Churchill, 11 May 1942, box 7, Gray Papers, AHC.
71 Handwritten letter from Joseph Walshe to Robert Brennan (Washington) 6 June 1942, Doc. No. 206 NAI DFA Washington Embassy Minister's File 1942, *Documents on Irish Foreign Policy* vol. VII, 1941–1945.
72 David Gray to Franklin Roosevelt, 6 June 1942, box 8, Gray Papers, AHC.
73 Typescript Translation of Intercepted message from Dublin (Hempel) via Bern to Berlin Foreign Ministry (Under Secretary of State Woermann) Dublin No. 168, sent 27 March, arrived 13 April 1942, box 7, Gray Papers, AHC.
74 Jean Edward Smith, *FDR* (New York: Random House, 2008), 541.
75 Letter, FDR to Winston S. Churchill, 18 March 1942, box 2, Map Room Papers: Messages: FDR-Churchill, March-April 1942, FDR Papers.
76 Lynne Olson, *Last Hope Island: Britain, Occupied Europe, and the Brotherhood that Helped to Turn the Tide of War* (London: Scribe Publications, 2018), 208.
77 Meacham, *Franklin and Winston*, 184.
78 *Ibid.*, 186.
79 Smith, *FDR*, 561–562.
80 Extract from Telegram from Joseph Walshe to Robert Brennan (Washington) (No. 203) 14 August 1942, Doc. No. 214 NAI DFA Secretary's Files P60, *Documents on Irish Foreign Policy* vol. VII, 1941–1945.
81 The Secretary of State (Hull) to the Ambassador in the UK (Winant) August 15, 1942, Document 651, *FRUS* 1942 vol. I.
82 David Gray to Ambassador John Winant (London), 23 August 1942, box 8, Gray Papers, AHC.
83 Confidential report from [Irish Minister to Spain] Leopold H. Kerney (Madrid) to Joseph Walshe, "Conversation with a German" [Veesenmayer] (SPC 19/4) 24 August 1942, Doc. No. 218 NAI DFA Secretary's Files A47, *Documents on Irish Foreign Policy* vol. VII, 1941–1945.
84 The US Ambassador to the UK (Winant) to the Secretary of State, 31 August 1942, Document 656, *FRUS* 1942 vol. I.
85 McCullagh, *De Valera*, 223.
86 US Minister to Ireland David Gray, Memorandum on the State of Ireland, to the State Department, 8 September 1942, box 40, President's Secretary's File: Ireland, May – December, 1942, FDR Papers.
87 *Ibid.*
88 *Ibid.*
89 *Ibid.* See also Extract from a personal code telegram from Robert Brennan to Joseph P. Walshe (No. 387) (Very Urgent) 14 November 1942, Doc. No. 241 NAI DFA Secretary's Files P2, *Documents on Irish Foreign Policy* vol. VII, 1941–1945: "There is evidence of concerted campaign here to put Ireland in the wrong light, particularly emphasising that country is centre of vast espionage and is imminent and vital danger to Allied cause.

Helen Kirkpatrick is now on unpublicised lecture tour, giving her personal experiences in Ireland, proving that Ireland's neutrality constitutes immediate danger to American and British forces. We have reports of Press and Radio activities on these lines recently from San Francisco, Chicago, Boston, New York."

90 David Gray to Franklin Roosevelt, 8 September 1942, box 8, Gray Papers, AHC. See also David Gray to Franklin Roosevelt, 16 September 1942, box 40, President's Secretary's File: Ireland, May – December, 1942, FDR Papers.
91 Franklin Roosevelt to David Gray, 16 September 1942, box 40, President's Secretary's File: Ireland, May – December, 1942 FDR Papers.
92 The Minister in Ireland (Gray) to the Secretary of State, 16 October 1942, Doc. 658, *FRUS* 1942 vol. I. See also Dwyer, *Irish Neutrality and the USA*, 157.
93 Memorandum of Conversation, the Under Secretary of State (Welles) and Minister of Ireland (Brennan), 29 October 1942, Doc. 660, *FRUS* 1942 vol. I.
94 Personal Code telegram from Joseph Walshe to Robert Brennan (No. 272) 28 October 1942, Doc. No. 235 NAI DFA Secretary's Files P2, *Documents on Irish Foreign Policy* vol. VII, 1941–1945.
95 O'Halpin, *Defending Ireland*, 191.
96 Translation of Transmission from German Legation in Dublin (Hempel) via Bern, to Berlin, Sent 22 October, arrived in Berlin 31 October 1942, box 8, Gray Papers, AHC.
97 *Ibid.*
98 Transcript of an intercepted phone conversation of 28 October 1942 between Joseph P. Walshe and Eduard Hempel with covering letter from Colonel Dan Bryan to Joseph Walshe (Secret) 3 November 1942 re. illicit use of radio transmitter in the German legation in Dublin], Doc. No. 237 NAI DFA Secretary's Files A20/4 G2, *Documents on Irish Foreign Policy* vol. VII, 1941–1945.
99 US Minister to Ireland David Gray, memo on "Discussion of Anglo-Irish Problems at Ambassador Winant's Dinner," 17 November 1942, box 40, President's Secretary's File: Ireland, May – December, 1942, FDR Papers.
100 Office of War Information to John Winant, 1 November 1942, box 211, John Gilbert Winant Papers, Franklin Roosevelt Presidential Library, Hyde Park, NY.
101 David Gray to Dan S. Terrell, Special Assistant to the American Minister, Office of War Information (Dublin), 12 January 1944, box 12, Gray Papers, AHC.
102 Tully, *Ireland and Irish Americans*, 116.
103 Letter from Robert Brennan to Joseph Walshe 25 November 1942, Doc. No. 246 NAI DFA Secretary's Files P2, *Documents on Irish Foreign Policy* vol. VII, 1941–1945.
104 *Ibid.*: "During the past couple of months we have had instances of grossly misleading information in such widely separated places as San Francisco, Chicago, New York and Boston, published by press and radio, on the matter of alleged activity of Nazi spies in Ireland. ... Miss Helen Kirkpatrick is at present on a lecture tour through the United States, her subject being Ireland and the War. We obtained a copy of her talk before the Chicago Council On Foreign

Relations. She gives experiences of her own, purporting to prove the success of the Nazi espionage in Ireland. When her statements are examined, it is found that there is no real evidence, and that her case is based entirely on conjecture and suspicion. The whole case made by Miss Kirkpatrick and others engaged in this propaganda is that because of this espionage Ireland's neutrality is a real danger to the Allies, and that that danger must be removed." See also Helen Kirkpatrick to David and Maude Gray, 24 January 1943, box 9, Gray Papers, AHC: "The Irish Minister in Washington wrote me a six-page single-spaced typewritten letter on the subject of my Irish speech in Chicago. Pittsburgh and Boston also had the great privilege of hearing men on that subject and Joe Kennedy's pals from South Boston came in. It was not a dull evening."

105 Personal code telegram from Joseph Walshe to Robert Brennan (No. 281) 17 November 1942, Doc. No. 242 NAI DFA Secretary's Files P2, *Documents on Irish Foreign Policy* vol. VII, 1941–1945.

106 US Minister to Ireland David Gray, memo on "Discussion of Anglo-Irish Problems at Ambassador Winant's Dinner," 17 November 1942, box 40, President's Secretary's File: Ireland, May – December, 1942, FDR Papers.

107 Franklin Roosevelt to David Gray, 18 December 1942, box 40, President's Secretary's File: Ireland, May – December, 1942, FDR Papers.

108 See for example, account of the joint Anglo-American bombing strategy determined at the Casablanca Conference: Sir Martin Gilbert, CBE, "Churchill Proceedings; Churchill and Bombing Policy," The fifth Churchill lecture, The George Washington University, Washington, DC, 18 October 2005, in *Finest Hour* 137 (Winter 2007–2008), www.winstonchurchill.org/publications/finest-hour/finest-hour-137/churchill-proceedings-churchill-and-bombing-policy/ (accessed 7 December 2020).

109 Hamby, "Democracy's Champions"; Smith, *FDR*, 565–568.

110 Telegram from Anthony Eden [in Washington, DC] to Churchill, 17 March 1943, CHAR: 20/108/20–22, Winston Churchill Archives online, The Chartwell Trust.

111 Meacham, *Franklin and Winston*, 238–239. See also Winston Churchill, Speech to Harvard University on receiving an honorary degree, 6 September 1943, https://winstonchurchill.org/resources/speeches/1941–1945-war-leader/the-price-of-greatness-is-responsibility/ (accessed 7 December 2020).

112 Letter from Sir John Maffey to Sir Eric Machtig (Dominions Office, London), 8 February 1943, DO 35/2062, British National Archives.

113 *Ibid.*

114 *Ibid.*

115 Dwyer, *Irish Neutrality and the USA*, 163–164. See also Brian Girvin, *The Emergency: Neutral Ireland 1939–45* (London: Pan Macmillan, 2007), 302–303.

116 Tully, *Ireland and Irish Americans*, 121.

117 *Ibid.*, 120.

118 Personal Code Telegram from John J. Hearne (Ottawa) to Joseph Walshe (No. 25), 3 April 1943, Doc. No. 278 NAI DFA Secretary's Files P4, *Documents*

on Irish Foreign Policy vol. VII, 1941–1945: Hearne reported on a conversation with Sir Anthony Eden and Malcolm MacDonald. Eden criticized Irish neutrality and predicted that Ireland would have no role in postwar international associations; MacDonald was more sympathetic to Ireland. See also Memorandum from Joseph Walshe to Eamon de Valera, 24 April 1943, Doc. No. 282 NAI DFA Secretary's Files A2, *Documents on Irish Foreign Policy* vol. VII, 1941–1945: Maffey seemed sympathetic to Irish neutrality, but warned that others in the British government, such as Winston Churchill, Clement Atlee, and Anthony Eden, resented Irish neutrality.

119 Girvin, *The Emergency*, 301–302. Girvin quoting Churchill in a document dated 5 May 1943.

120 "Memorandum by the Minister in Ireland (Gray) on Recommendations for the Adoption of a Joint Anglo-American Economic Policy Toward Eire Shaped with Reference to Political Consideration," 14 May 1943, Doc. 83 (711.41D/20), *FRUS* 1943 vol. III (Washington, DC: Government Printing Office, 1963).

121 Dwyer, *Irish Neutrality and the USA*, 168–169. See also Telegram from Lord Halifax, British Ambassador in the United States to Winston Churchill and Clement Atlee, reporting on a meeting he had with David Gray, 18 June 1943, CHAR: 20/113/87, Winston Churchill Archives online; The Secretary of State [Cordell Hull] to the President, 29 June 1943, Doc. 84 (811.34541D/11b.), *FRUS* 1943 vol. III; David Gray to Edward Mooney, Archbishop of Detroit, 16 August 1943, box 11, Gray Papers, AHC; Memorandum from Sean Nunan to Robert Brennan (Washington) 20 August 1943, Doc. No. 312 NAI DFA Secretary's Files P48A, *Documents on Irish Foreign Policy* vol. VII, 1941–1945.

122 David Gray, "Revised draft note to the Irish government," *c.* 16 August 1943, box 2, DG Papers, FDR Library; Telegram, The Secretary of State [Hull] to the Ambassador in the United Kingdom (Winant), 18 September 1943, Doc. 88 (811.3454D/11a), *FRUS* 1943 vol. III.

123 Telegram from Lord Halifax [British Ambassador in the U.S.] to Churchill and Anthony Eden, 8 July 1943, CHAR: 20/114/109, Winston Churchill Archives online.

124 The Secretary of State [Hull] to the Minister in Ireland (Gray), 5 October 1943, Doc. 94 (841D.01/206), *FRUS* 1943 vol. III.

125 Girvin, *The Emergency*, 304: "Eden, now foreign secretary, revealed to [U.S. Ambassador John] Winant that while Churchill was in favor of the initiative, a number of senior ministers had serious reservations. The Labor Party leader Clement Atlee was the most prominent cabinet member to oppose action on Ireland ... it was now widely accepted in Britain that if de Valera had achieved a united Ireland before the war, the entire island would have been neutral in the present conflict. This would have further disadvantaged the already hard-pressed British and perhaps even justified intervention. The argument now went that Britain had survived four years without Eire's ports or airfields, but had been able to use Northern Ireland for much needed bases, industrial production and airfields. The decision not to support Gray's initiative in 1943

Efforts to "break the backbone" of Irish neutrality

thus became a decision to maintain partition for the foreseeable future and was an unintended but not surprising consequence of Eire's neutrality ..."

126 Dwyer, *Irish Neutrality and the USA*, 177; McCullagh, *De Valera*, 239.
127 David Gray to Secretary of State Edward Stettinius, 22 October 1943, box 11, Gray Papers AHC. See also Telegram, "The Minister in Ireland (Gray) to the Secretary of State [Acting Secretary Stettinius], 1 November 1943, Doc. 100 (841D01/215) and Telegram, The Minister in Ireland (Gray) to the [Acting] Secretary of State [Stettinius], 9 November 1943, Doc. 101 (841D.01/217), *FRUS* 1943 vol. III.
128 David Gray to Franklin Roosevelt, 4 November 1943, box 11, Gray Papers, AHC.
129 Smith, *FDR*, 592–593.
130 Dwyer, *Irish Neutrality and the USA*, 180: "Gray sent the Secretary of State his arguments on the subject on 13 December 1943. He also enclosed a suggested draft for a formal note contending that Irish neutrality favored the Axis Powers because Ireland's geographic location afforded their representatives an opportunity for highly organized espionage, while it denied any such advantage to the Allies."
131 Telegram from Churchill (in Cairo) to Clement Atlee (Deputy Prime Minister), 8 December 1943, CHAR: 20/130/34, Winston Churchill Archives online.
132 Max Hastings, *The Secret War: Spies, Ciphers, and Guerrillas 1939–1945* (New York: HarperCollins, 2016), 334; John P. Duggan, *Herr Hempel and the German Legation in Dublin, 1937–1945* (Dublin: Irish Academic Press, 2003), 186-187.
133 Memorandum by Joseph Walshe for Eamon de Valera, "The German Wireless Transmitter," 15 December 1943, Doc. No. 355 NAI DFA, *Documents on Irish Foreign Policy* vol. VII, 1941–1945.
134 Dwyer, *Irish Neutrality and the USA*, 181–182.

7

Eire, neutral to the bitter end, January 1944 to June 1945

Diplomatic tensions in Dublin ran high in the spring of 1944, as they did in all the belligerent capitals. Planning was ramping up for Operation Overlord, the anticipated reopening of the European front in France, and security concerns were uppermost in the minds of the Allied leaders and their military generals at the London operational headquarters. The mammoth proportions of the planned invasion – an airborne assault of over 18,000 Allied paratroopers, over 130,000 ground troops, and 30,000 vehicles transported by 6,000 ships that all had to be landed in France at a point where the Germans were not ready to repel the invasion with an even greater military force[1] – demanded a mammoth degree of secrecy and subterfuge. German espionage in Eire could threaten the success of the operation, because, among other reasons, U.S. troops were amassing forces for the upcoming invasion on Northern Ireland bases again, reaching a total of 120,000 troops along with critical military equipment by January 1944.[2] The Irish government as well as the Anglo-American diplomats in Dublin were on high alert.

Although they weren't privy to any of the details of military planning for the D-Day invasion, David Gray and Sir John Maffey were focused on German activities in Eire as they worried about sabotage of the Allied operation.[3] At the end of December 1943, the Irish authorities had finally confiscated the German Legation's wireless radio transmitter that had been in the German Minister's possession since 1939. Joseph Walshe also officially informed the Anglo-Americans that two German agents had parachuted into the country in mid-December. These agents had been arrested and incarcerated and the wireless transmitters that they were delivering were also captured. Nonetheless, Gray remained deeply suspicious of further German intrigues.[4] Gray and the U.S. State Department went forward with their long-percolating plan to shame the Irish government into expelling the German and Japanese diplomats from Dublin, outlining the Allies' "security concerns" in an official diplomatic Note.[5]

British intelligence agencies had opposed the Americans' plan to shut down the German Embassy – by this time they had cracked the German message codes and were gathering information from the German Minister's communications with the Berlin Foreign Ministry. Prime Minister Winston Churchill and the British War Cabinet, however, endorsed the American plan to rid Dublin of the Axis governments' diplomats.[6] As Churchill persuaded his government to support the proposed American demands, he argued:

> Much more dangerous even than the information betrayed about the movements of Anglo-American troop convoys, is what will certainly be passing in a stream about our preparations for OVERLORD. If the German and Japanese ministers remain at their posts in Dublin, it may be necessary on military grounds to sever all contacts between Ireland and the Continent in the near future for a period of months. At present anyone can get in an Irish ship to Spain and give the latest news he has picked up in England about British and American preparations. Even if complete severance by sea was instituted, it would not prevent the German Ambassador from sending a wireless warning of zero, even though that was the last he was able to do.[7]

The first three weeks of February were marked by back-and-forth exchanges regarding the proposed American Note between Gray and Maffey, and the State Department and the British Foreign Office.[8] During these weeks, Britain also drafted a corresponding communiqué to be presented to Eamon de Valera endorsing the Americans' assertion that Irish neutrality policy in fact favored the Axis Powers and supporting American demands to expel the German and Japanese diplomats from Ireland. The American Note delivered to de Valera's government concluded:

> We [the U.S. government] request ... that the Irish Government take appropriate steps for the recall of German and Japanese representatives in Ireland. We should be lacking in candor if we did not state our hope that this action will take the form of severance of all diplomatic relations between Ireland and these two countries. You will, of course, readily understand the compelling reasons why we ask as an absolute minimum the removal of these Axis representatives whose presence in Ireland must inevitably be regarded as constituting a danger to the lives of American soldiers and to the success of Allied military operations.[9]

De Valera's copy of the Note includes the following comments, pushing back against the arguments the Americans made to justify their demands:

> The President, while conveying his appreciation for this expression of friendship, stated his confidence that the Irish Government and the Irish people whose freedom is at stake no less than ours would know how to meet their

responsibilities in this situation. [*Marginal note in de Valera's handwriting: 'we must judge that'.*]

It has become increasingly apparent that, despite the declared desire of the Irish Government that its neutrality should not operate in favor of either of the belligerents, it has in fact operated and continues to operate in favor of the Axis Powers and against the United Nations on whom your security [*de Valera: 'What ab[ou]t. their own invas.[ion] of our Security'*] and the maintenance of your national economy depend. [*de Valera: 'No'*] One of the gravest and most inequitable results of this situation is the opportunity for highly organized espionage [*de Valera: 'No evidence of this[;] at any rate w[oul]d be an excuse for every warring state against a neutral neighbor'*] which the geographical position of Ireland affords the Axis and denies the United Nations. ...[10]

The British persuaded the Americans not to publish the Note when it was delivered on February 21, or to publish de Valera's anticipated rejection.[11]

David Gray delivered the American Note to de Valera, who read it looking "very sour and grim," according to Gray.[12] De Valera immediately rejected the request, as predicted:

"Of course the answer will be no," he said before he had even finished reading the note; "as long as I am here it will be no ... we have done everything to prevent Axis espionage, going beyond what we might reasonably be expected to do and I am satisfied that there are no leaks from this country; for a year and a half you have been advertising the invasion of Europe and what has got out about it has not been from Eire; the German Minister, I am satisfied, has behaved very correctly and decently and as a neutral we will not send him away."[13]

De Valera then proceeded to meet with John Maffey and with Canadian High Commissioner to Ireland John Kearney to plead for their intervention to persuade Washington to withdraw the Note, which was, in fact, an "ultimatum," one that implied an American invasion of Eire if his government did not comply with American demands to expel the Axis diplomats. According to Maffey, "de Valera was 'white with indignation', saying, 'This is an ultimatum. This is an outrage.'"[14] David Gray reported what he had heard from John Kearney to Franklin Roosevelt: "[De Valera] told Kearney 'We will fight to the last man,'" if U.S. troops invaded Eire.[15] De Valera's plea for the Allies' support for Irish neutrality failed, however, and the British and Canadian representatives tried to cool the rhetoric on both sides.[16] David Gray waited for de Valera's refusal to expel the Axis diplomats to go public, as he knew U.S. public opinion would support the U.S. government's position with American troops' lives on the line in the anti-fascist war.[17] Publicity seemed inevitable, given the Irish government's reaction. After receiving the Note, de Valera called emergency meetings to inform his Cabinet and Defense Council. He also mustered the Irish Defence Forces and put them on patrol throughout Eire, anticipating a U.S. invasion. These actions ignited the rumor mill, in Dublin and beyond.[18]

Meanwhile, de Valera and Joseph Walshe plotted their government's next move. They dispatched Irish Minister Robert Brennan to the State Department to find out what would be the likely outcome if the Irish government refused to expel the Axis Powers from Dublin. The State Department assured Brennan that the U.S. military had no intention of invading Eire – however, they warned him that if the Irish government publicized their refusal in order to excite Irish nationalists, the move would backfire and they would surely incur "the angry curses of millions of American mothers, many of them Irish."[19] Gray also told his contacts in the Irish government that publicity of the Note, and the government's refusal to take action against the Axis diplomats, "is entirely in your hands. We have no desire to have you crucified by a press campaign and will not give the story out in any immediate future, but if you give it out and a storm breaks that is your affair."[20] Gray also asserted that publicity "is a matter of indifference to us."[21] But publicity is clearly what Gray counted on to put de Valera's government "on record" for maintaining its "immoral" neutrality policy and jeopardizing Allied security.[22]

De Valera and Walshe then instructed Robert Brennan to meet with the State Department again,[23] to formally reject the actions demanded in the American Note on March 7.[24] The Irish asserted that the American Note denied Eire its democratic rights to establish its own national neutrality policy, which the majority of Irish people supported.[25] With the formal rejection of the American Note, Gray and Roosevelt were anxious for Eire's position to go public. On March 10, Gray told Walshe that the Americans and British[26] *would* publish the official Note, "because word of it had leaked out." Now, "de Valera had little option but to publish his response."[27] De Valera's government insisted that either the Americans or the British had leaked the Note and the Irish response to the press.[28] Historian Brian Girvin has asserted, however, that de Valera's government was the source of the leak in an attempt to "create" a crisis that served de Valera's political interests.[29]

Not surprisingly, the American and Irish press seized upon the controversy. U.S. newspapers across the country focused on the threats that the active Axis spy network operating in Ireland posed to the Allied troops' security, and even branded de Valera's government a "'fascist-like' regime, one that was 'blind' and 'insulated' from the outside world."[30] The *Fort Worth Star-Telegram* expressed the views of the Anglo-American governments: "A Nation either is a friend of the Axis or the United Nations.

By not meeting cooperatively with the latter it becomes a friend of the former."[31] Sumner Welles also weighed in with an interview published on the front page of the *New York Herald Tribune*, casting aspersions on Irish manhood:

> The Irish are not going to be doing any fighting, ... It will be the men of the United Nations, whom they will not lift a finger to help, who will be fighting and dying to make it possible for the Irish to enjoy the peace of which they are "so fond." ... Those who will not lend a hand in the supreme effort to make it possible for a real peace once more to exist, ... have no right to expect to be heard by the victors when the war is won.[32]

And Helen Kirkpatrick, who had visited the Grays in Dublin in February, also filed a story on the controversy for the *Chicago Daily News*, and also charged that information leaks from the Dublin Axis Legations to their governments "could jeopardize the lives of [Allied] troops."[33]

Irish newspapers took the opposite tack. They supported de Valera's decision to reject American demands and reassert Ireland's sovereign rights. De Valera's response "went down extremely well," and effectively guaranteed his party winning a majority in the upcoming national elections.[34] Gray soon recognized that his plan to put de Valera on the defensive had backfired on him. At least, that was true in Ireland if not in America. He wrote to the State Department after the news broke that: "De Valera continues to take the line that our request was an affront to Irish sovereignty and an effort to intimidate the Irish people. He also asserts that acceding to our request would inevitably place Eire in the war. This is universally believed by the people."[35] Once again, Gray's manipulations so angered de Valera and Walshe that they tried to enlist the aid of the OSS officer who had been assigned to the U.S. Legation in Dublin, Ervin Marlin, in their plans to discredit Gray with the U.S. government in Washington.[36] Walshe also wrote to Robert Brennan: "This state of affairs is particularly dangerous since Gray is recognised even by his best friends as a pathological spy maniac. He has produced a new rumour almost every day since the crisis. ... You should talk to your close friends [referring to Irish American politicians] about this state of affairs which could so easily cause disaster between us."[37] Nonetheless, State Department officials who spoke with Brennan backed up Gray and insisted the American Note was warranted.[38] Brennan wrote to Walshe at the end of March that the State Department "emphasised that Gray was not responsible for the Note and that it did not emanate solely from State Department. The Chiefs of Army and Navy, that is superior officers of Security people you mention, were in on its drawing-up. ... They said, if I saw Secretary of State, [the] answer would be the same, and also there was not slightest chance Gray would be removed."[39] Brennan's discouraging message didn't stop Walshe from continuing his efforts to rid Dublin of Gray.[40] In the meantime, Gray orchestrated Marlin's removal from Dublin.[41]

While the American Note controversy occupied the Dubliners throughout the spring,[42] the Big Three United Nations leaders, Winston Churchill, Franklin Roosevelt, and Joseph Stalin, focused on military campaigns against the Germans, from the west led by the Anglo-American forces, and from the east led by the Soviet Army. The warlords had determined at the Tehran conference in late 1943 to launch several daring initiatives. The first, round-the-clock Anglo-American bombing raids on German aircraft production centers and industrial sites began on February 23. These raids inevitably caused many German civilian deaths, as well.[43] The second major 1944 campaign was Operation Overlord, the Allied invasion of France. In preparation for the invasion, the British government, at Churchill's directive, took several concrete steps to reduce security risks posed by neutral Ireland, beyond the ineffectual American Note. On March 13, Britain issued a travel ban between Britain and the Irish isle.[44] Further restrictions on telephone calls to foreign nations and bans on British newspapers that circulated in Ireland followed the travel ban. The British also announced that all diplomatic pouches destined for Ireland would be searched, and the Irish Minister in London, John Dulanty, was not allowed to travel abroad and was effectively confined to his London home. While the restrictions were imposed out of an abundance of caution in anticipation of the Allied invasion of France as Churchill told Roosevelt: "Spite against the Irish is not the intention of these measures but rather provision against our plans being betrayed by emissaries sent by sea or air from the German Minister in Dublin and preservation of British and American soldiers' lives,"[45] they also strengthened de Valera's popularity among Irish nationalists who resented the British-imposed restrictions.[46] From behind the scenes, Maffey sought to foster more "friendly cooperation" between Britain and Ireland and arranged for shipment of supplies from Britain to make up for some shortages of rationed goods.[47]

Operation Overlord was scheduled to launch from bases in the United Kingdom on May 1, 1944, if weather cooperated and planning operations went off without any hitches. Ultimately, Overlord's Supreme Commander, U.S. General Dwight Eisenhower, rescheduled the Allied Expeditionary Force invasion for June 5, and then delayed again for one more day due to foul weather on the English Channel, until June 6. The Allied troop landing proceeded through five Normandy beaches, surprising the Germans, who were ready for the attack to come through Calais, across the English Channel from Dover. Even with the element of surprise, the military campaign was costly. The Allies lost almost 16,000 troops in the invasion and during the succeeding campaign to retake France that continued through August, and the initial bombing campaign to clear the way for the Allied landing killed more than 4,000 French civilians.[48]

The military campaign launched on June 6 was critically important to the Allied war effort.[49] Churchill and Roosevelt were well aware of the stakes and the costs of the new European campaign. Roosevelt addressed the American nation on the night of June 6, and led "an estimated one hundred million Americans" in a prayer for the troops, "Our sons, pride of our Nation," and asked for God's blessing and success in battle.[50] In the end, Operation Overlord established a huge Allied army on European soil and marked a turning point in the war that forced the German retreat from France and that ultimately led to the defeat of Nazi Germany.

Helen Kirkpatrick played an important role on the war correspondents' committee that organized official press coverage of Operation Overlord. In November 1943, as the Allies began planning for the spring invasion, Kirkpatrick was in Italy reporting on British battles against the German Army that had occupied its former Axis ally and aiding medical personnel in the field hospital tents that were set up to treat the wounded soldiers. *Chicago Daily News* publisher and Secretary of the Navy Colonel Frank Knox called her in from the front to Allied army headquarters at Caserta, just north of Naples. Knox told Kirkpatrick to return to London. Giving her no specific reason other than a vague "there are things that you ought to be doing in London," Knox arranged Kirkpatrick's transport out of Italy.[51] Back in London in December, she learned of her new appointment to a select four-person press committee: "three men, for magazines, wire services, and radio, and Kirkpatrick for newspapers."[52] As historian Nancy Caldwell Sorel explained, Kirkpatrick's inclusion as a female journalist was truly exceptional in the male-dominated military establishment:

> Her presence there was a signal honor. The committee met once a week, with SHAEF [Supreme Headquarters Allied Expeditionary Force] ... personnel, including censors, and discussed how many reporters could be accommodated in the first wave of the invasion, how copy would get back to press headquarters, what kind of censorship they should expect. It was not their job to select the correspondents who would go in the first wave, nor was it their decision that none would be women. That unpopular call was made by the top command.[53]

On June 6, Kirkpatrick remained in London, waiting under the drone of the waves of planes heading for France to dispatch reports to the *Chicago Daily News* about the troop landings as she received them from the front.[54]

As planning for Operation Overlord went forward, seven women were included in the ranks of the forty-three Allied correspondents who were accredited to cover the campaign, although the women would not be among those embedded with the initial invasion forces.[55] Kirkpatrick could never pin down the U.S. Army's reasons for thwarting her efforts to join the combat troops in June, as she had already been reporting at the front lines in Italy. Military public relations officers told her at one point that it was because there were no "facilities" for women at the front. When Kirkpatrick disagreed and said: "You don't know what you're talking about when you say 'It poses problems for the commanding officers to have women there.' It doesn't pose problems at all," they answered, "Well, you know, the latrines."[56]

In mid-July, Kirkpatrick joined the Allied troops in France. Initially she was assigned to British General Bernard Montgomery's headquarters in Bayeux, near the Normandy coast. Several weeks later, she joined other American correspondents heading into Rennes, in Brittany, following General George Patton's forces. In the just-liberated city, the French residents lined the roads and showered the American jeep convoy with flowers. She attended an emotional ceremony in the town center, side by side with French Resistance fighters, as crowds cheered and sang the "Marseillaise." She continued to move with the troops as they liberated Normandy cities, and joined the French Second Armored Division as it advanced on Paris. By the end of August, the Germans had lost the city. Isolated German snipers, however, continued to target Allied forces who occupied the French capital.[57] Kirkpatrick witnessed the Paris liberation ceremony held in Notre Dame Cathedral, when German gunmen fired on the Free French generals, including Charles de Gaulle. The crowd in the church scrambled to take cover, while the generals, Kirkpatrick reported, "stood bareheaded before the altar" as the ceremony proceeded.[58] Kirkpatrick wrote to her parents describing these dramatic days:

> [W]e came to Paris, and being with the French division, I was among the first correspondents in. I was certainly the first woman – the others followed but didn't get in for 4 days. That too was something not to be missed. The street fighting – the fantastic reception – the flowers, tears, wine, the snipers, the surrender of the German garrison – and followed the next day by that incredible shooting in Notre Dame. Only a BBC man and I were there of the entire press corps, and I frankly admit that I have no idea why I'm alive today. I'm not one for believing in miracles but only a miracle saved the French generals and me, too, I suppose, from being killed. A miracle and the fact that the Germans and militia were such bad shots. Now I'm here, and glad to be, and unless I'm ordered out, I plan to stay on here.[59]

Kirkpatrick remained in Paris and reopened the *Chicago Daily News* bureau that had been closed since 1940. She was among the first of the

Allied war correspondents who toured some of the Gestapo's former torture chambers in the city and she interviewed some of the very few survivors, a preview of the horrors to come when the German concentration camps were liberated in spring 1945.[60] From her base office in Paris, Kirkpatrick also ventured out to the field, reporting on several fall and winter battles, including the Battle of the Bulge in December 1944–January 1945.[61]

The Big Three leaders focused on liberating Europe throughout the remainder of 1944 and into 1945. In Dublin, de Valera's government had been reaffirmed with its clear victory in the June 1944 general election, and David Gray reported the outcome in his regular letters to Franklin Roosevelt. Irish-American relations proceeded coolly, but without further conflicts until the fall.[62]

In late September, as the Allied troops pushed forward in Europe, recapturing German-occupied territory as they went, David Gray anticipated the Allied victory to come. His next move to unsettle de Valera's government came in the form of an official communication from the U.S. government to all neutral power governments, seeking pledges that Axis "war criminals and their henchmen" would not be given asylum when the war ended, but would be surrendered to the United Nations powers. Other neutral states – Switzerland, Sweden, Portugal, Spain, and the Argentine – had also received this message that Gray now delivered to Eire. Once again, de Valera's government gave Gray no satisfaction; they reserved the sovereign right to grant asylum at their discretion and gave no assurance of cooperation to the Allied Powers.[63] From the U.S. government's perspective, the Irish government's response confirmed a lack of moral clarity given that the Axis Powers' crimes against humanity were so well documented by this point.[64] The British, who seconded the Americans' call for the surrender of the Axis "war criminals," also drew angry defiance from the Irish government.[65]

By the end of 1944, Eire and its leader, Taoiseach de Valera, had become irritating, but minor, players in the end-of-war drama. The new U.S. Secretary of State, Edward Stettinius, generally "agreed with Gray that the only interests the United States had in Ireland were 'trade and possibly air traffic and the continuing interest in avoiding involvement in the partition issue.'"[66] President Roosevelt, whose re-election in November had been assured,[67] nonetheless had been put off by Irish nationalists who threatened to call out the Irish American vote against him if the Allies shut Ireland out of the postwar peace settlements. Like David Gray, Roosevelt deeply resented de Valera's refusal to join the anti-fascist fight.[68]

Roosevelt's main concerns as the new year, 1945, began were his failing health[69] and preparations for another Big Three conference to be held in the Soviet Union, at Yalta, in early February to determine postwar settlements that would shape global politics for the next generation.

Prior to the Yalta summit, Winston Churchill and Soviet Premier Joseph Stalin had met in Moscow in fall 1944, and had agreed upon their own power-sharing plan for postwar Europe. British influence would prevail in Greece; Soviet influence would prevail in Poland, Romania, Bulgaria, and Hungary; and the two nations would share influence "equally" over Yugoslavia. Churchill and Stalin also agreed, without Roosevelt's consent, to "dismember" postwar Germany and dismantle its industrial capacity. The U.S. and British governments had also reached agreement regarding prosecution of war criminals following the German defeat, but Churchill's attempts to pin down FDR on additional postwar Anglo-American settlements prior to meeting with Stalin were rebuffed: "At Yalta, Roosevelt, intent on securing Soviet entry into the war against Japan and participation in the planned new United Nations organization, displayed little interest in British objectives."[70]

Although the Allies agreed at Yalta to offer most of the remaining neutral nation-state holdouts one last chance to join the United Nations, Ireland was excluded from the Allies' outreach. Secretary of State for British Dominions Lord Cranborne expressed Britain's view: "her [Eire's] general policy of neutrality, her refusal to grant us bases and to remove the Axis Legations, and her unsatisfactory attitude over war criminals, put her quite out of court." The U.S. State Department's head of European Affairs John Hickerson expressed the U.S. government's similarly anti-Irish view: "the one time in history when Ireland had an opportunity to do something to assist this country the Irish government turned a deaf ear."[71] As news of the Yalta agreements became public and the setting-up conference for the proposed United Nations global governance organization was scheduled to open in San Francisco in April, Robert Brennan asked Joseph Walshe for guidance if he were asked whether an Irish delegation would attend the conference. Walshe told him: "You should reply 'Ireland's position as a neutral State is well known. In any case, question is purely hypothetical and there is nothing to be gained by such speculation.' Since we are not one of United Nations, we do not expect invitation and it would be bad thing to give remotest impression that we want one."[72]

That was the end of the Yalta discussion regarding Ireland. Yalta meetings had focused on other momentous decisions regarding the final stages of war in Europe and East Asia. On February 11, the closing day of the summit, the Big Three Allied leaders signed the Declaration of Liberated Europe:

> The establishment of order in Europe and the rebuilding of national economic life must be achieved by processes which will enable the liberated peoples to destroy the last vestiges of Nazism and fascism and to create democratic

institutions of their own choice. This is a principle of the Atlantic Charter – the right of all peoples to choose the form of Government under which they will live – the restoration of sovereign rights and self-government to those people who have been forcibly deprived of them by the aggressor nations.[73]

The high-minded words were intended once again to define the unified moral purpose of the war for the Allied warrior nations and for the victims liberated from Axis tyranny.[74] Observers in Ireland and elsewhere noted the "brazen cynicism" of the Declaration, as the independence of nations like Poland was traded away in postwar settlements.[75]

In February and March, now that the German defeat was almost secured, Winston Churchill continued to send a steady stream of letters and telegrams to Franklin Roosevelt, hoping to settle some outstanding disagreements between the Anglo-American governments and present a united front once again in planning for the postwar world. Regarding Eire, Churchill was certain that the United States would not intervene in the Anglo-Irish dispute over partition, but the U.S. had negotiated a civil aviation agreement with de Valera's government, independent from Britain, and over Churchill's objections.[76] Roosevelt, whose health was steadily failing, did not respond to many of Churchill's communications after the Yalta summit, which prompted Churchill to call on their personal friendship in order to reaffirm their governments' close state-to-state relations:

> I hope that the rather numerous telegrams that I have to send you on so many of our difficult and intertwined affairs are not becoming a bore to you. Our friendship is the rock on which I build for the future of the world so long as I am one of the builders, I always think of those tremendous days then you devised Lend-Lease, when we met at Argentia, when you decided with my heartfelt agreement to launch the invasion of Africa, and when you comforted me for the loss of Tobruk by giving me the 300 Shermans of subsequent Alamein fame. I remember the part our personal relations have played in the advance of the world cause now nearing its first military goal.
>
> I am sending to Washington and San Francisco [for the United Nations setting-up conference] most of my ministerial colleagues on one mission or another, and I shall on this occasion stay home to mind the shop. ...
>
> As I observed last time [we met], when the war of the giants is over, the wars of the pygmies will begin. There will be a torn ragged and hungry world to help to its feet: what will Uncle Joe or his successor say to the way we should both like to do it? ...[77]

By the end of March and beginning of April, the Allied troops were finally liberating the Nazi concentration camps as they advanced into German territory. Allied war correspondents, including Helen Kirkpatrick, documented the scenes of horror and the extent of the German depravity to the rest of the world.[78] On April 12, General Eisenhower entered one of the camps near Buchenwald:

> The general was so horrified, [Churchill biographer] Martin Gilbert wrote, that he "at once telegraphed Churchill to describe what he had seen, and then sent photographs of the dead prisoners to Churchill, who circulated them to the British Cabinet." "There is no doubt that this is probably the greatest and most horrible crime ever committed in the whole history of the world, and it has been done by scientific machinery by nominally civilized men in the name of a great State and one of the leading races of Europe," Churchill told Anthony Eden in the last year of the war.[79]

At Frank Aiken's directive, Irish censors had blocked publication of stories in Irish newspapers about German atrocities committed in the concentration camps throughout the war, although foreign reports of the liberation of Auschwitz, Belsen, and Buchenwald "death camps" in 1945 that were broadcast through the radio airwaves reached Irish listeners. In Aiken's view, censorship of Irish news outlets was justified; reports on the concentration camps may have weakened the Irish people's support for their government's neutrality policy and made it harder to maintain neutrality throughout the war.[80] The government's wartime censorship policy, however, had long-lasting consequences for the Irish nation: "Ireland's six years of neutral policy, with its official equidistance from the warring parties, made it all the harder for the Irish people to accept the facts of Nazi persecution and extermination, even when the eye-witness reports and newsreels started to appear at the end of the war."[81]

As "the world" read and heard the gruesome descriptions of mass death and destruction from the liberated camps, the troops, the war correspondents, and the world's people also heard the news of President Franklin Roosevelt's death on April 12. Here was a single individual whose death caused hundreds of millions of people in the United States and across the globe to mourn with deep and sincere sorrow.[82] American broadcast journalist Edward R. Murrow was reporting from the Buchenwald death camp when news of Roosevelt's death reached him. He told his radio audience what he witnessed and heard from the camp survivors:

> There were two rows of bodies stacked up like cordwood. They were thin and very white. Some of the bodies were terribly bruised, though there seemed to be little flesh to bruise. Some had been shot in the head, but they bled but little. ... I was there on Thursday and many men in many tongues blessed the name of Roosevelt. For long years his name meant the full measure of their hope. These men who had kept close company with death for many years did not know that Roosevelt would, within hours, join their comrades who had laid their lives on the scales of freedom.[83]

Roosevelt's fellow warlords, Winston Churchill and Joseph Stalin, openly mourned Franklin Roosevelt's death; FDR was their friend and was the world leader who "was critical to the founding of the Grand Alliance and to keeping it together."[84]

> "I was overpowered by a sense of deep and irrefutable loss," wrote Churchill. In Moscow, Averill Harriman drove to the Kremlin to inform Stalin. The Soviet leader was "deeply distressed" and held Harriman's hand for perhaps thirty seconds before asking him to sit down. "President Roosevelt has died but his cause must live on," he told Harriman and then agreed to send Molotov to represent the Soviet Union at the upcoming United Nations conference in San Francisco.[85]

In its April 23 issue, *Time Magazine* described the moment that Churchill heard the news: "The Prime Minister's face paled. He sat down, motionless for a full five minutes. Then he lifted his head, with the heaviness of a man who is suddenly very lonely. He whispered: 'Get me the Palace.' He informed the King, then called Washington, then labored with sad heart far into the night over the words he would speak in memoriam."[86] Winston Churchill eulogized Roosevelt in an eloquent tribute before the House of Commons, expressing his personal love for his great friend, but also sharing in the world's loss of a great leader:

> I conceived an admiration for him as a statesman, a man of affairs, and a war leader. I felt the utmost confidence in his upright, inspiring character and outlook and a personal regard – affection I must say – for him beyond my power to express today. His love of his own country, his respect for its constitution, his power of gauging the tides and currents of its mobile public opinion, were always evident, but, added to these were the beatings of that generous heart which was always stirred to anger and to action by spectacles of aggression and oppression by the strong against the weak. It is, indeed, a loss, a bitter loss to humanity that those heartbeats are stilled forever. ... For us, it remains only to say that in Franklin Roosevelt there died the greatest American friend we have ever known, and the greatest champion of freedom who has ever brought help and comfort from the new world to the old. ...[87]

Churchill also cabled his personal message to Eleanor Roosevelt: "I feel so deeply for you all. As for myself, I have lost a dear and cherished friendship which was forged in the fire of war. I trust you may find consolation in the magnitude of his work and the glory of his name."[88] And Joseph Stalin responded to Churchill's personal message to him, as well: "In President Franklin Roosevelt the Soviet people saw a distinguished statesman and a rigid champion of close cooperation between the three States. The friendly attitude of President Roosevelt to the U.S.S.R. will always be most highly valued and remembered by the Soviet people. So far as I am personally concerned I feel exceptionally deeply the burden of the loss of this great man that was our mutual friend."[89]

Even in Eire, where there was no love lost between Franklin Roosevelt and de Valera's government, David Gray wrote to Eleanor Roosevelt that the Irish people also seemed to feel the loss deeply:

> This is indeed a strange country. All this forenoon members of the government, their wives and leaders of the opposition have been coming in a stream to pay their respects. Mr. de Valera made a very moving tribute to the President in the Dáil this morning and moved adjournment till tomorrow. I thought I knew this country and its people, but this was something new. There was a great deal of genuine feeling.[90]

Gray's fond feelings for de Valera and the Irish government were short lived. The Irish Catholic government leaders refused to enter the Protestant church where a memorial service for Franklin Roosevelt took place, earning Gray's resentment for what he considered to be an act of disrespect for his nation's leader.[91] A few weeks later, with the German defeat imminent, Germany's Führer Adolf Hitler committed suicide in his Berlin bunker on April 30. Gray demanded that de Valera's government immediately confiscate the German Legation files and turn them over to the U.S. and British Foreign Offices. Once again, de Valera refused to accommodate the Allies: "'As I proceeded,' the American Minister reported, Mr de Valera grew red and looked very sour. He was evidently annoyed, but his manners were correct. When I finished, he slapped the copy of the memorandum, which I had presented him, on the desk and said 'This is a matter for my legal advisers. It is not a matter I can discuss with you now.'"[92] In de Valera's account of the meeting he rehashed the ongoing Irish American conflict, and the arguments that had been made many times over by the two men who had never understood each other's position: "He [Gray] said that a person who was rolling in the mud struggling with someone who was trying to kill him didn't appreciate the person who was standing aside saying I am friendly to you but I am friendly to the other fellow also, and was proceeding to argue further against our neutrality. Again, I told him that we had argued this matter with each other many times and that there was no point in going over it again."[93]

Then, on May 2, Eamon de Valera committed what was, from the Anglo-American perspective, the ultimate unforgivable act: the Taoiseach called on German Minister Eduard Hempel at the German Legation to express his nation's condolences on the death of Adolf Hitler. De Valera insisted on Ireland's rights as a neutral power to follow diplomatic protocol to its fullest expression.[94] He was supported in this decision by his deputy head of government, Sean T. O'Kelly, as well as by Frank Aiken and Frank

Gallagher.[95] Joseph Walshe, who accompanied de Valera and was a friend to Hempel, nonetheless had urged him not to take the provocative step.[96] A diplomatic storm followed. There was "international revulsion directed against him personally for treating Hitler as an average head of state,"[97] and the Allied press uniformly condemned de Valera's gesture: "Can it be that the moral myopia [the Irish government] imposed on themselves in the face of danger has now blinded them to all ethical values? Or that a preoccupation with protocol has atrophied their emotions?"[98] But "unrepentant"[99] Taoiseach de Valera never apologized. He justified his actions in a letter to Irish Minister Robert Brennan on May 21, during the controversy that unfolded over the next month:

> I acted very deliberately in this matter. So long as we retained our diplomatic relations with Germany to have failed to call upon the German representative would have been an act of unpardonable discourtesy to the German nation and to Dr. Hempel himself. During the whole of the war Dr. Hempel's conduct was irreproachable. He was always friendly and invariably correct – in marked contrast with Gray. I certainly was not going to add to his humiliation in the hour of defeat. ... I am anxious that you should know my mind on all this. I have carefully refrained from attempting to give any explanation in public. An explanation would have been interpreted as an excuse, and an excuse as consciousness of having acted wrongly. I acted correctly and I feel certain wisely.[100]

De Valera's condolence call might have passed from the news coverage quickly after a round of angry criticism played itself out. The German government surrendered to the United Nations on May 7, and Allied victory stories took over the global news outlets.[101] Then, on May 13, Winston Churchill broadcast his address summarizing "Five Years of War" for the British nation. He recounted the moments of national crisis when the German *blitzkrieg* attacks threatened the nation's survival, praised the British people's fortitude, and thanked the noble Allies who fought the Axis Powers alongside Great Britain. Within Churchill's litany of Britain's grimmest crisis points and list of extraordinary sacrifices, followed by moments of hope and aid from Allied comrades-in-arms, and ending with the triumphant victory of the West's democratic values, human rights, and freedom in Europe and resolute pledges to fight on against the Japanese fascist enemy in Asia, came a few lines to single out the moral failures of Eamon de Valera's leadership and Eire's wartime neutrality policy. Churchill reminded the world that during Britain's darkest days in 1940 and into 1941:

> The sense of envelopment, which might at any moment turn to strangulation, lay heavy upon us. We had only the northwestern approach between Ulster and Scotland through which to bring in the means of life and to send out the

forces of war. *Owing to the action of Mr. de Valera*, so much at variance with the temper and instinct of thousands of southern Irishmen, who hastened to the battlefront to prove their ancient valor, the approaches which the southern Irish ports and airfields could so easily have guarded were closed by the hostile aircraft and U-boats.

This was indeed a deadly moment in our life, and *if it had not been for the loyalty and friendship of Northern Ireland we should have been forced to come to close quarters with Mr. de Valera* or perish forever from the earth. However, with a restraint and poise to which, I say, history will find few parallels, we never laid a violent hand upon them, which at times would have been quite easy and quite natural, and left the de Valera Government to frolic with the German and later with the Japanese representatives to their heart's content.[102] (emphasis added)

According to historian T. Ryle Dwyer, in his delivery, "Churchill pulled out all the stops ... as he referred to the Irish leader with dismissive contempt. He emphasized the different syllables of de Valera's name in such a way as to conjure up a subliminal suggestion of the Taoiseach as the personification of the devil and evil in Eire by pronouncing his name as if it were D'evil Eire."[103]

Eamon de Valera's secretary, Kathleen O'Connell, reported that the Taoiseach was "seething" upon hearing Winston Churchill's speech.[104] De Valera answered Churchill's attack and rejected the Anglo-American version of Ireland's wartime neutrality policy in his broadcast to the Irish people on May 16, in an address he titled the "Day of Thanksgiving." As de Valera justified Ireland's neutrality, he reminded *his* nation: "The aim of our policy, I said [in 1939], would be to keep our people out of war." The Irish people were united behind the policy; the Irish Defence Forces resolutely guarded the nation "against the most serious dangers that threatened" to attack Ireland from all directions. And de Valera replied directly to Churchill's derogatory words to claim the moral high ground:

Mr. Churchill makes it clear that, in certain circumstances, he would have violated our neutrality and that he would justify his action by Britain's necessity. It seems strange to me that Mr. Churchill does not see that this, if accepted, would mean that Britain's necessity would become a moral code and that when this necessity became sufficiently great, other people's rights would not count. ...

Mr. Churchill is justly proud of his nation's perseverance against heavy odds. But we in this island are still prouder of our people's perseverance for freedom through all the centuries. ... [E]ven as a small partitioned nation, we shall go on and strive to play our part in the world, continuing unswervingly to work for the cause of true freedom and for peace and understanding between all nations. ...[105]

Some contemporary observers of the Churchill–de Valera feud, such as the Canadian High Commissioner John Hearne and even Sir John Maffey,[106] judged de Valera to have won a public relations victory, at least among the Irish people: "The public reaction to [de Valera's] address was overwhelming. 'With little exception', the Canadian representative reported, 'Mr. de Valera's broadcast is regarded in Ireland as a masterpiece, and it is looked upon as probably his best effort. It served to almost still the criticism which his visit to the German Minister provoked, and, insofar as I can judge, on balance, Mr. de Valera now stands in higher favor in Ireland than he did before his visit to the German Minister.'"[107] Maffey blamed Churchill for losing the day in the propaganda war: "Maffey admitted that the effect might be quite different outside of Ireland, but he thought that of little consequence to de Valera. 'So long as he can work his *mystique* over Irishmen in all parts of the world Mr. de Valera does not worry about the rest of humanity.'"[108]

Eamon de Valera had stood up to the Anglo-American warlords, and kept independent Eire neutral through to the bitter end of the world war. Despite this victory in the war of wills between the national leaders, Ireland as a nation-state experienced significant negative postwar consequences in terms of its diminished international standing and the minimal role it initially played in global governance, and in terms of deepening the Anglo-Irish divide and ensuring the continued partition of Ireland for many years to come. Irish American diplomatic relations also continued in their contentious vein as David Gray remained in his ministerial post at the U.S. Legation in Ireland until 1947, and the importance of Ireland's friendship to American leaders only regained importance in the context of the United States' global foreign policy strategy of containment of Soviet Russia's influence during the Cold War era.

Notes

1 Imperial War Museum Staff, "The 10 Things You Need to Know about D-Day," Imperial War Museums, online, www.iwm.org.uk/history/the-10-things-you-need-to-know-about-d-day (accessed 8 December 2020). See also Winston Churchill, "The Invasion of France, Speech to the House of Commons," 6 June 1944 (London: The Churchill Society), www.churchill-society-london.org.uk/InvaFrnc.html (accessed 8 December 2020).
2 John Potter, "Passing Through: The Story of the United States Army in Northern Ireland, 1942–1944," Northern Ireland War Memorial and Home Front Exhibition, Belfast, 2012, 8–9.
3 John P. Duggan, *Herr Hempel and the German Legation in Dublin, 1937–1945* (Dublin: Irish Academic Press, 2003), 189–190.

4 Clair Wills, *That Neutral Island: A Cultural History of Ireland During the Second World War* (London: Faber & Faber, 2007), 385–386.
5 David Gray, Memorandum [to State Department], 28 December 1943, box 11; David Gray to Ambassador John Winant, London, 7 January 1944, box 12, Coll. 03082, David Gray Papers, American Heritage Center, University of Wyoming (hereafter: Gray Papers, AHC).
6 David McCullagh, *De Valera: Rule, 1932–1972* (Dublin: Gill Books, 2018), 240.
7 Brian Girvin, *The Emergency: Neutral Ireland 1939–45* (London: Pan Macmillan, 2007), 306.
8 Telegram, "The Secretary of State [Hull] to the Ambassador in the United Kingdom (Winant), 3 February 1944, Doc. 144 (841D.01/235a), *Foreign Relations of the United States* (hereafter: *FRUS*), Diplomatic Papers, 1944, The British Commonwealth and Europe, vol. III (Washington, DC: Government Printing Office, 1965); Telegram, "The Minister in Ireland (Gray) to the Secretary of State [Hull], 5 February 1944, Doc. 145 (841D.01/236) *FRUS* 1944, vol. III; Telegram, The Ambassador in the United Kingdom (Winant) to the Secretary of State [Hull], 10 February 1944, Doc. 147 (841D.01/239) *FRUS* 1944, vol. III.
9 Letter from David Gray to Eamon de Valera (Dublin), "The American Note" (No. 410), 21 February 1944, Doc. No. 369 UCDA P150/2658, *Documents on Irish Foreign Policy* vol. VII, 1941–1945.
10 *Ibid.*
11 T. Ryle Dwyer, *Irish Neutrality and the USA, 1939–47* (Dublin: Gill & Macmillan, 1977), 182.
12 Telegram, The Minister in Ireland (Gray) to the Secretary of State [Hull], 21 February 1944, Doc. 149 (841D.01/244), *FRUS* 1944, vol. III.
13 *Ibid.*
14 McCullagh, *De Valera*, 241. See also Telegram, The Minister in Ireland (Gray) to the Secretary of State [Hull], 23 February 1944, Doc. 150 (841D.01/245), *FRUS* 1944, vol. III.
15 David Gray to Franklin Roosevelt, c. 24 February 1944, box 12, Gray Papers, AHC.
16 Code Telegram from John J. Hearne (Ottawa) to Joseph Walshe (No. 27), 28 February 1944, Doc. No. 377 NAI DFA Secretary's Files A53, *Documents on Irish Foreign Policy* vol. VII, 1941–1945.
17 David Gray to Franklin Roosevelt, c. 24 February 1944, box 12, Gray Papers, AHC. See also Telegram, The Minister in Ireland (Gray) to the Secretary of State [Hull], 25 February 1944, Doc. 152 (841D.01/248), *FRUS* 1944, vol. III.
18 Telegram, The Minister in Ireland (Gray) to the Secretary of State [Hull] 1 March 1944, Doc. 156 (841D.01/250), *FRUS* 1944, vol. III.
19 Code Telegram from Robert Brennan to Joseph Walshe (No. 63) (Confidential), 26 February 1944, Doc. No. 374 NAI DFA Secretary's Files A53, *Documents on Irish Foreign Policy* vol. VII, 1941–1945.

20 Telegram, The Minister in Ireland (Gray) to the Secretary of State [Hull], 1 March 1944, Doc. 156 (841D.01/250), *FRUS* 1944, vol. III.
21 *Ibid*. See also David Gray to Eamon de Valera, 2 March 1944, P150/2658, Eamon de Valera Papers (on microfilm), University College Dublin (hereafter: EdV Papers, UCD).
22 McCullagh, *De Valera*, 241.
23 Telegram from Joseph Walshe to Robert Brennan (Washington), "Reply to the American Note of 21st February, as cabled to Washington" (No. 51), 6 March 1944, Doc. No. 381 NAI DFA Secretary's Files A53, *Documents on Irish Foreign Policy* vol. VII, 1941–1945.
24 Dwyer, *Irish Neutrality and the USA*, 190.
25 Telegram from Frederick H. Boland to Robert Brennan (Washington) (No. 57) (Immediate), 10 March 1944, Doc. No. 384 NAI DFA Secretary's Files A53, and Telegram from Joseph Walshe to Robert Brennan (Washington), "Reply to the American Note of 21st February, as cabled to Washington" (No. 51), 6 March 1944, Doc. No. 381 NAI DFA Secretary's Files A53, *Documents on Irish Foreign Policy* vol. VII, 1941–1945.
26 Telegram, The Minister in Ireland (Gray) to the Secretary of State [Hull], 10 March 1944, Doc. 158 (841D.01/267), *FRUS* 1944, vol. III.
27 McCullagh, *De Valera*, 242–243.
28 Memorandum from Joseph Walshe to Eamon de Valera 14 March 1944, Doc. No. 388 NAI DFA Secretary's Files A53, *Documents on Irish Foreign Policy* vol. VII, 1941–1945.
29 Girvin, *The Emergency*, 249–250.
30 Wills, *That Neutral Island*, 387.
31 Dwyer, *Irish Neutrality and the USA*, 190–191.
32 *Ibid.*, 192. See also "Eire: Neutral Against Whom?" *Time Magazine* 43: 12 (20 March 1944), 36.
33 Helen Kirkpatrick, "Likely to Affect U.S. Invasion Plans," *Chicago Daily News* (11 March 1944), box 3, CA-MS-01132, Helen Paull Kirkpatrick Papers, Sophia Smith Collection, Smith College, Northampton, Massachusetts (hereafter: HPK Papers).
34 McCullagh, *De Valera*, 243. See also Wills, *That Neutral Island*, 388; Robert Fisk, *In Time of War: Ireland, Ulster and the Price of Neutrality, 1939–1945* (London: Andre Deutsch, 1983), 459; Dwyer, *Irish Neutrality and the USA*, 199, referencing May 1944 elections: "The time seemed right to capitalize on his defense of Irish neutrality. And it was. At the polls Fianna Fail gained seventeen seats to give the party a comfortable majority. At least one popular American news magazine believed that the Taoiseach had the United States government to thank for his victory. *Time* declared that American pressure had simply made the Irish people 'more devoted to their own belligerent neutrality than ever.'"
35 Telegram, The Minister in Ireland (Gray) to the Secretary of State [Hull], 18 March 1944, Doc. 166 (841D.o1/286), *FRUS* 1944, vol. III.
36 Memorandum from Joseph Walshe to Eamon de Valera (Most Secret), 18 March 1944, Doc. No. 396 NAI DFA Secretary's Files A3 and Handwritten

Memorandum by Joseph Walshe, 19 March 1944, Doc. No. 398 UCDA P150/2571, *Documents on Irish Foreign Policy* vol. VII, 1941–1945. See also Letter from Joseph Walshe to Ervin 'Spike' Marlin, 29 June 1944, Doc. No. 453 NAI DFA Secretary's Files A60, *Documents on Irish Foreign Policy* vol. VII, 1941–1945.

37 Code Telegram from Joseph Walshe to Robert Brennan (Washington) (No. 96), 22 March 1944, Doc. No. 402 NAI DFA Secretary's Files A 53, *Documents on Irish Foreign Policy* vol. VII, 1941–1945. See also Girvin, *The Emergency*, 311–312: "On one occasion Brennan was quoted as describing Gray as a dilettante with no diplomatic training who owed his post to the fact that he was related to Roosevelt. What Brennan wanted to get across, and thus has been the view of most Irish historians since, was Gray's unsuitability for his job."

38 Girvin, *The Emergency*, 313; McCullagh, *De Valera*, 243.

39 Code Telegram from Robert Brennan to Joseph Walshe (No. 127), 30 March 1944, Doc. No. 407 NAI DFA Secretary's Files A53, *Documents on Irish Foreign Policy* vol. VII, 1941–1945.

40 Memorandum from Joseph Walshe to Eamon de Valera, 3 April 1944, Doc. No. 408 NAI DFA Secretary's Files A2, *Documents on Irish Foreign Policy* vol. VII, 1941–1945; Code Telegram from Joseph Walshe to Robert Brennan (No. 114), 6 April 1944, Doc. No. 411 NAI DFA Secretary's Files A53, *Documents on Irish Foreign Policy* vol. VII, 1941–1945: "Gray has become a byword among ordinary people for dishonest anti-Irish exaggeration. You should not ask for his removal, but you could say that he is creating an atmosphere inimical to American interests."

41 Letters, David Gray to Colonel David E. K. Bruce, Officer in Charge of Strategic Services, American Embassy, London, 10 June 1944 and 17 June 1944, box 12, Gray Papers, AHC: "The mischief which Marlin made [befriending de Valera and Joseph Walshe and contradicting David Gray's reports on Axis activities in Ireland], … is so serious that the Department must be as adequately warned as possible. My own belief is that he is not a knave but a fool and that his vanity and sentiments have been played upon to the detriment of American interests. For this reason, I am anxious about what will happen if he returns to New York and is sought out by the Irish representation there, if not directly by Mr. Brennan in Washington. …"

42 Telegram, The Secretary of State [Hull] to the Ambassador in the United Kingdom (Winant), 4 April 1944, Doc. 171 (841D.01/325b), *FRUS 1944*, vol. III. This documents Hull's communication with de Valera; a copy also went to David Gray.

43 Sir Martin Gilbert, CBE, "Churchill Proceedings; Churchill and Bombing Policy," The fifth Churchill lecture, The George Washington University, Washington, DC, 18 October 2005, *Finest Hour* 137 (Winter 2007–2008), www.winstonchurchill.org/publications/finest-hour/finest-hour-137/churchill-proceedings-churchill-and-bombing-policy/ (accessed 8 December 2020).

44 Tony Gray, *The Lost Years: The Emergency in Ireland, 1939–1945* (London: Warner Books, 1998), 219–220. See also Telegram, The Ambassador in the

United Kingdom (Winant) to the Secretary of State [Hull], 14 March 1944, Doc. 163 (841D.01/268), *FRUS 1944*, vol. III: Winant reported on Churchill's explanation of travel bans and other restrictions on Ireland to the House of Commons, and on British press editorials that warned against "punishing" Ireland beyond what security imperatives demanded.

45 Telegram, The Prime Minister (Churchill) to President Roosevelt, 19 March 1944, Doc. 167 (841D,01/318), *FRUS 1944*, vol. III; Telegram from Winston Churchill to Franklin Roosevelt, 15 April 1944, CHAR: 20/162/35, Winston Churchill Archives online, The Chartwell Trust.

46 Gray, *The Lost Years*, 220, 271; Dwyer, *Irish Neutrality and the USA*, 194.

47 Code Telegram from Joseph Walshe to Robert Brennan (No. 126), 20 April 1944, Doc. No. 422 NAI DFA Washington Embassy File 73, *Documents on Irish Foreign Policy* vol. VII, 1941–1945.

48 Gilbert, "Churchill Proceedings."

49 Churchill, "The Invasion of France, Speech to the House of Commons."

50 Jon Meacham, *Franklin and Winston: An Intimate Portrait of an Epic Friendship* (New York: Random House, 2004), 284.

51 Interview with Helen Kirkpatrick Milbank by Anne Kasper, Women in Journalism, Oral History project of the Washington Press Club Foundation, April 3–5, 1990, p. 69, in the Oral History Collection of Columbia University and other repositories.

52 Nancy Caldwell Sorel, *The Women Who Wrote the War* (New York: Arcade Publishing, 1999), 219.

53 Sorel, *The Women Who Wrote the War*, 219.

54 *Ibid.*, 225.

55 Carolyn M. Edy, *The Woman War Correspondent, the U.S. Military, and the Press, 1846–1947* (Lanham, MD: Lexington Books, 2017), 95.

56 Edy, *The Woman War Correspondent*, 111.

57 Sorel, *The Women Who Wrote the War*, 250–257. See also Interview with Helen Kirkpatrick Milbank by Anne Kasper, April 3–5, 1990, pp. 71–75.

58 Sorel, *The Women Who Wrote the War*, 260.

59 Helen Kirkpatrick to Parents, 3 September 1944, box 9, HPK Papers.

60 Sorel, *The Women Who Wrote the War*, 267–269.

61 Interview with Helen Kirkpatrick Milbank by Anne Kasper, April 3–5, 1990, p. 76.

62 Dwyer, *Irish Neutrality and the USA*, 200–201.

63 Memoire for Conversation with the Irish Minister for External Affairs [Walshe, with David Gray]; Subject: Request for assurances from the Irish Government that Axis War Criminals and their Henchmen would be refused Irish Protection," 21 September 1944, P150/2672, EdV Papers, UCD. Aide Memoire from Eamon de Valera to David Gray regarding war criminals and the right to asylum, 9 October 1944, Doc. No. 483 NAI DFA Secretary's Files P78, *Documents on Irish Foreign Policy* vol. VII, 1941–1945.

64 McCullagh, *De Valera*, 249–250. Memorandum by Joseph Walshe regarding the United States attitude to asylum for war criminals, 23 October 1944,

Doc. No. 493 NAI DFA Secretary's Files P78, *Documents on Irish Foreign Policy* vol. VII, 1941–1945.
65 Memorandum by Joseph Walshe to Eamon de Valera regarding a conversation with Sir John Maffey concerning war criminals, 14 November 1944, Doc. No. 506 NAI DFA Secretary's Files P78, *Documents on Irish Foreign Policy* vol. VII, 1941–1945.
66 Girvin, *The Emergency*, 317.
67 Meacham, *Franklin and Winston*, 309. Roosevelt won the election with 53.5 percent of the popular vote, versus 46 percent for his Republican opponent, Thomas Dewey.
68 Girvin, *The Emergency*, 318.
69 Robert Brennan wrote to Joseph Walshe regarding Roosevelt's appearance at FDR's 20 January 1945 Inaugural Address: "though his voice was strong, [he] had a wretched pallor and his face was heavily lined." Letter from Robert Brennan to Joseph Walshe, 27 January 1945, Doc. No. 537 NAI DFA 313/2A, *Documents on Irish Foreign Policy* vol. VII, 1941–1945.
70 Alonso Hamby, "Democracy's Champions: Churchill and Roosevelt," *Finest Hour* 172 online (Spring 2016), https://winstonchurchill.org/publications/finest-hour/finest-hour-172/churchill-and-roosevelt/ (accessed 8 December 2020).
71 McCullagh, *De Valera*, 250–251.
72 Code telegram from Joseph Walshe to Robert Brennan (Washington) concerning Ireland's attendance at the San Francisco conference (No. 43), 24 February 1945, Doc. No. 547 NAI DFA 417/33, *Documents on Irish Foreign Policy* vol. VII, 1941–1945.
73 Meacham, *Franklin and Winston*, 322.
74 Helen Kirkpatrick, "French Hail Big Three Pact as Cementing Allied Unity," *Chicago Daily News* (14 February 1945), box 3, HPK Papers.
75 Michael Knightly, Chief Press Censor, Press Censor's Report for March 1945, P104/3505, Frank Aiken Papers (on microfilm), University College Dublin (hereafter: FA Papers, UCD).
76 Telegram from Winston Churchill to President Roosevelt, 27 January 1945, CHAR: 20/211/55, Winston Churchill Archives online. Churchill expressed surprise that the US Government has asked the Government of Southern Ireland to sign a bilateral Civil Aviation Agreement without telling the British Government beforehand; and requested these negotiations are postponed until they have a chance to talk the matter over. Telegram from Winston Churchill to President Roosevelt marked "Personal and Top Secret," 6 March 1945, CHAR: 20/212/68, Winston Churchill Archives online. Churchill expressed concern regarding the political repercussions of an Irish-American agreement on civil aviation, and appealed for the annulment of the agreement.
77 Telegram, Churchill to FDR, Map Room Papers; Messages: Churchill-FDR, Feb.–Apr. 1945, 17 March 1945, box 7, Franklin Delano Roosevelt Papers, Franklin Roosevelt Presidential Library, Hyde Park, NY (hereafter: FDR Papers).
78 Helen Kirkpatrick, "Allies Break Chains of Reich Slave Labor," *Chicago Daily News* (28 March 1945); "Frankfurt in Chaos," *Chicago Daily News*

(30 March 1945); "Slave Hordes Streaming to Rhine," *Chicago Daily News* (4 April 1945); "3000 Skeletons Come Slowly Back to Life," *Chicago Daily News* (24 April 1945); box 3, HPK Papers.
79 Meacham, *Franklin and Winston*, 355.
80 Michael Knightly, Press Censor's Report for April 1945, P104/3506, FA Papers, UCD. This report, for example, states that regarding reports of the killing of Jews in the concentration camps, "All these reports were stopped."
81 Wills, *That Neutral Island*, 397–398.
82 Sorel, *The Women Who Wrote the War*, 333, 336.
83 Meacham, *Franklin and Winston*, 355–356.
84 Frank Costigliola, *Roosevelt's Lost Alliances: How Personal Politics Helped Start the Cold War* (Princeton, NJ: Princeton University Press, 2012), 9, 284: "Molotov's plaintive query: 'Can you imagine how we felt?' [when FDR died]. As Stalin and Molotov affirmed many times in 1945–46, Roosevelt had functioned as the fulcrum of the alliance."
85 Jean Edward Smith, *FDR* (New York: Random House, 2008), 636.
86 "World's Man" *Time Magazine* 45: 17 (23 April 1945), 28–29.
87 Winston Churchill's tribute to Franklin Roosevelt, printed copy of Hansard recording [to the House of Commons], 17 April 1945, CHAR: 9/167/206–207, Winston Churchill Archives online.
88 Meacham, *Franklin and Winston*, 347.
89 Telegram from Joseph Stalin to Churchill, 15 April 1945, CHAR: 20/199/89, Winston Churchill Archives online.
90 David Gray to Eleanor Roosevelt, 13 April 1945, box 14, Gray Papers, AHC. See also Dwyer, *Irish Neutrality and the USA*, 202.
91 T. Ryle Dwyer, *Behind the Green Curtain: Ireland's Phoney Neutrality During World War II* (Dublin: Gill & Macmillan, 2009), 324.
92 *Ibid.*, 325.
93 Memorandum by Eamon de Valera, 30 April 1945, Doc. No. 569 UCDA P150/2687, *Documents on Irish Foreign Policy* vol. VII, 1941–1945.
94 Anthony J. Jordan, *Churchill: A Founder of Modern Ireland* (Dublin: Westport Books, 1995), 183.
95 Dermot Keogh, "Eamon de Valera and Hitler: An Analysis of International Reaction to the Visit to the German Minister, May 1945," *Irish Studies in International Affairs* 3: 1 (1989), 73.
96 *Ibid.*, 74; McCullagh, *De Valera*, 253.
97 Keogh, "Eamon de Valera and Hitler," 75.
98 John Day Tully, *Ireland and Irish Americans 1932–1945: The Search for Identity* (Dublin: Irish Academic Press, 2010), 134–135 (quoting a *Washington Post* editorial). See also Palash Ghosh, "The Irish Nationalist and the Nazi: When Eamon de Valera Paid his respects to Adolf Hitler," *International Business Times* [online] (10 September 2013), www.ibtimes.com/irish-nationalist-nazi-when-eamon-de-valera-paid-his-respects-adolf-hitler-1403768 (accessed 8 December 2020).

99 Ronan Fanning, *Eamon de Valera: A Will to Power* (Cambridge, MA: Harvard University Press, 2016), 196.
100 Letter from Eamon de Valera to Robert Brennan (Confidential), 21 May 1945, Doc. No. 590 UCDA P150/26/6, *Documents on Irish Foreign Policy* vol. VII, 1941–1945. See also McCullagh, *De Valera*, 254.
101 "The First Victory," *Time Magazine* 45: 20 (14 May 1945), 19–20.
102 Winston Churchill, "Five Years of War," Broadcast to the British Nation, 13 May 1945 (iBiblio, online information database, University of North Carolina at Chapel Hill) www.ibiblio.org/pha/policy/1945/1945–05–13a.html (accessed 8 December 2020).
103 Dwyer, *Behind the Green Curtain*, 330.
104 McCullagh, *De Valera*, 256.
105 "Taoiseach's Broadcast to the Nation at the Conclusion of the War in Europe," delivered on Wednesday 16 May 1945 (Dublin: The Irish Press).
106 Paul Bew, *Churchill and Ireland* (Oxford University Press, 2016), 162.
107 Dwyer, *Irish Neutrality and the USA*, 205.
108 McCullagh, *De Valera*, 257–258.

Conclusion

As the Second World War commenced in Europe, the British, American, and Irish leaders, Winston Churchill, Franklin Roosevelt, and Eamon de Valera, each set out to shape their nations' understandings of the causes and consequences of the conflict. Certainly, they each aimed to establish popular support for their wartime policies that were designed to achieve their ultimate goals of victory over their enemies – as they each defined what "victory" would entail and who their "enemies" were throughout the long and brutal war. Churchill, Roosevelt, and de Valera were also men whose egos convinced them that they personified "the nation" that they led, and that they exemplified the "dominant, culturally glorified form of masculinity," or the hegemonic masculinities as defined by their specific historical moments in time.[1] To be sure, their closest advisers and their governments' wartime propaganda campaigns helped to feed their manly egos and created the national myths that lionized them and delineated the exceptional and virile character traits that distinguished these men and their nations from enemy "others." But Churchill, Roosevelt, and de Valera fully participated in creating these gendered (and raced, classed, and sexualized) myths as they acted out their parts as wartime "Great Britain," "America," and "Ireland" in their personal relationships with one another, and through their proxies, that is, through their close foreign policy advisers on the ground in London, Washington, DC, and Dublin.

Although Franklin Roosevelt did not live to see the final surrender of the fascist enemies that the Western democracies fought against for six long years, his great fraternal friend Winston Churchill believed that Roosevelt knew victory over Nazi Germany was assured – and that Roosevelt knew he had played an integral part in bringing about that victory – before he died. Churchill shared with the world how he defined the meaning of Franklin Roosevelt's individual life and death – a "warrior's" life and death – in terms of how the "United States of America" as a nation had contributed to the Allied victory:

> What an enviable death was his. He had brought his country through the worst of its perils and the heaviest of its toils. Victory has cast its sure and steady beam upon him. He had broadened and stabilized in the days of peace the foundations of American life and union.
>
> In war he had raised the strength, might and glory of the great Republic to a height never attained by any nation in history. With her left hand she was leading the advance of the conquering Allied Armies into the heart of Germany and with her right, on the other side of the globe, she was irresistibly and swiftly breaking up the power of Japan. And all the time ships, munitions, supplies and food of every kind were aiding on a gigantic scale her Allies, great and small, in the course of the long struggle. ...
>
> For us, it remains only to say that in Franklin Roosevelt there lies the greatest American friend we have ever known and the greatest champion of freedom who has ever brought help and comfort from the new world to the old.[2]

The outpouring of grief at Roosevelt's passing and expressions of gratitude from his nation and the world for his leadership through the trials of war was marked with a sober and subdued funeral in Washington, DC, but hundreds of thousands of Americans bore witness to the trains that carried his body from his retreat in Warm Springs, Georgia where he died, to Washington, DC where he lay in state, and then on to his Hyde Park, New York home where he was buried.

When Winston Churchill died in 1965, and Eamon de Valera in 1975, their nations also collectively mourned their passing and paid them tribute with elaborate state funerals to celebrate their greatest contributions. For Churchill, his legacy as victorious Second World War "warlord" who led his nation through its fiercest existential battles to triumph over demonic fascist enemies was memorialized by many. General Dwight Eisenhower, Supreme Commander of the Allied Expeditionary Forces in Europe and former U.S. president, attended Churchill's funeral in London and represented Britain's great wartime ally. Among the high praise for Churchill, his "old friend," that Eisenhower shared with representatives of 120 countries and before Queen Elizabeth II in St Paul's Cathedral, was the assertion that, to the men who fought the war on the battlefields and sacrificed their lives, and to the world that was "saved" from fascist tyranny, "Churchill was Britain":

> ... he was the embodiment of British defiance to threat, her courage in adversity, her calmness in danger, her moderation in success. Among the allies his name was spoken with respect, admiration and affection. Although they loved to chuckle at his foibles, they knew he was a staunch friend. They felt his inspirational leadership. They counted him a fighter in their ranks.

Eisenhower also proclaimed that Churchill epitomized the manly ideal of soldier-statesman-citizen, would live on in the "world's" memory as a "champion of freedom."[3]

In Ireland, in August 1975, the Irish nation mourned the death of Eamon de Valera, the "most influential Irish political leader of this century."[4] The *Irish Times* memorialized "The Towering Figure" of de Valera in a special edition of the national newspaper that recounted de Valera's many achievements, as well as the many controversies he sparked in his long public life fighting for the independence and sovereignty of a united Irish nation, a fight that began with the 1916 Easter Rising:

> In one respect at least there will be no disagreement about Eamon de Valera: he was a great man. Great in controversy, it is true, but great also in his love for Ireland, in his vision, his tenacity, his independence of mind, his feeling for the people and his generosity. In a large measure his monument is the Republic of Ireland of today, with its weaknesses, its imperfections, its ends still to be tied off; but also, with its national pride realised, its sense of dynamism, its stability and its old divisions largely eradicated.[5]

The major achievement of his early years as Taoiseach was the 1937 Constitution that announced to the world de Valera's assertion of Ireland's masculine autonomy. The 1937 Constitution put Ireland on the unwavering path "to secure the sovereignty of parliament, assure the independence of the judiciary, and preserve the integrity of the institutions of State." The "first test" of Ireland's masculine autonomy "came at the outbreak of war in 1939," when de Valera declared Ireland's neutrality policy, standing up to the Anglo-American and German warlords and maintaining his nation's neutrality throughout the long war.[6]

Historians who have examined Ireland's experiences during the Second World War often note the substantial ways that de Valera's government aided the Anglo-American allies, even as Eire maintained its official status as a neutral power.[7] To counter the charges that Eire favored the Axis Powers, as the American Note outlined those charges in February 1944, Joseph Walshe enumerated the Irish government's many pro-Allied Powers actions.[8] These included significant collaborations between the British and Irish armies and intelligence forces, as well as release of British and American pilots whose planes landed within Eire's territory even as German pilots (and spies) were imprisoned for the duration of the war.[9] In addition, over 50,000 Irish volunteers fought in the British Army,[10] and 60,000 Irish citizens worked in British war production factories,[11] and they were not prohibited from doing so by de Valera's government. Historians also make the case that Churchill, Roosevelt, and de Valera all wanted to keep secret Ireland's friendly actions toward the Allied Powers – during the war *and* in the postwar period – for their own nationalist reasons. The Anglo-American leaders wanted to reinforce their wartime claims that they were fighting for the highest moral causes, and to make the indignant argument that Ireland had refused to join the righteous alliance against an evil and depraved enemy in order to rally their citizens' patriotism. De Valera, for his part, wanted to establish Ireland's nationalist credentials with its "strict neutrality" public posture in order to counter criticisms of his leadership from the militant IRA and to register his independence from Britain during and after the war.[12] Additionally, during the war de Valera's government certainly feared – with good reason – German reprisals if they joined the British alliance. In the first two and a half years of war, from September 1939 to December 1941 before the United States joined the war as an active belligerent, de Valera's close foreign policy advisers in Dublin, Joseph Walshe and Frank Aiken, also believed Britain's defeat was inevitable, and that Ireland's future as a "whole" nation which included restoration of the six northern counties "liberated" from British colonial rule, seemed to depend on currying Germany's favor.

The British, American, and Irish leaders' calculations of their wartime state-to-state relationships were based on strategic considerations, to be sure, but they were also determined by the fraternal friendships and the sometimes bitter animosities that developed among themselves and among their hand-picked Dublin advisers. Churchill's and Roosevelt's fraternal friendship cemented the wartime Anglo-American governmental alliance and established their British and American citizenries' positive feelings toward one another. Their antipathy toward Eamon de Valera and his "stubborn," "irrational," "dishonorable," and "unmanly" adherence to neutrality intensified the rift between the Anglo, American, and the Irish governments and national peoples during the war, and into the postwar period.

Although he had never hidden his resentment of Irish neutrality policy during the war, Winston Churchill's active dislike for Eamon de Valera was expressed in very public and personal terms during his address to the British nation on May 13, 1945. Churchill asserted that de Valera alone was responsible for preventing the Irish people from joining the British-led anti-fascist alliance, for withholding use of the Irish ports and other resources from the British armed forces that could have lost the war for Britain, and for "frolicking" with the Axis enemies in Dublin.[13] British diplomat Malcolm MacDonald, who had acted as go-between for the British Foreign Office when it tried to entice de Valera to join the British alliance in 1940, explained that Churchill's colonialist mindset would not let him view de Valera as anything but "an enemy, an enemy, an enemy" of the British Empire.[14] Because of de Valera's "amoral" insistence on Ireland's neutrality, Churchill also condemned the Irish nation on behalf of the British nation: "their conduct in this war will never be forgiven by the British people."[15] Churchill's personal and political support for the maintenance of Northern Ireland as "an integral part of the United Kingdom" was also ensured by Northern Ireland's national allegiance and Prime Minister Lord Craigavon's personal loyalty to Britain during the war. In consequence, the partition of Ireland was "solidified" in the postwar era, and became "institutionalized" by the close of the 1940s.[16] Moreover, throughout the war, Churchill had "nuture[d] Roosevelt's particular animus toward neutral Ireland."[17]

De Valera never forgave Churchill, either, for Churchill's part in the drafting the 1920 Government of Ireland Act that partitioned Ireland, as well as for Churchill's vitriolic criticism of Ireland's neutrality during the war. His answer to Churchill's May 13 address also snapped back at Churchill who had never respected Ireland's centuries-long fight for freedom, but rather continued "by the abuse of a people who have done him no wrong, trying to find in a crisis like the present, excuse for continuing mutilation of our country."[18] In 2007, historian Clair Wills wrote that "By war's end the [British and Irish people's] views of Irish neutrality were all but set in stone." This was a result, in large part, of their wartime leaders' "rhetorical battle [that] has cast a long shadow: attitudes toward wartime Ireland are still primarily determined by national allegiance. In Britain the story is still refusal to hand over the ports, and de Valera's condolences on Hitler's death. In Ireland it is a story of national survival."[19] Churchill and de Valera and their wartime governments were the primary authors of these stories, each side portraying their adversaries as living in amoral "darkness" and their own country representing "enlightened" moral values.

Although de Valera traveled to London and lunched with Churchill in 1953,[20] their first and only face-to-face meeting, when Churchill died, "De Valera declined an invitation to attend Churchill's funeral, but deigned to release the following statement: 'Sir Winston Churchill was a great Englishman, but we in Ireland had to regard him over a long period as a dangerous adversary.'"[21] Many Irish people emigrated to Britain when the war ended and mainly for economic reasons, but the Irish clergy and national politicians, Eamon de Valera in particular, tried to discourage his people from emigrating by focusing on the social problems, prejudice, and poor living conditions that the Irish would experience living in England.[22]

Franklin Roosevelt maintained cool relations with Eamon de Valera throughout the war. Not only was de Valera's strict neutrality policy a challenge to his own efforts to amend U.S. neutrality policy to aid Britain's anti-fascist war effort, but Roosevelt held a personal resentment toward de Valera and his closest advisers, too. De Valera's ministers in Dublin and Washington had threatened FDR's reelection in 1940 by calling on Irish Americans to vote against him, and they colluded with Roosevelt's isolationist political rivals throughout 1941, as they attempted to undercut

Roosevelt's pro-British actions before the United States officially entered the war.

Roosevelt's frosty relationship with de Valera was also strongly swayed by his uncle-by-marriage and personal emissary in Dublin, David Gray.[23] Gray was an avowed Anglophile who supported Britain's anti-fascist war from 1939 onward. He defined his mission as U.S. Minister in Dublin as one to persuade Ireland to abandon its neutrality policy and join the Western democracies' crusade against Nazi Germany's tyranny in Europe. To bring this about, Gray harbored dreams (or, in his critics' view, "delusions") that he could persuade Ireland to give up neutrality and bring Ireland into the anti-fascist alliance with Britain, in exchange for a promise of an end to partition of the Irish Isle and withdrawal of British colonial rule in Northern Ireland "in the future." His dream, however, was not realistic given the long and violent history of Anglo-Irish relations. As early as the summer of 1940, Gray began to denigrate de Valera and his advisers in his personal letters to Roosevelt as well as in his official communications with the State Department, and to criticize their stubborn refusal to "see reason" and accept his proposals. After his first five months as U.S. Minister in Dublin, from March to July 1940, when he was in near-daily contact with de Valera, Joseph Walshe, and Frank Aiken, Gray's own dream of negotiating an end to Ireland's partition and bringing Ireland into the anti-fascist alliance with Britain evaporated. By 1941, he was a bellicose critic of de Valera's government and openly plotted to put de Valera "in the wrong" with Franklin Roosevelt and his State Department supervisors. Gray engineered various propaganda campaigns against de Valera's neutrality policy that focused on the harm caused by Axis Legations and the German spies who schemed to invade Britain, and on de Valera's insistence on withholding access to critical ports and bases that hindered the Allies' abilities to wage war on their fascist foes.

Gray's campaigns were aided by American journalist Helen Kirkpatrick, who shared Gray's anti-fascist convictions and pro-Allied allegiance. Kirkpatrick as war correspondent for the *Chicago Daily News* crossed the border into the man's world of war – not only putting herself in the line of the enemies' gunfire to report firsthand on German attacks on Britain, France, and Italy, but also invading the male-only realm occupied by the governments' diplomatic and military elites. She certainly experienced opposition from the powerful men that she worked with since her mere presence challenged the "manliness of war,"[24] but she also served the interests of the Anglo-American leaders in publicizing the dangers of Irish neutrality to the Allied cause in news outlets in the United States and by sharing information with her influential contacts in Allied diplomatic offices and the U.S. military. Kirkpatrick's reporting on Irish neutrality, which was based on information David Gray shared with her from his post in Dublin as well as on her own interviews and investigations, helped to shape public opinion in the United States and Britain that was antagonistic to the Irish government's neutrality policy, and that, by extension, shaped Anglo-American people's opinions of the Irish people, during the war and into the postwar period.

During the last two years of the war, David Gray intensified his criticisms of de Valera and his government's aiding and abetting the Axis "war criminals" in Dublin in order to shut Ireland out of postwar global governance associations, and to undermine popular support in the United States for an end to partition of Ireland. Gray continued this campaign after the war, writing in 1946 to "prominent Irish-Americans, among them James A. Farley, John McCormack, and Joseph P. Kennedy. In each letter he enclosed an unsigned memorandum, 'The United States and Irish Partition', which was, in the words of a State Department official, 'a scathing indictment of the Irish government's attitude towards us during the war.'"[25] Gray believed that U.S. popular support for an end to partition could influence U.S. foreign relations, and could cause a rift in the Anglo-American alliance that he had promoted and valued throughout the years of war. This Anglo-American alliance, as Gray understood it, represented the best of Western civilization: that is, its democratic governing institutions and its Christian faith that valued human rights, human freedom, and human compassion. Irish and Irish American attacks on partition that focused on self-determination and the rights of "small" nations could appeal to democratic-minded Americans who might question the ongoing special relationship with British imperialism.

Gray was not completely mistaken about the popular appeal of the anti-partition arguments. Soon after the United Nations' fight against imperial Japan ended with the Japanese surrender on September 2, 1945, global governance organizations and nongovernmental international associations began organizing the postwar world. The Irish Anti-Partition League formed in fall 1945, and was soon supported by Fianna Fáil and all other Irish political parties. The League launched "a concerted effort to persuade foreign governments and the wider public of the moral case for a united Ireland," and was especially active in Britain, Australia, and the United States, the nations with the largest Irish immigrant populations. De Valera went on a tour of these nations to campaign against partition when Fianna Fáil lost its majority in the Dáil in 1948, and he lost his post as Taoiseach. The anti-partition campaign aimed to sway popular opinion in the United States and enlisted the political support of a few U.S. congressmen and senators in the late 1940s, but by the 1950s the Irish diaspora in America had reached a level of assimilation into the "mainstream" American culture, and interest in "Irish politics" waned.[26] Historian Diarmaid Ferriter has written that, even at the time, "De Valera embarked on an indulgent international anti-partition tour that achieved nothing." De Valera spoke to crowds of the already converted, and "the tour could not have come at a worse time in terms of interesting a wider world recovering from the Second World War."[27] When the British Parliament accepted the Dublin Dáil's declaration of independence with the passage of the Ireland Act of 1949, Parliament also declared "that Northern Ireland remains part of His Majesty's dominions and of the United Kingdom and it is hereby affirmed that in no event will Northern Ireland or any part thereof cease to be part of His Majesty's dominions and of the United Kingdom without the consent of the Parliament of Northern Ireland."[28] The "border issue" has persisted in Ireland and Northern Ireland to this day, flaring into violent conflict between IRA agents and British authorities at irregular intervals since the Second World War ended. The United States government, for the most part, kept its distance from the partition issue until 1998, when President Bill Clinton sent his emissary, Senator George Mitchell, to Belfast to help broker the Good Friday Peace Agreement between the Republic of Ireland and the United Kingdom. The agreement included a pledge by Sinn Féin and its Irish Republican Army to end its violent campaign against the British government and Ulster Protestants.

During the war, de Valera also held a low opinion of President Roosevelt and of his emissary, David Gray. And although de Valera's concerns for his nation's preservation justified his adherence to a strict neutrality policy, as he claimed in his public pronouncements throughout the conflict and into the postwar period, it was also fueled by personal resentment toward the Americans. De Valera's own account of his controversial condolence call to German Minister Eduard Hempel following Adolf Hitler's suicide, for example, demonstrates that Gray had provoked him to make the call with boorish demands for access to the German Legation's records, as well as other demands Gray made on de Valera's government over the war years for preferential treatment for the Allies.[29]

At war's end, Sir John Maffey also allowed himself to privately criticize de Valera's stubborn pride as the reason Eire maintained its neutrality policy, even as the Germans' wartime depravity was exposed with the Allied liberation of the Nazi concentration camps in 1945. Even at this late stage in the conflict, when it seemed to "the world" that the Allies' anti-fascist fight would go down in history as a "good war," fought in the name of justice and for the highest moral reasons, Maffey noted archly that de Valera "decided to get a mention for a conspicuous act of neutrality in the field. He would at least show that he was no 'band wagoner'."[30] Maffey also reported on a conversation he had with de Valera to the Dominions Office in the summer of 1945, when he and de Valera discussed the sorry state of Anglo-Irish relations. Maffey asked de Valera "what he considered to be the main factor" causing the rift. De Valera replied: "the Prime Minister," to which Maffey responded, "The Prime Minister was never likely to forget his period of heavy anxieties in defending the Atlantic approaches with no help from Eire."[31] In mid-June 1945, Maffey observed that the Irish people, who had generally supported de Valera's defense of Irish neutrality when Churchill attacked him publicly on May 13, were starting to express more critical views of their leader as censorship of news outlets relaxed and more accounts of Germany's wartime atrocities were published.[32] Joseph Walshe, not surprisingly, denied this was the case, and asserted that the majority of the Irish people still stood behind de Valera and defended the neutrality policy.[33]

After the war in Europe ended, Joseph Walshe also continued his personal vendetta to get David Gray recalled from his post in Dublin. He may have thought that without Franklin Roosevelt to "protect" Gray, he could be rid of the U.S. Minister, who "never missed an opportunity of showing his anti-Irish spleen."[34] Walshe lashed out in a letter to Robert Brennan in June 1945 that ended with the cry "What can you do about all this?":

> Perhaps you could talk strongly to some influential politician who would put an end to Gray's career. The general attitude of the Irish people towards David Gray is one of complete astonishment that the representative of the democratic United States of America should pass at least four days out of every seven with a group of effete nobles who are more violently anti-Irish than the worst John Bull in Britain. He is a toady of the very worst type, and the ordinary man-in-the-street is of the opinion that the Irish section in the State Department has gone completely daft or has deliberately set out to make America detested in Ireland.[35]

David Gray was ready to return home to the United States in summer 1945, too.[36] He had been more than willing to serve Franklin Roosevelt and pursue his mission to support the Allies during the anti-fascist war, but with Germany defeated he was ready to retire. The State Department, however, kept him in place to June 1947 as "American policymakers were largely unconcerned about Ireland" at that time. The acrimonious relations Gray established with de Valera, Walshe, and Aiken continued into the postwar period, however, and colored the remainder of his tenure as U.S. Minister to Ireland. By the time the State Department recalled Gray in mid-1947, his new supervisors blamed Gray for the poor bilateral relations that existed between the two states, during and after the war: "They expressed regret that the American perception of Irish neutrality during the war had been 'wrongly interpreted', again because of Gray. They said that Gray did not understand Irish nationalism and was unaware of Irish political realities." Indeed, Gray had continued his vindictive feud with de Valera and his ministers on into his retirement years, rehashing the charges he made during the war that neutrality had "served only Hitler's objectives," as German spies operated freely in Ireland throughout the war, and Dublin's lights "serv[ed] as a beacon to guide German bombers proceeding north to attack Belfast."[37] Gray continued to make his case against de Valera and Ireland's neutrality policy in a postwar memoir[38] and in public exchanges in letters to editors of Irish newspapers.[39]

Ireland's isolation from postwar global governance organizations that promoted collective security, free trade, and economic integration among Western European and Commonwealth nations was another continuing legacy of Ireland's wartime neutrality policy. According to historian Brian Girvin, de Valera's vision of an agricultural, self-sufficient nation held an "insidious influence" over the Republic of Ireland's national policies during the postwar decades, and Ireland remained a "poor country" until the 1990s.[40] In addition, Ireland's immediate postwar foreign relations were "in disarray and destined to get worse."[41] Ireland's membership in the United Nations (UN), a "victor's club,"[42] was blocked by the Soviet Union in 1946, and the Republic of Ireland did not join the UN until 1955. At that time, the United States and Soviet Union, as Cold War rivals, struck a deal to admit multiple nation-states to maintain an East–West balance of power in the global governance forum, and Ireland became a UN member as part of the "package deal" struck by the superpowers.[43] In 1949, Ireland turned down an opportunity to join the North Atlantic Treaty Alliance (NATO) because the six counties of Northern Ireland were not yet united with the Irish Republic, and Ireland's postwar leaders adopted a stance of "non-alignment" during the Cold War in the same way Ireland had remained neutral during the Second World War.[44] Ireland finally joined NATO in 1999, a decade after the Cold War ended, when NATO launched a new Partnership for Peace initiative to expand its nation-state membership in Europe.[45]

In the postwar period, Ireland remained outside the bond of Anglo-American friendship that Winston Churchill and Franklin Roosevelt established when joining their nations in anti-fascist alliance. The bilateral friendship between Britain and America would certainly ebb and flow during the Cold War years. After 1945, the United States became the world's acknowledged "superpower," and wielded an "unparalleled power" in geopolitics; at the same time, British imperial power eroded as its former colonies gained their independence.[46] Nonetheless, the friendship between the two nations has maintained its mythical power. The "fact" of the Anglo-American special relationship forged by Churchill and Roosevelt remains ingrained in the two nations' collective memories of the war. In the postwar period, Winston Churchill, for one, continued the mythmaking. In 1956, during his retirement from active political office, Churchill completed his four-volume opus, *A History of the English-Speaking Peoples*, begun in 1936. When the volumes were published, Churchill's preface to the first volume asserted the solid fraternal bonds of friendship between Britain and America, forged in war:

> For the second time in the present century the British Empire and the United States have stood together facing the perils of war on the largest scale known among men, and since the cannons ceased to fire and the bombs to burst we have become more conscious of our common duty to the human race. Language, law, and the process by which we have come into being, already afforded a unique foundation for drawing together and portraying a concerted task. I thought when I began that such a unity might well notably influence the destiny of the world. Certainly, I do not feel the need for this has diminished in any way in the twenty years that have passed.[47]

Decades later, in 2011, when U.S. President Barack Obama delivered his state address before the British Parliament, he also drew on long historical associations of Anglo-American friendship and the meaning of that friendship for the two nations and for the world, in words that both Winston Churchill and Franklin Roosevelt would have been proud to claim as their own:

> As two of the most powerful nations in the history of the world, we must always remember that the true source of our influence hasn't just been the size of our economies, or the reach of our militaries, or the land that we've claimed. It has been the values that we must never waver in defending around the world – the idea that all beings are endowed by our Creator with certain rights that cannot be denied.
>
> That is what forged our bond in the fire of war – a bond made manifest by the friendship between two of our greatest leaders. Churchill and Roosevelt had their differences. They were keen observers of each other's blind spots and shortcomings, if not always their own, and they were hard-headed about their ability to remake the world. But what joined the fates of these two men at that particular moment in history was not simply a shared interest in victory on the battlefield. It was a shared belief in the ultimate triumph of human freedom and human dignity – a conviction that we have a say in how this story ends.[48]

The wartime discourses laden with deeply felt emotions that the Anglo, American, and Irish leaders expressed during the Second World War defined their nation's manhood, their national identities, and their national purposes, and had far-reaching impacts at the time and for many decades afterward. Winston Churchill, Franklin Roosevelt, and Eamon de Valera

Conclusion 233

each attempted to shape the collective responses of their people to the war, to meet the challenges to their nations' survival, and to persuade their people to place the highest values on human freedom and justice, as they each understood the necessary conditions to attain freedom and justice. Their individual understandings of those conditions were certainly chauvinistic, parochial, racist, and gender biased as we understand these concepts today. But even as "we" reject their biased world views, their words and their understandings shaped the contours of postwar global politics and should be remembered and studied because they had a lasting and consequential power.

Notes

1 Carol Cohn, ed., *Women and Wars* (Malden, MA: Polity Press, 2013), 10.
2 Winston Churchill's tribute to Franklin Roosevelt, printed copy of Hansard recording [to the House of Commons], 17 April 1945, CHAR: 9/167/206–207, Winston Churchill Archives online, The Chartwell Trust.
3 Dwight D. Eisenhower, "Eisenhower's Tribute to Churchill, Delivered at St. Paul's Cathedral, January 30, 1965" (London: Marble Hill Press, 1965).
4 "Eamon de Valera is Dead," *Irish Times* special issue (30 August 1975), 1, KV-2-515-1, British National Archives, Kew, Richmond, Surrey, UK.
5 Ibid.
6 Ibid.
7 Alvin Jackson, *Ireland 1798–1998 War, Peace and Beyond* 2nd edition (Chichester: John Wiley & Sons, 2010), 300; Mervyn O'Driscoll, "Concluding Thoughts," in *Ireland in World War Two: Neutrality and Survival*, ed. Dermot Keogh and Mervyn O'Driscoll (Cork: Mercier Press, 2004), 291; T. Ryle Dwyer, *Behind the Green Curtain: Ireland's Phoney Neutrality During World War II* (Dublin: Gill & Macmillan, 2009), ix–x.
8 Files Memorandum to the Taoiseach 1944, Memorandum by the Department of External Affairs, "Cooperation with the British Government" (Secret) Dublin, Doc. No. 362 NAI DFA Secretary's Files, *Documents on Irish Foreign Policy* vol. VII, 1941–1945.
9 See Ronan Fanning, *Eamon de Valera: A Will to Power* (Cambridge, MA: Harvard University Press, 2016), 193. Fanning included the following list: Close liaison between Irish and British military authorities to plan against a possible German invasion of Ireland; exchange of information between British and Irish intelligence services; the use by British aircraft based on Lough Erne of a corridor over Irish territory and territorial waters for flying out over the Atlantic; "the immediate transmission to the United Kingdom Representative's Office in Dublin of reports of submarine activity received from their coast watching service"; transmission of meteorological reports and of reports of aircraft sightings over or approaching Irish territory; supplying particulars of German

crashed aircraft and personnel crashed or washed ashore or arrested on land; the internment of all German fighting personnel reaching Ireland while Allied service personnel were "allowed to depart freely and full assistance is given in recovering damaged aircraft"; de Valera's government's silent acquiescence in the wishes of the thousands of Irish citizens who fought in the Allied forces; and the establishment in February 1945 of a radar station in Irish territory for use against the latest form of German submarine warfare. (Although the war ended before it came into operation, it is the only example of de Valera agreeing to the establishment of a British military facility on Irish territory.)

10 Ibid., 198.
11 Brian Girvin, *The Emergency: Neutral Ireland 1939–45* (London: Pan Macmillan, 2007), 321. Girvin reported Joseph Walshe's claim that 150,000 Irish nationals served in the British military forces during the Second World War.
12 Fanning, *Eamon de Valera*, 195: "The Irish public knew nothing of de Valera's secret support for the Allies. Cocooned by the censor's cloak, it saw only what the government wanted it to see: a lonely stand against the combined might of British and American pressure."
13 Winston Churchill, "Five Years of War," Broadcast to the British Nation, 13 May 1945 (iBiblio, online information database, University of North Carolina at Chapel Hill), www.ibiblio.org/pha/policy/1945/1945-05-13a.html (accessed 8 December 2020).
14 Robert Fisk, *In Time of War: Ireland, Ulster and the Price of Neutrality, 1939–1945* (London: Andre Deutsch, 1983), 471.
15 Churchill quoted in Eunan O'Halpin, "The Second World War and Ireland," in *The Oxford Handbook of Modern Irish History*, ed. Alvin Jackson (Oxford: Oxford University Press, 2014), 715. See also Fanning, *Eamon de Valera*, 194: "Eamon de Valera never received, nor would he have wanted or expected, gratitude for his comprehensive secret support for the Allies throughout the war. Ireland's Neutrality instead attracted virulent British abuse not only during the war but for decades afterwards, in some quarters even to this day."
16 Anthony J. Jordan, *Churchill: A Founder of Modern Ireland* (Dublin: Westport Books, 1995), 188.
17 O'Halpin, "The Second World War and Ireland," 715.
18 "Taoiseach's Broadcast to the Nation at the conclusion of the War in Europe," delivered on Wednesday 16 May 1945 (Dublin: The Irish Press).
19 Clair Wills, *That Neutral Island: A Cultural History of Ireland During the Second World War* (London: Faber & Faber, 2007), 423.
20 Paul Bew, *Churchill and Ireland* (Oxford University Press, 2016), 172.
21 Palash Ghosh, "The Irish Nationalist and the Nazi: When Eamon de Valera Paid his respects to Adolf Hitler," *International Business Times* [online] (10 September 2013), www.ibtimes.com/irish-nationalist-nazi-when-eamon-de-valera-paid-his-respects-adolf-hitler-1403768 (accessed 8 December 2020).
22 Mary Daly, "Nationalism, Sentiment, and Economics: Relations between Ireland and Irish America in the Postwar Years," *Eire-Ireland* 37: 1&2 (Spring/Summer 2002), 76.

23 John Day Tully, *Ireland and Irish Americans 1932–1945: The Search for Identity* (Dublin: Irish Academic Press, 2010), 140. Tully has asserted: "David Gray was the prime mover of events in British-Irish-American relations during the period of American involvement in World War Two. His motivation, however, was not the advancement of war aims, but a forestalling of the efforts of Irish Americans to play a role in post war politics and to discredit Irish neutrality and de Valera enough to prevent the Irish from interfering in postwar British-American relations."
24 Cohn, *Women and War*, 22–23.
25 T. Ryle Dwyer, *Irish Neutrality and the USA, 1939–47* (Dublin: Gill & Macmillan, 1977), 207.
26 Daly, "Nationalism, Sentiment, and Economics," 82–83.
27 Diarmaid Ferriter, *The Border: The Legacy of a Century of Anglo-Irish Politics* (London: Profile Books, 2019), 47.
28 Jordan, *Churchill: A Founder of Modern Ireland*, 194.
29 Letter from Eamon de Valera to Robert Brennan (Confidential), 21 May 1945, Doc. No. 590 UCDA P150/26/6, *Documents on Irish Foreign Policy* vol. VII, 1941–1945. See also David McCullagh, *De Valera: Rule, 1932–1972* (Dublin: Gill Books, 2018), 254.
30 David McCullagh quoting Sir John Maffey to Sir Eric Machtig, British Dominions Office, in *De Valera*, 253. See also Joe Carroll, "De Valera's Condolences Given Out of Courtesy," *Irish Times* online (26 January 2005), www.irishtimes.com/news/de-valera-s-condolences-given-out-of-courtesy-1.409409 (accessed 8 December 2020).
31 Memorandum by Sir John Maffey, UK Representative to Eire of conversation with Mr. de Valera, 6 July 1945, DO 35/2088, British National Archives.
32 Wills, *That Neutral Island*, 394.
33 Letter from Joseph Walshe to Sean Murphy (Irish Minister in Paris) 7 June 1945, Doc. No. 602 NAI DFA Secretary's Files P12/1, *Documents on Irish Foreign Policy* vol. VII, 1941–1945.
34 Letter from Joseph Walshe to Robert Brennan (Washington) 11 June 1945, Doc. No. 603 NAI DFA Secretary's Files P48A, *Documents on Irish Foreign Policy* vol. VII, 1941–1945.
35 *Ibid.*
36 Girvin, *The Emergency*, 318.
37 Tully, *Ireland and Irish Americans*, 146–150.
38 Gray never completed or published his memoir, but it has since been published by Paul Bew. See Paul Bew, *A Yankee in De Valera's Ireland: The Memoir of David Gray* (Dublin: Royal Irish Academy, 2012).
39 David Gray, "Mr. de Valera Refused 'Join Allies' Plea," *Irish Times* (October 2, 1946), box 16; "Notes on de Valera," April 27, 1947, box 2; "Hitler's Blueprint for Landing in Ireland, Hoped for Southern Aid in Air Invasion of North, Revelations in Captured Documents," *Sunday Independent* (Dublin), July 30, 1950, box 7; "Dangerous Delusions," Letter to the Editor in *Irish Times*, c. 1950, box 16; "Former Minister Attacks Ireland," *Irish*

Times, c. 1950, box 16, David Gray Papers, 1855–1962, Franklin Roosevelt Presidential Library, Hyde Park, New York. See also Dwyer, *Irish Neutrality and the USA*, 211.
40 Girvin, *The Emergency*, 327–328.
41 Francis M. Carroll, "Ireland Among the Nations of the Earth: Ireland's Foreign Relations from 1923 to 1949," *Irish Studies* (2016), 15.
42 *Ibid.*
43 Tully, *Ireland and Irish Americans*, 151.
44 Carroll, "Ireland Among the Nations if the Earth," 17.
45 Tully, *Ireland and Irish Americans*, 153.
46 Mark A. Stoler, "The Second World War in U.S. History and Memory," *Diplomatic History* 25: 3 (Summer 2001), 384–388.
47 Winston Churchill, *A History of the English-Speaking Peoples*, quoted in João Carlos Espada, "Winton Churchill: The English-Speaking Peoples and the Free World," *Finest Hour* 173 (Summer 2016), https://winstonchurchill.org/publications/finest-hour/finest-hour-173/english-speaking-peoples/ (accessed 8 December 2020).
48 Barack Obama, "Speech before British Parliament in Westminster Palace," 21 May 2011. https://obamawhitehouse.archives.gov/the-press-office/2011/05/25/remarks-president-parliament-london-united-kingdom (accessed 8 December 2020).

Bibliography

Manuscript collections

Franklin D. Roosevelt Presidential Library, Hyde Park, New York
    Franklin Roosevelt Papers, Map Room Papers, 1945, Official Files, Ireland, 1939–1945 and President's Secretary's Files, Ireland, 1939–1945; David Gray Papers, 1855–1962; John Gilbert Winant Papers, 1916–1947.

Sophia Smith Collection, Smith College, Northampton, Massachusetts
    Helen Paull Kirkpatrick Papers, CA-MS-01132.

University of Wyoming American Heritage Center, Laramie, Wyoming
    David Gray Papers, 1857–1960, Coll. 03082.

University College Archives, Dublin, Ireland
    Eamon de Valera Papers (on microfilm, P150); Frank Aiken Papers (on microfilm, P104).

The Chartwell Papers, Chartwell Trust, Churchill College, University of Cambridge, United Kingdom
    The Papers of Sir Winston Churchill (online).

Documents on German Foreign Policy, 1918–1945, from the Archives of the German Foreign Ministry
    Volumes 7–11 (Washington, DC: Government Printing Office, 1956–1960).

Documents on Irish Foreign Policy
    Volume VI, 1939–1941; Volume VII, 1941–1945.

Foreign Relations of the United States
    Diplomatic Papers 1940 Volume III (Washington, DC: US Government Printing Office, 1958); Diplomatic Papers 1941 Volume III (Washington, DC: US Government Printing Office, 1959); Diplomatic Papers 1942 Volume I (Washington, DC: US Government Printing Office, 1960); Diplomatic Papers 1944 Volume III (Washington, DC: Government Printing Office, 1965).

The National Archives, Kew, Richmond, Surrey, United Kingdom
   Dominions Office and Successors, United Kingdom Representative to Eire, and Embassy, Republic of Ireland: Archives, Correspondence, DO 130, 1939–1969; Prime Minister's Office PREM 3 and 4 (Winston Churchill); War Cabinet Meeting Minutes CAB 66; Intelligence and Security Services, KV Name Reports: Eamon de Valera.

The Public Records Office of Northern Ireland, Belfast, Northern Ireland
   Cabinet Records and War Records (General and Communications with Newspapers), 1941–1942; 1939–1943.

Secondary sources

"A Declaration of the United Nations." 1 January 1941. The United Nations, Section 1: Origin and Evolution. Chapter A, *The Yearbook of the United Nations*. www.unmultimedia.org/searchers/yearbook/page.jsp?volume=1946–47&page=36&searchType=advanced (accessed 9 December 2020).

Alison, Miranda. "Wartime Sexual Violence: Women's Human Rights and Questions of Masculinity." *Review of International Studies* 33 (2007), 75–90.

Anderson, Benedict. *Imagined Communities: Reflections on the Origin and Spread of Nationalism*. London: Verso, 1983.

"Atlantic Charter," August 14, 1941. The Avalon Project, Documents in Law, History and Diplomacy. New Haven, CT: Lillian Goldman Law Library, Yale Law School, 2008. https://avalon.law.yale.edu/wwii/atlantic.asp (accessed 9 December 2020).

Banerjee, Sikata. *Muscular Nationalism: Gender, Violence and Empire in India and Ireland, 1914–2004*. New York: New York University Press, 2012.

Barton, Brian. *Northern Ireland in the Second World War*. Belfast: Ulster Historical Foundation, 1995.

Bendinger, Elmer. *No Time for Angels: The Tragicomic History of the League of Nations*. New York: Alfred A. Knopf, 1975.

Bew, Paul. *A Yankee in De Valera's Ireland: The Memoir of David Gray*. Dublin: Royal Irish Academy, 2012.

Bew, Paul. *Churchill and Ireland*. Oxford: Oxford University Press, 2016.

Bew, Paul. *Ireland: The Politics of Enmity, 1789–2006*. New York: Oxford University Press, 2007.

Bowen, Elizabeth. *"Notes on Eire": Espionage Reports to Winston Churchill 1940–2*. 3rd ed. With a review of Irish Neutrality in World War 2 by Jack Lane and Brendan Clifford. Cork: Aubane Historical Society, 2009.

Burns, James MacGregor. *Roosevelt: The Soldier of Freedom, 1940–1945*. Open Road media, e-book, 2012.

Carroll, Francis M. "Ireland Among the Nations of the Earth: Ireland's Foreign Relations from 1923 to 1949." *Irish Studies* (2016), 35–52.

Carroll, Joe. "De Valera's Condolences Given Out of Courtesy." *Irish Times* online (26 January 2005). www.irishtimes.com/news/de-valera-s-condolences-given-out-of-courtesy-1.409409 (accessed 9 December 2020).

Carter, Carolle J. *The Shamrock and the Swastika: German Espionage in Ireland in World War II*. Palo Alto, CA: Pacific Books, 1977.

Chamberlain, Neville, Prime Minister. "Radio Address, September 3, 1939." The Avalon Project Documents in Law, History and Diplomacy, Yale Law School. https://avalon.law.yale.edu/wwii/gb3.asp (accessed 9 December 2020).

Churchill, Winston. "Five Years of War," Broadcast to the British Nation, 13 May 1945. iBiblio, online information database, University of North Carolina at Chapel Hill. www.ibiblio.org/pha/policy/1945/1945–05–13a.html (accessed 9 December 2020).

Churchill, Winston S. *Into Battle, 1941.* RosettaBooks, 2013.

Churchill, Winston. Speech to Harvard University on receiving an honorary degree. 6 September 1943. https://winstonchurchill.org/resources/speeches/1941–1945-war-leader/the-price-of-greatness-is-responsibility/ (accessed 9 December 2020).

Churchill, Winston. Speech to the House of Commons, "Their Finest Hour." 18 June 1940. The International Churchill Society, 2020. https://winstonchurchill.org/resources/speeches/1940-the-finest-hour/their-finest-hour/ (accessed 9 December 2020).

Churchill, Winston. "The Invasion of France, Speech to the House of Commons." 6 June 1944. London: The Churchill Society, 2020. www.churchill-society-london.org.uk/InvaFrnc.html (accessed 9 December 2020).

Cohn, Carol, ed. *Women and Wars.* Malden, MA: Polity Press, 2013.

Cole, Robert. *Propaganda, Censorship and Irish Neutrality in the Second World War.* Edinburgh: Edinburgh University Press, 2006.

Connell, R. W. and James W. Messerschmidt. "Hegemonic Masculinity: Rethinking the Concept." *Gender & Society* 19: 6 (December 2005), 829–859.

Coogan, Tim Pat. *Eamon de Valera: The Man Who Was Ireland.* New York: HarperCollins, 1993.

Cook, Blanche Wiesen. *Eleanor Roosevelt: The War Years and After*, vol. 3, *1939–1962*. New York: Viking, 2016.

Costigliola, Frank. "Pamela Churchill, Wartime London and the Making of a Special Relationship." *Diplomatic History* 36: 4 (September 2012), 753–762.

Costigliola, Frank. *Roosevelt's Lost Alliances: How Personal Politics Helped Start the Cold War.* Princeton, NJ: Princeton University Press, 2012.

Cull, Nicholas J. *Selling War: The British Propaganda Campaign Against American 'Neutrality' in World War II.* Oxford: Oxford University Press, 1996.

Dallek, Robert. *Franklin D. Roosevelt and American Foreign Policy, 1932–1945.* New York: Oxford University Press, e-book edition, 1995.

Dallek, Robert. *Franklin D. Roosevelt: A Political Life.* New York: Penguin, 2018.

Daly, Mary. "Nationalism, Sentiment, and Economics: Relations between Ireland and Irish America in the Postwar Years." *Eire-Ireland* 37: 1&2 (Spring/Summer 2002), 74–91.

Dean, Robert D. *Imperial Brotherhood: Gender and the Making of Cold War Foreign Policy.* Amherst, MA: University of Massachusetts Press, 2001.

D'Este, Carlo. *Warlord: A Life of Winston Churchill at War, 1874–1945.* New York: HarperCollins, 2008.

Devere, Heather and Graham M. Smith. "Friendship and Politics." *Political Studies Review* 8 (2010), 341–356.

Dilks, David. *Churchill and Company: Allies and Rivals in War and Peace.* London: I. B. Tauris, 2012.

Dobson, Alan P. *Anglo-American Relations in the Twentieth Century: Of Friendship, Conflict and the Rise and Decline of Superpowers.* New York: Routledge, 1995.

Dower, John W. *War Without Mercy: Race and Power in the Pacific War.* New York: Pantheon, 1986.
Duggan, John P. *Herr Hempel and the German Legation in Dublin, 1937–1945.* Dublin: Irish Academic Press, 2003.
Dwyer, T. Ryle. *Behind the Green Curtain: Ireland's Phoney Neutrality During World War II* Dublin: Gill & Macmillan, 2009.
Dwyer, T. Ryle. *Irish Neutrality and the USA, 1939–47.* Dublin: Gill & Macmillan, 1977.
Edy, Carolyn M. *The Woman War Correspondent, The U.S. Military and the Press, 1846–1947.* Lanham, MD: Lexington Books, 2017.
Egofske, Leah Susan. "A Contested Policy: Irish and American Perspectives on Eire's Neutrality." MA Thesis. Graduate School of Clemson University (May 2013).
Eisenhower, Dwight D. "Eisenhower's Tribute to Churchill, Delivered at St. Paul's Cathedral, January 30, 1965." London: Marble Hill Press, 1965.
English, Richard. *Irish Freedom: The History of Nationalism in Ireland.* London: Pan Macmillan, 2007.
Espada, João Carlos. "Winton Churchill: The English-Speaking Peoples and the Free World." *Finest Hour* 173 online (Summer 2016). https://winstonchurchill.org/publications/finest-hour/finest-hour-173/english-speaking-peoples/ (accessed 9 December 2020).
Fanning, Ronan. *Eamon de Valera: A Will to Power.* Cambridge, MA: Harvard University Press, 2016.
Ferriter, Diarmaid. *Judging Dev: A Reassessment of the Life and Legacy of Eamon de Valera.* Dublin: Royal Irish Academy, 2007.
Ferriter, Diarmaid. *The Border: The Legacy of a Century of Anglo-Irish Politics.* London: Profile Books, 2019.
Fisk, Robert. *In Time of War: Ireland, Ulster and the Price of Neutrality, 1939–1945.* London: Andre Deutsch, 1983.
"George Washington's Farewell Address, 1796." Milestones 1784–1800. Washington, DC: U.S. Department of State Office of the Historian. https://history.state.gov/milestones/1784–1800/washington-farewell (accessed 9 December 2020).
"German Declaration of War Against the United States." 11 December 1941. The History Place. www.historyplace.com/worldwar2/timeline/germany-declares.htm (accessed 9 December 2020).
"German Territorial Losses, Treaty of Versailles, 1919." United States Holocaust Memorial Museum. https://encyclopedia.ushmm.org/content/en/map/german-territorial-losses-treaty-of-versailles-1919 (accessed 9 December 2020).
Ghosh, Palash. "The Irish Nationalist and the Nazi: When Eamon de Valera Paid His Respects to Adolf Hitler." *International Business Times* online (10 September 2013). www.ibtimes.com/irish-nationalist-nazi-when-eamon-de-valera-paid-his-respects-adolf-hitler-1403768 (accessed 9 December 2020).
Gilbert, Martin. *Churchill: A Life.* New York: Henry Holt, 1991.
Gilbert, Sir Martin, CBE. "Churchill Proceedings; Churchill and Bombing Policy." The fifth Churchill lecture, The George Washington University, Washington, DC, 18 October 2005. *Finest Hour* 137 online (Winter 2007–2008). www.winstonchurchill.org/publications/finest-hour/finest-hour-137/churchill-proceedings-churchill-and-bombing-policy/ (accessed 9 December 2020).
Girvin, Brian. *The Emergency: Neutral Ireland 1939–45.* London: Pan Macmillan, 2007.

Goldstein, Joshua S. *War and Gender: How Gender Shapes the War System and Vice Versa*. New York: Cambridge University Press, 2001.

Gray, Tony. *The Lost Years: The Emergency in Ireland, 1939–1945*. London: Warner Books, 1998.

Green, David B. "This Day in Jewish History: A Jewish Writer Commits Suicide at the League of Nations," *Jewish World* online. (3 July 2013). www.haaretz.com/jewish/.premium-this-day-a-suicide-at-the-league-of-nations-1.5290616 (accessed 9 December 2020).

Hamby, Alonso. "Democracy's Champions: Churchill and Roosevelt." *Finest Hour* 172 online (Spring 2016). https://winstonchurchill.org/publications/finest-hour/finest-hour-172/churchill-and-roosevelt/ (accessed 9 December 2020).

Hastings, Max. *The Secret War: Spies, Ciphers, and Guerrillas 1939–1945*. New York: HarperCollins, 2016.

Hatchley, Thomas E. and Lawrence J. McCaffrey. *The Irish Experience Since 1800: A Concise History*. New York: Routledge, 2010.

Hollihan, Kerrie Logan. *Women of Action, Reporting Under Fire: 16 War Correspondents and Photojournalists*. Chicago, IL: Chicago Review Press, 2014.

"Home from the Sea." *Time Magazine* 38: 8 (August 25, 1941), 13–17.

Hooper, Charlotte. *Manly States: Masculinities, International Relations, and Gender Politics*. New York: Columbia University Press, 2001.

Hopkins, June. "Churchill and Three Presidents – Churchill and Hopkins: The Main Prop and Animator of Roosevelt Himself." *Finest Hour* 160 online (Autumn 2013). https://winstonchurchill.org/publications/finest-hour/finest-hour-160/churchill-and-three-presidents-3-churchill-and-hopkins-the-main-prop-and-animator-of-roosevelt-himself/ (accessed 9 December 2020).

Hull, Mark M. "A Tale of German Espionage in Wartime Ireland." In *Ireland in World War Two: Neutrality and Survival*, ed. Dermot Keogh and Mervyn O'Driscoll. Cork: Mercier Press, 2004, 81–92.

Imperial War Museum Staff. "The 10 Things You Need to Know About D-Day." United Kingdom: Imperial War Museums online (4 January 2018). www.iwm.org.uk/history/the-10-things-you-need-to-know-about-d-day (accessed 9 December 2020).

"Ireland and America: A Special Supplement on Ireland's Position in the Battle of the Atlantic." *Nation* 154: 5, part 2 (31 January 1942).

Jackson, Alvin. *Ireland 1798–1998 War, Peace and Beyond*, 2nd ed. Chichester: John Wiley & Sons, 2010.

James, Pearl, ed. *Picture This: World War I Visual Culture*. Lincoln, NB: University of Nebraska Press, 2009.

Jordan, Anthony J. *Churchill: A Founder of Modern Ireland*. Dublin: Westport Books, 1995.

Kaiser, David. *No End Save Victory: How FDR Led the Nation into War*. New York: Basic Books, 2014.

Kaplan, Danny. *The Men We Loved: Male Friendship and Nationalism in Israeli Culture*. New York: Berghahn Books, 2006.

Kaplan, Danny. "What Can the Concept of Friendship Contribute to the Study of Nationalism?" *Nations and Nationalism* 13: 2 (2007), 225–244.

Kasper, Anne. "Interview with Helen Kirkpatrick Milbank." Women in Journalism oral history project of the Washington Press Club Foundation, April 3–5, 1990, Oral History Collection of Columbia University and other repositories.

Kaufman, Joyce P. and Kristen P. Williams. "Nationalism, Citizenship, and Gender." In *Oxford Research Encyclopedia of International Studies*, online edition. Oxford: Oxford University Press, November 2017.

Kennedy, Greg. "Neville Chamberlain and Strategic Relations with the US During His Chancellorship." *Diplomacy & Statecraft* 13: 1 (March 2002), 95–120.

Kennedy, Michael. *Guarding Neutral Ireland: The Coast Watching Service and Military Intelligence, 1939–1945*. Dublin: Four Courts Press, 2008.

Keogh, Dermot. "Eamon de Valera and Hitler: An Analysis of International Reaction to the Visit to the German Minister, May 1945." *Irish Studies in International Affairs* 3: 1 (1989), 69–92.

Keogh, Dermot. "Profile of Joseph Walshe, Secretary, Department of Foreign Affairs, 1922–46." *Irish Studies in International Affairs* 3: 2 (1990), 59–80.

Keogh, Dermot and Mervyn O'Driscoll, eds. *Ireland in World War Two: Neutrality and Sustainability*. Cork: Mercier Press, 2004.

Keylor, William R. *The Twentieth Century World and Beyond, An International History Since 1900*, 6th ed. New York: Oxford University Press, 2011.

Kimball, Warren F., ed. *Churchill and Roosevelt, The Complete Correspondence*, vol. 1, *Alliance Emerging, October 1933–November 1942*. Princeton, NJ: Princeton University Press, 1984.

Kirkpatrick, Helen Paull with Foreword by Victor Gordon Lennox. *This Terrible Peace*. London: Rich & Cowan, 1939.

Kirkpatrick, Helen Paull. *Under the British Umbrella*. New York and London: Charles Scribner's Sons, 1939.

Koschut, Simon and Andrea Oelsner, eds. *Friendship and International Relations*. New York: Palgrave Macmillan, 2014.

LaFeber, Walter. *The American Age: United States Foreign Policy at Home and Abroad since 1750*. New York: W. W. Norton, 1989.

Larson, Erik. *The Splendid and the Vile: A Saga of Churchill, Family, and Defiance during the Blitz*. New York: Crown, 2020.

Malešević, Siniša. "The Chimera of National Identity." *Nations and Nationalism* 17: 2 (2011), 272–290.

Manning, Maurice. *James Dillon, A Biography*. Dublin: Wolfhound Press, 1999.

McCullagh, David. *De Valera: Rule*, vol. II, *1932–1975*. Dublin: Gill Books, 2018.

McEvoy, Dermot. "What if Michael Collins Had Been Irish Leader the Night Pearl Harbor was Bombed?" *Irish Central*, 7 December 2018. www.irishcentral.com/opinion/others/what-if-michael-collins-had-been-irish-leader-the-night-pearl-harbor-was-bombed (accessed 9 December 2020).

McKercher, B. J. C. "National Security and Imperial Defense: British Grand Strategy and Appeasement, 1930–1939." *Diplomacy & Statecraft* 19: 3 (September 2008), 391–442.

Meacham, Jon. *Franklin and Winston: An Intimate Portrait of an Epic Friendship*. New York: Random House, 2004.

"Mr. Roosevelt's War." *Time Magazine* 38: 2 (14 July 1941), 13–15.

Nagel, Joane. "Masculinity and Nationalism: Gender and Sexuality in the Making of Nation." *Ethnic and Racial Studies* 21: 2 (1998), 242–269.

"National Ordeal." *Time Magazine* 38: 24 (15 December 1941), 20–21.

Nolan, Aengus. "'A Most Heavy and Grievous Burden': Joseph Walshe and the Establishment of Sustainable Neutrality, 1940." In *Ireland in World War Two:*

Neutrality and Survival, ed. Dermot Keogh and Mervyn O'Driscoll. Cork: Mercier Press, 2004, 126–143.
Obama, Barack. "Speech before British Parliament in Westminster Palace." 21 May 2011. https://obamawhitehouse.archives.gov/the-press-office/2011/05/25/remarks-president-parliament-london-united-kingdom (accessed 9 December 2020).
O' Drisceoil, Donal. *Censorship in Ireland, 1939–1945*. Cork: Cork University Press, 1996.
O'Driscoll, Mervyn. *Ireland, Germany and the Nazis: Politics and Diplomacy, 1919–1939*, 2nd ed. Dublin: Four Courts Press, 2017.
O'Halpin, Eunan. "'According to the Irish Minister in Rome ...': British Decrypts and Irish Diplomacy in the Second World War." *Irish Studies in International Affairs* 6 (1995), 95–105.
O'Halpin, Eunan. *Defending Ireland: The Irish State and its Enemies Since 1922*. New York: Oxford University Press, 2000.
O'Halpin, Eunan, ed. *MI5 and Ireland, 1939–1945*. Dublin: Irish Academic Press, 2003.
O'Halpin, Eunan. "The Second World War and Ireland." In *The Oxford Handbook of Modern Irish History*, ed. Alvin Jackson. Oxford: Oxford University Press, 2014, 711–725.
Olson, Lynne. *Citizens of London: The Americans Who Stood with Britain in Its Darkest, Finest Hour*. New York: Random House, 2011.
Olson, Lynne. *Last Hope Island: Britain, Occupied Europe, and the Brotherhood That Helped to Turn the Tide of War*. London: Scribe Publications, 2018.
Olson, Lynne. *Those Angry Days: Roosevelt, Lindbergh, and America's Fight Over World War II*. New York: Random House, 2013.
Peterson, V. Spike, ed. *Gendered States: Feminist (Re)Visions of International Relations Theory*. Boulder, CO: Lynne Rienner, 1992.
Pickett, Clarence E. "Difficulties in the Placement of Refugees." *Annals of the American Academy of Political and Social Science* 203 (May 1939), 94–98.
Plain, Gill. *John Mills and British Cinema: Masculinity, Identity and Nation*. Edinburgh: Edinburgh University Press, 2006.
Potter, John. "Passing Through: The Story of the United States Army in Northern Ireland, 1942–1944." Belfast: Northern Ireland War Memorial and Home Front Exhibition, 2012.
Purnell, Sonia. *Clementine: The Life of Mrs. Winston Churchill*. New York: Viking Penguin, 2015.
"Radio Address by Neville Chamberlain, Prime Minister, September 3, 1939." The Avalon Project Documents in Law, History and Diplomacy, Yale Law School. https://avalon.law.yale.edu/wwii/gb3.asp (accessed 9 December 2020).
Rock, William R. "Review of Richard Crockett, Twilight of Truth: Chamberlain, Appeasement, and the Manipulation of the Press." *American Historical Review* 95: 5 (December 1990), 1547–1548.
Roi, Michael. "Introduction: Appeasement: Rethinking the Policy and Policy-Makers." *Diplomacy & Statecraft* 19: 3 (September 2008), 383–390.
Roosevelt, Franklin. "Address to Congress Requesting a Declaration of War." 8 December 1941. Presidential Speeches, Franklin D. Roosevelt Presidency. University of Virginia Miller Center, 2019. https://millercenter.org/the-presidency/presidential-speeches/december-8-1941-address-congress-requesting-declaration-war (accessed 9 December 2020).

Roosevelt, Franklin. "Fireside Chat 15: On National Defense." 26 May 1940. Presidential Speeches, Franklin D. Roosevelt Presidency. University of Virginia Miller Center, 2019. https://millercenter.org/the-presidency/presidential-speeches/may-26-1940-fireside-chat-15-national-defense (accessed 9 December 2020).

Roosevelt, Franklin. "Fireside Chat 19: On the War with Japan." 9 December 1941. Presidential Speeches, Franklin D. Roosevelt Presidency. University of Virginia Miller Center, 2019. https://millercenter.org/the-presidency/presidential-speeches/december-9-1941-fireside-chat-19-war-japan (accessed 9 December 2020).

Roosevelt, Franklin. "State of the Union (Four Freedoms)." 6 January 1941. Presidential Speeches, Franklin D. Roosevelt Presidency. University of Virginia Miller Center, 2019. https://millercenter.org/the-presidency/presidential-speeches/january-6-1941-state-union-four-freedoms (accessed 9 December 2020).

Roosevelt, Franklin Delano. "The Great Arsenal of Democracy." 29 December 1940. American Rhetoric,com. www.americanrhetoric.com/speeches/fdrarsenalofdemocracy.html (accessed 9 December 2020).

Roosevelt, Franklin. "Third Inaugural Address." 20 January 1941. Presidential Speeches, Franklin D. Roosevelt Presidency. University of Virginia Miller Center, 2019. https://millercenter.org/the-presidency/presidential-speeches/january-20-1941-third-inaugural-address (accessed 9 December 2020).

Runyan, Anne Sisson and V. Spike Peterson. *Global Gender Issues in the New Millennium*, 3rd ed. Boulder, CO: Westview Press, 2009.

Sheehan, Vincent. "Covering Hell's Corner: While Bombers Hurl their Deadly Loads, Correspondents Dig In." *Current History* (22 October 1940), 18–20.

Sherwood, Robert E. *Roosevelt and Hopkins: An Intimate History*. New York: Grosset & Dunlap, 1948.

Smith, Jean Edward. *FDR*. New York: Random House, 2008.

Smith, Kevin. "Reassessing Roosevelt's View of Chamberlain After Munich: Ideological Affinity in the Geoffrey Thompson–Claude Bowers Correspondence." *Diplomatic History* 33: 5 (November 2009), 839–864.

Sorel, Nancy Caldwell. *The Women Who Wrote the War*. New York: Arcade Publishing, 1999.

Spencer, John H. "The Italian–Ethiopian Dispute and the League of Nations." *American Journal of International Law* 31 (October 1937), 614–630.

Stoler, Mark A. "The Second World War in U.S. History and Memory." *Diplomatic History* 25: 3 (Summer 2001), 383–392.

Stone, Lawrence. "Prosopography." *Daedalus* 100: 1 in *Historical Studies Today* (Winter 1971), 46–79.

"The Japanese Attack on Pearl Harbor, December 7, 1941." United States Library of Congress, America's Story. www.americaslibrary.gov/jb/wwii/jb_wwii_pearlhar_1.html (accessed 9 December 2020).

"The President Speaks." *Time Magazine* 37: 1 (6 January 1941), 11–14.

Thompson, John A. "Conceptions of National Security and American Entry into World War II." *Diplomacy & Statecraft* 16: 4 (December 2005), 671–697.

Tonra, Ben. *Global Citizen and European Republic: Irish Foreign Policy in Transition*, e-book ed. Manchester: Manchester University Press, 2007.

"Treaty of Nonaggression Between Germany and the Union of Soviet Socialist Republics." The Avalon Project Documents in Law, History and Diplomacy, Yale Law School. https://avalon.law.yale.edu/20th_century/nonagres.asp; "Secret

Additional Protocol." https://avalon.law.yale.edu/20th_century/addsepro.asp (both accessed 9 December 2020).
Tully, John Day. *Ireland and Irish-Americans, 1932–1945: The Search for Identity.* Dublin: Irish Academic Press, 2010.
Voss, Frederick S. *Reporting the War: The Journalistic Coverage of World War II.* Washington, DC: Smithsonian Institution Press, 1994.
White, Timothy J. "Nationalism vs Liberalism in the Irish Context: From a Postcolonial Past to a Postmodern Future." *Eire-Ireland* 37: 3&4 (Fall/Winter 2002), 25–38.
Wills, Clair. *That Neutral Island: A Cultural History of Ireland During the Second World War.* London: Faber & Faber, 2007.
Wilson, Woodrow. War Messages. 65th Cong., 1st Sess. Senate Doc. No. 5, Serial No. 7264. Washington, DC, 1917. https://wwi.lib.byu.edu/index.php/Wilson%27s_War_Message_to_Congress (accessed 9 December 2020).
Wood, Ian S. *Britain, Ireland, and the Second World War.* Edinburgh: Edinburgh University Press, 2010.
Yuval-Davis, Nira. *Gender & Nation.* London: Sage, 1997.

Index

Abwehr 10, 62, 83, 84, 169
Aiken, Frank 10, 54, 55, 59, 62, 63, 84, 86, 114, 119, 209, 225
   to United States (1941) 120–127
American Friends of Irish Neutrality (AFIN) 112, 126, 152
American Note controversy (1944) 187, 198–203
Anglo-American special relationship 5–8, 11, 15, 143, 231, 232
Anglo-Irish Treaty (1921) 4, 30, 34 49
Anglo-Irish Treaty (1938) 30–32, 34, 40 n. 46
appeasement policy (Britain) 24, 26–29, 32–34
Atlantic Charter 142, 145

Belfast Blitz 127
bombing of County Wexford 96
bombing of Dublin 130
Bowen, Elizabeth 75 n. 74, 173, 174
Brennan, Robert 55, 56, 89, 91, 98, 112, 123, 124, 130, 157, 177, 179, 183, 201, 202, 207, 212

Chamberlain, Neville 15, 24, 26–34, 36, 38 n. 24, 44, 58–61, 85, 87
   resignation as Prime Minister 68, 69
Churchill, Winston 1–3, 7, 8, 15, 16, 24, 26, 27, 34–37, 43, 48, 49, 85, 86, 90–92, 109, 115–117, 128, 129, 131
   and Allied victory in Europe 212, 213, 225, 226
   and Irish neutrality 58, 59, 66, 67, 69, 97, 98
   and London Blitz 95, 96, 127, 128
   death of 223, 226
   elevated to Prime Minister 68, 81
   meetings with Franklin Roosevelt 142–146, 158–160, 178, 179, 184, 187
   outbreak of war 44–46
   United States entry into war 155, 156
conscription controversy (Northern Ireland) 36, 128, 129
Craig, James (Lord Craigavon) 56, 66, 85–87, 226
Cudahy, John 28, 29, 61, 97

de Valera, Eamon 1–5, 9, 10, 15, 29–33, 35, 36, 50, 59, 60, 67, 69, 85–88, 98, 109, 112, 120, 125, 126, 141, 142
   and Allied victory in Europe 213, 226, 229
   and Irish Republican Army 35, 36
   and U.S. entry into war 156, 157
   condolence call to German Legation 211, 212, 229
   death of 224
   outbreak of war 51–53
   rejection of American Note 200–202
Dillon, James 112, 119, 122, 141, 142, 173, 174
Donovan, William J. (Bill) 116, 122, 123, 152
Dulanty, John 96, 128, 129, 203

Index

Dunkirk evacuation 82, 101 n.7, 101 n. 13

Eisenhower, Dwight D. 203, 209, 223
Emergency Powers Act (1939) 53

fraternal friendship 2, 11–13, 67, 109, 225
  Churchill and Roosevelt 8, 15, 48–50, 140, 143, 144, 158–160, 162 n. 25, 168, 177–179, 184, 208, 210, 211, 225

Gallagher, Frank 149, 150, 212
Goertz, Hermann 70, 83, 84, 147, 163 n. 40, 147, 169–171, 176
Gray, David 10, 11, 64–67, 70, 82, 83, 88, 89, 112, 123, 125, 130, 141, 168
  and American Note (1944) 187, 188, 199–202, 206
  and postwar relations with Ireland 230, 231
  break with de Valera 172, 173, 176, 177, 180, 181, 211, 227, 228
  on death of Roosevelt 211
  on German spies in Ireland 89, 147–152, 169, 176, 198
  U.S. propaganda campaigns in Ireland 174, 175, 183
  vision of postwar Anglo-American relations 184–187, 228

Held, Stephen 70, 83, 84
Hempel, Eduard 51, 52, 60, 69, 70, 84, 112–114, 130, 147, 169, 170, 176, 177, 182, 183, 211
Hopkins, Harry 99, 114–117

Irish-American special relationship 3, 9, 10
Irish foreign relations 141, 142, 231
Irish Republican Army (IRA) 4, 35, 36, 41 n. 72, 54, 62, 67, 77 n. 109, 83, 84, 148, 169, 171, 179, 180
Irish Treaty Ports 30, 34, 58, 69, 90, 98, 112, 113, 147

Kirkpatrick, Helen Paull 10, 11, 14, 16, 21–25, 27, 33, 43, 44, 61, 63, 64, 68, 175
  reporting on Irish neutrality 62, 88–90, 118, 119, 122, 149–151, 158, 170, 171, 183, 227, 228
  reporting on liberation of concentration camps 206, 208, 209
  reporting on London Blitz 92–95
  reporting on Operation Overlord 204, 205

Lend-Lease aid to Britain 99, 110, 114, 116, 117, 124, 130, 142

MacDonald, Malcolm 30, 31, 85–87, 89, 225
Maffey, Sir John Loader 10, 56–60, 75 n. 72, 82, 83, 85, 88, 120, 121, 129, 151, 156, 172, 174, 184, 185, 203
  and Allied victory in Europe 214, 229, 230
  and American Note 199, 200
manhood/masculinity 2, 4, 8, 13, 14, 46, 48, 50, 86, 87, 91, 126, 173, 174, 222, 224, 227
Munich Agreement (1938) 24, 32, 33, 35, 36

national identity 3–5, 12, 185, 222, 224, 225, 232, 233
nationalism 11–13
Nazi-Soviet Pact 43, 131
neutrality (Ireland) 5, 51–54, 62, 63, 68, 74 n. 68, 86–88, 111, 112, 118, 119, 127, 130, 141, 142, 156, 157, 173, 184, 185, 207, 213, 224, 225, 233 n. 9
neutrality (United States) 7, 47, 61, 91, 97, 98, 100, 111, 152, 153

Operation Overlord 15, 16, 187, 198, 199, 203, 204

partition of Ireland 4, 29–31, 35, 85, 86, 228, 229

Roosevelt, Franklin D. (FDR) 1–3, 7, 8, 15, 16, 27, 28, 31, 33, 35, 49, 50, 61, 64, 81, 90, 91, 97, 99, 100, 131, 142
  death of 209–211, 222, 223
  Four Freedoms address 109–111
  hostility towards de Valera 146, 181, 182, 184, 206, 226, 227
  meeting with Frank Aiken 124, 125
  outbreak of war 47, 48
  war address to Congress, to American people 154, 155

Tehran Conference (1943) 187

United States entry into war 153–155
United States Military in Northern Ireland 140, 141, 152, 171, 172, 174, 176, 182

Walshe, Joseph 10, 51, 56, 59, 63, 67–70, 84, 85, 89, 112–114, 119, 120, 130, 148, 149, 151, 152, 169, 170, 177, 179, 183, 202, 203, 207, 212, 224, 225, 230
Willkie, Wendell 97, 116, 117, 120
Winant, John Gilbert (Gil) 97, 117, 118, 149, 155, 172, 179, 180

Yalta Conference (1945) 206–208

EU authorised representative for GPSR:
Easy Access System Europe, Mustamäe tee 50,
10621 Tallinn, Estonia
gpsr.requests@easproject.com

www.ingramcontent.com/pod-product-compliance
Lightning Source LLC
Chambersburg PA
CBHW070325240426
43671CB00013BA/2360